THE

FOOTBALL QUIZ BOOK

THE FOOTBALL QUIZ BOOK

THOUSANDS OF BRAIN-TEASING QUESTIONS TO TEST YOUR KNOWLEDGE TO THE LIMIT

COMPILED BY
JOE CAMERON

This is a Parragon Book
This edition published in 2000

Parragon
Queen Street House
4 Queen Street
Bath BA1 1HE
UK

Printed and bound in the UK
Cover photos: Allsport UK Ltd

ISBN 0-75253-205-7

CONTENTS

CONTENTS

CONTENTS

CONTENTS

CONTENTS

CONTENTS

QUIZ 1

Answers on page 13

1 Who became the chief executive of the English Premier League in 1997?

2 Shaun Teale went to which club after leaving Aston Villa?

3 Which former Leeds United manager scored a goal for Brighton after only 15 seconds?

4 Which Manchester Utd legend scored 49 goals in 106 appearances for England?

5 During the 97-98 season which Northern Ireland manager was sacked?

6 Where was the 1963 European Cup Winners' Cup Final held?

7 Howard Wilkinson followed Billy Bremner as manager of which club?

8 In which decade was Danny Blanchflower born?

9 Which England cricketer played in the 1950 FA Cup Final for Arsenal?

10 Name the only two countries in the 1998 World Cup to have 100% records in their group matches?

11 John Scales moved from Wimbledon to which club for £3.5m in August 1994?

12 Which club did Mike Phelan leave to join Manchester Utd?

13 Kevin Moran left Manchester Utd in 1988 for which club?

14 Which defender was 18 years and 183 days old when he made his England debut?

15 Keith Weller played for which Cup Winners' Cup trophy winners?

Answers to page 13

1 Gary Lineker, **2** 1-1, **3** Peter Osgood, **4** Hampshire, **5** Port Vale, **6** Liverpool, **7** Leicester City (1969), **8** David Seaman, **9** Chelsea, **10** Scunthorpe Utd, **11** Billy Wright, **12** Hull City, **13** Manchester City, **14** 1947, **15** 1992, Liverpool, Rush (Ian) v Sunderland, Rush (David).

QUIZ 2

Answers on page 14

1 Kevin Keegan was the first British player to be involved in a half-million pound transfer. Which club did he join?

2 Which Sporting Lisbon player won the 1973-74 Golden Boot award?

3 David Hayes made a record 358 appearances, for which Scottish club between 1969-84?

4 At which club did Chris Woods make his League debut?

5 During the 97-98 season who resigned as manager of Swansea City, just 13 days after taking over?

6 Gates and McCall scored Euro goals in the same game for which club?

7 Angus and Elder formed a fullback pairing at which club?

8 Fullback Chris Lawler scored goals for Liverpool, Stockport and which other club?

9 Which is the only country to have taken part in every World Cup finals stage?

10 Which club did Karel Poborsky leave to join Manchester Utd?

11 Who is the highest goal-scorer for Republic of Ireland?

12 Who lost to Leeds Utd in the 1968 Fairs Cup Final?

13 Where was the 1970 European Cup Final held?

14 Which country did John Mahoney play for?

15 Grant and Rideout scored Euro goals in the same 1990s game for which club?

Answers to page 14

1 1960s, **2** 'Anfield Rap', **3** Berti Vogts, **4** Brad Friedel, **5** Craig Johnston, **6** Everton, **7** Graeme Souness, **8** Jim Beglin, **9** Juventus, **10** Luton Town, **11** Neil Ruddock, **12** Phil Neal, **13** Ron Yeats, **14** Steve Nichol, **15** West Ham United.

QUIZ 3

Answers on page 11

1 Who was top scorer in the 1986 World Cup finals with six goals?

2 What was the 90 minute score in the 1989 Mersey FA Cup Final?

3 Which Chelsea player has scored in every round, including the FA Cup Final?

4 Which county did England centre forward Ted Drake play cricket for?

5 At which club did Mark Bright make his League debut?

6 Gary Gillespie first played in an FA Cup Final for which team?

7 Andy Lochhead first played in an FA Cup Final for which club?

8 Who played every League game in his first season with the club as Arsenal won the 1990-91 title?

9 Which London club did Englan'd World Cup hero Geoff Hurst manage?

10 Manchester City recorded a 6-0 League Cup win over which club in September 1974?

11 Who was the first man to win 100 caps for England?

12 Which club did Billy Bremner move to after Leeds Utd glory days?

13 Matt Busby won the FA Cup as a player at which club?

14 When did Bob Paisley play in a Championship-winning side at Liverpool?

15 Which 1990s FA Cup Final had opposing players with the same surname?

Answers to page 11

1 Peter Leaver, **2** Tranmere Rovers, **3** Howard Wilkinson, **4** Bobby Charlton, **5** Bryan Hamilton, **6** Rotterdam, **7** Leeds Utd, **8** 1920s, **9** Denis Compton, **10** France and Argentina, **11** Liverpool, **12** Norwich City, **13** Sporting Gijon, **14** Duncan Edwards, **15** Chelsea.

LIVERPOOL 1

Answers on page 12

1 In which decade did Liverpool first win the FA Cup?

2 Which Liverpool record reached No.3 in the charts in 1988?

3 Which German player had the task of trying to mark Kevin Keegan in Liverpool's victory in the 1977 European Cup Final?

4 Name the player bought by Liverpool from Columbus Crew?

5 Who had been brought to Liverpool as Keegan's replacement before Kenny Dalglish's arrival?

6 What is the middle name of ex-Liverpool ace Mark Walters?

7 Who resigned as manager of Liverpool following their FA Cup defeat by Bristol City?

8 Who replaced Alan Kennedy for Liverpool in 1985-86?

9 Which club beat Liverpool to win the European Super Cup in 1984?

10 Liverpool player Ian Rush scored 5 goals in a match in October 1983. Who were the opponents?

11 Who wanted a 'Loyalty' payment from Tottenham Hotspur after spending season 1992-93 with them before moving to Liverpool?

12 Which Liverpool player made 366 consecutive First Division appearances between 1974-1983?

13 Which Liverpool skipper said of Bill Shankley, "His Motivation could move mountains"?

14 Who moved to Liverpool from Ayr Utd for £300,000 in 1981?

15 Which club did Julian Dicks join on leaving Liverpool?

Answers to page 12

1 Hamburg, **2** Hector Yazalde, **3** Greenock Morton, **4** QPR, **5** Micky Adams, **6** Ipswich Town, **7** Burnley, **8** Portsmouth, **9** Brazil, **10** Slavia Prague, **11** Frank Stapleton, **12** Ferecvaros, **13** Milan, **14** Wales, **15** Everton.

WOLVES

Answers on page 17

1 Who moved from Bradford in 1995 to Wolves to set a club record for a transfer fee received?

2 Which player scored 34 League goals for Wolves in 1987-88?

3 How many times did Wolve's Billy Wright play for England?

4 What is the highest position Wolves have ever achieved in the League?

5 Which Wolves player moved for £1 million to Manchester City in 1979?

6 In which decade did Wolves first win the FA Cup?

7 Which Tommy became boss of Wolves?

8 Who succeeded Graham Hawkins as manager of Wolves in 1984?

9 In which decade did Wolves first win the Championship?

10 Wolves appointed which former England manager in April 1994?

11 In the only all-English European final ever, which side beat Wolverhampton Wanderers in the 1972 UEFA Cup

12 Which TV expert scored a League Cup Final winner for Wolves?

13 Which team were beaten 3-1 by Wolves in the 1949 FA Cup Final?

14 Wolves was the starting place for which two former England captains?

15 Against which country did Wolves teenager Ryan Green make his international debut?

Answers to page 17

1 Scunthorpe Utd, **2** Barcelona, **3** Darwen, **4** 1962, **5** Millwall, **6** Ron Atkinson, **7** Unsuitable pitch (plastic), **8** Walter Abbott, **9** Arsenal, **10** Trinidad & Tobago, **11** Mechelen, **12** Sheffield Utd, **13** Brondby, **14** John, **15** Leeds Utd.

QUIZ 4

Answers on page 18

1 Trevor Francis moved from Manchester City to which club for £800,000 in July 1982?

2 Who scored the winner for AC Milan in the 1990 European Cup Final?

3 How many times did Stan Cullis guide Wolves to League Championship victory?

4 Which Barcelona player was European footballer of the Year in 1974?

5 Who was Arsenal's top scorer for six consecutive seasons?

6 What is the highest position Hull City have ever achieved in the League?

7 Which commentator said, "Stuart Pearce has got the taste of Wembley in his nostrils"?

8 How many home matches did Manchester Utd play on their way to the 1990 FA Cup Final?

9 Where was the 1997 European Cup Winners' Cup Final held?

10 What was introduced in 1878 to help control the game?

11 Which team did West Ham Utd beat 2-0 in the 1975 FA Cup Final?

12 Which club did Barcelona buy Ronaldo from for £18m?

13 Which club reached three consecutive Cup Winners' Cup finals in the 1970s?

14 Spurs player Alf Stokes scored 5 goals in a match in September 1957. Who were the opponents?

15 Which was the first club to achieve the so-called 'New Double' of League Championship and League Cup?

Answers to page 18

1 Igor Stimac, **2** Frank Burrows, Bobby Smith, Jimmy Rimmer, Kevin Cullis, Jan Molby, **3** 28, **4** Black, **5** Jairzinho (Brazil), **6** Darlington, **7** Gabriel Batistuta, **8** Celtic, **9** 1-22, **10** Ally McCoist, **11** 1982, **12** Ron Harris, **13** Southampton, **14** 42, **15** Billy Foulkes.

QUIZ 5

Answers on page 15

1 In 1959 Neil Lambton managed only three days as boss of which club?

2 Where was the 1972 European Cup Winners' Cup Final held?

3 Birmingham City player Walter Abbott scored 5 goals in a match in November 1898. Who were the opponents?

4 In which year did Liverpool last gain promotion?

5 Which club did Wimbledon buy John Fashanu from?

6 Which manager said "It was a game of two halves, and we were crap in both of them"?

7 Why were Luton expelled from the Littlewoods Cup in the 1986-87 season?

8 Which player scored 34 League goals for Birmingham City in 1898-99?

9 Which soccer team does punk singer Johnny Rotten support?

10 Which country does Dwight Yorke play for?

11 What is the more familiar Flemish name of the Belgian club known in France as FC Malines?

12 Tony Currie was at which club when he made his international debut?

13 Which club did Peter Schmeichel leave to join Manchester Utd?

14 What is Niall Quinn's middle name?

15 Rodney Wallace moved from Southampton to which club for £1.6m in July 1991?

Answers to page 15

1 Dean Richards, **2** Steve Bull, **3** 105, **4** Division 1 Champions 3 times, **5** Steve Daley, **6** 1890s, **7** Docherty, **8** Tommy Docherty, **9** 1950s, **10** Graham Taylor, **11** Tottenham Hotspur, **12** Andy Gray, **13** Leicester City, **14** Billy Wright and Stan Cullis, **15** Malta.

QUIZ 6

Answers on page 16

1 Who was the first Croatian international to play in the English League?

2 Swansea City went through five managers in 1995-96. Can you name them all?

3 How old was Steve Coppell when he retired from playing?

4 What colour are Southampton's home shorts?

5 Only one player has scored in every match of a World Cup finals. Who was he?

6 Gary Pallister went on loan to which north-east club during his first spell at Middlesborough?

7 In the 1988 World Cup finals who was the only player to score a hat-trick in the group matches?

8 Who beat Dundee Utd 3-0 in the 1974 Scottish FA Cup Final?

9 What number sequence was worn by players in the 1933 FA Cup Final?

10 Who scored Scotland's only goal of Euro '96?

11 Which year in the 1980s saw the first English League soccer match played on an artificial pitch?

12 Who holds Chelsea's record for most League appearances?

13 Which club did Bill Shankly nickname The Ale-House Brawlers?

14 To two each way, how many caps did Phil Thompson win?

15 In Manchester Utd's 1968 Euro trail who scored their last goal against Real Madrid?

Answers to page 16

1 Sampdoria, **2** Frank Rijkaard, **3** Three, **4** Johan Cruyff, **5** Ian Wright, **6** 3rd Division 2, (1909-10), **7** John Motson, **8** None, **9** Rotterdam, **10** Referees whistle, **11** Fulham, **12** Inter Milan, **13** Anderlecht, **14** Birmingham, **15** Nottingham Forest.

QUIZ 7

Answers on page 21

1 Who followed David Hay as Celtic manager?

2 Name the Munich air crash survivor who played on until 1966?

3 Where was the 1954 World Cup held?

4 Who followed Neil Warnock as boss of Huddersfield Town in 1995?

5 Luton Town recorded a 7-2 League Cup win over which club in October 1989?

6 Who won the European Champions Cup three times between 1989-1994?

7 Which team are know as The Greens - Les Verts?

8 Luton Town chairman David Kohler demanded £300,000 compensation after which manager moved?

9 Which club did David Platt leave to join Arsenal?

10 Who succeeded Ron Tindall as manager of Portsmouth in 1974?

11 In season 1992-93 who scored 9 goals in 10 England appearances?

12 Which two clubs from the same British city played in the same European Cup Competition?

13 Tottenham Hotspur player Bobby Smith scored 5 goals in a match in March 1958. Who were the opponents?

14 Blackburn Rovers recorded a 6-1 League Cup win over which club in December 1992?

15 Nayim scored a last minute Cup Winners' Cup Final goal for which club?

Answers to page 21

1 Fred Everiss, **2** Ron Atkinson, **3** West Ham, **4** 1880s, **5** John Osbourne, **6** Ron Saunders, **7** 1920s, **8** John Reynolds, **9** Sheffield Wednesday, **10** Aston Villa, **11** Johnny Giles, **12** Strollers, **13** Aston Villa, **14** Laurie Cunningham, **15** Tony Brown.

ARSENAL 1

Answers on page 22

1 What was the score after normal time in the 1971 Arsenal v Liverpool FA Cup Final?

2 How many times did Arsenal win the championship in the 1930s?

3 Who became Britain's most expensive player when he moved from Preston North End to Arsenal in 1929?

4 Which Arsenal player held the club's scoring record before Ian Wright?

5 Ian Wright moved to Arsenal for £2.5m from which club?

6 Which club did Kenny Sansom leave to join Arsenal?

7 Clive Allen moved from Arsenal to which club for £1.25 million in August 1980?

8 Arsenal recorded a 11-1 FA Cup win over which club in January 1932?

9 Which Arsenal player in the 1997-98 season missed an away match in Greece because of his fear of flying?

10 Who was Arsenal's most successful manager?

11 Who beat Arsenal 1-0 in the 1978 FA Cup Final?

12 Who did Tony Adams replace as Arsenal skipper in 1988?

13 Which team did Arsenal pip to the league title in their first double winning season?

14 David Rocastle moved from Arsenal to which club for £2 million in July 1992?

15 Arsenal recorded a 7-0 League Cup win over which club in September 1979?

Answers to page 22

1 Lincoln City, **2** Marseille, **3** Paul Elliott, **4** Dundee, **5** Liverpool, **6** Rangers and Leeds Utd, **7** Ayr Utd, **8** Leeds Utd, **9** George Ramsey, **10** Alex Ferguson, **11** Paul Gascoigne, **12** Jim Beglin, **13** Malmo, **14** Jason, **15** Nigel Martyn.

WEST BROM 1

Answers on page 19

1 Which WBA manager held the job for 46 years?

2 Who said "I don't care if he's black or white or yellow with purple spots, if he can do a job for West Bromwich Albion he's in the team."?

3 Who did WBA beat in the last two-legged League Cup Final?

4 In which decade did WBA first win the FA Cup?

5 Who was in goal when WBA won the FA Cup in the 1960s?

6 Who succeeded Nobby Stiles as manager of WBA in 1986?

7 In what decade did WBA first win the Championship?

8 Which West Brom star of the 1890s, nicknamed 'Baldy' won five caps for Northern Ireland and then eight with England?

9 Who beat WBA 4-2 in the 1935 FA Cup Final?

10 WBA recorded a 6-1 League Cup win over which club in September 1966?

11 Which ex-WBA manager said, "the only certainty about management is the sack"?

12 What followed West Bromwich before the name Albion was introduced?

13 Who beat WBA 2-0 in the 1887 FA Cup Final?

14 Which player did Real Madrid sign from WBA for £1 million in 1979?

15 Which WBA player became the first player to score in every round of the League Cup?

Answers to page 19

1 Billy McNeill, **2** Harry Gregg, **3** Switzerland, **4** Brian Horton, **5** Mansfield, **6** AC Milan, **7** St Etienne, **8** David Pleat, **9** Sampdoria, **10** Ian St John, **11** David Platt, **12** Manchester City and Utd, **13** Aston Villa, **14** Watford, **15** Real Zaragoza.

QUIZ 8

Answers on page 20

1 Who became the first club to be relegated from the English League?

2 Which French club were stripped of their title and relegated to the Second Division for match-fixing in 1993-94?

3 Which Celsea player sued Dean Saunders for damages over a tackle that ended his playing career?

4 Who were the first club to retain the Scottish League Cup?

5 Which English club reached the semi-finals of the 1996-97 Cup Winners' Cup?

6 Which two British clubs played against each other in the European Cup in 1992?

7 Who plays at home at Somerset Park?

8 Which was Denis Irwin's first League club?

9 Aston Villa became only the second club to do the League and Cup 'double' in 1897. Who was their manager at the time?

10 Who said, "The Old Trafford job was one I simply could not turn down"?

11 Who said, "They say injuries come in threes. In my case it seems to be 33s"?

12 Who replaced Alan Kennedy for Liverpool in 1985-86?

13 Who lost 1-0 to Nottingham Forest in the 1979 European Cup Final?

14 What forename is shared by defenders Dodd and McAteer?

15 Who moved from Bristol Rovers in November 1989 to set a club record for a transfer fee received?

Answers to page 20

1 0-0, **2** 5, **3** Alex james, **4** Cliff Bastin, **5** Crystal Palace, **6** Crystal Palace, **7** Crystal Palace, **8** Darwen, **9** Dennis Bergkamp, **10** George Graham (six trophies in eight years), **11** Ipswich Town, **12** Kenny Sansom, **13** Leeds Utd, **14** Leeds Utd, **15** Leeds Utd.

QUIZ 9

Answers on page 25

1 Who plays at home at Love Street?

2 What was the name of Bill Shankly's brother who was also a soccer manager?

3 Howard Wilkinson followed Jack Charlton as boss of which club?

4 Les Ferdinand moved from QPR to which club for £6m in June 1995?

5 Ipswich Town player Ray Crawford scored 5 goals in a match in September 1962. Who were the opponents?

6 Which player scored his 100th Manchester Utd goal in the 1992 League Cup Final?

7 Who did Liverpool beat on penalties in the 1984 European Cup Final?

8 Which Scottish club plays at Pittodrie Stadium?

9 Rufus Brevett moved for £250,000 to QPR in 1991 to set a record for a transfer fee received at which club?

10 Dave Sexton followed Gordon Jago's first spell as manager of which club?

11 Which is the most southerly English League club?

12 Which team is TV cook Delia Smith a director of?

13 Who beat Sunderland 2-0 in the 1992 FA Cup Final?

14 Who succeeded Dave Ashworth as manager of Liverpool in 1923?

15 Alex Ferguson managed which two Cup Winners' Cup winners?

Answers to page 25

1 Paul Rideout, **2** Nat Lofthouse, **3** Ron Greenwood, **4** Liverpool, **5** Italy, **6** Barnsley, **7** Mark Hughes, **8** Michel Platini, **9** Danny Blanchflower, **10** Alex Smith, **11** 3, **12** Clarke, **13** Mansfield, **14** Crystal Palace, **15** Liverpool.

QUIZ 10

Answers on page 26

1 Which was the first English team to participate in the Cup Winners' Cup?

2 What colour are Hearts home shirts?

3 Which club had a fanzine called *Fly Me To The Moon*?

4 Which club did Ron Greenwood become a director of in 1983?

5 Bury's commercial manager has two famous sons playing for another club. Who are they?

6 Which Manchester Utd and Republic of Ireland player was known as 'Gentleman John'?

7 At which Scottish club did John Spencer make his League debut?

8 Jim Smith replaced Gordon Lee as manager of which club?

9 At which club did Dion Dublin make his League debut?

10 Which players book *A Double Life* appeared in 1990?

11 Which team lost 2-0 to Manchester Utd in the 1994 FA Charity Shield?

12 Which Leeds Utd midfielder hit a 1995 hat-trick against Coventry City?

13 Who were the first team to retain the Scottish League Cup?

14 Who is the most capped German player?

15 Who was the first player to be sent off in a match shown live on television?

Answers to page 26

1 4, **2** Andy Cole, **3** Barcelona, **4** Bobby Charlton, **5** David May, **6** Dion Dublin, **7** Fourth, **8** It was the only one to be replayed (Manchester Utd won it 4-0), **9** Leicester city, **10** Mark Hughes, **11** Norwich City, **12** Ron Atkinson, **13** Steve Bruce, **14** WBA, **15** 1-1

QUIZ 11

Answers on page 23

1 In the 1994-95 FA Cup winning season, who was Everton's top League scorer?

2 Which former player became President of Bolton?

3 Which England manager gave Bryan Robson his first cap?

4 Dean Saunders moved from Derby County to which club for £2.9m in July 1991?

5 An extra time goal by which country sent Nigeria out of the 1994 World Cup?

6 Which team does TV chat show host Michael Parkinson support?

7 Which football player is known as 'Sparky'?

8 Which French player finished as the top scorer in the 1984 European Championship tournament?

9 Which Northern Ireland skipper said, "Our tactics are to equalize before the other side scores"?

10 Who succeeded Ian Porterfield as manager of Aberdeen?

11 How many games did Billy Wright miss between his first and last appearance for England?

12 What is the surname of strikers Allan, Frank and Wayne?

13 Who plays at home at the Field Mill Ground?

14 From 1895 to the First World War where were FA Cup Finals played?

15 Which club finished second to Everton, nine points adrift, in the race for the 1986-87 title?

Answers to page 23

1 St Mirren, **2** Bob, **3** Sheffield Wednesday, **4** Newcastle United, **5** Florina, **6** Brian McClair, **7** AS Roma, **8** Aberdeen, **9** Doncaster Rovers, **10** QPR, **11** Plymouth Argyle, **12** Norwich City, **13** Liverpool, **14** Matt McQueen, **15** Manchester Utd and Aberdeen.

• MANCHESTER UTD 1 •

Answers on page 24

1 How many Championships did Bobby Charlton win with Manchester Utd?

2 Who scored a hat-trick in Manchester Utd's 7-0 Premiership defeat of Barnsley?

3 Mark Hughes moved from Manchester Utd to which club for £2.5m in June 1986?

4 Who scored 199 of League goals in 606 appearances for Manchester Utd between 1956 and 1973?

5 Who scored for Manchester Utd in the Cantona Kung-Fu game?

6 Manchester Utd paid £1m to Cambridge for which player in August 1992?

7 What was the lowest position Manchester Utd finished in the League under Ron Atkinson?

8 What was unique about about the first Charity Shield match, a 1-1 draw between Manchester Utd and Queens Park Rangers?

9 Which team did Manchester Utd beat 3-1 in the 1963 FA Cup Final?

10 Who scored a last gasp equaliser for Manchester Utd v Oldham in a 1990s semi-final?

11 Which club did Mike Phelan leave to join Manchester Utd?

12 Who was sacked to be replaced by Alex Ferguson at Manchester Utd?

13 Who was Manchester Utd's Cup Winners' Cup skipper in 1991?

14 Which club did Bryan Robson play for before joining Manchester Utd?

15 What was the 90 minute score in the Manchester Utd v Liverpool Charity Shield game?

Answers to page 24

1 Wolverhampton Wanderers, **2** Maroon, **3** Middlesborough, **4** Brighton, **5** Manchester United players Gary & Philip Neville, **6** Johnny Carey, **7** Morton, **8** Blackburn Rovers, **9** Norwich City, **10** Phil Neal, **11** Blackburn Rovers, **12** Gary McAllister, **13** Dundee, **14** Lothar Matthaus, **15** Paul Gascoigne.

RANGERS 1

Answers on page 29

1 Which team did Rangers beat 4-1 after extra time in the 1982 Scottish FA Cup Final?

2 Who beat Rangers 1-0 to after extra time in the 1967 Cup-Winners' Cup Final?

3 Which team did Rangers beat 1-0 in the 1994 Scottish FA Cup Final?

4 Who did Rangers beat 3-1 in the 1976 Scottish FA Cup Final?

5 Who did Rangers beat 5-0 in the 1964 Scottish League Cup Final?

6 What did Rangers achieve in season 1898-99?

7 How many League goals did Gazza score in his 28 games for Rangers in 1995-96?

8 Who did Rangers beat 1-0 in the 1953 Scottish FA Cup Final replay?

9 Which team with a ground in England knocked Rangers out of the 1967 Scottish FA Cup?

10 Who did Rangers beat 3-1 in the 1964 Scottish FA Cup Final?

11 Apart from Rangers, which other Scottish League club did Ray Wilkins play for?

12 Who lost 3-2 to Rangers in the 1972 Cup-Winners' Cup Final?

13 In what decade did rangers first win the Championship?

14 Who did Rangers beat 2-1 in the 1978 Scottish FA Cup Final?

15 Who was manager of Rangers from 1920 to 1957?

Answers to page 29

1 Just Fontaine, **2** Steve Daley, **3** Monaco, **4** Dean Saunders, **5** Manchester Utd, **6** Tottenham Hotspur, **7** Nottingham Forrest, **8** 83, **9** Bury, **10** Arsenal, **11** Charlton Athletic, **12** 10, **13** Jimmy Rimmer, **14** Eoin Jess, **15** 13.

QUIZ 12

Answers on page 30

1 Where was the 1958 European Cup Final held?

2 Who scored Arsenal's first goal in the title decider at Anfield in 1989?

3 World champions West Germany were beaten 2-1 by which home international team in 1991?

4 Which team lost a play-off Final yet still went up in 1990?

5 Which soccer team does prime minister Tony Blair support?

6 Which club has a fanzine called *Garibaldi*?

7 Which English club did Jock Stein manage?

8 Who scored 20 goals in 70 appearances for Arsenal, Manchester Utd, Ajax, Derby County, Le Harvre, Blackburn Rovers?

9 Fernando Nelson moved from Sporting Lisbon to which club in 1996?

10 What is the highest position Wrexham have ever achieved in the League?

11 Eddie McGoldrick first played in an FA Charity Shield for which club?

12 Which Liverpool player scored his first international goal in Brazil?

13 In which Stadium was the 1986 World Cup Final played?

14 Which club did Ray Houghton leave to join Liverpool?

15 Which manager said"Newcastle United supporters have, in the last few years, been through thick and thin"?

Answers to page 30

1 Gaelic football, **2** Bayern Munich, **3** Division 1 champions (9 times), **4** Kenny Dalglish, **5** 1991, **6** 48, **7** Sterland, **8** George Ramsey (Aston Villa), **9** Nottingham Forest, **10** 1880s, **11** East Fife, **12** Windsor and Eton, **13** Lawrence, **14** Clarrie Bourton, **15** 5 days.

QUIZ 13

Answers on page 27

1 Which French player finished as a top scorer in the 1958 World Cup?

2 Who moved from Wolves to Manchester City for over £1 million in 1979 to set a club record for a transfer fee received?

3 Which club did Jurgen Klinsmann join after leaving Inter Milan?

4 Who moved from Oxford Utd to Derby County in 1988 to set a club record for a transfer fee received?

5 For which club did Stuart Pearson scored in an FA Cup final?

6 Chris Waddle first played in an FA Cup Final for which team?

7 Which English club did Celtic's fullback Tommy Gemmell play for?

8 How many goals did Ferenc Puskas score for Hungary?

9 West Ham Utd recorded a 10-0 League Cup win over which club in 1984?

10 Ian Wright moved from Crystal Palace to which club for £2.5m in September 1991?

11 With which soccer club did actor Glen Murphy have trials with?

12 How many international goals did Billy Bingham score?

13 Who played every game in goal for Aston Villa in the 1981 side?

14 Coventry City paid £1.75m for which Aberdeen player in 1996?

15 How many international goals did John Toshack score?

Answers to page 27

1 Aberdeen, **2** Bayern Munich, **3** Dundee Utd, **4** Hearts, **5** Morton, **6** Won all their League games, **7** 14, **8** Aberdeen, **9** Berwick Rangers, **10** Dundee Utd, **11** Hibernian, **12** Moscow Dynamo, **13** 1890s, **14** Aberdeen, **15** Bill Struth.

QUIZ 14

Answers on page 28

1 Apart from soccer, Kevin Moran was a star in which sport?

2 Boris Becker had soccer trials for which club?

3 What is the highest position Everton have ever achieved in the League?

4 Who hit Liverpool's last league goal in the 1985-86 double season?

5 Which year did Tranmere Rovers win the Play-Off final to gain promotion to Division two?

6 How many goals did Gary Lineker score for England?

7 Which Mel was with Sheffield Wednesday when he made his only England appearance in 1988 against Saudi Arabia?

8 Which manager has won the FA Cup six times, all with the same club?

9 Who beat Malmo 1-0 in the 1979 European Cup Final?

10 In which decade did Hibernian first win the Scottish FA Cup?

11 Who beat Partick Thistle 3-2 in the 1954 Scottish League Cup Final?

12 Wimbledon recorded a 7-2 FA Cup win over which club in November 1980?

13 Which Lennie became boss of Luton Town in December 1995?

14 Which player scored 49 League goals for Coventry City in 1931-32?

15 Forfar employed Steve Murray as manager in 1980 for how long?

Answers to page 28

1 Brussels, **2** Alan Smith, **3** Wales, **4** Sunderland, **5** Newcastle Utd, **6** Nottingham Forest, **7** Leeds Utd, **8** Frank Stapleton, **9** Aston Villa, **10** 15th Division 2, (1978-79), **11** Arsenal, **12** John Barnes, **13** The Azteca in Mexico City, **14** Oxford Utd, **15** Kevin Keegan.

QUIZ 15

Answers on page 33

1 Which Real Madrid player won the 1989-90 Golden Boot award?

2 How many Hereford players were sent off in their match against Northampton in September 1992?

3 Who was the Italian skipper in the 1994 World Cup Final?

4 Bobby Gould followed Dave Sexton as manager of which club?

5 Who signed Stuart Pearce at Coventry City?

6 Who was given a jail sentence, later squashed on appeal, for attacking a taxi-driver?

7 What was the first club that Brian Clough managed?

8 Which team were beaten 2-1 by Aston Villa in the 1957 FA Cup Final?

9 Who beat Fulham 2-0 in the 1975 FA Cup Final?

10 Which team won the 1967 UEFA Cup?

11 How old was Kenny Dalglish when he first played for Celtic?

12 Who beat Arsenal 1-0 in the 1978 FA Cup Final?

13 At which club did Peter Reid start his playing career?

14 Who lost 3-1 to Everton in the 1985 Cup-Winners' Cup Final?

15 Who beat West Brom 4-2 in the 1935 FA Cup Final?

Answers to page 33

1 Andreas Thom, **2** Danny McGrain, **3** Feyenoord, **4** Internazionale, **5** Lou Macari, **6** St Johnstone, **7** 1890s, **8** Andy Walker, **9** Danny McGrain, **10** Five, **11** Ipswich Town, **12** Lou Macari, **13** Steve Chalmers, **14** 1906-07, **15** Billy McNeill.

KEVIN KEEGAN 1

Answers on page 34

1 How much to the nearest million did Keegan spend in transfer fees as manager of Newcastle Utd?

2 How many different England managers did Keegan play for?

3 Keegan moved to Southampton from which German side?

4 Who was appointed Fulham manager by Keegan in his role of Director of Football at Craven Cottage?

5 How many times did Keegan play for England?

6 What was the name of Keegan's chart single of the 1970s?

7 Keegan moved from Liverpool to which club for £500,000 in June 1977?

8 Which German player had the task of marking Keegan in Liverpool's victory in the 1977 European Cup Final?

9 Which Welshman was Keegan's main strike partner at Liverpool?

10 With which league club did Keegan start his career?

11 Which manager took Keegan to Liverpool?

12 Which manager brought Keegan back to England after playing in Germany?

13 Which club was Keegan with when he was First Division leading scorer in 1981-82?

14 Which aftershave did Keegan advertise with boxer Henry Cooper?

15 In 1996 Kevin Keegan was incensed by Alex Ferguson's comments concerning which opposing team?

Answers to page 34

1 Juventus, **2** West Ham Utd, **3** David Platt, **4** Division 1 Champions 3 times, **5** Stan Flashman (Barnet), **6** Tow Law Town, **7** Ray Wilkins, **8** Leeds Utd, **9** 1920s, **10** Zinedine Zidane, **11** Gillingham, **12** Manchester Utd, **13** Oleg Salenko, **14** Boston United, **15** Wally Ardron.

CELTIC 1

Answers on page 31

1 Which German international joined Celtic in July 1995?

2 Which Celtic player fractured his skull against Falkirk in 1972?

3 Who beat Celtic 2-1 in the 1970 European Cup Final?

4 Who did Celtic beat 2-1 in the 1967 European Cup Final?

5 Who was the first manager of Celtic to be sacked by Fergus McCann?

6 Who did Celtic beat 1-0 in the 1970 Scottish League Cup Final?

7 In which decade did Celtic first win the Scottish FA Cup?

8 Who moved from Bolton to Celtic in 1994 to set a club record for a transfer fee received?

9 Which Celtic star was diagnosed diabetic after playing in the 1974 World Cup squad?

10 How many players were sent off in the 1967 World Club Championship between Celtic and Racing Club?

11 Which club did Tony Mowbray join on leaving Celtic?

12 Which manager, still living in England, was dismissed by Celtic in June 1994?

13 Who scored Celtic's 1967 European Cup Final winner?

14 What season did Celtic achieve Scotland's first double?

15 Which Celtic player was Scottish Footballer of the Year in 1965?

Answers to page 31

1 Hugo Sanchez, **2** 4, **3** Franco Baresi, **4** Coventry City, **5** Bobby Gould, **6** Dennis Wise, **7** Hartlepool Utd, **8** Manchester Utd, **9** West Ham Utd, **10** Dynamo Zagreb, **11** 20, **12** Ipswich Town, **13** Bolton Wanderers, **14** Rapid Vienna, **15** Sheffield Wednesday.

QUIZ 16

Answers on page 32

1 Which team won the 1977 UEFA Cup?

2 Alan Devonshire made his international debut while at which club?

3 Who was made skipper in Terry Venables' first game in charge of England?

4 What is the highest position Wolves have ever achieved in the League?

5 Which club chairman sacked manager Barry Fry eight times?

6 Which non-League side did Chris Waddle play for?

7 Which England player was sent off in the Mexico 1986 World Cup?

8 At which club did Terry Phelan make his League debut?

9 In which decade was Tom Finney born?

10 Which French player was sent off for stamping against Saudi Arabia in the first round of the World Cup Finals in 1998?

11 Which club has a fanzine called *Brian Moores Head (Looks Uncannily Like The London Planetarium)*?

12 Which team does Angus Deayton support?

13 Who scored six goals for Russia in the 1994 World Cup Finals?

14 Which non-league side does TV commentator John Motson support?

15 Which player scored 36 League goals for Nottingham Forest in 1950-51?

Answers to page 32

1 £60 million, **2** 4, **3** Hamburg, **4** Ray Wilkins, **5** 63, **6** 'Head Over Heels In Love', **7** S V Hamburg, **8** Berti Vogts, **9** John Toshack, **10** Scunthorpe Utd, **11** Bill Shankly, **12** Lawrie McMenemy, **13** Southampton, **14** Brut, **15** Leeds Utd.

QUIZ 17

Answers on page 37

1 Who were the first British team to compete in the European Cup?

2 Which Liverpool player was widely reported to have been offered £110,00 per week tax-free wages at which Spanish club?

3 Who started his second spell as Stoke City boss in September 1994?

4 Who became Britain's first £100 - a-week footballer?

5 How did goalkeeper Frank Swift die?

6 Which club did Gordon Strachan join on leaving Aberdeen?

7 Where was the Chelsea v Leeds Utd replayed FA Cup final held?

8 Which former England striker is known as 'Bully'?

9 Where did Dean Saunders move to when he left Oxford Utd?

10 Which was the only seeded country not to qualify for the second round of the 1998 World Cup Finals?

11 Which university played in the second and third FA Cup Finals?

12 Which ground is Floyd Road?

13 Which country does John McGinlay play for?

14 What was remarkable about the Home International Championship of 1955-56?

15 What is John Aldridge's middle name?

Answers to page 37

1 One, **2** Bobby Gould, **3** USA, **4** Southampton, **5** Bury, **6** Wignall, **7** The Crowd, **8** Norwich City, **9** Roberto Baggio, **10** Sheffield Wednesday, **11** Blue and White, **12** 349, **13** 1930-31, **14** Everton, **15** Stuttgart.

QUIZ 18

Answers on page 38

1 In the 1970s, which keeper went 1,143 minutes in international soccer without conceding a goal?

2 David Larter made a record 426 appearances for which Scottish club between 1987-98?

3 Which team are known as the Shrews?

4 Which club was Kevin Keegan with when he was First Division leading scorer in 1981-82?

5 Who were the first brothers to be at an English double-winning club?

6 What was England's biggest win over Scotland?

7 Which club has a fanzine called *Hey Big Spender*?

8 Who were the only team to beat West Germany in the 1974 World Cup finals?

9 Who succeeded Dally Duncan as boss of Blackburn Rovers in 1961?

10 Which was the last team to win the European Cup in their first ever season in the competition?

11 Which French player scored two goals against Croatia in the 1998 World Cup Semi-Final?

12 Who succeeded Phil Neal as manager of Coventry City in 1995?

13 Which Sir Norman produced the 1980s report "The State of Football"?

14 How many days was Jock Stein in charge of Leeds Utd?

15 'The Famous Five' helped which Scottish club to the Championship just after the Second World War?

Answers to page 38

1 Andy Cole, **2** David Kelly, **3** John Beresford, **4** Manchester Utd, **5** Portsmouth, **6** Wimbledon, **7** £60 million, **8** Barcelona, Dynamo Kiev, PSV Eindhoven, **9** Derby County, **10** Kevin Keegan, **11** Mark Lawrenson, **12** Robert Lee, **13** 1900s, **14** Blackpool, **15** Douglas Hall and Freddie Shepherd.

QUIZ 19

Answers on page 35

1 How many international goals did Mike Summerbee score?

2 Who was manager of Wimbledon when they won the FA Cup Final in 1988?

3 Against which country was Leonardo of Brazil sent off in 1994?

4 Which club released Dennis Wise because he was too small?

5 In 1981-82 Craig Madden established a record for most League goals in a season at which club?

6 Which Steve became boss of Colchester Utd in January 1995?

7 The Bradford City fire disaster led to a June 1985 No.1 for various artists under which name?

8 Dave Stringer followed Ken Brown as manager of which club?

9 Who was Italy's top scorer in the 1994 World Cup in the USA?

10 Which club's ground is near the River Don?

11 What two colours are on Hartlepool's home shirts?

12 How many League goals did Dixie Dean score for Everton?

13 In which season did Manchester Utd lose the first 12 games?

14 Kevin Richardson first played in an FA Cup Final for which team?

15 Who did Napoli beat in the 1989 UEFA Cup Final?

Answers to page 35

1 Leeds Utd, **2** Miner, **3** Fulham, **4** Chester City, **5** 1900, **6** Jan Ceulemans, **7** Because he had been convicted of a drink-driving offence, **8** Tom Boyd, **9** Burnley, **10** Fettis, **11** Stoke City, **12** Barcelona, **13** Alan Shearer, **14** Blackburn Rovers, **15** Kennington Oval.

NEWCASTLE 1

Answers on page 36

1 Which player scored 34 League goals for Newcastle Utd in 1993-94?

2 Who was Newcastle Utd's top scorer in the 1992-93?

3 Which defender scored both goals for Newcastle Utd in their 2-2 draw away to Dynamo Kiev in the 1997-98 Champions League?

4 Who were Newcastle Utd's opponents in Alan Shearer's first Wembley game for the club?

5 On February 22 1956, Newcastle Utd visited which club for the first English League game to be played under floodlights?

6 Which club did Andy Thorn leave to join Newcastle Utd?

7 How much did Kevin Keegan spend in transfer fees at Newcastle Utd?

8 Which three other clubs were in Newcastle Utd's 1997-98 Champions' League Group?

9 Which club did Paul Kitson leave to join Newcastle Utd?

10 Which manager said "Newcastle supporters have, in the last few years, been through thick and thin"?

11 Which ex-Liverpool defender did Keegan get to advise Newcastle Utd about their defence?

12 Who did Charlton sell to Newcastle for £750,000 in September 1992?

13 In what decade did Newcastle Utd first win the Championship?

14 Which team did Newcastle Utd beat 2-0 in the 1951 FA Cup Final?

15 Which two Newcastle Utd directors resigned after tabloid press revelations about their behaviour in Spain?

Answers to page 36

1 Dino Zoff, **2** Montrose, **3** Shrewsbury Town, **4** Southampton, **5** Gary and Phil Neville, **6** 9-3, **7** Derby County, **8** East Germany, **9** Jack Marshall, **10** Aston Villa in 1982, **11** Lilian Thurman, **12** Ron Atkinson, **13** Chester, **14** 44, **15** Hibernian.

WALES 1

Answers on page 41

1 In which decade did Wales first win at Wembley?

2 Who made his debut for Wales aged 18 years 71 days?

3 Who is the youngest player to earn a full Welsh Cap?

4 By what score did England beat Wales at Cardiff in 1896?

5 Who was manager of Wales for 47 days?

6 Which team did Wales beat 5-0 in their first game in the 1998 World Cup campaign?

7 Where was Welsh international Mark Crossley born?

8 Who started the game in goal for Wales when they drew against Jamaica in a friendly in March 1998?

9 Who scored 5 goals in a game for Derby County against Wales in March 1896?

10 Which Welsh player was 45 years and 229 days old when he won a cap for England in 1920?

11 Who started the game in goal for Wales when they beat Malta in a friendly in June 1998?

12 Who was the first Welsh player to be sent off in an international?

13 Who was the young Middlesborough striker who made his England debut against Wales in 1959?

14 Which London side defeated Wales in a friendly in May 1996?

15 While at Crystal Palace, who was the first fourth division player to be picked for Wales?

Answers to page 41

1 Chelsea, **2** Charlie George, **3** Milija Aleksic, **4** Chelsea, **5** Rome, **6** Leicester City, **7** Newcastle United, **8** Feyenoord in 1970, **9** 12, **10** Dooley, **11** Sunderland, **12** Celtic, **13** Alex McLeish, **14** Eric, **15** Tottenham Hotspur.

QUIZ 20

Answers on page 42

1 Did Sir Matt Busby ever play international soccer?

2 In which decade did Notts County first win the FA Cup?

3 Who was the first Englishman to manage a European Cup-winning side?

4 In which year did FIFA decree that linesmen be called Referee's Assistants?

5 In 1946, which Charlton Athletic player became the first player to score for both teams in an FA Cup Final?

6 Who did Scotland face in their first 1998 World Cup qualifying game?

7 How many captains had England had before Alan Shearer?

8 Who was Sporting Lisbon's English coach when they won the Portugese League Championship in 1982?

9 Where was the 1978 European Cup Winners' Cup Final held?

10 Which Dutch player scored the winning goal to knock Argentina out of the 1998 World Cup at the quarter-finals stage?

11 Which John became boss of Preston in 1992?

12 Which Scottish team appeared as Tannochbrae in an episode of the 1960s' BBC drama serial *Doctor Finlay's Casebook*?

13 Who holds the Arsenal League appearance record?

14 Webb and Wallace lined up together for which trophy-winning team?

15 Port Vale used to have which word at the front of their name?

Answers to page 42

1 Barnsley, **2** Vinnie Jones, **3** Monaco, **4** West Ham Utd, **5** Eusebio, **6** Ferenc Puskas, **7** Southport, **8** Aston Villa, **9** John Wark, **10** . . . his knees have gone all trembly", **11** Liverpool, **12** The Bees, **13** Leicester Fosse, **14** Richard Parker, **15** Drink driving.

QUIZ 21

Answers on page 39

1 Who were the first London side to win the League Cup?

2 Which English player lost a finger in an accident with a lawnmower?

3 Who was in goal for Spurs when they won the FA Cup in 1981?

4 Which club has a fanzine called *The Red Card*?

5 Which city hosted the European Cup Final when Liverpool won it for the first time?

6 David Nish became the youngest FA Cup Final skipper with which team?

7 Richard Dinnis was manager of which club in 1977?

8 Which were the first team from Holland to win the European Cup?

9 How many games did Blackburn play in 1996 without a win?

10 Which Derek scored most goals in a season for Sheffield Wednesday?

11 Who was George Chisholm playing for when he scored a League Cup Final own goal?

12 Chris Morris was at which club when he made his international debut?

13 Which defender won 77 caps for Scotland between 1980 and 1991?

14 What is David Hirst's middle name?

15 Steve Sedgley first played in an FA Cup Final for which team?

Answers to page 39

1 1970s, **2** John Charles, **3** Ryan Green (Wolves), **4** 9-1, **5** John Toshack, **6** San Marino, **7** Barnsley, **8** Jones, **9** Steve Bloomer, **10** Billy Meredith, **11** Jones, **12** Trevor Hockey, **13** Brian Clough, **14** Leyton Orient, **15** Vic Rouse.

QUIZ 22

Answers on page 40

1 Who beat West Brom 1-0 in the 1912 FA Cup Final replay?

2 Who received a £20,000 fine from the FA for voicing a video nasty?

3 In 1992 Jurgen Klinsmann left Inter Milan to join which club?

4 Sheffield Utd player Harry Johnson scored 5 goals in a match in December 1927. Who were the opponents?

5 Which Benfica player won the 1967-68 Golden Boot award?

6 Who scored the first European Cup Final hat-trick?

7 Oldham Athletic player Bert Lister scored 7 goals in a match in December 1962. Who were the opponents?

8 John and James Cowan played for which double winners?

9 Who was the first British player to score a hat-trick of penalties in a Euro game?

10 Complete the chorus from a silly FA Cup song written about Ossie Ardiles. "Ossie's going to Wembley . . .

11 Which club first won the League Cup three years in a row?

12 What is Barnet's nickname?

13 Grimsby Town player Tommy McCairns scored 6 goals in a match in April 1896. Who were the opponents?

14 Which player scored 37 League goals for Millwall in 1926-27?

15 What crime was Tony Adams found guilty of and sent to prison in December 1990?

Answers to page 40

1 Yes (He played once for Scotland), **2** 1890s, **3** Bob Paisley, **4** 1996, **5** Bert Turner, **6** Austria, **7** He was the 100th, **8** Malcolm Allison, **9** Paris, **10** Denis Bergkamp, **11** Beck, **12** Alloa Athletic, **13** David O'Leary, **14** Manchester Utd, **15** Burslem.

QUIZ 23

Answers on page 45

1 In which year did Wales reach the World Cup Finals for the only time?

2 Which player scored 43 League goals for Sunderland in 1928-29?

3 David Rocastle moved from Arsenal to which club for £2 million in July 1992?

4 Which club has a fanzine called *Follow The Yellow Brick Road*?

5 What was the outcome of the penalty shoot-out in the Brazil v Holland 1998 World Cup semi-final?

6 Who made his twelfth and last visit to Wembley as a manager for the 1983 League Cup Final?

7 Rioch and George scored Euro goals in the same 1970s match for which club?

8 Gary Crosby first played in an FA Cup Final for which team?

9 Which defender played for Nottingham Forest, Sampdoria and Sheffield Wednesday?

10 Don Welsh and Phil Taylor have both managed which club?

11 Who succeeded Stan Anderson as manager of Middlesborough in 1973?

12 Kevin Keegan moved to Southampton from which German side?

13 Which Liverpool defender made his England debut at the age of 20?

14 Who was Blackburn Rovers's only League ever present in 1994-95?

15 Who succeeded Joe Royle as manager of Oldham Athletic in 1994?

Answers to page 45

1 Valencia, **2** RSC Anderlecht, **3** Tottenham Hotspur, **4** Bruges, **5** RSC Anderlecht, **6** Billy Thompson, **7** Espanol, **8** Stuttgart, **9** Fiorentina, **10** AS Roma, **11** Torino, **12** Fairs Cup, **13** Borussia Dortmund, **14** Tottenham Hotspur, **15** Parma and Juventus.

SCOTLAND 1

Answers on page 46

1. What was the score of Wembley's England v Scotland game in 1967?
2. Who, during the 1974 World Cup Finals, was the first player to make 55 appearances for Scotland?
3. Who was the goalkeeper called up at short notice by Scotland when Andy Goram made his shock withdrawal from the 1998 World Cup?
4. Which Gordon scored Scotland's only World Cup goal in Mexico?
5. How many goals did Andy Gray score for Scotland?
6. Which two players are joint top scorers for Scotland?
7. Which ex-Liverpool player holds Scotland's most capped record?
8. Which country did Scotland beat in the 1990 World Cup tournament?
9. What was Scotland's biggest win over England?
10. Whose last game for Scotland was the 1978 World Cup defeat by Peru in which he missed a penalty?
11. Who were Scotland's joint top scorers in Italia '90?
12. How many goals did Billy Bremner score for Scotland?
13. Who was Scotland's caretaker manager in the mid 1980s?
14. From 1974, how many consecutive World Cup tournaments did Scotland reach?
15. How many points did Scotland win in their 1998 World Cup group final matches?

Answers to page 46

1 Ralph Hunt, **2** Jimmy Greaves, **3** Leicester City, **4** Franz Beckenbauer, **5** Andy Cole, **6** West Ham Utd v Crystal Palace, **7** Luton Town, **8** Liverpool, **9** John Toshack, **10** Norwich City, **11** Bayern Munich, **12** Sheffield Wednesday, **13** Carlos Alberto, **14** Argentina, **15** Harry Gregg.

UEFA CUP FINALS

Answers on page 43

1 Which Spanish side was the first team to reach three consecutive UEFA Cup finals?

2 Who lost to Arsenal in the 1970 UEFA Cup Final?

3 Which British team lost to Feyenoord in the 1974 UEFA Cup Final?

4 Who lost to Liverpool in the 1976 UEFA Cup Final?

5 Who did Tottenham Hotspur beat in the 1984 UEFA Cup Final?

6 Who was in goal for both legs of Dundee Utd's 1987 UEFA Cup Final?

7 Which Spanish side lost the 1988 UEFA Cup Final after being three up from the first leg?

8 Who did Napoli beat in the 1989 UEFA Cup Final?

9 Who did Juventus beat in the 1990 UEFA Cup final?

10 Who did Internazionale beat in the 1991 UEFA Cup final?

11 Who lost to Ajax on away goals in the 1992 UEFA Cup Final?

12 What was the UEFA Cup originally called?

13 Who lost to Juventus in the 1993 UEFA Cup Final?

14 Who won the first UEFA Cup Final?

15 Which two Italian teams contested the UEFA Cup Final in 1995?

Answers to page 43

1 1958, **2** Dave Halliday, **3** Leeds Utd, **4** Mansfield Town, **5** Brazil won 4-2, **6** Bob Paisley, **7** Derby County, **8** Nottingham Forest, **9** Des Walker, **10** Liverpool, **11** Jack Charlton, **12** Hamburg, **13** Rob Jones, **14** Alan Shearer, **15** Graham Sharpe.

QUIZ 24

Answers on page 44

1 Which player scored 31 League goals for Norwich City in 1955-56?

2 Which Chelsea star finished as the League's top scorer in 1959?

3 Which club did Alan Shearer score his first Newcastle United hat-trick against?

4 Which Bayern Munich player was European footballer of the Year in 1976?

5 Who did Bristol City buy from Arsenal for £500,000 and sell to Newcastle United for £1.75m nine months later?

6 Which was the second Premiership match of the 1997-98 season to be abandoned through floodlight failure?

7 Steve Claridge joined Cambridge in November 1992 from which club?

8 Craig Johnston moved from Middlesborough to which club for £575,000 in April 1981?

9 Which British manager did Real Madrid sack in 1990?

10 Jon Newsome moved from Leeds Utd to which club for £1m in June 1994?

11 Who beat St Etienne 1-0 in the 1976 European Cup Final?

12 Andy Sinton moved from QPR to which club for £2.7m in August 1993?

13 Who was the captain of Brazil when they lifted the World Cup for the third time?

14 Who won the 1978 World Cup?

15 Who kept goal for Northern Ireland in the 1958 World Cup?

Answers to page 44

1 3-2 to Scotland, **2** Denis Law, **3** Jonathan Gould (Celtic), **4** Strachan, **5** 7, **6** Denis Law and Kenny Dalglish, **7** Kenny Dalglish, **8** Sweden, **9** 7-2, **10** Don Masson, **11** McCall and Johnston (1each), **12** Three, **13** Alex Ferguson, **14** Five, **15** one.

QUIZ 25

Answers on page 49

1 Who started the game in goal for Wales when they beat Malta in a friendly in June 1998?

2 Who were winners in 1992 in the first game where a top flight team went out of the FA Cup competition in a shoot out?

3 Who was fined £20,000 by the FA for doing the voice-over on a video nasty?

4 Which Benfica player was European footballer of the Year in 1965?

5 Up to the late 1980s, which club played at The Old Showground?

6 Which Arsenal player was Footballer of the Year in 1971?

7 Which team were beaten 3-2 by Everton in the 1966 FA Cup Final?

8 Who beat Hibernian 6-2 in the 1969 Scottish League Cup Final?

9 At which club did Steve McMahon make his League debut?

10 Who succeeded Gordon Hurst as manager of Oldham Athletic in 1966?

11 Where was the replayed Mersey League Cup Final of the 1980s held?

12 Which player scored 33 League goals for Oldham Athletic in 1936-37?

13 Who hit five goals for Ipswich Town against Southampton in 1981-82?

14 Who lost to Nottingham Forest in the 1979 Super Cup?

15 Where was the 1993 European Cup Final held?

Answers to page 49

1 72, **2** Southampton, **3** Four, **4** Sunderland, **5** Sheffield Wednesday, **6** East Fife, **7** York City, **8** Leeds Utd, **9** Chelsea, **10** AC Milan, **11** Gary Pallister, **12** 1875, **13** Jan Molby, **14** Everton, **15** West Ham Utd.

QUIZ 26

Answers on page 50

1 What was Ray Houghton's first League club?

2 Which Scot took over as manager of Benfica during the 1997-98?

3 Who was the Sunderland goalkeeper in the 1973 FA Cup Final?

4 Oldham Athletic player Frank Bunn scored 6 goals in a League Cup match in October 1989. Who were the opponents?

5 Which player, suffering from a broken nose, scored for Spurs in the 1993 FA Cup Final replay?

6 Who was the manager of Belgium during the 1998 World Cup qualifying play-off's?

7 How many World Cup Finals have Argentina appeared in?

8 Which Cliff set a career goals record at Arsenal?

9 Which ex-Manchester Utd player became Jack Charlton's assistant with the Republic of Ireland?

10 Which Spanish international played in European Cup Finals for both Barcelona and Inter Milan in the 1960s?

11 Which club had a fanzine called *Beesotted*?

12 Which club does television presenter Terry Christian support?

13 Which is the only team to have won the European Cup more often than its own domestic championship?

14 What was unique about the positions of the two captains in the 1934 World Cup Final between Italy and Uruguay?

15 Which player will be forever connected with the 1953 FA Cup Final?

Answers to page 50

1 24, **2** Bobby Charlton, **3** Eight, **4** Jackie Milburn, **5** Ray Wilkins, **6** Tommy Lawton, **7** 3, **8** Bobby Charlton, **9** Elland Road, **10** Johnny Haynes, **11** Rob Jones, **12** Tommy Lawton, **13** 48, **14** Bobby Robson, **15** Four.

QUIZ 27

Answers on page 47

1 How many internationals did Alan Ball play for England?

2 Francis Benali played over 200 games for which club?

3 Before the World Cup Finals in 1990, how many years had gone by without an England being awarded a penalty?

4 Jim Montgomery set a League appearance record at which club?

5 On the day of the 1995 FA Cup Final which Premiership club announced that their manager was leaving?

6 Which club played at Bayview park?

7 Alphabetically, which is the last English League team?

8 Allan Clarke followed Jimmy Adamson as manager of which club?

9 Who were the first post-war English champions to have won less than half their fixtures?

10 Which Italian team did Luther Blissett play for?

11 Who moved from Middlesborough in August 1989 to set a club record for a transfer fee received?

12 When did FA Cup Final go to extra time for the first time?

13 Which midfielder sent a glorious pass up to Ian Rush for his first goal in the 1986 FA Cup final?

14 Earl Barrett first played in an FA Charity Shield for which club?

15 Which club used to play at the Recreation Ground, Canning Town?

Answers to page 47

1 Jones, **2** Southampton, **3** Vinnie Jones, **4** Eusebio, **5** Scunthorpe Utd, **6** Frank McLintock, **7** Sheffield Wednesday, **8** Celtic, **9** Everton, **10** Jimmy McIlroy, **11** Maine Road, **12** Tom Davis, **13** Alan Brazil, **14** Barcelona, **15** Munich.

ENGLAND 1

Answers on page 48

1 How many England goals did Geoff Hurst score?

2 Who is England's all-time record goalscorer?

3 How many goals did England score against Turkey in 1984?

4 Who scored England's first ever hat-trick in a World Cup match?

5 Which England player was sent off in the Mexico 1986 World Cup?

6 Which England player scored 22 times in 23 appearances?

7 How many games did Billy Wright miss between his first and last appearance for England?

8 Who scored for England in his 100th international?

9 The first home England international since 1966 to be played away from Wembley was in 1995 against Sweden. Where was it played?

10 Who was skipper of England from 1960 until involved in a serious car accident in 1962?

11 Which Liverpool defender made his England debut at the age of 20?

12 Timed at 17 seconds in 1947, who scored England's fastest goal?

13 How many goals did Gary Lineker score for England?

14 Which England manager has won most World Cup games?

15 Walter Winterbottom led England into how many World Cups?

Answers to page 48

1 West Ham Utd, **2** Graeme Souness, **3** Jim Montgomery, **4** Scarborough, **5** Andy Linighan, **6** Georges Leekens, **7** 4, **8** Bastin, **9** Maurice Setters, **10** Luis Suarez, **11** Bretford, **12** Manchester Utd, **13** Nottingham Forest, **14** They were both goalkeepers, **15** Stanley Matthews.

• CUP WINNERS' CUP •

Answers on page 53

1 The 1981 Cup Winners' Cup final was the only one to have been contested by two Eastern European clubs. Which ones?

2 Who came off the substitutes bench to score Chelsea's winner in the 1998 European Cup Winners Cup Final?

3 What happened to the referee after Leeds Utd's defeat in the 1973 Cup Winners' Cup Final?

4 Who scored Aberdeen's winner in the 1983 Cup Winners' Cup Final?

5 Who scored Manchester Utd's goals in the 1991 European Cup Winners' Cup Final against Barcelona?

6 In what year was the first Euro Cup Winner's Cup Final first played?

7 Nayim scored a last minute Cup Winners' Cup Final goal for whic club?

8 What was the scoreline in the 1963 Cup Winners' Cup Final, in which an English club won for the first time?

9 In which city has the Cup Winners' Cup Final been played most often?

10 Who beat Leeds Utd in the 1973 Cup Winners' Cup Final?

11 Who lost 1-0 to Chelsea in the 1998 Cup Winners' Cup Final?

12 Which club reached three consecutive Cup Winners' Cup finals in the 1970s?

13 1860 Munich and Anderlecht have both played which English team in Euro Cup Winners' Cup Finals?

14 Where was the 1964 European Cup Winners' Cup Final replay held?

15 Who won the first Cup Winners Cup Final played at Wembley?

Answers to page 53

1 Dave Basset (Nottingham Forest), **2** Ian Wright, **3** Uruguay, **4** Shamrock Rovers, **5** 1901, **6** Aston Villa, **7** Walter Tait, **8** Notts County, **9** Keith Branagan, **10** The Manor, Oxford Utd, **11** 1920s, **12** 1940s, **13** Wolves, **14** Billy Bonds, **15** Frank Skinner.

QUIZ 28

Answers on page 54

1 Who said "If Liverpool is a danger to your health, try managing Barnet"?

2 Which Blackburn Rovers and England defender suffered a long-term injury against Middlesborough in December 1995?

3 Where was Ron Atkinson's first League managers job from November 1974 to January 1978?

4 Who beat Hibernian 3-2 in the 1979 Scottish FA Cup Final 2nd replay?

5 Which two English internationals helped Monaco to the Championship in 1988?

6 Which team has won the Bulgarian League Championship most often?

7 Brian Talbot followed Ron Atkinson's second spell as boss of which club?

8 What was the offence for which Kanchelskis was sent off in Manchester Utd's 1994 League Cup Final?

9 Which defender was the last skipper to lift the Jules Rimet Trophy after a World Cup Final?

10 Who plays at home at the Belle Vue Ground?

11 Which country did Alfred Strange play for?

12 Which Celtic star was diagnosed diabetic after playing in the 1974 World Cup squad?

13 Danny Blanchflower followed Ken Shellito as manager at which club?

14 At which club did Terry Paine finish his playing career?

15 Which was Steve Bruce's first League club?

Answers to page 54

1 QPR, **2** Lincoln City, **3** Dave Magnall, **4** Karl Heinz Rummenigge, **5** Southampton, **6** Manchester City, **7** Argentina, **8** Billy Bremner, **9** Rinus Michels, **10** Red, **11** Robbie Savage, **12** Lancashire and Yorkshire Railway, **13** Parma, **14** Alloa, **15** Atletico Madrid.

QUIZ 29

Answers on page 51

1 Which manager was the first to be sacked in 1999?

2 Who came off of the bench to hit two goals in a Final for Crystal Palace?

3 The world's most played international fixture is played between Argentina and which other country?

4 Which team has won the Irish League most often?

5 In which year did Spurs first win the FA Cup?

6 Portsmouth player Peter Harris scored 5 goals in a match in September 1958. Who were the opponents?

7 Who, in 1888, scored the first League hat-trick (for Burnley against Blackburn Rovers)?

8 Which was Mark Draper's first League club?

9 Who went down from the top flight with Millwall in 1990 and Bolton in 1996?

10 Which was the first ground to have floodlights permanently installed?

11 In which decade was Nat Lofthouse born?

12 In which decade was George Best born?

13 Andy Gray moved from Aston Villa to which club for £1.75 million in September 1979?

14 Which defender made a record 663 appearances for West Ham Utd between 1967 and 1988 and later managed the club?

15 Which famous comedian and TV star is a supporter of West Brom?

Answers to page 51

1 Dynamo Tibilisi and Carl Zeiss Jena, **2** Gianfranco Zola, **3** He was Suspended by UEFA, **4** Hewitt, **5** Mark Hughes, **6** 1961, **7** Real Zaragoza, **8** 5-1, **9** Rotterdam (four times), **10** AC Milan, **11** Stuttgart, **12** Anderlecht, **13** West Ham Utd, **14** Antwerp, **15** West Ham Utd (1965).

QUIZ 30

Answers on page 52

1 Which English club was the first to install an artificial pitch?

2 Who were Bradford city's opponents in the fire disaster game?

3 Which player scored 33 League goals for Huddersfield Town in 1931-32?

4 Which Bayern Munich player was European footballer of the Year in 1980 and 1981?

5 Nick Holmes was a long serving player with which club?

6 Kevin Reeves hit an FA Cup Final goal for which club?

7 In which country were the 1978 World Cup Finals held?

8 Which player describing his upbringing said "There's only one word to describe Raploch, and that's hard"?

9 Who was the Dutch coach for Euro 88?

10 What colour are Aberdeen's home shorts?

11 Which Welsh international was disciplined by manager Bobby Gould for disrespectful behaviour towards Paolo Maldini?

12 In Manchester Utd's founding days what did the letters LYR stand for?

13 Which club beat AC Milan to win the European Super Cup in 1994?

14 Which Scottish side plays home games at Recreation Park?

15 At which Spanish club did Abel Resino go 1,275 minutes without conceding a goal?

Answers to page 52

1 Barry Fry, **2** Graham Le Saux, **3** Cambridge Utd, **4** Rangers, **5** Mark hateley and Glenn Hoddle, **6** CSKA Sofia, **7** West Brom, **8** Deliberate handball, **9** Daniel Passarella (Trophy was then awarded to Argentina), **10** Doncaster Rovers, **11** England, **12** Danny McGrain, **13** Chelsea, **14** Hereford Utd, **15** Gillingham.

QUIZ 31

Answers on page 57

1 Who scored nine goals in a 1970s FA Cup match against Margate?

2 Chelsea won the 1998 Coca-Cola cup. Dennis Wise was captain, but who stepped up to receive the trophy?

3 What is the highest position Derby County have ever achieved in the League?

4 What is the main colour of Carlise Utd's home shirts?

5 Which goalkeeper was called up at short notice by Scotland when Andy Goram made his shock withdrawal from the 1998 World Cup?

6 Which player left West Brom for £1.5m in 1981?

7 Which Dutchman hit a Euro 88 hat-trick against England?

8 What is the highest position QPR have ever achieved in the League?

9 Alan Taylor scored twice in an FA Cup Final for which club?

10 Barry Horne first played in an FA Charity Shield for which club?

11 Who started the game in goal for England when they drew against Saudi Arabia in a friendly in May 1998?

12 In which decade did Celtic first win the Scottish FA Cup?

13 Which West Brom and Manchester Utd player was forced to retire through injury in 1988?

14 At which club did George Curtis set a League appearance record that stood until the mid-90s?

15 Which John became boss of Norwich City in 1994?

Answers to page 57

1 AC Milan, **2** Ajax, **3** AS Roma, **4** Bayern Munich, **5** Bob Houghton, **6** Bobby Charlton, **7** Brian Kidd, **8** Eddie and Frank Gray, **9** John Robertson, **10** Juventus in 1996, **11** Liverpool, **12** Manchester Utd, **13** Marseille, **14** Real Madrid in 1957, **15** Reims.

• NORTHERN IRELAND 1 •

Answers on page 58

1 Who is the Luton Town and Everton forward who went on to manage Northern Ireland?

2 Who kept goal for Northern Ireland in the 1958 World Cup?

3 Who scored the winning goal against Spain to take Northern Ireland through to the second round of the 1982 World Cup finals?

4 Which Northern Ireland player scored to defeat West Germany in a European qualifier in 1983?

5 Which Northern Ireland player became the first to receive a red card in a British Home International match?

6 How many international goals did Northern Ireland's Johnny Crossan score in the 1960s?

7 Who became manager of Northern Ireland in 1994?

8 Which Northern Ireland skipper said, "Our tactics are to equalise before the other side scores"?

9 Which Arsenal and Tottenham Hotspur manager was also team boss of Northern Ireland in 1996?

10 Who was the first non-Ulsterman to manage Northern Ireland?

11 During the 97-98 season which Northern Ireland manager was sacked?

12 Who is Northern Irelands most-capped player?

13 Who is Northern Irelands top goal-scorer?

14 Against which country did Northern Ireland record a 7-0 victory?

15 Who is the youngest player to represent Northern Ireland in the World Cup Finals?

Answers to page 58

1 Phelan, **2** Newcastle Utd, **3** Lazio, **4** Jack Charlton, **5** Burnley, **6** Romford, **7** Leeds Utd, **8** Stockport (1994 Play-off final against Burnley), **9** Boca Juniors, **10** Teacher, **11** FC Koln, **12** George Graham, **13** Aston Villa, **14** Liberia, **15** John Wark.

• EUROPEAN CUP FINALS •

Answers on page 55

1 Which team appeared in the European Cup Final in 1993,1994 and 1995?

2 Who were the first Dutch club to reach the European Cup Final?

3 Who lost on penalties to Liverpool in the 1984 European Cup Final?

4 Which team won the first European Cup Final to go to a replay?

5 Who was Malmo's English manager when they met Nottingham Forest in the European Cup Final?

6 Who scored first for Manchester Utd in the 1960s European Cup Final against Benfica?

7 Which British player played in a European Cup Final on his 19th birthday?

8 Which brothers played in the 1976 European Cup Final?

9 Who scored Nottingham Forest's goal in the European Cup final to beat Hamburg?

10 Before Borussia Dortmund in 1997, which was the last team to win the European Cup Final in their own country?

11 Michel Platini inspired Juventus to European Cup Final victory over which English side?

12 Who beat Benfica 4-1 after extra time in the 1968 European Cup Final?

13 Who beat AC Milan 1-0 in the 1993 European Cup Final before being stripped of the title?

14 Which was the first club to play a European Cup Final on their own ground?

15 Which French team became the first to lose two European Cup Finals?

Answers to page 55

1 Ted MacDougall, **2** Gianluca Vialli (player/manager), **3** Division 1 Champions (1971-72, 1974-75), **4** Blue, **5** Jonathan Gould (Celtic), **6** Bryan Robson, **7** Marco van Basten, **8** Division 1 (2nd 1975-76), **9** West Ham Utd, **10** Everton, **11** Seaman, **12** 1890s, **13** Remi Moses, **14** Coventry City, **15** Deehan.

QUIZ 32

Answers on page 56

1 Which Mike of Manchester Utd won his only England cap in 1989?

2 Kevin Carr and Martin Thomas have both played for which club?

3 For which Italian Serie A club was Pierluigi Casiraghi playing for at the time of the 1998 World Cup?

4 After a check up and brain scan, who said, “It proves that I do have a brain”?

5 Which Lancashire side won the championship in 1960?

6 Where was Tony Adams born?

7 Who lost 1-0 to AC Milan in the 1973 Cup-Winners’ Cup Final?

8 Who are the only club to have had two players sent off in a game at Wembley?

9 Diego Maradona made his name playing for which Argentine team?

10 What was Bob Wilson’s job before he turned pro?

11 Which team won the first Bundesliga championship in Germany in 1963?

12 Who was boss of Millwall between 1982 and 1986?

13 Which club did Derek Moutfield join on leaving Everton?

14 In which country was former European Player of the Year George Weah born?

15 Which Scottish player has joined Ipswich Town on three occasions?

Answers to page 56

1 Billy Bingham, **2** Harry Gregg, **3** Gerry Armstrong, **4** Norman Whiteside, **5** Billy Ferguson, **6** 10, **7** Bryan Hamilton, **8** Danny Blanchflower, **9** Terry Neill, **10** Lawrie McMenemy, **11** Bryan Hamilton, **12** Pat Jennings (119), **13** Colin Clarke (13), **14** Wales, **15** Norman Whiteside.

QUIZ 33

Answers on page 61

1 What nationality is Kim Milton Nielsen, the referee who sent Beckham off in the 1998 World Cup finals?

2 In which decade was John Aldridge born?

3 Who scored for Nottingham Forest in the 1991 Final?

4 Which teams played in the 1962 World Cup Final?

5 What do the initials USSF stand for?

6 At which club did Mick Harford make his League debut?

7 Who scored for PSV Eindhoven as they beat Newcastle United 1-0 in the 1997-98 Champions' League?

8 Who scored the goals that took Aston Villa through 2-1 in the second leg of their second round UEFA Cup tie with Athletico Bilbao?

9 Which club had a fanzine called *City Gent*?

10 Which club did Iain Dowie leave to join Southampton?

11 Which two German-speakers had a row in the Tottenham Hotspur tunnel?

12 Who beat Dundee Utd 1-0 in the 1987 Scottish FA Cup Final?

13 Which Roger was First Division leading scorer in 1965-66?

14 Who is Chris Casper's footballing father?

15 Which soccer team does former tennis star John Lloyd support?

Answers to page 61

1 Swansea City, **2** Porterfield, **3** Queen's Park, **4** Kevin Keegan, **5** 7th Division 1 (1986-87), **6** 3rd Division 1 (1990-91), **7** Division 1 (1st), **8** Everton in 1890-91, before Liverpool were formed, **9** Oldham Athletic, **10** Steve McMahon, **11** Manchester Utd, **12** Leicester City, **13** Manchester City, **14** Dislocated shoulder, **15** Stuart Pearson.

QUIZ 34

Answers on page 62

1 Which player scored 35 League goals for Millwall in 1960-61?

2 Which player scored 44 League goals for Leicester City in 1956-57?

3 Which player scored 37 League goals for Derby County in 1930-31?

4 Which player scored 33 League goals for Tottenham Hotspur in 1986-87?

5 Which player scored 60 League goals for Everton in 1927-28?

6 How old was Dino Zoff when he was in Italy's World Cup-winning side?

7 Who scored 5 goals in a game for Derby County against Wales in March 1896?

8 What is Ray Wilkins middle name?

9 Which England player was sent off in 1973 against Poland?

10 Which country failed to score in the USA 1994?

11 In the 1994 World Cup finals Jack Charlton, manager of the Republic of Ireland was fined and given a touchline ban by FIFA. What offence did he commit?

12 What was the name of the trophy Brazil won outright in 1970?

13 Gary Lineker played his last game against which country?

14 Beating Dunferline in the 1991 League Cup Final gave which club its first major trophy for 19 years?

15 Which players appeared in every England game of the 1966 World Cup finals?

Answers to page 62

1 Dennis Irwin, **2** Lansdowne Road, **3** Roy Keane, **4** Eamon Dunphy, **5** Liam Brady, **6** To the second round, **7** England, **8** Malta, **9** Wales, **10** 1949, **11** Eoin Hand, **12** Maurice Setters, **13** 1964 European Championships, **14** Frank Stapleton, **15** Mick McCarthy.

QUIZ 35

Answers on page 59

1 Kevin Cullis was briefly boss of which League club in 1996?

2 Which Ian became Chelsea manager in 1991?

3 Which team won the Scottish FA Cup ten times then managed to go 100 years without winning it?

4 Which Hamburg player was European Footballer of the Year in 1978 and 1979?

5 What is the highest position Luton Town have ever achieved in the League?

6 What is the highest position Crystal Palace have ever achieved in the League?

7 What is the highest position Sheffield Wednesday have ever achieved in the League?

8 Who won the League Championship first - Liverpool or Everton?

9 Which club was Mike Milligan bought from and sold back to?

10 The book *Macca Can* was about which player?

11 Which club did Mark Robins leave to Join Norwich City?

12 Brian Little followed David Pleat as manager of which club?

13 Birmingham City recorded a 6-0 League Cup win over which club in December 1962?

14 Which injury forced Bryan Robson out of the 1986 World Cup?

15 Who was the 1970s favourite 'Pancho'?

Answers to page 59

1 Danish, **2** 1950s, **3** Stuart Pearce, **4** Brazil and Czechoslovakia, **5** United States Soccer Federation, **6** Lincoln City, **7** Wim Jonk, **8** Ian Taylor and Dwight Yorke, **9** Bradford City, **10** Crystal Palace, **11** Christian Gross and Jurgen Klinsmann, **12** Motherwell, **13** Hunt, **14** Frank, **15** Wolverhampton Wanderers.

• REPUBLIC OF IRELAND •

Answers on page 60

1 Who scored the Republic of Ireland's goal in their 1-1 draw with Belgium in the first leg of the 1998 World Cup qualifying play-off?

2 At which ground do the Republic of Ireland play home matches?

3 Who was stripped of the captaincy of the Republic of Ireland in 1996 for taking a holiday without informing his boss?

4 Which Republic of Ireland international wrote the book *Only A Game*?

5 Which Republic of Ireland player was nicknamed 'Chippy'?

6 How far did the Republic of Ireland progress in the 1994 World Cup finals?

7 Against which team did Jack Charlton's Republic of Ireland record a 1-0 victory and three 1-1 draws?

8 The Republic of Ireland record an 8-0 win over which country in 1983?

9 Against which country did John Aldridge make his international debut?

10 In what year did the Republic of Ireland become the first team outside the UK to defeat England in England?

11 Who did Jack Charlton succeed as boss of the Republic of Ireland?

12 Which ex-Manchester United player became Jack Charlton's assistant with the Republic of Ireland?

13 Apart from the 1990 World Cup, in which other tournament did the Republic of Ireland reach the quarter-finals stage?

14 Who is the highest goal-scorer for Republic of Ireland?

15 Who succeeded Jack Charlton as manager of Republic of Ireland?

Answers to page 60

1 Peter Burridge, **2** Arthur Rowley, **3** Jack Bowers, **4** Clive Allen, **5** William 'Dixie' Dean, **6** 40, **7** Steve Bloomer, **8** Colin, **9** Alan Ball, **10** Greece, **11** He argued with the referee, **12** The Jules Rimet Trophy, **13** Sweden, **14** Hibernian, **15** Banks, Cohen, Wilson, Stiles, J. Charlton, Moore, R. Charlton, Hunt.

LIVERPOOL 2

Answers on page 65

1 What was the score after normal time in the 1971 Arsenal v Liverpool FA Cup Final?

2 When did Liverpool last gain promotion?

3 Which team lost 1-0 to Liverpool in the 1989 FA Charity Shield?

4 Which Liverpool manager was boss of Huddersfield from 1956-59?

5 Which Liverpool outfield player was the only one not to score in the 11-0 rout of Stromsgodset in 1974?

6 Which South African-born Australian footballer was bought by Liverpool in 1981?

7 Which club did Peter Beardsley join on leaving Liverpool?

8 Who lost to Liverpool in the 1977 Super Cup?

9 Which television personality took over when a linesmen was injured during an Arsenal and Liverpool match in 1972?

10 Which Italian team did Ian Rush join from Liverpool?

11 Which Kevin played for Liverpool in the 1985-86 double season?

12 Which Liverpool player was fined £2,000 for exceeding 45 disciplinary points during the 1995-96 season?

13 Who was Liverpool skipper for the 1981 European Cup victory in 1981?

14 Which former Liverpool star is manager of Greek side Panionios?

15 Liverpool player Andy McGuigan scored 5 goals in a match in January 1902. Who were the opponents?

Answers to page 65

1 Leeds Utd, **2** Miner, **3** Fulham, **4** Chester City, **5** 1900, **6** Jan Ceulemans, **7** Because he had been convicted of a drink-driving offence, **8** Tom Boyd, **9** Burnley, **10** Fettis, **11** Stoke City, **12** Barcelona, **13** Alan Shearer, **14** Blackburn Rovers, **15** Kennington Oval.

QUIZ 36

Answers on page 66

1 From 1965 to 1974 what was the lowest position that Leeds Utd finished in the First Division?

2 Who was in goal for England in the 1997 World Cup qualifier v Italy at Wembley?

3 In Steve Bruce's first season with Manchester Utd who played most times as his central defensive partner?

4 Paul Goddard was at which club when he made his international debut?

5 Who is Steve Howey's soccer-playing brother?

6 What was the first club that John Sillett managed?

7 What is the main stadium used for French home internationals?

8 Howard Kendall followed Mel Machin as manager of which club?

9 Who was the first keeper to skipper a World Cup winning side?

10 Who beat Celtic 1-0 in the 1971 Scottish League Cup Final?

11 Which England international scored in both the FA and Coca-Cola Cup Finals of 1993?

12 Who scored the two goals to win Euro '96?

13 Italian Gianluigi Lentini moved from which club to AC Milan in a £12.5m deal?

14 To which French club was Fabrizio Ravanelli eventually transferred from Middlesborough for £5 million?

15 In which decade was Sam Hamman born?

Answers to page 66

1 Cameroon, **2** 1970, **3** Manchester City, **4** 1968, **5** Real Madrid (seven), **6** Chelsea, **7** Crystal Palace, **8** Hearts, **9** 7-2, **10** Patrik Berger, **11** Chelsea, **12** Gary Lineker, **13** Manager Frank Clark, **14** Leicester City, **15** Aberdeen.

QUIZ 37

Answers on page 63

1 West Ham Utd player Vic Watson scored 6 goals in a match in February 1929. Who were the opponents?

2 What was Matt Busby's occupation before he became a footballer?

3 Jimmy and John Conway were at which club together in the 1970s?

4 Coventry City player Cyril Regis scored 5 goals in a match in October 1985. Who were the opponents?

5 When did Bury first win the FA Cup?

6 Who set a record by playing 96 times for Belgium?

7 Why was West Ham Utd's Rio Ferdinand dropped from the England squad for the game against Moldova?

8 Which Scot scored an own goal against Brazil in the 1998 World Cup Finals?

9 Which club have a ground with the Bob Lord Stand?

10 Who started the game in goal for Northern Ireland when they beat Slovakia in a friendly in March 1998?

11 Which was Steve Bould's first League club?

12 Gary Lineker moved from Everton to which club for £2.8m in June 1986?

13 In July 1992, the move of which player to Blackburn Rovers broke the British transfer record?

14 Which Club's ground is by the River Darwen?

15 At which ground was the first FA Cup Final played?

Answers to page 63

1 0-0, **2** 1962, **3** Arsenal, **4** Bill Shankly, **5** Brian Hall, **6** Craig Johnston, **7** Everton, **8** Hamburg, **9** Jimmy Hill, **10** Juventus, **11** MacDonald, **12** Neil Ruddock, **13** Phil Thompson, **14** Ronnie Whelan, **15** Stoke City.

QUIZ 38

Answers on page 64

1 Who did England beat in the 1990 World Cup quarter-final?

2 In which year did the Charlton brothers play their last international?

3 Colin Bell was at which club when he made his international debut?

4 When did AC Milan first win the Cup Winners' Cup?

5 Which team has won the European Cup the most often?

6 Which soccer club seriously considered penning in supporters behind electric fences?

7 Steve Coppell followed Alan Mullery as manager at which club?

8 Which Scottish side did Neil Pointon move to?

9 What was Scotland's biggest win over England?

10 Who scored from the penalty spot to give the Czech Republic the lead in the Euro '96 Final against Germany?

11 Which soccer team does comedian David Baddiel support?

12 Who scored 24 goals for Tottenham Hotspur in the 1989-90 season?

13 In the 1997-98 season who was given the vote of confidence by the board of Manchester City?

14 Which club did Mark Draper leave to join Aston Villa?

15 Who beat Hamburg to win the European Super Cup in 1983?

Answers to page 64

1 Fourth, **2** Ian Walker, **3** Mal Donaghy, **4** West Ham Utd, **5** Lee Howey, **6** Hereford Utd, **7** Parc des Princes, **8** Manchester City, **9** Gianpietro Combi (1934 Italy), **10** Rangers, **11** Chris Waddle, **12** Olivier Bierhoff, **13** Torino, **14** Olympique Marseille, **15** 1950s.

QUIZ 39

Answers on page 69

1 In which decade did Leeds Utd first win the FA Cup?

2 In which decade was Kevin Keegan born?

3 George Cohen was with which club when he played for England?

4 Which was Alan Wright's first League club?

5 Alan Shearer's first Wembley game for Newcastle United was against which club?

6 Who was the last player before Alan Shearer to score more than 30 League goals in three consecutive seasons?

7 Who scored half of Southampton's 74 First Division goals in the 1966-67 season?

8 Which tournament had only Brazil, England and Scotland competing?

9 Who beat Cardiff 1-0 in the 1925 FA Cup Final?

10 Tottenham Hotspur recorded a 5-0 FA Cup win over which club in September 1990?

11 What was Clive Allen's first League club?

12 Which relegated London team reached the semi-finals of the League Cup in 1993?

13 Who scored a hat-trick for Blackpool in the 1953 FA Cup Final?

14 Which John became boss of Lincoln City in 1995?

15 Which player and manager Brian was born in Peterlee in November 1953?

Answers to page 69

1 7, **2** Andy Cole, **3** Barcelona, **4** Bobby Charlton, **5** David Trezeguet, **6** Dundee, **7** Gary Walsh, **8** John Aston, **9** Les Sealey, **10** Matt Busby, **11** Norwich City, **12** Ron Atkinson, **13** Stuart Pearson, **14** West Ham Utd, **15** 1900s.

• WORLD CUP 1966 1 •

Answers on page 70

1 Who were Argentina playing against in the 1966 World Cup when their captain Rattin was sent off?

2 Before hitting his Final hat-trick how many goals had Geoff Hurst scored in the 1966 World Cup?

3 Who did West Germany beat 4-0 in the quarter-finals of the 1966 World Cup?

4 Who hosted the 1966 World Cup?

5 Who scored the first goal of the 1966 World Cup tournament?

6 Which club provided three England players for the World Cup-winning squad of 1966?

7 Who was leading scorer in the 1966 World Cup tournament?

8 What was the name of the dog who found the stolen World Cup?

9 What nickname was given to the England team after they adopted a 4-3-3 formation?

10 How many players did England use in the 1966 World Cup Finals?

11 Which country lost 2-1 to England in the 1966 World Cup semi-final?

12 How many goals did Geoff Hurst score for England in the 1966 World Cup?

13 Which three countries were in Englands group in the 1966 World Cup?

14 Who was left back in the 1966 World Cup winning side?

15 How many goals did Eusebio score against North Korea in the 1966 World Cup finals?

Answers to page 70

1 Malcolm Crosby, **2** Crewe Alexandra, **3** Celtic and Albion Rovers, **4** Kenny Dalglish, **5** El Loco, **6** Steve Nichol, **7** John McSeventy, **8** Brian and Jimmy Greenhoff, **9** Hearts, **10** Hamburg, **11** Aberdeen, **12** Gordon Banks, **13** Karlsruhe, **14** Smith, **15** Hearts.

• MANCHESTER UTD 2 •

Answers on page 67

1 What was Robson's shirt number for most of his Manchester Utd career?

2 Who hit a 1997-98 Champions League hat-trick for Manchester Utd in their 3-1 win at Feyenoord?

3 Who lost 2-1 to Manchester Utd in the 1991 Cup-Winners' Cup Final?

4 Which Manchester Utd player was voted European footballer of the Year in 1966?

5 Whose goal for Monaco knocked Manchester Utd out of the 1997-98 Champion's League?

6 Which club did goalkeeper Jim Leighton join when he finally left Manchester Utd?

7 Peter Schmeichel played all but two games for Manchester Utd in the 1993-94 season. Who played in those games?

8 Who played on the left wing when Manchester Utd beat Benfica in the European Cup Final of 1968?

9 Who was in goal for Manchester Utd in the Final replay against Crystal Palace in 1990?

10 Who was manager of Manchester Utd when they won the European Cup in 1968?

11 Mark Robins moved from Manchester Utd to which club for £800.000 in August 1982?

12 Which Manchester Utd manager signed Gordon Strachan?

13 Who began his career in 1969 at Hull City, moved to Manchester Utd in 1974 where he won 15 England caps then moved to West Ham in time for their 1980 FA Cup victory?

14 A win in the final game of the 1994-95 season would have made Manchester Utd Premiership winners. Which team held them to a draw?

15 In what decade did Manchester Utd first win the Championship?

Answers to page 67

1 1970s, **2** 1950s, **3** Fulham, **4** Blackpool, **5** Manchester Utd, **6** Jimmy Greaves, **7** Ron Davies, **8** The Rous Cup, **9** Sheffield Utd, **10** Hartlepool Utd, **11** QPR, **12** Crystal Palace, **13** Stan Mortensen, **14** Beck, **15** Little.

QUIZ 40

Answers on page 68

1 Who was caretaker manager of Sunderland when he took them to the 1992 FA Cup Final?

2 Dario Gradi became manager of which club in 1983?

3 Which two Scottish clubs did Jock Stein play for?

4 Who was manager at Blackburn Rovers when they won the premiership in 1994-95?

5 What was the nickname of Peru's Ramon Quiroga?

6 Ayr's record fee received was £300,000 in 1981 when which player moved to Liverpool?

7 Who succeeded John Steel as manager of Barnsley in 1971?

8 Which brothers played together in a 1970s FA Cup Final?

9 Bauld, Conn and Wardhaugh formed 'The Terrible Trio' at which club in the 1950s?

10 Which German city is home to St Pauli?

11 Alphabetically, which is the first Scottish League team?

12 Who was the keeper for the losing Leicester City side in the 1961 FA Cup Final?

13 Which club did West Ham Utd sign Slavic Bilic from?

14 Which Alan became manager of Crystal Palace in March 1993?

15 Which club lost out in both the Scottish League and FA Cup in 1986?

Answers to page 68

1 England, **2** One, **3** Uruguay, **4** England, **5** Pele, **6** West Ham United, **7** Eusebio, **8** Pickles, **9** Wingless Wonders, **10** 15, **11** Portugal, **12** 4, **13** France, Mexico and Uruguay, **14** Ray Wilson, **15** 4.

QUIZ 41

Answers on page 73

1 Which former Liverpool player invented the Predator boot?

2 What was unique about about the first Charity Shield match, a 1-1 draw between Manchester Utd and Queens Park Rangers?

3 Which player opened the scoring for Tottenham Hotspur in the 1961 FA Cup Final?

4 Who quit as Celtic boss after winning the League in 1998?

5 With 583 games, which goalkeeper established Charlton's League appearance record?

6 Neil Warnock succeeded John Barnwell as manager of which club?

7 Which Scottish team are known as The Sons?

8 Which club did Kevin Richardson leave to join Arsenal?

9 Which Barry became manager of Birmingham City in 1993?

10 What is the highest position Coventry City have ever achieved in the League?

11 Which two teams met in the 1994 World Cup Final?

12 Which club won the League Cup four times during the 1980s?

13 What is Robbie Fowler's middle name?

14 Who succeeded Lou Macari as manager of Stoke City in 1993?

15 Who beat Dundee Utd 2-1 in the 1988 Scottish FA Cup Final?

Answers to page 73

1 Arsenal, **2** Norwich City, **3** Eddie and Frank, **4** Craig Johnston, **5** European Cup, **6** Watford, **7** Division 1 Champions, **8** Crystal Palace, **9** Brentford, **10** Newcastle Utd, **11** Real Madrid, **12** Sophus Nielsen, **13** Mike Smith, **14** West Brom, **15** London.

QUIZ 42

Answers on page 74

1 Who was sacked as Manchester City boss just 12 days into the 1993-94 season?

2 Jimmy Dickinson succeeded Ian St John as manager of which club?

3 Which current Premiership club has spent the most time in the top flight?

4 Which soccer team does England cricketer Mike Atherton support?

5 Where was the 1972 European Cup Final held?

6 In which country were the 1970 World Cup Finals held?

7 Brazilian star Ronaldo moved from which club to Intenazionale for £18m in July 1997?

8 Who was voted European Player of the Year for the third time in 1993?

9 Where was the 1998 European Cup Final held?

10 Against which team did West Ham's Joe Cole make his debut?

11 Which goalkeeper said, "It's not nice going down to the supermarket and the woman at the till thinking 'dodgy keeper'"?

12 Which Chris played for Leicestershire at cricket in the day and for Doncaster Rovers in an evening match on the same date?

13 Which country did goalkeeper Bruce Grobbelaar play for?

14 What is the highest position Oxford Utd have ever achieved in the League?

15 Who was signed by Manchester City from Liverpool in January 1996?

Answers to page 74

1 Jairzinho, **2** Carlos Alberto, **3** Karl-Heinz Schnellinger, **4** Brazil (1970), **5** Peter Bonetti, **6** Alan Mullery, **7** Gerson, **8** Brian Labone, **9** Gerd Muller, **10** Bobby Moore, **11** Mexico, **12** West Germany, **13** Uruguay, **14** Brazil, Czechoslovakia and Romania, **15** Sir Alf Ramsey.

QUIZ 43

Answers on page 71

1 Don Howe was manager of which team in 1984?

2 Which Third Division giant-killers reached the 1959 FA Cup semi-final?

3 Which Gray brothers were in the Leeds Utd team of the 1970s?

4 Which South African-born Australian footballer was bought by Liverpool in 1981?

5 Kevin Keegan's last game for Liverpool was in which competition?

6 At which club did twin brothers Dean and David Holdsworth start their careers?

7 What is the highest position Arsenal have ever achieved in the League?

8 With which football club did Ian Wright make his League debut?

9 Steve Perryman followed Frank McLintock as boss of which club?

10 Manchester Utd recorded a 7-2 League Cup win over which club in October 1976?

11 Which Spanish football club plays its home matches in the Bernbeu Stadium?

12 Who scored 10 goals in a game for Denmark against France in October 1908?

13 Who was Welsh boss for the vital 1977 World Cup qualifier v Scotland?

14 Stuart Williams won 33 of his Welsh caps while at which club?

15 In which city do QPR play?

Answers to page 71

1 Craig Johnston, **2** It was the only one to be replayed (Manchester Utd won it 4-0), **3** Bobby Smith, **4** Wim Jansen, **5** Sam Bartram, **6** Notts County, **7** Dumbarton, **8** Watford, **9** Fry, **10** Division 1 (6th) 1969-70, **11** Brazil v Italy, **12** Liverpool, **13** Bernard, **14** Joe Jordan, **15** Celtic.

WORLD CUP 1970 1

Answers on page 72

1 Who scored in the 1970 England V Brazil World Cup game?

2 Who was the skipper of the 1970 Brazilian World Cup team?

3 Which defender hit West Germany's last minute equaliser in the 1970 World Cup semi-final?

4 Felix was in goal for which World Cup winners?

5 Who kept goal as England lost to West Germany in the 1970 World Cup?

6 Which Player was outjumped by Pele before Banks made his save in Mexico 1970?

7 Which heavy-smoking midfielder scored Brazil's second goal in the 1970 World Cup Final?

8 Which Everton centre-back played in the 1970 World Cup in Mexico?

9 Who scored ten goals for Germany in the 1970 World Cup finals?

10 Who was voted best defender in the world by journalists after the 1970 World Cup?

11 In which country were the 1970 World Cup finals held?

12 Which country lost 4-3 to Italy in the 1970 World Cup semi-final?

13 Which country lost 3-1 to Brazil in the 1970 World Cup semi-final?

14 Which other countries were in England's group in the 1970 World Cup finals?

15 Who was England's manager in the 1970 World Cup finals?

Answers to page 72

1 Peter Reid, **2** Portsmouth, **3** Arsenal, **4** Manchester Utd, **5** Rotterdam, **6** Mexico, **7** Barcelona, **8** Marco van Basten, **9** Amsterdam, **10** Swansea City (FA Cup third round, January 1999), **11** David James, **12** Balderstone, **13** Zimbabwe, **14** 18th Division 1, (1983-4, 1986-87), **15** Nigel Clough.

LEEDS UTD 1

Answers on page 77

1 Why did the second leg of Leeds Utd's 1992 first round tie against Stuttgart have to be replayed?

2 Leeds Utd recorded a 4-0 League Cup win over which club in November 1977?

3 Which Gray brothers were in the Leeds Utd team of the 1970s?

4 Which former Leeds Utd manager scored a goal for Brighton after only 15 seconds?

5 Who lost to Leeds Utd on the away goals rule in the 1971 UEFA Cup Final?

6 Jon Newsome moved from Leeds Utd to which club for £1m in June 1994?

7 What did Leeds Utd's shirts have written on them when they won the 1992 Championship?

8 In which decade did Leeds Utd first win the Championship?

9 Name the former Leeds Utd and Scotland star who died in December 1997?

10 Which giant-killers knocked Leeds Utd out of the 1970-71 FA Cup?

11 Which club did Tony Yeboah leave to join Leeds?

12 Which club did Billy Bremner move to after Leeds Utd glory days?

13 Which striker was sent off on his on-loan return to Leeds Utd in 1996?

14 Which club did Lee Chapman leave to join Leeds Utd the first time?

15 In 1966, which Leeds Utd defender won his only Scottish cap?

Answers to page 77

1 QPR, **2** Bristol Rovers, **3** West Germany, **4** Just Fontaine, **5** Josef Masopust, **6** RSC Anderlecht, **7** Michael Thomas, **8** Everton, **9** Steve Pears, **10** Plymouth Argyle, **11** Dave Bassett, **12** Burnden Park, **13** Watford, **14** John Cameron, **15** Lisbon.

QUIZ 44

Answers on page 78

1 Which South American team beat New Zealand 4-0 in the 1982 World Cup finals?

2 Which country lost 3-1 to Czechoslovakia in the 1934 World Cup Semi-Final?

3 Who received a £1,000 fine for giving a 'Hitler Salute' to the crowd at Tottenham in 1996?

4 Who lost 4-0 to Anderlecht in the 1978 Cup-Winners' Cup Final?

5 Which club has won the Spanish Cup most often?

6 Where was the 1991 European Cup Winners' Cup Final held?

7 Which ex-Newcastle United player committed suicide on a railway track?

8 Which Leeds Utd striker was known as 'The Shark'?

9 Why did the second leg of Leeds Utd's 1992 first round tie against Stuttgart have to be replayed?

10 Phil Boyer was Division One top scorer in the 1980s with which club?

11 In which decade did Leicester City win the FA Cup?

12 Which club has a fanzine called On the 2nd May?

13 What is the highest position Barnsley have ever achieved in the League?

14 In the 1954 World Cup finals Turkey had a surprise victory beating South Korea 7-0, they then lost their next match 7-2. Who beat them?

15 Who were the beaten semi-finalists in the 1995-96 FA Cup?

Answers to page 78

1 Nuremberg, **2** 4th Division 1 (1935-36, 1946-47), **3** Argentina, **4** Crystal Palace and Sheffield Wednesday, **5** Wembley, **6** John Barnes, **7** Pittodrie (Aberdeen), **8** Sergei Baltacha, **9** Emerson, **10** 12 yards, **11** Liam Brady, **12** 10th Division 2, (1892-93), **13** Dino Zoff, **14** Bobby Charlton, **15** Nottingham Forest.

QUIZ 45

Answers on page 75

1 If you were walking down South Africa Road, which London club's ground would you be nearest?

2 Which team were once known as Eastville Rovers?

3 Geoff Hurst hit his first England hat-trick against which team?

4 Who holds the record for the highest individual scoring aggregate in World Cup final?

5 Which Dukla Prague player was European footballer of the Year in 1962?

6 Who lost to Arsenal in the 1970 UEFA Cup Final?

7 Who beat Liverpool with the last kick of the 1988-89 season?

8 Kevin Sheedy played in a Cup Winners' winning team with which club?

9 Who was the regular keeper for Middlesborough in their 1992-93 relegation season?

10 Which club has a fanzine called Rub of the Greens?

11 Who said on promotion to the top flight, "Contrary to popular opinion I don't tell my players to kick the opposition in the nuts"?

12 33 spectators died in 1946 after crash barriers gave way at which ground?

13 Which Division 3 team placed an advert in The Times in 1983, looking for players between 18 and 80' preferably with 2 arms and 2 legs?

14 Who succeeded Frank Brettall as manager of Tottenham Hotspur in 1888?

15 Where was the 1992 European Cup Winners' Cup Final held?

Answers to page 75

1 Because Stuttgart fielded four foreign players, rather than the maximum permitted three, **2** Colchester, **3** Eddie and Frank, **4** Howard Wilkinson, **5** Juventus, **6** Norwich City, **7** Top Man, **8** 1960s, **9** Billy Bremner, **10** Colchester Utd, **11** Eintracht Frankfurt, **12** Hull City, **13** Lee Chapman, **14** Nottingham Forest, **15** Willie Bell.

QUIZ 46

Answers on page 76

1 Where was the 1967 European Cup Winners' Cup Final held?

2 What is the highest position Stoke City have ever achieved in the League?

3 Which was the last host nation before France to win the World Cup?

4 Mark Bright has played in Finals for which two clubs?

5 Where was the 1971 European Cup Final held?

6 Which England winger has the middle name Charles Bryan?

7 Which stadium became Britain's first-ever all-seater stadium?

8 Which Ukrainian played in Britain for Ipswich Town and St Johnston?

9 Which Brazilian star could not settle in Middlesborough?

10 How far must the penalty spot be from the goal line?

11 Which former Celtic manager became manager of Brighton?

12 What is the highest position Crewe Alexandra have ever achieved in the League?

13 Who was the oldest player to receive a World Cup winners' medal?

14 Which Manchester Utd player was European footballer of the Year in 1966?

15 Gary Charles was at which club when he made his international debut?

Answers to page 76

1 Brazil, **2** Germany, **3** Mark Bosnich (Aston Villa), **4** Austria/WAC, **5** Athletico Bilbao, **6** Rotterdam, **7** Hughie Gallacher, **8** Joe Jordan, **9** Because Stuttgart fielded four foreign players, rather than the maximum permitted three, **10** Southampton, **11** Never, **12** Bristol Rovers, **13** 3rd Division 2 (1914-15, 1921-22), **14** West Germany, **15** Chelsea and Aston Villa.

QUIZ 47

Answers on page 81

1 Which ex-England player made 824 League appearances?

2 Which player scored 32 League goals for Stoke City in 1927-28?

3 Newcastle United recorded a 7-1 League Cup win over which club in October 1993?

4 Liverpool's legendary striker Billy Liddell came from which country?

5 Who was David Sullivan talking about when he said, " After three years and 61 players, we think it's time someone else is entitled to a go"?

6 Which brother was at Aston Villa with Bruce Rioch?

7 Which Hungarian player was nicknamed 'The Galloping Major'?

8 When was Tommy Lawton born?

9 Who beat Leeds Utd 1-0 in the 1973 FA Cup Final?

10 Which club had a fanzine called *Our Days Are Numbered*?

11 Which Wimbledon player joined Leyton Orient from Brentford in 1992?

12 Which keeper can list Birmingham, Watford and Sunderland among his clubs?

13 What is the highest position Shrewsbury Town have ever achieved in the League?

14 Which Arsenal player was voted Footballer of the Year in 1971?

15 What was the score after 90 minutes in the Final of the 1994 World Cup?

Answers to page 81

1 Wimbledon, **2** 0-2, **3** 1970s, **4** Arsenal, **5** Bill Shankly, **6** Brighton, **7** Crystal Palace, **8** Everton, **9** Home Farm, **10** Joe Fagan, **11** Juventus, **12** Mark Lawrenson, **13** Newcastle Utd, **14** Port Vale, **15** RSC Anderlecht.

• WORLD CUP 1974 1 •

Answers on page 82

1 In the 1974 World Cup Final who scored a first minute penalty for Holland?

2 Who played in goal for Holland in the 1974 World Cup Final?

3 Which country faced West Germany in the opening game of the 1974 World Cup tournamenet?

4 Which English referee was in charge of the 1974 World Cup Final?

5 Who retired from international soccer after the 1974 World Cup game against Zaire?

6 Who captained West Germany in the 1974 World Cup Final?

7 At the time of the 1974 World Cup, Dutch players Rep, Han and Krol were all with which club?

8 Name the successor to Sir Stanley Rous, who took over as president of FIFA just before the 1974 World Cup?

9 Who captained Holland in the 1974 World Cup Final?

10 Who was in goal for Holland in the 1974 World Cup Final?

11 The 1974 World Cup saw the first black African country to reach the finals, who were they?

12 How many goals did Poland's Grzegorz Lato score in the 1974 World Cup finals?

13 Who were the only team to beat West Germany in the 1974 World Cup?

14 In which country were the 1974 World Cup finals held?

15 Which German player scored a penalty in the 1974 World Cup Final?

Answers to page 82

1 Brian McClair, **2** None, **3** Stan Collymore, **4** Five, **5** England, **6** Jimmy Cookson, **7** Weah, **8** 0-0, **9** Hillsborough, **10** Partick Thistle, **11** Assistant Manager, **12** Manchester Utd, **13** Leicester City, **14** Buenos Aires, **15** Walsall.

LIVERPOOL 3

Answers on page 79

1 Which team lost 2-1 to Liverpool in the 1988 FA Charity Shield?

2 What was the half time score in the Chelsea v Liverpool 1997 4th Round FA Cup game, which the home side won 4-2?

3 In which decade did Liverpool win the UEFA Cup for the first time?

4 Which team won the 1988-89 Football League Championship with a 2-0 win in their final match against Liverpool?

5 Which manager took Kevin Keegan to Liverpool?

6 Who was Jimmy Case playing for when he knocked his old club Liverpool out of the FA Cup in 1983?

7 In 1990, Liverpool beat which club 9-0 in the League and lost to them in an FA Cup semi-final?

8 Which team were beaten 3-2 by Liverpool in the 1989 FA Cup Final?

9 Which Irish club did Ronnie Whelan come from?

10 Who took over at Liverpool when Bob Paisley retired in 1983?

11 Ian Rush moved from Liverpool to which club for £3.2m in June 1987?

12 In August 1981 Brighton received £900,00 from Liverpool for which player?

13 Which team were beaten 3-0 by Liverpool in the 1974 FA Cup Final?

14 Who was beaten 3-0 by Liverpool in the 1998-99 Third Round FA Cup tie?

15 Which club beat Liverpool to win the European Super Cup in 1978?

Answers to page 79

1 Terry Paine, **2** Charles Wilson, **3** Notts County, **4** Scotland, **5** Barry Fry, **6** Neil, **7** Ferenc Puskas, **8** 1919, **9** Sunderland, **10** Liverpool, **11** Dean Holdsworth, **12** Tony Coton, **13** 8th Division 2, (1983-84, 1984-85), **14** Frank McLintock, **15** 0-0.

QUIZ 48

Answers on page 80

1 Which Celtic player was Footballer of the Year in 1987?

2 How many home League games did Manchester Utd lose in 1995-96?

3 Who held the British transfer record before Alan Shearer's 1996 move?

4 Discounting penalties, how many goals did Alan Shearer score in Euro 96?

5 Which Country did Colin Viljoen play for?

6 Which player scored 44 League goals for Chesterfield in 1925-26?

7 Which George of AC Milan was European Footballer of the Year in 1996?

8 What was the 90-minute score in the 1971 Arsenal v Liverpool FA Cup Final?

9 Owlerton was the original name of which ground?

10 Alan Rough made a record 410 appearances, for which Scottish club between 1969-82?

11 What was Gordon Strachan's position at Coventry when he refused to leave the pitch during a reserve match?

12 Which soccer team does snooker player Ken Doherty support?

13 Which club had goalkeepers Banks and Shilton on their books in the 1960s?

14 In which city do Boca Juniors play?

15 With 467 League games from 1964 to 1982 Colin Harrison set an appearance record at which club?

Answers to page 80

1 Johan Neeskens, **2** Jongbloed, **3** Chile, **4** Jack Taylor, **5** Denis Law, **6** Beckenbauer, **7** Ajax, **8** Joao Havelange, **9** Johan Cruff, **10** Jan Jongbloed, **11** Zaire, **12** 7, **13** East Germany, **14** West Germany, **15** Breitner.

QUIZ 49

Answers on page 85

1 Which club did Paul Furlong join on leaving Chelsea?

2 Which team were beaten 1-0 by Dundee Utd in the 1994 Scottish FA Cup Final?

3 Who succeeded Bobby Gould as manager of West Brom in 1992?

4 Who won the 1954 World Cup?

5 Which giant-killers knocked Leeds Utd out of the 1970-71 FA Cup?

6 How many times was Dave Bassett capped when he played for England as a semi pro?

7 Which GM Vauxhall Conference club were first to gain automatic promotion to the league?

8 Heslop and Towers played for which Cup Winners' Cup trophy winning team?

9 Who moved from Cardiff to Sheffield Utd for £300,000 in 1994 to set a club record for a transfer fee received?

10 Which club did Jack Kelsey play for?

11 With which club did Neville Southall make his League debut?

12 Gary Lineker first played in an FA Cup Final for which team?

13 In which city do East Fife play?

14 How did John White of Spurs die?

15 In the 1998 World Cup finals which team was the only one not to concede a goal in their three group matches?

Answers to page 85

1 Each goal was scored against a different goalkeeper. (The first against Martin Thomas, then outfield substitute Chris Hepworth and finally Peter Beardsley), **2** Jack Charlton, **3** Bolton Wanderers, **4** Sunderland, **5** 18, **6** Terry Bly, **7** Stranraer, **8** Bond, **9** Brian Clough, **10** Aston Villa, **11** Scunthorpe United, **12** Denmark, **13** Wrexham, **14** Twice - in 1920 and 1929, **15** Joe Fagan.

QUIZ 50

Answers on page 86

1. Tony Cottee moved from West Ham Utd to which club for £2m in July 1988?
2. Norwich City coach David Williams took charge of which country for one game?
3. Bobby Charlton's last Manchester Utd League appearance was at which ground?
4. Which veteran striker is known as 'Aldo'?
5. Who were the first team to win the First Division title on its formation in 1892-93?
6. What was the goalkeeper afraid of, according to the title in the film directed by Wim Wenders?
7. What was the nationality of the referee in the 1966 World Cup Final?
8. Which club was goalkeeper Andy Goram with when he scored against Morton?
9. Which defender played in all Aston Villa's 1995-96 League games?
10. Tottenham Hotspur recorded a 5-0 League Cup win over which club in September 1990?
11. Where did Alan Shearer move to on leaving Southampton?
12. Which English referee controlled the 1974 World Cup Final?
13. Which Liverpool manager sold Peter Beardsley?
14. Who was the first British player to move for £1,000?
15. Derek Parkin set a league appearance record at which club?

Answers to page 86

1 Argentina 6 Peru 0, **2** Krol, **3** Score for both teams, **4** Argentina, **5** Passarella, **6** Austria, **7** Argentina, **8** Italy, **9** River Plate Stadium, **10** Archie Gemmill, **11** Holland, **12** Kempes, **13** Rene Van Der Kerkhof, **14** Willie Johnston, **15** Holland, Iran and Peru.

QUIZ 51

Answers on page 83

1 What was unusual about West Ham defender Alvin Martin's hat-trick in the 8-1 thrashing of Newcastle United in 1987?

2 Which manager took Middlesborough into the top flight for the first time?

3 Brian Kidd finished his playing career in England with which club?

4 Which club were promoted instead of Swindon when they were penalised for financial irregularities in 1991?

5 How many teams play in the German Bundesliga?

6 Which Peterborough forward hit 52 goals in a season?

7 Danny McDonald made a record 256 appearances, for which Scottish club?

8 If dad John is the boss and son Kevin is a defender, what is the surname?

9 Which manager dealt with four fans who invaded the pitch in a League Cup match at the City ground in 1989?

10 Who beat West Brom 2-0 in the 1887 FA Cup Final?

11 In 1959 Neil Lambton lasted just three days as boss of which club?

12 Which country does Claus Thomsen come from?

13 The Welsh Cup was first competed for in 1878. Who were the winners?

14 How many times have Kilmarnock won the Scottish FA Cup?

15 Who took over at Liverpool when Bob Paisley retired in 1983?

Answers to page 83

1 Birmingham City, **2** Rangers, **3** Ossie Ardiles, **4** West Germany, **5** Colchester Utd, **6** 10, **7** Scarborough, **8** Manchester City, **9** Nathan Blake, **10** Arsenal, **11** Bury, **12** Everton, **13** Methil, Fife, **14** Struck by lightning, **15** Argentina.

WORLD CUP 1978 1

Answers on page 84

1 In 1978 hosts Argentina met Peru in a quarter-final match. What was the score?

2 Who captained Holland in the 1978 World Cup Final?

3 What did Erny Brandts do in the Italy v Holland game in the 1978 World Cup finals?

4 Peru's goalkeeper in the 1978 quarter-final match against Argentina in which Peru lost 6-0 was born in which country?

5 Who captained Argentina in the 1978 World Cup Final?

6 Which country beat West Germany 3-2 to send them out of the 1978 World Cup finals?

7 Who won the 1978 World Cup?

8 Who did Brazil beat in the third place play-off in the 1978 World Cup finals?

9 Which stadium in Buenos Aires was used for the 1978 World Cup finals?

10 Which Scottish player scored against Holland in the 1978 World Cup?

11 Who were Argentina's opponents in the 1978 World Cup Final in which they won 3-1 after extra-time?

12 Who was the top-scorer in the 1978 World Cup finals?

13 In the 1978 World Cup Final, which Dutchman wore a cast on his arm?

14 Which British player was sent home from the 1978 World Cup tournament after being found guilty of taking illegal substances?

15 Which countries were in Scotland's group in the 1978 World Cup finals?

Answers to page 84

1 Everton, **2** Wales, **3** Stamford Bridge, **4** John Aldridge, **5** Sunderland, **6** The Penalty, **7** Swiss, **8** Hibernian, **9** Alan Wright, **10** Hartlepool Utd, **11** Blackburn Rovers, **12** Jack Taylor, **13** Graeme Souness, **14** Alf Common, **15** Wolves.

SPURS 1

Answers on page 89

1 Alf Ramsey was the only player bought by which Spurs boss?

2 Which team was beaten 3-1 by Spurs in the 1962 FA Cup Final?

3 Who scored within 120 seconds of the 1987 Spurs v Coventry City FA Cup Final?

4 A club record fee received stood for ten years when which player left Everton for Spurs in the mid 1980s?

5 Who moved from Ipswich Town to Spurs in 1993 to set a club record for a transfer fee received?

6 Which side beat Spurs 7-0, inflicting their worst League defeat in history?

7 Which club did Ossie Ardiles join on loan from Spurs during the Falklands War?

8 How did John White of Spurs die?

9 Which Scottish international defender played both for Arsenal and Spurs under Terry Neill in the 1970s?

10 How much did Spurs pay for Ossie Ardiles when he signed from Huracan in 1978?

11 Which club did Danny Blanchflower play for before he joined Spurs?

12 Which team were beaten 2-1 by Spurs in the 1967 FA Cup Final?

13 Who were the first team to beat Spurs in an FA Cup Final?

14 Who scored 24 goals for Spurs in the 1989-90 season?

15 When Martin Peters joined Spurs, who moved the other way?

Answers to page 89

1 Five, **2** Bernard Lama, **3** FA Cup Final, **4** 1982, **5** Fiorentina, **6** Jack Charlton, Republic of Ireland manager, **7** Charlton Athletics, **8** Erik Thorstvedt, **9** Osman, **10** Northern Ireland, **11** Preston North End, **12** Michael Ricketts, **13** Paris, **14** Peter Ward, **15** None.

QUIZ 52

Answers on page 90

1 Mel Sterland moved from Sheffield Wednesday to which club for £800,000 in March 1989?

2 Which Kevin was a scoring machine for Derby County in the 1970s?

3 What is the highest position Watford have ever achieved in the League?

4 Where was the 1960 European Cup Final held?

5 Who did Liverpool sign from Bolton in September 1995?

6 What was England winger Mark Chamberlain's soccer playing brother called?

7 Tony Barton followed Ron Saunders as boss of which club?

8 Which team appeared in the European Cup Final in 1993,1994 and 1995?

9 Who was the first player to be capped for England while on the books of a foreign team?

10 Charlie Nicholas left which club to join Arsenal?

11 Which Scottish manager suffered only three defeats in his twelve games?

12 How many goals did Gary Lineker score for England?

13 Which referee sent off Manchester Utd's Kevin Moran in an FA Cup Final?

14 Cec Podd set an appearance record at which club?

15 Which country do Sampdoria come from?

Answers to page 90

1 Oldham Athletic, **2** English, **3** Rangers, **4** Leeds Utd (1974) Arsenal (1993), **5** England, **6** Division 1 (2nd 1983-84), **7** Birkenhead, **8** Holland, **9** Norwich City, **10** Chile, **11** Dario Gradi, **12** Holland, **13** Bill Walsh, **14** Lawrie McMenemy, **15** Allan Simonsen.

QUIZ 53

Answers on page 87

1 How many different clubs in France did Eric Cantona play for before coming to England?

2 Who kept goal for France in their quarter-final victory over Holland during Euro '96?

3 What was Gazza's last competitive match of 1991?

4 New Zealand had their World Cup moment of glory with one finals appearance. In which year was that?

5 Which Italian side were the first to win the European Cup Winners' Cup?

6 Who was fined £10,000 and received a one-match touchline ban during the 1994 World Cup finals?

7 Aston Villa player Gerry Hitchens scored 5 goals in a match in November 1959. Who were the opponents?

8 Who was in goal for Tottenham Hotspur in the 1991 FA Cup Final?

9 Which Russell became boss of Bristol City in 1993?

10 Which country did Dave Clements play for?

11 At which club did Bobby Charlton end his career?

12 Which Walsall striker, coming on as a sub against Brighton in May 1996, scored with his first touch of the ball in his first game for the club?

13 Where was the 1981 European Cup Final held?

14 Which player scored 32 League goals for Brighton 1976-77?

15 How many goals did Alan Shearer score in his first full season?

Answers to page 87

1 Arthur Rowe, **2** Burnley, **3** Clive Allen (Spurs), **4** Gary Lineker, **5** Jason Dozzell, **6** Liverpool, **7** PSG, **8** Struck by lightning, **9** Willie Young, **10** £300,000, **11** Aston Villa, **12** Chelsea, **13** Coventry City, **14** Gary Lineker, **15** Jimmy Greaves.

QUIZ 54

Answers on page 88

1 Andy Goram was at which club when he made his international debut?

2 A FIFA ruling stated that all international referees must be able to speak what language?

3 Who beat Dundee Utd 4-1 in the 1981 Scottish FA Cup Final replay?

4 Name the only two teams to have lost the Charity Shield on penalties?

5 Who hosted the 1966 World Cup?

6 What is the highest position Southampton have ever achieved in the League?

7 In which city do Tranmere Rovers play?

8 Argentina conceded two goals in each of their final matches of the 1998 finals. England was one of there opponents, who was the other?

9 Butterworth and Culverhouse were in the same team at which club?

10 Which country was the venue for the 1962 World Cup?

11 Who succeeded Allen Batsford as manager of Wimbledon in 1978?

12 Who were Argentina's opponents in the 1978 World Cup Final in which they won 3-1 after extra time?

13 Who succeeded Bill Shankly as manager of Grimsby Town in 1954?

14 Who was the first non-Ulsterman to manage Northern Ireland?

15 Which Borussia Moenchengladbach player was European footballer of the Year in 1977?

Answers to page 88

1 Glasgow Rangers, **2** Hector, **3** 2nd Division 1, (1982-83), **4** Glasgow, **5** Jason McAteer, **6** Neville, **7** Aston Villa, **8** AC Milan, **9** Gerry Hitchens, **10** Celtic, **11** Tommy Docherty, **12** 48, **13** Peter Willis, **14** Bradford City, **15** Italy.

QUIZ 55

Answers on page 93

1 Which club was Steve Stone with when he made his international debut?

2 Which team lost 1-0 to Manchester Utd in the 1985 FA Cup Final?

3 Cantona scored for Manchester Utd in his 1995 October comeback against which team?

4 Which former player became Director of Football at Blackpool?

5 Who did Arsenal beat in the final league game of the 1970s double-winning season?

6 Which referee was pushed to the ground by Sheffield Wednesday's Paulo di Canio in a league match with Arsenal in September 1998?

7 Who inspired the starting of the European Championship?

8 Which Trevor came on as an English substitute in the 1990 World Cup semi-final?

9 Which country does Mikkel Beck play for?

10 What is Vinnie Jones' middle name?

11 How many substitues could be used in the Premiership?

12 What was strange about the West Ham Utd v Castilla European Cup Winners' Cup game in 1980?

13 Who made his debut for Wales aged 18 years 71 days?

14 Which county did Raich Carter play cricket for?

15 Terry Phelan was at which club when he made his international debut?

Answers to page 93

1 AC Milan, **2** Arnold Muhren, **3** Benfica (Portugal), **4** Bobby Charlton, **5** Deliberate handball, **6** Eric Cantona, **7** George, **8** John Fitzpatrick, **9** Liverpool, **10** Maurice Setters, **11** Paul Ince, **12** Ron Atkinson, **13** Swindon Town, **14** Wilf McGuinness, **15** 1909.

• WORLD CUP 1982 1 •

Answers on page 94

1 What was the England squad's song for Spain 1982 called?

2 How many teams competed in the 1982 World Cup in Spain?

3 What was the score after extra-time in the France v West Germany 1982 World Cup semi-final?

4 Which South American team beat New Zealand 4-0 in the 1982 World Cup finals?

5 In 1982, what was the nickname of England's mascot?

6 Who was Italy's captain when they won the World Cup in 1982?

7 Which country went out of the 1982 World Cup Finals at the round robin quarter-final stage, despite not losing a match in the tournament?

8 Which team scored within 27 seconds against France in the 1982 World Cup?

9 Which country lost 5-4 on penalties to West Germany in the 1982 World Cup semi-final?

10 The Irish played five games during the 1982 World Cup finals losing just one. Which country did they lose to?

11 England's 1982 World Cup campaign was marred by injuries to which two key players?

12 How many games did England lose in Spain in 1982?

13 Who was Italy's top scorer in the 1982 World Cup tournament?

14 Which country lost 2-0 to Italy in the 1982 World Cup semi-final?

15 Who was English boss in Spain in 1982?

Answers to page 94

1 Ron Atkinson, **2** Blackburn Rovers, **3** Peter Osgood, **4** Windsor Park, **5** David Wagstaffe, **6** 1920s (Cardiff), **7** Steaua Bucharest, **8** Tony Adams, **9** Middlesborough, **10** Frank Swift, **11** Chesterfield, **12** Robert, **13** Bobby Moore, **14** The Republic of Ireland, **15** Stoke City.

• MANCHESTER UTD 3 •

Answers on page 91

1 Ray Wilkins moved from Manchester Utd to which club for £1.5m in June 1984?

2 Who scored the 1980s FA Cup Final replay penalty for Manchester Utd?

3 Who were Manchester Utd's opponents in the 1968 European Cup Final?

4 Which Manchester United legend scored 49 goals?

5 What was the offence for which Kanchelskis was sent off in Manchester Utd's 1994 League Cup Final?

6 Which Manchester Utd player was PFA Player of the Year in 1994?

7 Who was Mark Buchan's Manchester Utd playing brother?

8 Who was Manchester Utd's first ever League substitute?

9 Cantona scored for Manchester Utd in his 1995 October comeback against which team?

10 Which ex-Manchester Utd player became Jack Charlton's assistant with the Republic of Ireland?

11 Who was sent off in Manchester Utd's 1990s European Champions League 3-1 defeat in Gothenburg?

12 Who succeeded Dave Sexton as manager of Manchester Utd in 1981?

13 Manchester Utd player Harold Halse scored 6 goals in a match in the 1911 Charity Shield. Who were the opponents?

14 Who followed Sir Matt Busby as manger of Manchester Utd?

15 When did Manchester Utd first win the FA Cup?

Answers to page 91

1 Nottingham Forest, **2** Everton, **3** Liverpool, **4** Billy Bingham, **5** Tottenham Hotspur, **6** Paul Alcock, **7** Henri Delauney, **8** Steven, **9** Denmark, **10** Peter, **11** Two, **12** Played behind closed doors, **13** John Charles, **14** Derbyshire, **15** Wimbledon.

QUIZ 56

Answers on page 92

1 Who succeeded Dave Sexton as manager of Manchester Utd in 1981?

2 David Batty moved from Leeds Utd to which club for £2.7m in October 1993?

3 In Chelsea's 13-0 win over Jeunesse Hautcharage in the European Cup Winners' Cup in September 1971, which player scored five goals?

4 At which ground do Linfield play?

5 Which English League player was the first to be shown the Red Card?

6 In which decade was the FA Cup won by a team not from England?

7 Which was the only Eastern European team ever to win the European Cup?

8 Who was Arsenal's youngest ever captain when he took over in 1988?

9 Hednsford Town took the lead against which Premiership side in a 1997 4th Round tie?

10 Which ex-England keeper, working as a journalist, lost his life in the Munich air disaster?

11 Port Vale player Stewart Littlewood scored 6 goals in a match in September 1932. Who were the opponents?

12 What is Keith Gillespie's middle name?

13 Who succeeded Peter Morris as manager of Southend Utd in 1984?

14 Which country did Chris Houghton play for?

15 Liverpool player Andy McGuigan scored 5 goals in a match in January 1902. Who were the opponents?

Answers to page 92

1 "This Time (We'll Get it Right)", **2** 24, **3** 3-3, **4** Brazil, **5** Bulldog Bobby, **6** Dino Zoff, **7** England, **8** England, **9** France, **10** France 4-1, **11** Keegan and Brooking, **12** None, **13** Paolo Rossi, **14** Poland, **15** Ron Greenwood.

QUIZ 57

Answers on page 97

1 Which club has the smallest pitch in the Premiership?

2 Who was Rangers' manager for thirty-seven years from 1920 to 1957?

3 Which country did Graham Rix go to play football in?

4 Who were the first club from the top flight to go out of the FA Cup on penalties?

5 In the 1960s David Herd left which club to Join Manchester Utd?

6 Which was the first club to play a European Cup Final on their own ground?

7 Which boss took Newcastle United into the Premier League?

8 Who was boss when Swindon Town went down in 1994-95?

9 Who took over as an emergency keeper in the 1957 FA Cup Final?

10 What is the highest position Leicester City have ever achieved in the League?

11 Which manager developed the 'push and run' style of playing?

12 Who scored for the Republic of Ireland in their 2-1 defeat in the second leg of the World Cup qualifying play-off against Belgium?

13 Which Spanish club knocked holders Manchester Utd out of the 1991-92 Cup Winners' Cup in the second round?

14 Who was sacked as manager of Queens Park Rangers in the 1997-98 season?

15 Which important spectator created a first at the Burnley v Liverpool 1914 FA Cup Final?

Answers to page 97

1 Peter Bonetti, **2** Canada, **3** AC Milan, **4** 68, **5** Emlyn Hughes, **6** David Platt, **7** Turkey, **8** Ron Greenwood, **9** Ipswich Town, **10** Neale, **11** Brentford, **12** Manchester Utd, **13** Gordon marshall, **14** Dino Zoff, **15** Oldham Athletic.

QUIZ 58

Answers on page 98

1 Who holds the West Brom League appearance record?

2 Who was the regular keeper in Crystal Palace's 1994-95 relegation season?

3 Which soccer team does Big Country's Stuart Adamson support?

4 Which soccer team does TV chef Gary Rhodes support?

5 Who beat Kilmarnock 2-0 in the 1953 Scottish League Cup Final?

6 Which former Arsenal manager is said to haunt the corridors of Highbury?

7 Which Tottenham Hotspur star played his only international game in 1982 against Iceland?

8 Who holds Chelsea's record of 41 goals in a season?

9 What is the inscription above the Bill Shankly gates at Anfield?

10 What was Barry Venison's first League club?

11 In which city has the Cup Winners' Cup Final been played most often?

12 Which football player was known as 'Sniffer'?

13 How many goals did Peter Osgood score for England?

14 What is the highest position Southend Utd have ever achieved in the League?

15 Which Yorkshire team went out of the League in 1993?

Answers to page 98

1 Gary Stevens, **2** Denmark, Uruguay and West Germany, **3** Carlos Bilardo, **4** Ray Wilkins, **5** Belgium, **6** Bryan Robson and Peter Shilton, **7** Six, **8** France, **9** Bryan Robson, **10** Aztec Gold, **11** Colombia, **12** Bryan Robson, **13** Three, **14** Franz Beckenbauer, **15** Gary Lineker.

QUIZ 59

Answers on page 95

1 Which football player was known as 'The Cat' ?

2 Which country does Frank Yallop come from?

3 Who beat Barcelona 4-0 in the 1994 European Cup Final?

4 How many goals did Gerd Muller score for Germany?

5 Which football player was known as 'Crazy Horse'?

6 Which international star moved to Bari in August 1992?

7 Who were the only team not to score in Euro 96?

8 Who was English boss in Spain in 1982?

9 In the 1970s, David Johnson was at which club when he made his international debut?

10 Which Phil skippered both Lincoln and Worcester CCC in the 1980s?

11 With which soccer club did singer Rod Stewart have trials with?

12 Which club did cricketer Arnold Sidebottom play for in the mid-1970s?

13 Who was league ever-present for Celtic in 1995-96?

14 Which goalkeeper helped Juventus win seven league titles and the UEFA Cup?

15 Ian Wood set a League appearance record for which club?

Answers to page 95

1 Arsenal, **2** Bill Struth, **3** France, **4** Manchester Utd, **5** Arsenal, **6** Real Madrid in 1957, **7** Kevin Keegan, **8** John Gorman, **9** Jackie Blanchflower, **10** 2nd Division 1 (1928-29), **11** Arthur Rowe, **12** Ray Houghton, **13** Atletico Madrid, **14** Bruce Rioch, **15** George V was the first monarch at a Final.

• WORLD CUP 1986 1 •

Answers on page 96

1 In the 1986 World Cup which two England players in the squad had the same name?

2 Which other countries were in Scotland's group for the 1986 World Cup finals?

3 Who was manager of Argentina in the 1986 World Cup finals?

4 Which England player was sent off in the Mexico 1986 World Cup?

5 Which country lost 2-0 to Argentina in the 1986 World Cup semi-final?

6 Which two players captained England during the 1986 World Cup finals?

7 How many goals did Gary Lineker score in the 1986 World Cup?

8 Which country lost 2-0 to West Germany in the 1986 World Cup semi-final?

9 Which England player dislocated his shoulder during the 1986 World Cup finals?

10 What was the name of the ITV theme for the 1986 World Cup finals?

11 Which country was originally chosen to host the 1986 World Cup finals?

12 Which player was substituted in both of England's opening games in the 1986 World Cup finals?

13 How many quarter-finals went to extra time in the 1986 World Cup?

14 Who was manager of West Germany in the 1986 World Cup finals?

15 Which player got a hat-trick as England beat Poland 3-0 in the 1986 World Cup finals?

Answers to page 96

1 Tony Brown, **2** Nigel Martyn, **3** Dunfermline Athletic, **4** Manchester Utd, **5** Dundee, **6** Herbert Chapman, **7** Steve Perryman, **8** Jimmy Greaves, **9** *You'll Never Walk Alone*, **10** Sunderland, **11** Rotterdam (four times), **12** Allan Clarke, **13** None, **14** 12th Division 2, (1991-92), **15** Halifax Town.

ARSENAL 2

Answers on page 101

1 Who beat Arsenal 1-0 in the 1972 FA Cup Final?

2 Who was affectionately known as 'Big Ead' by his Arsenal fans?

3 Who scored Arsenal's last minute goal against Liverpool at Anfield to win the League title in 1989?

4 Who was Arsenal's captain when they won the double for the first time?

5 Which ex-Arsenal player was sent off in a Sweden v Romania World Cup quarter-final match?

6 Who was captain of Arsenal's FA Cup winning side of 1930?

7 Which Arsenal defender brought Paul Allen down from behind in 1980 when he was clear on goal?

8 Name the Scottish international defender who played both for Arsenal and Tottenham Hotspur under Terry Neill in the 1970s?

9 What was the score in the 1991 Arsenal v Tottenham Hotspur FA Charity Shield?

10 How old was Charles Buchan when he went to Arsenal?

11 Which club beat Arsenal to win the European Supercup in 1995?

12 Which Scotland and Arsenal player was 'The Wee Wizard'?

13 Who was the first ever non-British manager to take charge of Arsenal?

14 Which Newcastle player was sent off in a 1996 Coca-Cola quarter-final after clashing with Arsenals Lee Dixon?

15 Who is Arsenal's most expensive signing?

Answers to page 101

1 Red Star Belgrade, **2** Recreation Park (Alloa), **3** Oldham Athletic, **4** Sweden, **5** John White, **6** Aime Jacquet, **7** 3rd Division 2, (1954-55), **8** Everton, **9** Sean, **10** Durie, **11** Leeds Utd, **12** Torquay Utd, **13** Howard Wilkinson, **14** European Cup Winners' Cup, **15** South Korea 9-0 and West Germany 8-3.

QUIZ 60

Answers on page 102

1 Which soccer team does politician and author Jeffery Archer support?

2 What colour goes with amber on Cambridge United's home shirts?

3 Paul Davis and Anders Limpar were in the same team at which club?

4 Which club won the French League Championship seven times between 1967 and 1976?

5 What did Blackburn Rovers do immediately before the 1883 Cup Final that no other cup Final team had done before?

6 Who scored Middlesborough's first goal in the second leg of their Coca-Cola Cup semi-final against Liverpool?

7 Who moved from Grimsby Town to Blackburn Rovers for £1 million to set a club record for a transfer fee received?

8 Which club did Kenny Sansom leave to join Arsenal?

9 Tom Cargill made a record 445 appearances, for which Scottish club between 1966-81?

10 What was Leighton James' first League club?

11 In which decade was Bobby Gould born?

12 Where was the 1965 European Cup Final held?

13 Tony Cottee and Peter Beardsley were in the same team at which club?

14 Which club did Russell Hoult leave to join Derby County?

15 Mark Hately was at which club when he made his international debut?

Answers to page 102

1 Steve McManaman, **2** Chelsea v Leeds (1970), **3** Wimbledon, **4** Arsenal, **5** Bobby Mimms **6** 1940s, **7** Liverpool, **8** Bertie Mee, **9** Middlesborough, **10** Professional player, (A Scot paid to play in England), **11** Blackburn Rovers, **12** Pat Jennings, **13** 1970s, **14** Carlisle United, **15** QPR.

QUIZ 61

Answers on page 99

1 Who did Manchester Utd beat to win the European Super Cup in 1991?

2 At which ground do Rangers play their reserve team games?

3 Ian Marshall and Graeme Sharpe were in the same team at which club?

4 In which country were the 1958 World Cup Finals held?

5 Which famous player was killed by lightning on a golf course in 1965?

6 Name the French coach who announced his retirement after leading his team to their 1998 World Cup triumph in Paris?

7 What is the highest position Rotherham United have ever achieved in the League?

8 Which club did Alan Ball join on leaving Blackpool in 1966?

9 What is Tim Breaker's middle name?

10 Which Gordon was Gary Lineker's regular strike partner in his last League season in England?

11 Which soccer team does tennis player Stefan Edberg support?

12 Who plays at home at Plainmoor?

13 Who was appointed the FA's Technical Director in 1996?

14 What was the only major European Trophy Gary Lineker won?

15 In the 1954 World Cup finals Hungary had two impressive victories. Who were the countries and what were the scores?

Answers to page 99

1 Leeds Utd, **2** Leslie Compton, **3** Michael Thomas, **4** Pat Rice, **5** Stefan Schwartz, **6** Tom Parker, **7** Willie Young, **8** Willie Young, **9** 0-0 after extra time, **10** 33, **11** AC Milan, **12** Alex James, **13** Arsene Wenger, **14** David Ginola, **15** Dennis Bergkamp.

QUIZ 62

Answers on page 100

1 Which England attacking midfielder was born in Bootle in February 1972?

2 What was the first FA Cup Final to be drawn at Wembley?

3 Clive Goodyear played in an FA Cup Final for which team?

4 Who beat Manchester Utd 3-2 in the 1979 FA Cup Final?

5 Who was in goal for Everton in the 1986 FA Cup Final?

6 In which decade was commentator Barry Davies born?

7 Michel Platini inspired Juventus to European Cup Final victory over which English side?

8 Who was Graham Taylor's assistant when Watford reached the FA Cup Finals in 1984?

9 With which club did Graeme Souness make his League debut?

10 In footballing terms what was a 'Scottish Professor'?

11 Kenny Dalglish followed Don Mackay as manager of which club?

12 Which goalkeeper scored a goal in the 1967 Charity Shield match?

13 In which decade did Chelsea first win the FA Cup?

14 Which club was once known as Shaddongate United?

15 John Byrne played in a League Cup Final for which club?

Answers to page 100

1 Bristol Rovers, **2** Black, **3** Arsenal, **4** St Etienne, **5** Train, **6** Paul Merson, **7** Gary Croft, **8** Crystal Palace, **9** Arbroath, **10** Burnley, **11** 1940s, **12** Milan, **13** Everton, **14** Leicester City, **15** Portsmouth.

QUIZ 63

Answers on page 105

1 Gary Bailey played in an FA Cup Final for which team?

2 Wimbledon player Alan Cork scored 4 goals in a match in February 1979. Who were the opponents?

3 Who was in goal for Holland in the 1974 World Cup Final?

4 How many Scottish premier titles did Alex Ferguson win as manager of Aberdeen?

5 In November of the 1997-98 season it was widely reported that the world's richest man was interested in buying Everton. Who was he?

6 Who moved from Hereford Utd to QPR in 1990 to set a club record for a transfer fee received?

7 Who lost 5-1 to Spurs in the 1963 Cup-Winners' Cup Final?

8 Barrie Williams was boss of which 1989 giant-killers?

9 Which member of the Italian squad for Euro '96 played his club football in the USA?

10 Which defender hit West Germany's last minute equaliser in the 1970 World Cup semi-final?

11 Who were England's first choice fullbacks for Italia 90?

12 Which country did Alex Elder play for?

13 Who were Argentina playing against in the 1966 World Cup when their captain Rattin was sent off?

14 What was the attendance of the first Scottish FA Cup Final?

15 In which decade did Sheffield Utd first win the FA Cup?

Answers to page 105

1 Crystal Palace, **2** Burnley, **3** Everton, **4** John Gregory, **5** Neil, **6** Six, **7** 14, **8** Charlton Athletics, **9** Exeter, **10** Jozef Venglos, **11** Neil Cox, **12** Stan Collymore, **13** 1880s, **14** Chelsea, **15** Gary Shaw.

WORLD CUP 1990 1

Answers on page 106

1 Which player scored the only goal of the 1990 World Cup Final?

2 Who qualified for the 1990 World Cup finals after a 0-0 draw with Poland?

3 Who was the Republic of Ireland's keeper in the penalty shootout against Romania in the 1990 World Cup finals?

4 Who did Cameroon beat in the 1990 World Cup opener?

5 England and the Republic of Ireland were in which group in Italia '90?

6 Which player burst into tears after England's World Cup semi final defeat in 1990?

7 In Italia '90 which country played extra-time in both the quarter-finals and semi-finals?

8 Which country beat England in the third place play-off game in the 1990 World Cup?

9 Who were England's first choice fullbacks for Italia '90?

10 Which team knocked Italy out of Italia '90?

11 Which Englishman had a 'goal' disallowed in game against Belgium in Italia '90?

12 Who was England's first choice goalkeeper in the 1990 Word Cup finals?

13 Which African side reached the 1990 World Cup quarter-finals?

14 Who captained West Germany in the 1990 World Cup Final?

15 What was Scotland's World Cup record in 1990?

Answers to page 106

1 Dion Dublin, **2** Hibernian, **3** Notts County, **4** Preston North End, **5** Nigel, **6** Aston Villa, **7** South Africa, **8** Stanley Mathews, **9** Jimmy Dickson, **10** Dean Richards, **11** 8, **12** Wembley, **13** John Barnes, **14** Hearts, **15** Alex Ferguson.

ASTON VILLA 1

Answers on page 103

1 Which club did Gareth Southgate leave to join Aston Villa?

2 Aston Villa player Len Capwell scored 5 goals in a match in August 1925. Who were the opponents?

3 Who were Aston Villa's opponents in the first League Cup Final needing a second replay?

4 Who took over from Brian Little as manager of Aston Villa?

5 Which brother was at Aston Villa with Bruce Rioch?

6 How many goals did Stan Collymore score in his first season at Villa?

7 How many players were used by Aston Villa during their Championship -winning season of 1980-81?

8 Aston Villa player Gerry Hitchens scored 5 goals in a match in November 1959. Who were the opponents?

9 Which club did Villa beat 8-1 in the League Cup in October 1985?

10 Who has managed Czechoslovakia, Slovakia and Aston Villa?

11 Which defender went from Scunthorpe to Aston Villa in 1991 to set a club record for a transfer received?

12 Who scored a UEFA Cup hat-trick for Aston Villa against Stromsgodset in September 1998?

13 In which decade did Aston Villa first win the FA Cup?

14 Tony Hateley moved to which club for £100,000 in October 1966?

15 Who scored a European Cup hat-trick for Aston Villa against Dinamo Bucharest in November 1982?

Answers to page 103

1 Manchester United, **2** Torquay Utd, **3** Jan Jongbloed, **4** 3, **5** The Sultan of Brunei, **6** Darren Peacock, **7** Atletico Madrid, **8** Sutton Utd, **9** Roberto Donadoni, **10** Karl-Heinz Schnellinger, **11** Paul Parker and Stuart Pearce, **12** Northern Ireland, **13** England, **14** 3,500, **15** 1890s.

QUIZ 64

Answers on page 104

1 In 1996-97 which Coventry City player was dismissed in successive League games?

2 Which soccer team does Marillion's Fish support?

3 Neil Warnock took which side up to the top flight in 1991?

4 Blackpool player Jimmy McIntosh scored 5 goals in a match in May 1948. Who were the opponents?

5 What is much-travelled Gleghorn's first name?

6 Which 1970s League Cup-winning side was cricketer Jimmy Cumbes in?

7 In July 1992, which country was re-elected to FIFA after an absence of 18 years?

8 Who played his first England game in 1935 and his last in 1957?

9 Which Portsmouth and England wing-half retired in 1965?

10 Who moved from Bradford in 1995 to Wolves to set a club record for a transfer fee received?

11 How many times did Alex James play for Scotland?

12 Where was the 1978 European Cup Final held?

13 Which Englishman had a 'goal' disallowed in the Belgium game in Italia 90?

14 Who beat Kilmarnock 1-0 in the 1963 Scottish League Cup Final?

15 Which manager declared, "Goal keepers are a more protected species than the Golden eagle"?

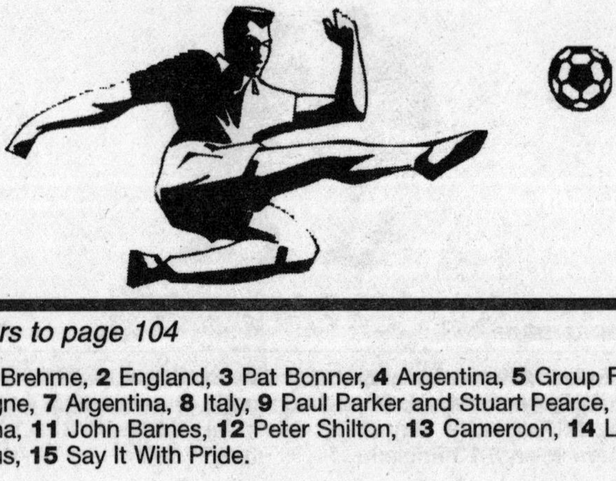

Answers to page 104

1 Andy Brehme, **2** England, **3** Pat Bonner, **4** Argentina, **5** Group F, **6** Paul Gascoigne, **7** Argentina, **8** Italy, **9** Paul Parker and Stuart Pearce, **10** Argentina, **11** John Barnes, **12** Peter Shilton, **13** Cameroon, **14** Lothar Matthaus, **15** Say It With Pride.

QUIZ 65

Answers on page 109

1 Who succeeded Andy Beattie as manager of Huddersfield Town in 1956?

2 Which British countries took part in the 1974 World Cup Finals?

3 Where was the 1959 European Cup Final held?

4 In which city do Heart of Midlothian play?

5 Robins and Ekoku started the season as strikers, but left before which club went out of the Premiership?

6 Ipswich Town recorded a 5-0 League Cup win over which club in August 1977?

7 Who beat Rangers 2-1 in the 1971 Scottish FA Cup Final replay?

8 Who said that there were only two teams on Merseyside-Liverpool and Liverpool Reserves?

9 At which club did Colin Griffin set a League appearance record?

10 Which Welsh club used to play at Acton Park?

11 Who scored England's first ever hat-trick in a World Cup match?

12 Who was the regular keeper for Norwich City in their 1994-95 relegation season?

13 What was the highest score in a Charity Shield?

14 Southend Utd recorded a 10-1 FA Cup win over which club in December 1968?

15 What name did Dixie Dean give his daughter, born on the day in 1931 that his club Everton, beat Southampton 9-1?

Answers to page 109

1 Andy Walker, **2** Chris Armstrong, **3** Manchester City, **4** Charlton Athletic, **5** Lisbon, **6** Leeds Utd, **7** West Brom, **8** Bristol Rovers, **9** England, **10** Manchester City, **11** Boca Juniors, **12** Fettis, **13** 13, **14** Tommy Lawrence, **15** 1940s.

QUIZ 66

Answers on page 110

1 Who joined Arsenal for a record British fee in December 1971?

2 Which Scottish captain was banned for life from playing for his country?

3 Which former Bolton centre-half Alan was born in Liverpool in 1971?

4 Burnley recorded a 6-0 League Cup win over which club in September 1968?

5 Which club once had Fosse at the end of its name?

6 Maurice Malpass was assistant manager and a player for which team in 1996?

7 Who moved from Manchester City to Tottenham Hotspur for £1.7m in 1988 to set a club record for a transfer received?

8 Which country did Ashley Grimes play for?

9 How is Jimmy Gardener better known?

10 Charlton Athletic player John Summers scored 5 goals in a match in October 1960. Who were the opponents?

11 Birmingham City's Managing Director Karen Brady is married to which former Blues player?

12 Who followed Matt Busby at Manchester Utd?

13 In which Swiss city do Servette play their home matches?

14 Who, in the 1990s saved five penalties in three days - three against Tranmere in a League Cup semi-final and two v Tottenham Hotspur?

15 Chris Waddle was at which club when he played in Italia 90?

Answers to page 110

1 Bulgaria, **2** Jack Charlton, Republic of Ireland manager, **3** Sweden, **4** Bulgaria, **5** John Aldridge, **6** The Pasadena Rose Bowl, **7** Bulgaria, **8** Mexico, **9** To the second round, **10** Franco Baresi, **11** Oleg Salenko, **12** USA, **13** 0-0, **14** GianFranco Zola, **15** Ray Houghton.

QUIZ 67

Answers on page 107

1 Who moved from Bolton to Celtic in 1994 to set a club record for a transfer fee received?

2 Which Crystal Palace player was tested positive for cannabis in March 1995?

3 Against which side did Ryan Giggs score his first League goal?

4 A 1940s extra time FA Cup goal by Duffy won the cup for which club?

5 In which city do Benfica play?

6 An extra-time goal by Ian St John beat which team in an FA Cup Final?

7 Alan Ashman was manager of which FA Cup winners?

8 Who plays at home at Twerton Park?

9 Which country did Ralph Coates play for?

10 Mike Doyle scored a League Cup Final goal for which club?

11 Diego Maradona made his name playing for which Argentinian club?

12 Who started the game in goal for Northern Ireland when they beat Switzerland in a friendly in April 1998?

13 How many international goals did Martin Chivers score?

14 Which Liverpool player was affectionately known as 'The Flying Pig'?

15 In which decade was Gerson born?

Answers to page 107

1 Bill Shankly, **2** Scotland only, **3** Stuttgart, **4** Edinburgh, **5** Norwich City, **6** Northampton, **7** Celtic, **8** Bill Shankly, **9** Shrewsbury Town, **10** Wrexham, **11** Jackie Milburn, **12** Bryan Gunn, **13** Manchester Utd 8 Swindon Town 4, **14** Brentwood, **15** Nina.

• WORLD CUP 1994 1 •

Answers on page 108

1 Which country finished fourth in the 1994 World Cup?

2 Who was fined £10,000 and received a one-match touchline ban during the 1994 World Cup finals?

3 Which country lost 1-0 to Brazil in the 1994 World Cup semi-final?

4 Which country knocked Germany out of the 1994 World Cup tournament?

5 Which player was involved in the substitute row in the Mexico v Republic of Ireland 1994 World Cup game?

6 Which stadium held the 1994 World Cup Final?

7 Which country lost 2-1 to Italy in the 1994 World Cup semi-final?

8 Which country were top of the Republic of Ireland's Group in USA 1994?

9 How far did the Republic of Ireland progress in the 1994 World Cup finals?

10 Who was the Italian skipper in the 1994 World Cup Final?

11 Who scored six goals for Russia in the 1994 World Cup finals?

12 In 1994, Leonardo of Brazil was sent off against which country?

13 What was the score after 90 minutes in the Final of the 1994 World Cup?

14 Which Italian was sent off against Nigeria in the 1994 World Cup?

15 Which Irish player scored the winning goal against Italy in the 1994 World Cup finals match?

Answers to page 108

1 Alan Ball, **2** Billy Bremner, **3** Stubbs, **4** Grimsby Town, **5** Liecester City, **6** Dundee Utd, **7** Paul Stewart, **8** The Republic of Ireland, **9** 'Five Bellies', **10** Portsmouth, **11** Paul Peschisolido, **12** Wilf McGuinness, **13** Geneva, **14** Mark Bosnich, **15** Marseille.

ENGLAND 2

Answers on page 113

1 Which Arsenal defender was capped 86 times for England between 1979 and 1986?

2 Who took over as England skipper from Billy Wright?

3 How many of his 29 games did Ron Revie lose as England boss?

4 Who beat England in the quarter-finals of the 1962 World Cup?

5 How many England managers did Kevin Keegan play for?

6 Who is the youngest player this century to play for England?

7 Against which country did David Platt score his first England hat-trick?

8 How many caps did Gordon Banks win?

9 Which father and son strikers played a total of 16 games for England without managing to score a goal?

10 Who scored England's first hat-trick in the 90s, and against which country?

11 Which English player scored twice in the 3-0 defeat of China in 1996?

12 How many times did Joe Mercer serve as caretaker manager for England?

13 How many times did Wolve's Billy Wright play for England?

14 In how many games was Bobby Moore skipper of England?

15 Against which country did Glenn Hoddle scored on his 1979 England debut?

Answers to page 113

1 Franz Beckenbauer, **2** 4, **3** R Gray, **4** Parma, **5** 1940s, **6** Derek Dooley, **7** Sheffield Wednesday, **8** Aston Villa, **9** Adam Tanner, **10** Bill McGarry, **11** Sunderland, **12** Pierluigi Pairetto - Italy, **13** Southampton, **14** Alfie Conn, **15** Real Madrid.

QUIZ 68

Answers on page 114

1 What is the highest position AFC Bournemouth have ever achieved in the League?

2 Which team won the 1982 UEFA Cup?

3 Which English club does former Soviet President Mikhail Gorbachev support?

4 Who scored the first goal of the 1998 World Cup Finals?

5 In which city do Castilla play?

6 Which French player went head to head with Stuart Pearce in Euro 92?

7 Which club was Roger Stanislaus with when he failed a random drug test?

8 Who were the first brothers to win European Championship medals?

9 What is the main colour of Walsall's home shirts?

10 In which city do Port Vale play?

11 Which Brian became boss of Huddersfield Town in June 1995?

12 A late goal by which team meant the Republic of Ireland failed to reach the semi-finals of the Euro '88 Championship?

13 Against which of the Home countries did Ian Rush make his debut?

14 In which country did France first win the European Championship?

15 Kevin Campbell and Chris Bart-Williams both moved on the same day to which club?

Answers to page 114

1 Division 1 Champions, **2** 6th Division 1, (1981-82), **3** Liverpool, **4** Mohammed Tinam one of the 16 Ethiopian footballers who defected, **5** Sheffield Wedneday, **6** 42, **7** West Ham Utd, **8** 1992-93, **9** Brentford, **10** John O'Hare, **11** Chelsea, **12** Mike Walker, **13** Norwich City, **14** Wallace, **15** Wilf Gillow.

QUIZ 69

Answers on page 111

1 Who became the first person to captain and manage World Cup winning sides?

2 How many international goals did Steve Archibald score?

3 Who succeeded Jim Smith as manager of Millwall in 1961?

4 Which club did Gianfranco Zola leave to join Chelsea?

5 In which decade was Johan Cruyff born?

6 Who scored 46 League goals for Sheffield Wednesday in 1951-52?

7 Derby County player Steve Bloomer scored 6 goals in a match in January 1899. Who were the opponents?

8 Charlton Athletic player Eddie Fermani scored 5 goals in a match in February 1955. Who were the opponents?

9 Which Ipswich Town player was banned after a drug test?

10 Who succeeded Jackie Milburn as manager of Ipswich Town in 1964?

11 West Ham Utd player Geoff Hurst scored 6 goals in a match in October 1968. Who were the opponents?

12 Give the name and nationality of the Referee that awarded the Czech Republic a penalty against Germany in the Euro '96 Final?

13 Ipswich Town player Alan Brazil scored 5 goals in a match in February 1982. Who were the opponents?

14 In 1977 who became the first player to win Scottish FA Cup medals with both Rangers and Celtic?

15 Who beat Stade de Reims 2-0 in the 1959 European Cup Final?

Answers to page 111

1 Kenny Sansom, **2** Ronnie Clayton, **3** 7, **4** Brazil, **5** Four, **6** Michael Owen, **7** San Marino, **8** 73, **9** Brian and Nigel Clough, **10** Gary Lineker v Malaysia, **11** Nick Barmby, **12** Seven, **13** 105, **14** 90, **15** Bulgaria.

QUIZ 70

Answers on page 112

1. What is the highest position Aston Villa have ever achieved in the League?
2. What is the highest position Swansea City have ever achieved in the League?
3. Jim Beglin first played in an FA Cup Final for which team?
4. Which football player said, "We have been able to realise our dreams in Italy because for once the officials accompanying us left us our passports"?
5. Which club signed Chris Waddle from Marseille for £1m in 1992?
6. How many league games did Paul Gascoigne play for Lazio over three years?
7. Which club lost the first ever FA Cup Final to be played at Wembley?
8. What season was the new back-pass law seen for the first time?
9. Which club plays at Griffin Park?
10. Which Nottingham Forest player was fouled in the incident leading to the penalty in the 1970s League Cup Final replay v Liverpool?
11. Which soccer team does politician David Mellor support?
12. Who succeeded Dave Stringer as manager of Norwich City in 1992?
13. Ken Brown followed John Bond as boss of which club?
14. Which Danny played his only England game in 1986 against Egypt?
15. Who succeeded Peter McWilliam as manager of Middlesborough in 1934?

Answers to page 112

1 12th Division 2 (1988-89), **2** Gothenburg, **3** Wigan Athletic, **4** Cesar Sampaio, **5** Madrid, **6** Basil Boli, **7** Leyton Orient, **8** Erwin and Ronald Koeman, **9** Red, **10** Stoke-on-Trent, **11** Horton, **12** Holland, **13** Scotland, **14** France, **15** Nottingham Forest.

QUIZ 71

Answers on page 117

1 Which Welshman signed a three-year contract as coach to Sporting Lisbon in July 1984

2 Which team does Archbishop of Canterbury George Carey support?

3 Who succeeded Charlie Hurley as manager of Reading in 1977?

4 Trevor Steven won a total of eight Championship medals with which English club did he win two of them?

5 In 1904, which keeper made the first of his 564 appearances for Notts County?

6 What colours are Colchester Utd's striped shirts?

7 Which Arsenal player was booked for the first time in his career in the 1993 FA Cup Final replay?

8 Which club had a fanzine called *Beyond the Boundary*?

9 Which Dutch club were the first to win a major European trophy?

10 Who beat Partizan Belgrade 2-1 in the 1966 European Cup Final?

11 Which club was once known as Boscombe St Johns?

12 What colour are Chesterfield's home shirts?

13 Who was the only League ever present for Rangers in 1995-96?

14 Who did Stanley Matthews play for in the 1953 FA Cup 'Matthews Final'?

15 Which Catholic international was signed by Graeme Souness at Rangers?

Answers to page 117

1 Strasbourg, **2** Wimbledon, **3** 1-1, **4** 1981, **5** Arsenal, **6** Bill Shankly, **7** Bristol Rovers, **8** David James, **9** Everton in 1890-91, before Liverpool were formed, **10** Ian Callaghan, **11** John Barnes, **12** Juventus, **13** Mark Lawrenson, **14** Nicholas, **15** Real Madrid.

WORLD CUP 1998 1

Answers on page 118

1 Who was shown the first yellow card of the 1998 World Cup finals?

2 How many Carling Premiership club players were in the 1998 World Cup winning side?

3 Which English official was assistant referee in the 1998 World Cup final?

4 In the 1998 World Cup final who was playing his 18th World Cup tie?

5 How many times were England beaten in the 1998 World Cup tournament, and by which countries?

6 Who stepped down as boss of Italy after the World Cup finals in 1998?

7 Name the only two countries in the 1998 World Cup to have 100% records in their group matches?

8 Who scored England's goal against Romania in the 1998 World Cup?

9 Which England player was pictured in a Portugese nightclub shortly before the 1998 World Cup finals?

10 Name the French coach who announced his retirement after leading his team to their 1998 World Cup triumph in Paris?

11 Which Brazilian won his 111th cap in the 1998 Final?

12 Who missed the fourth spot kick for Holland during their semi-final shoot-out against Brazil in the 1998 World Cup?

13 Before the 1998 World Cup, how many of England's chosen 22 finals players had previous World Cup finals experience?

14 Which Scot scored an own goal against Brazil in the 1998 World Cup?

15 In the 1998 World Cup finals who was the first of 22 players to receive the red card?

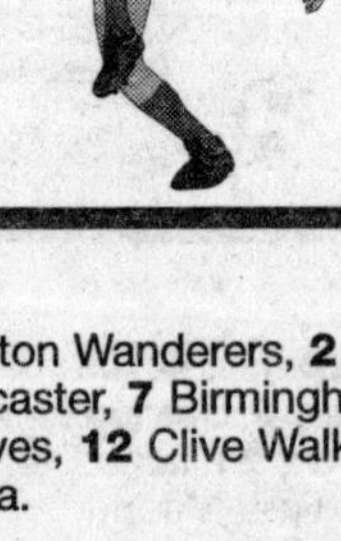

Answers to page 118

1 Blackburn Rovers and Bolton Wanderers, **2** Rangers, **3** Sagittarius, **4** Andy Cole, **5** Shaun, **6** Doncaster, **7** Birmingham City, **8** Rest of UK X1, **9** Darren, **10** Japan's, **11** Wolves, **12** Clive Walker, **13** Luton Town, **14** Clapton Orient, **15** Barcelona.

LIVERPOOL 4

Answers on page 115

1 Who beat Liverpool 3-0 in the 1997-98 UEFA Cup second round first leg?

2 Who beat Liverpool 1-0 in the 1988 FA Cup Final?

3 What was the 90 minute score in the Manchester Utd v Liverpool Charity Shield game?

4 In which year in the 1980s did Liverpool and Everton not contest the Charity Shield?

5 Who beat Liverpool 2-0 in the 1950 FA Cup Final?

6 Which famous former Liverpool manager died in 1981?

7 Liverpool player John Evans scored 5 goals in a match in September 1954. Who were the opponents?

8 Steve McManaman and which other player were league ever-presents for Liverpool in 1995-96 season?

9 Who won the League Championship first - Liverpool or Everton?

10 Who is Liverpool's longest serving player, with 640 appearances between 1960 and 1978?

11 Who was Liverpool's top scorer in the the 1989-90 season?

12 Who beat Liverpool 1-0 in the 1985 European Cup Final?

13 Who was Liverpool's only English born player in the 1986 FA Cup Final?

14 Which Charlie scored the winner against Liverpool in the 1987 League Cup Final?

15 Who lost 1-0 to Liverpool in the Final of the 1981 European Cup?

Answers to page 115

1 John Toshack, **2** Arsenal, **3** Maurice Evans, **4** Everton, **5** Albert Ironmonger, **6** Blue and White, **7** Alan Smith, **8** Oldham Athletic, **9** Feyenoord, **10** Real Madrid, **11** Bournmouth, **12** Blue, **13** Alan McLaren, **14** Blackpool, **15** Mo Johnston.

QUIZ 72

Answers on page 116

1. Which two teams beginning with B were relegated to the Third Division for the first time ever in 1971?
2. Which team did Kenny Dalglish support as a boy?
3. What is Gary Lineker's star sign?
4. Who hit three plus as Manchester Utd beat Ipswich Town 9-0 in 1995?
5. Who is Peter reid's soccer playing manager?
6. Where was Kevin Keegan born?
7. Neil Whatmore moved from Bolton Wanderers to which club for £340,000 in August 1981?
8. Who did wales beat 3-2 to celebrate their FA's centenary in 1951?
9. What is Clive Allen's middle name?
10. Which country's supporters cleaned up the stadia after each match they attended at the World Cup Finals in 1998?
11. Paul Bradshaw was ever present in goal as which team were relegated in 1982?
12. Who was the first player to score 100 goals in League and Non-league football?
13. Liverpool player Ian Rush scored 5 goals in a match in October 1983. Who were the opponents?
14. What was Leyton Orient known as between the time they entered the League and the end of the Second World War?
15. Where was the 1982 European Cup Winners' Cup Final held?

Answers to page 116

1 Cesar Sampaio, **2** Five, **3** Mark Warren, **4** Taffarel, **5** 3, Italy, Romania, Argentina, **6** Cesare maldini, **7** France and Argentina, **8** Michael Owen, **9** Teddy Sheringham, **10** Aime Jacquet, **11** Claudio Taffarel, **12** Frank De Boer, **13** None, **14** Tom Boyd, **15** Anatoli Nankov (Bulgaria).

QUIZ 73

Answers on page 121

1 Who lost 2-1 to Dynamo Tibilisi in the 1981 Cup-Winners' Cup Final?

2 Who succeeded Graham Hawkins as manager of Wolves in 1984?

3 Ron Atkinson took over as manager of Sheffield Wednesday during the 1997-98 season. Who did he replace?

4 Where was the 1957 European Cup Final held?

5 Alan Rough set a League appearance record at which club?

6 Which Welsh player was 45 years and 229 days old when he won a cap for England in 1920?

7 In what year was the Scottish FA Cup withheld after two draws between Rangers and Celtic?

8 Which Bolton Wanderers boss got the sack on the 2nd January 1996?

9 Who said in 1997, "The temptation of a job like this was too much"?

10 Which club was previously called Argyle Athletic Club?

11 What are the first names of Juventus' 1993 UEFA Cup-winning Baggios?

12 Who started the game in goal for England when they beat Portugal in a friendly in April 1998?

13 Where was the 1975 European Cup Final held?

14 Who managed Wolves to three League Championships in the 1950s?

15 Which club did John Spencer leave to join Chelsea?

Answers to page 121

1 Arsenal, **2** Billy, **3** Arsenal, **4** Both Goalkeepers, **5** Graeme Souness, **6** Ipswich Town, **7** Hereford Utd, **8** Hamburg, **9** Glasgow, **10** Charlton Athletic, **11** Liverpool, **12** Nat Lofthouse, **13** Rangers, **14** Watford, **15** Luton Town.

QUIZ 74

Answers on page 122

1 Who beat Rangers 4-0 in the 1969 Scottish FA Cup Final?

2 Which two teams appeared in the first Milk Cup?

3 When did Rangers first achieve the treble?

4 What is Clayton Blackmore's middle name?

5 Who became England's most expensive goalkeeper when he moved to Crystal Palace in 1989?

6 Mark Robins was leading scorer for which Premiership side when they finished third?

7 How many international goals did Maradonna score for Argentina?

8 What season was the back-pass law introduced?

9 Which club received the money when Trevor Francis became Britain's first million pound player?

10 Which soccer team does Mikhail Gorbachev support?

11 Which Phil became Bolton manager in 1985?

12 Who was Keith Edwards playing for when he was the League's top scorer in 1981-82?

13 Brian Marwood moved from Sheffield Wednesday to which club for £600,000 in March 1988?

14 Paul Parker moved from QPR to which club for £1.7m in July 1991?

15 Which is the oldest surviving club in Wales?

Answers to page 122

1 5, **2** Howard Kendall, **3** Sweden, **4** Alan Smith, **5** Johan Cruyff, **6** Winston, **7** Barcelona, **8** Mark Crossley, **9** *They Think It's All Over*, **10** Barcelona & Grampus Eight, **11** Nagoya Grampus 8, **12** Walkers, **13** Brazil, **14** None, **15** Turkey.

QUIZ 75

Answers on page 119

1 Who lost a Euro Cup Winners' Final to Valencia in 1980 on a penalty shoot-out?

2 What was the name of the white horse who helped avert disaster at the first Wembley FA Cup Final in 1923?

3 Rioch, Graham and Mee have all managed which club?

4 What is the footballing link between Pope John Paul II and Albert Camus?

5 In 1990 which Scot said " You cannot guarantee a thing in this game"?

6 Which team won the 1981 UEFACup?

7 Which club has a fanzine called *Talking Bull*?

8 Who lost 2-0 to AC Milan in the 1968 Cup-Winners' Cup Final?

9 Which university did Brian McClair attend?

10 Carl Leaburn and John Humphries were in the same side at which club?

11 Which team won the 1976 UEFA Cup?

12 Who scored 30 goals for England in 33 appearances?

13 Which soccer team did Kenny Dalglish support as a boy?

14 Glenn Roeder left as boss of which club in February 1996?

15 Brian Stein hit a late League Cup Final winner for which club?

Answers to page 119

1 Carl Zeiss Jena, **2** Tommy Docherty, **3** David Pleat, **4** Madrid, **5** Partick Thistle, **6** Billy Meredith, **7** 1909, **8** Roy McFarland, **9** Kenny Dalglish, **10** Plymouth Argyle, **11** Dino and Roberto, **12** Seaman, **13** Paris, **14** Stan Cullis, **15** Rangers.

GARY LINEKER

Answers on page 120

1 How many hat-tricks did he score for England?

2 Which boss took Gary Lineker to Everton in 1985?

3 Against which country did Gary Lineker play his last international game?

4 Who went on when Gary Lineker was sustituted in his last game for England?

5 Which manager sold Gary Lineker to Tottenham Hotspur?

6 What is Gary Lineker's middle name?

7 Gary Lineker moved from Everton to which club for £2.8m in June 1986?

8 Who saved Gary Lineker's penalty in an FA Cup Final?

9 Which sports-based TV show is Gary Lineker a team captain on?

10 Which two foreign teams did Gary Lineker play for?

11 At which club was Gary Lineker playing when he retired from soccer?

12 Which brand of crisps does he advertise?

13 Gary Lineker missed a penalty against which team in 1992?

14 How many red cards was Gary Lineker given in his playing career?

15 Against which country did he score his first international hat-trick?

Answers to page 120

1 Celtic, **2** Liverpool v Spurs, **3** 1948-49, **4** Graham, **5** Nigel Martyn, **6** Norwich City, **7** 33, **8** 1992-93, **9** Birmingham City, **10** Wigan Athletic, **11** Neal, **12** Sheffield United, **13** Arsenal, **14** Manchester Utd, **15** Wrexham.

RED CARD 1

Answers on page 125

1 How many players were sent off in the 1997 Chesterfield v Plymouth Argyle league game?

2 Darren Peacock was sent off as which London club knocked Newcastle Utd out of the 1995-96 FA Cup?

3 Which Arsenal defender was sent off in a Premiership match against Aston Villa for handling the ref?

4 Which Manchester Utd Star got a red card after the final whistle in 1993?

5 Which Blackburn player was sent off after three minutes of his debut against Everton?

6 Who was the first player to be convicted of feigning an injury to try to get an opponent sent off?

7 Who in 1996 was fined £2,000 for refusing to leave the field when sent off in a reserve game?

8 What was unusual about the dismissal of Ian Banks in December 1989?

9 Which Scottish winger Willie of the 1960s to the 1980s was sent off 15 times?

10 Who in January 1991 became the first player to be sent off in a live TV League match?

11 Who was Peter Shilton playing for when he was sent off for the first time in his career?

12 John Burns became the first British player to be sent off on his debut. What club was he playing for on this eventful day in 1923?

13 In 1971 Nottingham Forest had a player sent off for the first time in 32 years. Who was the player involved?

14 Who are the only club to have had two players sent off in a game at Wembley?

15 How many times was Wimbledon hardman Vinnie Jones sent off whilst playing for The Dons?

Answers to page 125

1 Liverpool, **2** Graeme Souness, **3** Chelsea, **4** Argentina, **5** Alan Gilzean, **6** Tottenham Hotspur, **7** Liverpool, **8** Hamburg, **9** Crystal Palace, **10** Reading, **11** Davie Cooper, **12** Manchester United, **13** Galatasaray, **14** Liverpool, Tranmere Rovers, **15** Black and White.

QUIZ 76

Answers on page 126

1 In June 1994 Swedish player Martin Dahlin turned down a transfer to which English club?

2 Who played their home games at the Baseball Ground until May 1997?

3 Who had the nickname the *Clown Prince*?

4 Which team won the 1980 UEFA Cup?

5 Which soccer team does politician Gordon Brown support?

6 Who was keeper Mark Smith playing for when he was sent off after 19 seconds in a 1993-94 match against Darlington?

7 Which Aberdeen player was sent off in the 1979 Scottish League Cup Final?

8 Leicester City player Arthur Chandler scored 6 goals in a match in October 1928. Who were the opponents?

9 Who scored 41 league goals for Chelsea in 1960-61?

10 Who beat Real Madrid 1-0 in the 1981 European Cup Final?

11 Norwich City player Roy Hollis scored 5 goals in a match in December 1951. Who were the opponents?

12 Which club originally played at the Red House ground?

13 Which soccer team does singer Alison Moyet support?

14 With which soccer club did comedian Eddie Large have trials with?

15 Republic skipper Roy Keane was red carded in 1996 against which country?

Answers to page 126

1 Joe Kinnear, **2** Porto, **3** QPR, **4** Everton, **5** Bryan Robson, **6** Burslem, **7** John Deehan, **8** Walsall, **9** Southampton, **10** South Africa, **11** England, **12** Hungary, **13** Everton, **14** Ian Rush, **15** Tottenham Hotspur.

QUIZ 77

Answers on page 123

1 Stan Colymore moved from Nottingham Forest to which club for £8.5m in July 1995?

2 Whose biography is called *No Half Measures*?

3 Gavin Peacock moved from Newcastle United to which club for £1.25m in July 1993?

4 Peru's goalkeeper in the 1978 quarter-final match against Argentina in which Peru lost 6-0 was born in which country?

5 Who is Dundee's all time top League scorer?

6 Greame Souness was at which club for three years without playing in the first team?

7 Who beat Moenchengladbach 3-1 in the 1977 European Cup Final?

8 Which German club did Uwe Seeler play for?

9 With which club did TV Presenter Angus Deyton have trials with?

10 Tottenham Hotspur player Ted Harper scored 5 goals in a match in August 1930. Who were the opponents?

11 Which former Scotland and Rangers winger died from a brain haemorrhage at the age of 39 in March 1995?

12 Anderlecht's worst ever result was in 1956 when they lost 10-0 in the first round of the European Cup. Who were their opponents?

13 Which Turkish side did Graeme Souness become boss of in 1995?

14 With which club did comedian Stan Boardman have trials with?

15 What two colours are on Hereford United's home shirts?

Answers to page 123

1 5, **2** Chelsea, **3** Emmanuel Petit, **4** Eric Cantona, **5** Garry Flitcroft, **6** Gordon Durie (Tottenham), **7** Gordon Strachan (Coventry City), **8** He was a sub on the bench, **9** Johnston, **10** Paul Gascoigne, **11** Plymouth Argyle, **12** Rochdale, **13** Sammy Chapman, **14** Stockport (1994 Play-off final against Burnley), **15** Twelve.

QUIZ 78

Answers on page 124

1 Who succeeded Peter Withe as manager of Wimbledon in 1992?

2 Who lost 2-1 to Juventus in the 1984 Cup-Winners' Cup Final?

3 Tony Currie first played in an FA Cup Final for which team?

4 Who was Andy Gray playing for when he hit a mid - 1980s European Cup Winner's Cup treble?

5 According to FIFA who has scored the fastest goal in a World Cup final?

6 Port Vale used to have which word at the front of their name?

7 Who succeeded Mike Walker as manager of Norwich City in 1994?

8 Bolton Wanderers player T Caldwell scored 5 goals in a match in September 1983. Who were the opponents?

9 Which was Alf Ramsey's first club as player?

10 In which country was Mark Stein born?

11 Which country did Mike O'Grady play for?

12 In the Final of the 1954 World Cup West Germany played against which country?

13 Which team took part in the Charity Shield from 1984 to 1987?

14 Who did Chester City sell to Liverpool for £300,000 in May 1980?

15 Gordon Durie moved from Chelsea to which club for £2.2 million in August 1991?

Answers to page 124

1 Everton, **2** Derby County, **3** Len Shackleton, **4** Eintracht Frankfurt, **5** Raith Rovers, **6** Crewe Alexandria, **7** Doug Rougvie, **8** Portsmouth, **9** Jimmy Greaves, **10** Liverpool, **11** Walsall, **12** Rotherham United, **13** Southend Utd, **14** Manchester City, **15** Russia.

QUIZ 79

Answers on page 129

1 How many Scottish League clubs did Denis Law play for?

2 Who hit a hat-trick when Chelsea beat Manchester City 5-4 in the Full Members Cup?

3 Which keeper did a goalmouth sit-in at half time in 1990?

4 How many international goals did Andy McEvoy score?

5 Who was in goal for both legs of Dundee Utd's 1987 UEFA Cup Final?

6 Who became manager of Wimbledon in January 1992?

7 Bobby Charlton scored in a 1956 Youth Cup Final against which Chesterfield goalkeeper?

8 Which player of the 1930s has scored most goals in a season for Luton Town?

9 Who was England's first choice goalkeeper in the 1990 Word Cup Finals?

10 Which soccer team does TV presenter Eamonn Holmes support?

11 Who lost 4-2 to Anderlecht in the 1976 Cup-Winners' Cup Final?

12 Who is the only Manchester Utd boss never to have lost a game to Manchester City?

13 Who was the first manager in the world to pay £15m for a player?

14 Who lost 2-1 to Aberdeen after extra time in the 1983 Cup-Winners' Cup Final?

15 Which Dutch side did Bobby Robson manage after leaving England?

Answers to page 129

1 Celtic, **2** Hibernian, **3** Rangers, **4** St Mirren, **5** Celtic, **6** Ian Porterfield, **7** Rangers, **8** Stenhousemuir, **9** 1950s, **10** 1980, **11** Celtic, **12** Jim Leighton, **13** Rangers, **14** Willie Miller, **15** Celtic.

QPR 1

Answers on page 130

1 QPR recorded a 8-1 League Cup win over which club in October 1983?

2 What was unique about about the first Charity Shield match, a 1-1 draw between Manchester Utd and QPR?

3 Who was QPR's top league scorer in 1995-96?

4 In which city do QPR play?

5 Which player scored 30 League goals for QPR in 1966-67?

6 Who moved from Hereford Utd to QPR in 1990 to set a club record for a transfer fee received?

7 Paul Parker moved from QPR to which club for £1.7m in July 1991?

8 Andy Sinton moved from QPR to which club for £2.7m in August 1993?

9 Which goalkeeper did QPR sell for £1.3m in 1989-90?

10 Les Ferdinand moved from QPR to which club for £6m in June 1995?

11 Who scored 11 goals for QPR in the 1976-77 UEFA Cup campaign?

12 Which Northern Ireland star is QPR's most capped player?

13 What is the highest position QPR have ever achieved in the League?

14 Darren Peacock moved from QPR to which club for £2.7m in March 1994?

15 Who scored 11 goals in QPR's first European season?

Answers to page 130

1 Arsenal, **2** Arsenal, **3** William Murray, **4** 1906-07, **5** 1910's, **6** Chris Turner, **7** Carl, **8** Oldham Athletic, **9** Juventus, **10** Dixie, **11** None, **12** Scunthorpe, **13** Norwich City, **14** Coventry City, **15** Bertie Mee.

ABERDEEN 1

Answers on page 127

1 Who did Aberdeen beat 2-1 in the 1984 Scottish FA Cup Final?

2 Who did Aberdeen beat 3-0 in the 1985-86 Scottish League Cup Final?

3 Which team was beaten 4-1 after extra time by Aberdeen in the 1982 Scottish FA Cup Final?

4 Who beat Aberdeen 3-1 in the 1959 Scottish FA Cup Final?

5 Who did Aberdeen beat 9-8 in the 1990 Scottish FA Cup Final on penalties?

6 Who followed Alex Smith as manager of which club?

7 Who beat Aberdeen 1-0 in the 1953 Scottish FA Cup Final replay?

8 Which side provided a great Scottish Cup shock by knocking Aberdeen out in 1995?

9 In what decade did Aberdeen first win the Championship?

10 In which year did Alex Ferguson win the Scottish Premier Division title for the first time as Aberdeen manager?

11 Who beat Aberdeen 2-1 in the 1954 Scottish FA Cup Final?

12 Which keeper did Alec Ferguson sign from his former club Aberdeen?

13 Who beat Aberdeen 2-1 in the 1978 Scottish FA Cup Final?

14 Which Scottish international made 556 league appearances for Aberdeen between 1973-90?

15 Who beat Aberdeen 2-0 in the 1967 Scottish FA Cup Final?

Answers to page 127

1 None, **2** David Speedie (Chelsea), **3** Neville Southall, **4** Six, **5** Billy Thompson, **6** Joe Kinnear, **7** Gordon Banks, **8** Joe Payne, **9** Peter Shilton, **10** Manchester Utd, **11** West Ham Utd, **12** Ron Atkinson, **13** Kevin Keegan (for Alan Shearer), **14** Real Madrid, **15** PSV Eindhoven.

QUIZ 80

Answers on page 128

1 Who beat Liverpool 2-0 in the 1950 FA Cup Final?

2 Who beat Sheffield Utd 1-0 in the 1936 FA Cup Final?

3 Who succeeded Johnny Cochrane as manager of Sunderland in 1939?

4 What season did Celtic achieve Scotland's first double?

5 In which decade did Blackburn Rovers first win the championship?

6 Who succeeded Mark Lawrenson as manager of Peterborough United?

7 What is the name of Glenn Hoddle's brother, once with Barnet?

8 Which club was once known as Pine Villa?

9 Which team won the 1993 UEFA Cup?

10 What was the nickname of William Ralph Dean?

11 Of the six games England played during the 1966 World Cup finals how many resulted in defeat?

12 What was Kevin Keegan's first club?

13 Andy Townsend was at which club when he made his international debut?

14 Phil Babb was at which club when he made his international debut?

15 Which Arsenal boss said "I hadn't planned to be a football manager"

Answers to page 128

1 Crewe, **2** It was the only one to be replayed (Manchester Utd won it 4-0), **3** Daniel Dichio, **4** London, **5** Rodney Marsh, **6** Darren Peacock, **7** Manchester Utd, **8** Sheffield Wednesday, **9** David Seaman, **10** Newcastle Utd, **11** Stan Bowles, **12** Alan McDonald, **13** Division 1 (2nd 1975-76), **14** Newcastle Utd, **15** Stan Bowles.

QUIZ 81

Answers on page 133

1 Which seaside resort once included Sir Stanley Matthews in its soccer team?

2 Which three Sheffield Wednesday players were involved in the 1962 match-fixing scandal?

3 Which Adrian moved to Espanol from Everton in the 1980s?

4 Which club beat Hamburg to win the European Super Cup in 1977?

5 Which country has Fredi Bobic played for?

6 In a 1993 Champions League game, which club were leading German champions Werder Bremen 0-3 at half-time only to end up losing 5-3?

7 Which Lancashire soccer team were the first to achieve the League and Cup double?

8 Who plays at home at Sincil Bank?

9 Which country lost 2-1 to Italy in the 1994 World Cup Semi-Final?

10 Which player captained England a record 90 times, second in number only to Bobby Moore?

11 Which Jimmy of Celtic hit the first hat-trick in a Scottish FA Cup Final?

12 In what year was the first European Championship Final played?

13 Who has won most Scottish caps during their time with Rangers?

14 Who was bought by Ipswich Town in 1994 at a club record fee?

15 Tony Parkes was caretaker manager of which Premiership club?

Answers to page 133

1 Bergamo, **2** William, **3** 1920s, **4** Frank Stapleton, **5** Jimmy Greaves, **6** Liverpool, **7** Hearts, **8** 5, **9** Sheffield Wednesday, **10** Joseph, **11** Pierluigi Casiraghi, **12** Arsenal, **13** Sheffield Wednesday (1993), **14** John Scales, **15** Rotherham Utd.

QUIZ 82

Answers on page 134

1 Who is the only player to have scored in every division of the league, from Fourth to Premiership, with the same club?

2 Who was the first goalkeeper to captain his side to victory in an FA Cup Final?

3 Who started the game in goal for England when they drew against Belgium in a friendly in May 1998?

4 Who started the game in goal for Northern Ireland when they lost to Spain in a friendly in June 1998?

5 Which Manchester Utd keeper was club joint top scorer in mid-season 1974-75 because of his spot kick success?

6 Which country beat England 6-3 and 7-1 in the 1950s?

7 How many international goals did Lou Macari score?

8 Who was the first footballer to be knighted?

9 Brothers Danny, Rodney and Ray Wallace were together at which club?

10 Which Scottish Steve played for Barcelona in the 1980s?

11 What was the first English club that Ted McMinn played for?

12 What acheivement wins the annual Golden Boot for footballers?

13 Tony Fitzpatrick made a record 351 appearances, for which Scottish club between 1973-88?

14 Which English football club was originally known as Newton Heath?

15 Which soccer team does actor Leslie Phillips support?

Answers to page 134

1 Aston Villa, **2** Crystal Palace, **3** Gary Lineker, **4** Joe Parkinson, **5** Oldham Athletic, **6** Steve Burtenshaw, **7** 1930, **8** Barcelona, **9** Deportivo La Coruna, **10** Glasgow Rangers, **11** John Morrissey, **12** Paul Rideout, **13** Telford Utd, **14** 1981, **15** Bill Kenwright.

QUIZ 83

Answers on page 131

1 In which Italian city do Atlanta play their home matches?

2 What is Ian Bishop's middle name?

3 In which decade did Burnley first win the Championship?

4 Which ex-Arsenal player played for Ajax and Le Havre?

5 When Martin Peters joined Spurs, who moved the other way?

6 Which side beat Tottenham 7-0, inflicting their worst league defeat in history?

7 Who won the Scottish cup in 1998?

8 How many times did Arsenal win the championship in the 1930s?

9 Pugh, Fantham and Quinn played for which 1960s FA Cup Finalists?

10 What is Denis Irwin's first name?

11 Who scored the only goal of the 1998 World Cup qualifying play-off second leg that enabled Italy to go through to the finals at the expense of Russia?

12 Which club does Jeremy Beadle support?

13 Which club became the first English side to lose both domestic Cup Finals in the same season?

14 Which defender played 240 games for Wimbledon before going to Liverpool?

15 In 1991 who became the first club to win an FA Cup shoot out?

Answers to page 131

1 Blackpool, **2** Tony Kay, David Layne, Peter Swan, **3** Heath, **4** Liverpool, **5** Germany, **6** Anderlecht, **7** Preston North End, **8** Lincoln City, **9** Bulgaria, **10** Billy Wright, **11** Quinn, **12** 1960, **13** George Young, **14** Steve Sedgley, **15** Blackburn.

EVERTON 1

Answers on page 132

1 Which club did Derek Moutfield join on leaving Everton?

2 At which ground did Everton gain their first FA Cup win in 1906?

3 A club record fee received stood for ten years when which player left Everton for Tottenham Hotspur in the mid 80s?

4 Who moved from Bournmouth to Everton in 1994 to set a club record for a transfer fee received?

5 Which club did Mike Milligan leave to join Everton?

6 Who succeeded Billy Bingham as manager of Everton in 1977?

7 In what year were Everton first relegated?

8 Gary Lineker moved from Everton to which club for £2.8m in June 1986?

9 From which Spanish club did Everton aquire French international striker Mickael Medar?

10 Trevor Steven moved from Everton to which club for £1.5m in June 1989?

11 Who is the soccer playing son of former Everton star Johnny Morrissey?

12 In the 1994-95 FA Cup winning season, who was Everton's top League scorer?

13 Which non-League side did Everton beat in 1985 in the FA Cup?

14 In which year in the 1980s did Liverpool and Everton not contest the Charity Shield?

15 At the start of 1998 -99, which theatre impresario was listed as one of Everton's directors?

Answers to page 132

1 Alan Cork (Wimbledon), **2** Dave Beasant (Wimbledon), **3** Martyn, **4** Fettis, **5** Alec Stepney, **6** Hungary, **7** Five, **8** Sir Stanley Matthews, **9** Southampton, **10** Archibald, **11** Derby County, **12** Europe's leading goal scorer, **13** St Mirren, **14** Manchester United, **15** Tottenham Hotspur.

LEAGUE HAT-TRICKS

Answers on page 137

1 Who is the youngest scorer of a hat-trick in top flight English soccer?

2 Who scored a hat-trick in Manchester Utd's 7-0 Premiership defeat of Barnsley?

3 Ian Wright broke Arsenal's goal-scoring record with a hat-trick against which team?

4 Whose hat-trick at Wembley in 1998 helped Charlton secure a place in the Premiership?

5 Who marked his 1986 debut for Southampton with a hat-trick?

6 Who scored a hat-trick for Coventry on the opening day of the 1997-98 season at home against Chelsea?

7 Who has scored more hat-tricks in his career than any other British footballer?

8 What was unusual about West Ham defender Alvin Martin's hat-trick in the 8-1 thrashing of Newcastle in 1987?

9 Which Leeds Utd midfielder hit a 1995 hat-trick against Coventry City?

10 Which club did Alan Shearer score his first Newcastle United hat-trick against?

11 Who scored a double hat-trick on his debut for Newcastle United in the 1950s?

12 Which player hit his first Newcastle Utd hat-trick against Wimbledon in October 1995?

13 Adcock, Stewart and White each hit three for which team in the same game in 1987?

14 Who finished Southampton's joint top scorer in 1995-96 with 7 goals, having hit a hat-trick in the first game?

15 Who scored a first-half hat-trick for Liverpool against Newcastle in Ruud Gullits first game in charge?

Answers to page 137

1 Liverpool (18 times), **2** Paul Ince, **3** Diego Maradona, **4** Peter McParland, **5** Nottingham Forest, **6** Maritimo, **7** Red, **8** Chelsea, **9** Bournmouth, **10** 1900s, **11** Andrei Kanchelskis, **12** Scotland, **13** Davies, **14** West Ham Utd, **15** Jonathan.

QUIZ 84

Answers on page 138

1 Who succeeded Kenny Dalglish as manager of Blackburn Rovers in 1995?

2 Which country was the first to appear in three consecutive European Championship Finals?

3 In the 80s which League-championship winning manager was labelled "A Young Pup" by Brian Clough?

4 Who scored 6 goals in a game for Linfield against Wales in February 1930?

5 Norman Deeley scored twice in an FA Cup Final for which club?

6 What nickname was given to striker Charlie Fleming?

7 What was the result of Scotland's Group four game against Iran in the 1978 World Cup?

8 Which club beat Sampdoria to win the European Super Cup in 1990?

9 Which club did Peter Beardsley join on leaving Liverpool?

10 Who has been manager at Bristol City, Oxford, Sunderland and York?

11 Which England manager accused his players of "running around like headless chickens"?

12 What was Grimsby Town once known as?

13 Who was appointed Fulham manager by Director of Football at Craven Cottage Kevin Keegan?

14 When Juventus were beaten in the 1971 UEFA Cup Final what unfamiliar colour did they play in?

15 Which club did Ray Wilkins finish his playing career at?

Answers to page 138

1 1950s, **2** Lothar Matthaus, **3** Borussia Dortmund, **4** Leeds Utd, **5** USA, **6** Arsenal, **7** Glasgow, **8** John Hartson, **9** Patrik Kluivert, **10** 1948-49, **11** 1920s, **12** Rodney Marsh, **13** Barcelona, **14** Bayern Munich, **15** Tom Moody.

QUIZ 85

Answers on page 135

1 Which team has appeared in the Charity Shield most often?

2 Who was sent off in Manchester Utd's 1990s European Champions League 3-1 defeat in Gothenburg?

3 Gianofranco Zola took over the number 10 shirt at Napoli from which superstar?

4 Who was Aston Villa's two goal hero in the 1957 FA Cup Final?

5 Which soccer team does Tory politician Kenneth Clarke support?

6 Which club from Madeira plays in the Portugese League?

7 What colour are Charlton's home socks?

8 Stoke City recorded a 6-2 League Cup win over which club in October 1974?

9 Southend Utd recorded a 6-1 League Cup win over which club in August 1968?

10 In which decade did Sheffield Wednesday first win the Championship?

11 Who moved from Manchester United to Everton for £5.5m in August 1995?

12 In the 1930s, which country did HM Wales play for?

13 1970s international centres Ron and Wyn share what surname?

14 Which soccer team does Newcastle United and England mid-fielder Rob Lee support?

15 What is Nick Barmby's middle name?

Answers to page 135

1 Alan Shearer, **2** Andy Cole, **3** Bolton, **4** Clive Mendonca, **5** Colin Clarke, **6** Dion Dublin, **7** Dixie Dean - 37, **8** Each goal was scored against a different goalkeeper. (The first against Martin Thomas, then outfied substitute Chris Hepworth and finally Peter Beardsley), **9** Gary McAllister, **10** Leicester City, **11** Len Shackleton, **12** Les Ferdinand, **13** Manchester City, **14** Matt Le Tissier, **15** Michael Owen.

QUIZ 86

Answers on page 136

1 In which decade did the Germans first win the World Cup?

2 Who was skipper of the winning German team in the 1990 World Cup?

3 Which club were the German champions in 1995-96?

4 Davis Batty was at which club when he made his international debut?

5 Who beat England in a Group Two 1950 World Cup match in Belo Horizonte?

6 Which side narrowly failed to win the double in the 1951-52 season?

7 Where was the 1976 European Cup Final held?

8 Which Welsh international scored Arsenal's goal in their 2-1 defeat by Real Zaragoza in the 1995 Cup Winners' Cup Final?

9 Which Dutchman who was sent off in Hollands match with Belgium in the 1998 World Cup finals?

10 When did Rangers first achieve the treble?

11 In which decade was Tommy Docherty born?

12 Which player scored 30 League goals for QPR in 1966-67?

13 Who were the first club to eliminate Real Madrid from the European Cup competition?

14 Who lost to Dynamo Kiev in the 1975 Super Cup?

15 Who was Oxford United's top league scorer in 1990-90?

Answers to page 136

1 Ray Harford, **2** West Germany. (1972 1976,1980), **3** Howard Kendall, **4** Joe Bambrick, **5** Wolves, **6** Cannonball, **7** 1-1, **8** AC Milan, **9** Everton, **10** Dennis Smith, **11** Graham Taylor, **12** Grimsby Pelham, **13** Ray Wilkins, **14** All Blue, **15** Leyton Orient.

QUIZ 87

Answers on page 141

1 Player/manager Ian Bowyer was in the same side as his son Gary at which club?

2 Which soccer striker played for the MCC against the Germans, scored a run and said "It's always nice to score one against the Germans"?

3 Playing from 1947 to 1959, Denis Lewis set a League appearance record at which seaside club?

4 Against which team did West Ham's Joe Cole make his League debut?

5 Who was the first player to make 700 English League apppearances?

6 With which soccer club did singer Julio Iglesias have trials with?

7 Bobby Charlton came out of retirement to play for which League club?

8 Who scored both AC Milan's goals when they won the European Cup in 1963 and also played for Juventus when they lost the 1973 Final to Ajax?

9 Who was in goal when West Ham Utd won the FA Cup in 1980?

10 In which city do East Stirlingshire play?

11 Ian Rush moved from Liverpool to which club for £3.2m in June 1987?

12 Who were the first Dutch club to win the European Cup?

13 Who was known as 'the last of the Busby Babes' after becoming the final signing of the Old Trafford legend?

14 Tony Dorigo moved from Chelsea to which club for £1.7 million in June 1991?

15 Who beat Panathinaikos 2-0 in the 1971 European Cup Final?

Answers to page 141

1 Forty-four, **2** Geoff Hurst, **3** Ian St John, **4** £80,000, **5** OFK Belgrade, **6** 3, **7** Peru, **8** 6, **9** The Sun, **10** Barnet, **11** West ham Utd, **12** Bill Nicholson, **13** West Ham Utd, **14** Charlie Nicholas, **15** Chelsea.

SHEFF WED 1

Answers on page 142

1 Who did Ron Atkinson replace as manager of Wednesday?

2 Who scored the winning goal in the 1993 all Sheffield FA Cup semi-final?

3 Who succeeded Derek Dooley as manager of Wednesday in 1974?

4 In which decade did Wednesday first win the FA Cup?

5 Who was the Wednesday striker who had a leg amputated?

6 In the pre shoot-out days, how many hours of play did the 1979 FA Cup tie between Arsenal and Wednesday last for?

7 Which three Wednesday players were involved in the 1962 match-fixing scandal?

8 In which decade did Wednesday first win the Championship?

9 Which player scored 46 League goals for Wednesday in 1951-52?

10 Wednesday player Douglas Hunt scored 6 goals in a match in November 1938. Who were the opponents?

11 Which club did Ian Nolan move from in August 1994?

12 Wednesday recorded an 8-0 League Cup win over which club in October 1989?

13 Which defender played for Nott Forest, Sampdoria and Wednesday?

14 Which referee was pushed to the ground by Wednesday's Paulo di Canio in a league match with Arsenal in September 1998?

15 Which West Ham Utd player had his red card reduced to yellow after TV evidence showed he was wrongly dismissed in a game against Wednesday?

Answers to page 142

1 Manchester Utd, **2** Hartlepool, **3** 1980s, **4** 1980, **5** 1960s, **6** Barcelona, **7** Celtic, **8** Stanley Mortensen, **9** China and Hong Kong, **10** Newcastle United, **11** Chelsea, **12** Crosby, Liverpool, **13** Dean Holdsworth, **14** Exeter City, **15** Glasgow.

JIMMY GREAVES

Answers on page 139

1 Jimmy Greaves played for England 57 times. How many goals did he score for them?

2 Which player replaced the injured Jimmy Greaves in the 1966 World Cup quarter finals?

3 Who was Jimmy Greaves' television partner on ITV?

4 How much did AC Milan pay Chelsea in 1961 for the goal-scoring services of Jimmy Greaves?

5 Against which side did he become the first Tottenham Hotspur player to be sent off for 35 years?

6 How many internationals did Jimmy Greaves play after the 1966 World Cup?

7 Against which country did Jimmy Greaves make his scoring debut?

8 How many times did Jimmy Greaves score three or more goals for England?

9 For which tabloid newspaper does Jimmy Greaves write a column?

10 At which non-League club did Jimmy Greaves play out his career?

11 At which club did Jimmy Greaves finish his League career?

12 Which manager brought Jimmy Greaves back from Italy?

13 What was the third London Side that Jimmy Greaves played for?

14 Which player's leaving caused Jimmy Greaves to say, "Stringfellows will miss him"?

15 At which club did Jimmy Greaves set a goal-scoring record of 41 goals in a season?

Answers to page 139

1 Hereford Utd, **2** Gary Lineker, **3** Torquay Utd, **4** Manchester Utd (January 1999), **5** Jimmy Dickson, **6** Real Madrid, **7** Preston North End, **8** Jose Altafini, **9** Phil Parkes, **10** Falkirk, **11** Juventus, **12** Feyenoord, **13** Sammy McIlroy, **14** Leeds Utd, **15** Ajax.

QUIZ 88

Answers on page 140

1 Danny Wallace first played in an FA Cup Final for which team?

2 In 1992/93 which English club set a new record by not scoring a goal for 13 league and Cup matches?

3 In what decade did Dundee Utd first win the Championship?

4 In which year did Alex Ferguson win the Scottish Premier Division title for the first time as Aberdeen manager?

5 In which decade did Liverpool first win the FA Cup?

6 Rivaldo moved from D. La Coruna for £16.1m in August 1997. To which club did he go?

7 Who beat Airdrieonians 3-1 in the 1975 Scottish FA Cup Final?

8 Who hit a hat-trick in the Matthew's Final?

9 In their pre-Euro 96 tour, which countries did England visit?

10 Jim Smith followed Willie McFaul as manager of which club?

11 Who beat Bolton Wanderers in their last Premiership match of the 1997-98 season, resulting in their relegation?

12 In which city do Marine play?

13 Who moved from Brentford to Wimbledon in 1992 to set a club record for a transfer fee received?

14 Who was Fred Binney playing for when he was the League's leading scorer in 1972-73?

15 In which city do Partick Thistle play?

Answers to page 140

1 David Pleat, **2** Mark Bright, **3** Steve Burtenshaw, **4** 1890s, **5** Derek Dooley, **6** Nine, **7** Tony Kay, David Layne, Peter Swan, **8** 1900s, **9** Derek Dooley, **10** Norwich, **11** Tranmere Rovers, **12** Aldershot, **13** Des Walker, **14** Paul Alcock, **15** Alvin Martin.

QUIZ 89

Answers on page 145

1 Which manager took Kevin Keegan to Liverpool?

2 In what month was Alan Shearer born?

3 Dixie McNeil followed Bobby Roberts as manager of which club?

4 How many international goals did Peter Beardsley score?

5 Which team were beaten 1-0 by Ipswich Town in the 1978 FA Cup Final?

6 Alan Wright and Scott Sellars were in the same team at which club?

7 Oman Biyik played in the World Cup for which country?

8 Which England midfielder played in white boots for Everton?

9 Which player scored 42 League goals for Portsmouth in 1992-93?

10 Which club broke their own transfer record to buy Paul Bernard from Oldham Athletic in 1995?

11 Steve Hodge was at which club when he made his international debut?

12 Who scored for England in his 100th international?

13 At which club did Gianfranco Zola make his name as understudy to Diego Maradonna?

14 Which David was a Yorkshire wicket keeper and Bradford City player?

15 Who scored six goals for Italy in the 1990 World Cup Finals?

Answers to page 145

1 Arthur and Jack Rowley, **2** South Africa, **3** Luton Town, **4** Bob Stokoe, **5** Sheffield Wednesday, **6** Phil Neal, **7** Liverpool, **8** Brian Laudrup, **9** Rotherham, **10** John Aldridge, **11** Bolton Wanderers, **12** Grimsby Town, **13** Jairzinho, **14** Strachan, **15** Norwich City & Sunderland.

QUIZ 90

Answers on page 146

1 In which country were the 1966 World Cup Finals held?

2 Who scored the goal for Sweden that finally put paid to England's hopes in the 1992 European Championship finals?

3 Who beat Fulham in the Division Two promotion play-off semi-finals?

4 With 215 goals Harry Hampton is all-time top League scorer at which club?

5 Ossie Ardiles followed Jim Smith as boss of which club?

6 Which Red Star Belgrade player won the 1990-91 Golden Boot award?

7 Which team were beaten 2-0 by Everton in the 1984 FA Cup Final?

8 Who was the regular goalkeeper for Notts County in their 1991-92 relegation season?

9 Where was the 1956 European Cup Final held?

10 Who was the first player to win England Caps at all five levels - schoolboy, youth, amateur, Under 23 and full?

11 Who was the longest-serving England manager?

12 Which side is known as The Pars?

13 In which city do Real Sociedad play?

14 What was Tony Daley's first league club?

15 Which soccer team does TV presenter Jim Bowen support?

Answers to page 146

1 Derby County, **2** Frank Stapleton, **3** Glenn Cockerill, **4** Inter Milan, **5** Jimmy Hill, **6** Marwood, **7** Never, **8** Parma, **9** Preston North End, **10** Sheffield Wednesday, **11** Steve Morrow, **12** Terry Neill, **13** Tom Whittaker, **14** 1913, **15** 1951.

QUIZ 91

Answers on page 143

1 In the 1950's which brothers each reached 200 League goals on the same day?

2 Which country does Lucas Radbe come from?

3 Which club had a fanzine called *Mad As A Hatter*?

4 Who succeeded Frank Hill as boss of Charlton Athletic in 1965?

5 Leppings Lane runs by which club's ground?

6 Who was boss when Bolton Wanderers went down to the Fourth Division for the first time ever?

7 Which club did Mark Kennedy join after leaving Millwall?

8 Which member of a footballing family became the first non-British Scottish PFA Footballer of the Year?

9 Which club had a fanzine called *Windy and Dusty*?

10 Which player was involved in the substitute row in the Mexico v the Republic of Ireland 1994 World Cup game?

11 At which club did Jimmy Phillips make his League debut?

12 With 448 League games in the 1950s and 1960s, Keith Jobling set an appearance record at which club?

13 Who scored in the 1970 England v Brazil World Cup game?

14 Which Gordon scored Scotland's only World Cup goal in Mexico?

15 Both finalists in the 1975 League Cup were relegated from the top flight that season. Can you name them both?

Answers to page 143

1 Bill Shankly, **2** August, **3** Wrexham, **4** 9, **5** Arsenal, **6** Blackburn Rovers, **7** Cameroon, **8** Alan Ball, **9** Guy Whittingham, **10** Aberdeen, **11** Aston Villa, **12** Bobby Charlton, **13** Napoli, **14** Bairstow, **15** Toto Schillachi.

ARSENAL 3

Answers on page 144

1 Where did Charlie George go when he left Arsenal?

2 Which ex-Arsenal player played for Ajax and Le Havre?

3 In 1988, TV film evidence showed that Paul Davis of Arsenal had broken which Southampton player's jaw?

4 Before joining Arsenal for £7.5m, Dennis Bergkamp played for which Italian club?

5 Which television personality took over when a linesmen was injured during an Arsenal and Liverpool match in 1972?

6 Which Brian of Arsenal won his only England cap in 1988?

7 How many times did Arsenal win the FA Cup in the 1980s?

8 Who lost 1-0 to Arsenal in the 1994 Cup Winners' Cup Final?

9 Which Division Two team led Arsenal 2-0 at home before losing 2-4 in the third round of the 1998-99 FA Cup?

10 Which team were beaten 2-1 by Arsenal in the 1993 FA Cup Final?

11 Which Arsenal player broke his arm in a fall after being hoisted in the air by Tony Adams at the end of the 1993 League Cup Final?

12 Who succeeded Bertee Mee as manager of Arsenal in 1976?

13 Who succeeded George Allison as manager of Arsenal in 1947?

14 In which year were Arsenal relegated to the second division having only won three matches all season?

15 In which year did Arsenal install floodlights at Highbury?

Answers to page 144

1 England, **2** Tomas Brolin, **3** Grimsby Town, **4** Aston Villa, **5** Newcastle United, **6** Darko Pancev, **7** Watford, **8** Steve Cherry, **9** Paris, **10** Terry Venables, **11** Walter Winterbottom, **12** Dunfermline, **13** San Sebastian, Spain, **14** Aston Villa, **15** Blackburn Rovers.

EURO '96 1

Answers on page 149

1 Which English headmaster was a referee in Euro '96?

2 Who was the captain of winners Germany in Euro '96?

3 Who took England's fifth penalty in the shoot-out against Germany in the Euro '96 tournament?

4 How many games had Alan Shearer not scored for England before Euro '96?

5 Which country won the Euro '96 tournament Fair Play Award?

6 Who was Germany's top scorer in Euro '96 and with how many goals?

7 How many games were their in Euro '96?

8 How many minutes of extra-time were needed in the Euro '96 Final?

9 Whose amazing Euro '96 lob knocked out Portugal?

10 Which player scored England's first goal in Euro '96?

11 Bernard Lama Played for which country in Euro '96?

12 At which two grounds were the Euro '96 semi-finals held?

13 Who was the leading scorer in Euro '96, with five goals in the tournament?

14 Apart from England, which other country took part in two penalty shoot-outs in Euro '96?

15 Who scored for the Czech Republic in the Final of Euro '96?

Answers to page 149

1 Manchester Utd, **2** Manchester Utd, **3** 100 yards, **4** Terry Venables, **5** Wednesday Old Athletic, **6** Matt Busby, **7** Leyton Orient, **8** Blackburn Rovers, **9** Mark, **10** Exeter City, **11** Wolves, **12** Joe Mercer, **13** Blackburn Rovers, **14** Burnley, **15** Queens Park.

QUIZ 92

Answers on page 150

1 Who moved from Chelsea to Manchester United in 1979 for a record £825,000 before moving to AC Milan in 1984?

2 Which country did Scotland beat in the 1990 World Cup tournament?

3 Which Liverpool player won the 1983-84 Golden Boot award?

4 Which former Liverppol goalkeeper was accused of match-fixing?

5 Which country did Paul Bodin play for?

6 Which club did Bob Stokoe manage on three separate occasions?

7 Who scored nine goals for Portugal in the 1966 World Cup Finals?

8 Who succeeded David Pleat as manager of Leicester City in 1991?

9 In Italy, the import of what was banned in 1964, only to be lifted in 1980?

10 Apart from Rangers, which other Scottish League club did Ray Wilkins play for?

11 Who beat Bayern Munich 1-0 in the 1982 European Cup Final?

12 Who was the first Briton to win the World Manager of the Year award?

13 Who knocked out Blackburn, West Ham and Southampton before losing to Middlesborough in the Semi-Finals of the 1996-97 Coca-Cola Cup?

14 Which club ended Milan's 58-match unbeaten run in the Italian League?

15 At which club did Warren Barton make his League debut?

Answers to page 150

1 Alan Shearer, **2** Manchester Utd, **3** Bolton, **4** Plymouth Argyle, **5** Oxford Utd, **6** Alan Wright, **7** Dennis Irwin, **8** Arnold Muhren, **9** Crystal Palace, **10** Liverpool, **11** Tottenham Hotspur, **12** Reynald Pedros, **13** 10 minutes, **14** Earle Barrett, **15** Alan Ball.

QUIZ 93

Answers on page 147

1 Andy Cole was at which club when he made his international debut?

2 Mal Donaghy and Denis Irwin were in the same team at which club?

3 What is the maximum width of a soccer pitch?

4 Who was boss at Tottenham Hotspur when Gazza arrived?

5 Aston Villa recorded a 13-0 FA Cup win over which club in October 1886?

6 Who was manager of Manchester Utd when they won the European Cup in 1968?

7 Which club did Mervyn Day leave to join Aston Villa?

8 Which club has a fanzine called *Loadsamoney*?

9 Which forename is shared by ex-keepers Grew and Wallington?

10 Which club had a fanzine called *In Exile*?

11 Who were the first English club to play in the Cup Winners' Cup competition?

12 Which former England soccer captain and manager died on his 76th birthday in 1990?

13 For which club did Graeme Le Saux leave Chelsea?

14 Jimmy Mullen Followed Frank Casper as manager of which club?

15 Which Scottish club is nicknamed the Spiders?

Answers to page 147

1 David Elleray, **2** Jurgen Klinsmann, **3** Teddy Sherringham, **4** 12, **5** England, **6** Jurgen Klinsmann, three, **7** 31, **8** Five, **9** Karel Poborsky, **10** Alan Shearer, **11** France, **12** Old Trafford and Wembley, **13** Alan Shearer, **14** France, **15** Patrick Berger.

QUIZ 94

Answers on page 148

1 Which Southampton player became the youngest to score a First Division hat-trick in April 9, 1988?

2 Who went down in 1974 after 37 years in the top flight?

3 In which town was Nat Lofthouse born?

4 Who plays their home games at Home Park?

5 Which League Cup Final winning side did Alan Judge play for?

6 Which left-back was displaced by Graeme Le Saux at Blackburn Rovers?

7 Which Manchester Utd player scored the Republic of Ireland's goal in their 1-1 draw with Belgium in the first leg of the 1998 World Cup qualifying play-off?

8 Which Dutch master joined Manchester Utd from Ipswich Town?

9 Which club has a fanzine called *Eastern Eagle*?

10 Comedian Stan Boadman was once on the books of which club?

11 Which club paid £2 million to sign Paul Gascoigne?

12 In Euro '96, whose penalty for France was saved in the semi-final shoot-out against the Czech Republic?

13 Under the new Premiership arrangements, the half time interval was to be 15 minutes long. How long had it previously been?

14 Who moved from Oldham Athletic for £1,700,000 in February 1992 to set a club record for a transfer fee received?

15 Who joined Arsenal for a record British transfer fee in December 1971?

Answers to page 148

1 Ray Wilkins, **2** Sweden, **3** Ian Rush, **4** Bruce Grobbelaar, **5** Wales, **6** Carlisle United, **7** Eusebio, **8** Gordon Lee, **9** Foreign players, **10** Hibernian, **11** Aston Villa, **12** Terry Venables, **13** Stockport County, **14** Parma, **15** Maidstone Utd.

QUIZ 95

Answers on page 153

1 Who scored Ipswich Town's 1978 FA Cup winner against Arsenal?

2 Liverpool player Robbie Fowler scored 5 goals in a match in October 1993. Who were the opponents?

3 In which decade was Brian Clough born?

4 Who was the manager of Hereford Utd in 1972, the year they won election to the Football League?

5 Which was Neil Webb's first League club?

6 Which club used to play at Sheepfoot Lane?

7 In 1967, who became the first British team to win the European Cup?

8 What was Alan Kennedy's nickname at Liverpool?

9 Who has scored more hat-tricks in his career than any other British footballer?

10 Who scored 30 goals in 102 appearances for Scotland?

11 Ray Wilkins first played in an FA Cup Final for which team?

12 Chelsea recorded a 7-0 League Cup win over which club in November 1960?

13 Who was manager of Ipswich Town's championship winning team of the sixties?

14 In what year was Paul Gascoigne?

15 What is the highest position Blackburn Rovers have ever achieved in the League?

Answers to page 153

1 Decorate his kitchen, **2** Sweden, **3** John Jensen, **4** Rudi Voller, **5** Germany and Holland, **6** David Platt, **7** Richard Gough, **8** Stockholm, Gothenburg, Malmo and Norrkoping, **9** Lars Olsen, **10** Germany, **11** Switzerland, **12** Yugoslavia, **13** Thomas Brolin, **14** Stockholm, Gothenburg, Malmo and Norrkoping, **15** Gothenburg.

LIVERPOOL 5

Answers on page 154

1 Kevin Keegan moved from Liverpool to which club for £500,000 in June 1977?

2 Which former Bolton centre-half Alan was born in Liverpool in 1971?

3 Which club did Joey Jones leave to join Liverpool?

4 How many times did Bob Paisley take Liverpool to Wembley?

5 Kenny Dalglish's last game in charge of Liverpool was a 5th round FA Cup game against Everton. What was the score?

6 Who beat Liverpool 2-1 in the 1971 FA Cup Final?

7 Who said that there were only two teams on Merseyside-Liverpool and Liverpool Reserves?

8 Who was Liverpool's only League ever-present in the 1985-86 double-winning season?

9 Which former Liverpool player was Blackburn Rover's top scorer in their 1992 promotion season?

10 What is Jamie Redknapp's middle name?

11 Who did Chester City sell to Liverpool for £300,000 in May 1980?

12 Which Liverpool player scored his first international goal in Rio?

13 Which Liverpool player appeared three times at Wembley in 1977-78, his first season in England?

14 Which ex-Liverpool defender did Kevin Keegan get to advise Newcastle Utd about their defence?

15 Who was signed by Manchester City from Liverpool in January 1996?

Answers to page 154

1 Reading, **2** Pat Nevin, **3** PSV Eindhoven and Barcelona, **4** Coventry, **5** Chelsea, **6** Swindon Town, **7** Boris Stankovic, **8** "Escape To Victory", **9** Racecourse Ground, **10** Newcastle Utd, **11** Swanse City, **12** Barnsley, **13** Black, **14** Arnold Muhren, **15** Manchester City.

EURO '92

Answers on page 151

1. What had Denmark's manager Richard Moller Nielsen reputedly planned to do during Euro 92, before his team's surprise late call up?
2. Which country hosted the 1992 European Championship Competition?
3. Who scored a Final Euro 92 goal and then moved to play in London?
4. Who was the German skipper who broke his arm in his first game in the1992 European Championship in Sweden?
5. Which two countries in Euro 92 did not contain any English based players?
6. Who scored England's only goal in Euro 92?
7. Which member of the Scotland squad in the 1992 European Championship finals in Sweden was born in Sweden?
8. In which four Swedish cities were European Championship finals matches played in 1992?
9. Who was the captain of the Denmark team that won the 1992 European Championship in Sweden?
10. Who did Denamrk beat in the final?
11. From which country did Galler, the referee in the Euro 92 Final come?
12. Which country did Denmark replace in the Euro 92 Championships?
13. Who scored the goal for Sweden that finally put paid to England's hopes in the 1992 European Champioship finals?
14. Which four cities hosed the Euro 92 Championship?
15. In which city was the Euro 92 Final held?

Answers to page 151

1 Roger Osbourne, **2** Fulham, **3** 1930s, **4** Colin Addison, **5** Reading, **6** Oldham Athletic, **7** Celtic, **8** "Barney", **9** Dixie Dean - 37, **10** Kenny Dalglish, **11** Manchester Utd, **12** Doncaster Rovers, **13** Alf Ramsey, **14** 1967, **15** 1994-95 Premiership Champions.

QUIZ 96

Answers on page 152

1 Bulgarian Boris (Bobby) Mikhailov first played in England for which club?

2 Which Scottish Pat was on Tranmere's books at the start of 1996-97?

3 With which two clubs did Dutch international star Ronald Koeman win European Cup medals?

4 At which club did Les Sealey make his League debut?

5 What was Tommy Docherty's first club as manager?

6 Manchester Utd player Harold Halse scored 6 goals in a match in the 1911 Charity Shield. Who were the opponents?

7 Who was the first player to be sent off at Wembley?

8 Which film featured Bobby Moore and Pele?

9 What is Wrexham's ground called?

10 Tony Blair is a fan of which club?

11 Which club has made seven appearances in the European Cup-Winners' Cup despite never finishing higher than sixth in the League?

12 Which soccer team does bowler Darren Gough support?

13 What colour are Brentford's home shorts?

14 Which Dutch outfield player was 37 when Holland won Euro 88?

15 Which club has the largest pitch in England?

Answers to page 152

1 S V Hamburg, **2** Stubbs, **3** Wrexham, **4** 12, **5** 4-4, **6** Arsenal, **7** Bill Shankly, **8** Bruce Grobbelaar, **9** David Speedie, **10** Frank, **11** Ian Rush, **12** John barnes, **13** Kenny Dalglish, **14** Mark Lawrenson, **15** Nigel Clough.

QUIZ 97

Answers on page 157

1 Who was keeper Roger Freestone playing for when he scored two penalty goals in 1995-96?

2 Which club has a fanzine called *Tripe 'N' Trotters*?

3 Which year first saw FA Cup Final receipts top two million pounds?

4 What are the usual qualifications for the two teams that contest the FA Charity Shield?

5 What was the nickname of Manchester Utd's early 20th century player Enoch Walker?

6 Which club lost in the final of the League Cup and Semi-Final of the FA Cup in 1989-90?

7 West Brom recorded a 6-1 League Cup win over which club in November 1965?

8 What was Colin Cooper's first league club?

9 What did Meadowbank Thistle change its name to?

10 Why were Leeds City expelled from the League in 1919?

11 Which club has a fanzine called *The Seadog Bites Back*?

12 Who lost to Ajax in the 1972 Super Cup?

13 How many international goals did Alan Ball score?

14 Hankin and Hart scored in the same European game for which club?

15 Southampton recorded a 5-0 League Cup win over which club in August 1979?

Answers to page 157

1 Portsmouth, **2** Tommy Docherty, **3** Aldershot (A), **4** Gresley Rovers, **5** Gateshead, **6** 1940s, **7** Manchester City, **8** Liverpool, **9** Rotterdam, **10** Benfica (Portugal), **11** Swindon Town, **12** Harry Cripps, **13** Swindon Town, **14** Reading, **15** Stockport County.

QUIZ 98

Answers on page 158

1 Who lost 2-0 to Magdeburg in the 1974 Cup-Winners' Cup Final?

2 When Scotland hammered England 5-1 at Wembley in 1928 what nickname were they given?

3 What was the name of Derby County's old ground?

4 How long was John Cochrane manager of Reading for?

5 Which Ted became secretary of the FA in September 1973?

6 Which Jimmy became manager of Brighton in November 1995?

7 How many FA Cup winners medals did George Best win?

8 Which soccer team does actor Sean Bean support?

9 Which side inflicted a 10-4 thrashing on Everton in season 1958-59?

10 Who was Manchester City's keeper in the 1989 promotion to top flight?

11 How many keepers did Oldham Athletic use in 1993-94?

12 Who managed West Germany in the 1966 World Cup Final?

13 In which decade did Aberdeen first win the Scottish FA Cup?

14 In which city do Feyenoord play?

15 Bryan Hamilton was boss of which club twice in the 1980s?

Answers to page 158

1 Liverpool, **2** QPR, **3** Ted Ditchburn, **4** 0-0 after extra time, **5** Aston Villa, **6** Chelsea, **7** Coventry City, **8** Gerry Francis, **9** Johan Cruyff, **10** Mackay, **11** QPR, **12** Terry Fenwick, **13** 11, **14** Atletico Madrid, **15** Chris Armstrong.

QUIZ 99

Answers on page 155

1 Darren Anderton first played in a semi-final for which club?

2 Who said in 1977, "I have been punished for falling in love"?

3 Sheffield Wednesday recorded an 8-0 League Cup win over which club in October 1989?

4 Crewe Alexandra recorded a 7-1 FA Cup win over which club in November 1994?

5 Which team, third from bottom of the League in 1960 applied for re-election for the first time in over twenty years, yet still got voted out?

6 In which decade did Charlton Athletic first win the FA Cup?

7 Which soccer team does goalkeeper Alex Stepney support?

8 Which club was Peter Beardsley with when he first won the FA Cup?

9 Where was the 1974 European Cup Winners' Cup Final held?

10 Who were Manchester Utd's losing opponents in the 1968 European Cup Final?

11 John Trollope made 770 League appearances for which club between 1960 and 1980?

12 Which Millwall defender scored over 40 goals during the 1960s and early 1970s?

13 Which club originally had the nickname 'The Moonrakers' after an old legend?

14 John Arlott, the voice of cricket, was a fan of which club?

15 At which club did Eric Cantona's brother Joel make his English debut?

Answers to page 155

1 Swansea City, **2** Bolton Wanderers, **3** 1990, **4** League Champions versus FA Cup Winners, **5** "Knocker", **6** Oldham, **7** Coventry City, **8** Middlesborough, **9** Livingston, **10** Making illegal payments, **11** Scarborough, **12** Rangers, **13** 9, **14** Leeds Utd, **15** Wrexham.

SPURS 2

Answers on page 156

1 Which club beat Spurs after extra time in a League Cup Final?

2 Which team were beaten 3-2 by Spurs in the replayed 1982 FA Cup Final?

3 Which Spurs keeper of the 1940s and 1950s made over 450 appearances and was capped six times by England?

4 What was the score in the 1991 Arsenal v Spurs FA Charity Shield?

5 Spurs player Bobby Smith scored 5 goals in a match in March 1958. Who were the opponents?

6 By winning 6-1 at White Hart Lane, which team inflicted Spurs' worst home defeat since 1935?

7 Who beat Spurs 3-2 in the 1987 FA Cup Final?

8 Who was Spurs boss when Klinsmann left the club?

9 Which manager sold Gary Lineker to Spurs?

10 Which Dave of Spurs broke his left leg twice in a year in the 1960s?

11 Which club did Clive Wilson leave to join Spurs?

12 Which Spurs player was jailed for four months in September 1991 for drink-driving offences?

13 In 1960-61 Spursstarted by winning how many League games in a row?

14 Who lost 5-1 to Spurs in the 1963 Cup-Winners' Cup Final?

15 Who became Spurs most expensive player when he moved from Crystal Palace in the summer of 1995?

Answers to page 156

1 AC Milan, **2** Wembley Wizards, **3** Baseball Ground, **4** 13 days, **5** Croker, **6** Case, **7** None, **8** Sheffield Utd, **9** Tottenham Hotspur, **10** Andy Dibble, **11** Four, **12** Helmut Schon, **13** 1940s, **14** Rotterdam, **15** Wigan.

BOBBY CHARLTON

Answers on page 161

1 How many appearances did Bobby Charlton make for England?

2 When did Bobby Charlton first play for Manchester United?

3 In which year was he voted European footballer of the Year?

4 How many league goals did Bobby Charlton score for Manchester Utd?

5 How many Championships did Bobby Charlton win with Manchester Utd?

6 How many goals did Bobby Charlton score for England?

7 How many appearances did Bobby Charlton make for Manchester Utd?

8 In which Northumberland Village was Bobby Charlton born?

9 Bobby Charlton scored in a 1956 Youth Cup Final against which Chesterfield goalkeeper?

10 Bobby Charlton came out of retirement to play for which League club?

11 Which club did Bobby Charlton manage between 1973 and 75?

12 Bobby Charlton's first international goal was against which country?

13 Bobby Charlton's last Manchester Utd League appearance was at which ground?

14 According to Bobby Charlton who "still had his magic" when nearing 50?

15 Against which country did Bobby Charlton score to became England's all-time leading scorer when he netted against Sweden in 1968?

Answers to page 161

1 Leyton Orient, **2** Celtic, **3** Eddie and Frank Gray, **4** Crystal Palace (V Leicester City), **5** Roger Kenyon, **6** Chelsea, **7** Dynamo Kiev, **8** Stuttgart, **9** Real Madrid, **10** Burnley, **11** Third Lanark, **12** Ross County, **13** Oldham Athletic, **14** Andrew, **15** Vancouver Whitecaps.

QUIZ 100

Answers on page 162

1 In which decade did Hearts first win the Scottish FA Cup?

2 Which keeper did Alec Ferguson sign from his former club Aberdeen?

3 In which city do St Mirren play?

4 What colour goes with black stripes on Swansea's home shirts?

5 Which striker was involved in Britain's first £300,000 transfer?

6 Who beat Hearts 3-1 in the 1968 Scottish FA Cup Final?

7 Which player scored 38 League goals for Manchester City in 1928-29?

8 In which decade was Tony Adams born?

9 What was Alan Cork's first League club?

10 Brighton and Hove Albion recorded a 10-1 FA Cup win over which club in November 1965?

11 Which Bulgarian striker was banned for life after a brawl in 1985 to be reinstated six months later?

12 Which club has a fanzine called 'Yidaho'?

13 How many times did Bolivia compete in the World Cup finals?

14 Who was the English Player of the Year in 1994-95?

15 Who succeeded Alf Ramsey as manager at Ipswich Town?

Answers to page 162

1 Chris Woods, **2** Celtic, **3** Port Vale, **4** Brighton, **5** Arsenal, **6** George, **7** Runcorn, **8** Todd, **9** Bury, **10** Amsterdam, **11** Rangers, **12** Juventus, **13** Port Vale, **14** Luton Town, **15** Wolves.

QUIZ 101

Answers on page 159

1 Who plays at home at Brisbane Road?

2 Billy McNeill made a record 486 appearances, for which Scottish club between 1957-75?

3 Which brothers played in the 1976 European Cup Final?

4 A last-gasp Steve Claridge goal for Leicester City beat which team in a Wembley play-off?

5 Which Everton player scored an own goal in the League Cup final replay against Aston Villa?

6 Darren Peacock was sent off as which London club knocked Newcastle United out of the 1995-96 FA Cup?

7 Who lost to Steaua Bucharest in the 1986 Super Cup?

8 Where in Germany was Jurgen Klinsmann born?

9 Julio Iglesias was reserve team goalkeeper for which club?

10 Which Lancashire town team represented England in the European Cup in 1960-61?

11 Which club left the League in 1967?

12 Who joined the League in 1994 along with Caledonian Thistle?

13 Joe Royale followed Jimmy Frizzell as boss of which club?

14 What is Steve Bould's middle name?

15 Which foreign team did Peter Beardsley play for?

Answers to page 159

1 106, **2** 1956, **3** 1966, **4** 199, **5** 4, **6** 49, **7** 606, **8** Ashington, **9** Gordon Banks, **10** Preston North End, **11** Preston North End., **12** Scotland, **13** Stamford Bridge, **14** Stanley Mathews, **15** Sweden.

QUIZ 102

Answers on page 160

1 Who in July 1986 moved to Rangers for £600,000, a new record fee for a keeper?

2 Who beat Dundee Utd 2-1 in the 1985 Scottish FA Cup Final?

3 Who was beaten 3-0 by Liverpool in the 1998-99 Third Round FA Cup tie?

4 Who was Jimmy Case playing for when he knocked his old club Liverpool out of the FA Cup in 1983?

5 Which team won the 1970 UEFA Cup?

6 What was the name of Mark Buchan's Manchester Utd playing brother?

7 Ian Woan joined Nottingham Forest from which non-league club?

8 Which Colin became Middleborough manager in 1991?

9 Which club did Martin Dobson manage between 1984-1989?

10 In which city do Ajax play?

11 Who beat Raith Rovers 2-0 in the 1948-49 Scottish League Cup Final?

12 Who beat Manchester United at Old Trafford in their first European defeat of the 1990s?

13 Against which club did Michael Owen score his first FA Cup goal?

14 Which was Iain Dowie's first league club?

15 Gary Pierce was in goal as which club won the League Cup?

Answers to page 160

1 1890s, **2** Jim Leighton, **3** Paisley, **4** White, **5** Bob Latchford, **6** Dunfermline, **7** Tom Johnson, **8** 1960s, **9** Wimbledon, **10** Wisbech, **11** Hristo Stoichkov, **12** Wimbledon, **13** Three, **14** Jurgen Klinsmann, **15** Jackie Milburn.

QUIZ 103

Answers on page 165

1 Which was the first World Cup tournament that Holland qualified for after the Second World War?

2 Which country lost 1-0 to Brazil in the 1994 World Cup Semi-Final?

3 Which team won the 1992 UEFA Cup on away goal difference?

4 Ray Wilkins was player/coach at Crystal Palace for one game in 1994. Who were the opponents for that game and what was the score?

5 Which team lost 2-1 to Liverpool in the 1988 FA Charity Shield?

6 What was the name of the ITV theme for the 1986 World Cup Finals?

7 Who scored Wimbledon's goal that won the FA Cup Final in 1988?

8 Who became Chelsea's record signing when he joined the club for £1.6m in 1990?

9 Who beat Hibernian 6-1 in the 1972 Scottish FA Cup Final?

10 At which club did Mark Hateley make his League debut?

11 Who lost 2-0 to Sampdoria after extra time in the 1990 Cup-Winners' Cup Final?

12 Which ex-Liverpool star was boss at Oxford Utd for a short time in 1988?

13 George Eastham was at which club when he made his international debut?

14 Which country did Harry Daft play for?

15 Which England manager has won most World Cup games?

Answers to page 165

1 Bury, **2** Jack Baynes, **3** Manchester Utd, **4** Stuart Pearce, **5** 1890s, **6** Carl Tiler, **7** John O'Hare, **8** Mark Crossley, **9** Tottenham Hotspur, **10** 1970s, **11** Coventry City, **12** John Robertson, **13** Newcastle Utd, **14** Tottenham Hotspur, **15** Alf-Inge Haaland.

REFEREES

Answers on page 166

1 What nationality is Kim Milton Nielsen, the referee who sent Beckham off in the 1998 World Cup finals?

2 Which English headmaster was a referee in Euro '96?

3 Which former League referee became a government minister?

4 Which language must all FIFA referees be able to speak?

5 In the first season of the Premiership, what colour strip did referees wear?

6 What happened to the referee after Leeds Utd's defeat in the 1973 Cup Winners' Cup Final?

7 Who got into bother for calling referee Robbie Hart a "Muppet"?

8 Which English referee was in charge of the 1974 World Cup Final?

9 Which soccer team does referee Paul Durkin support?

10 Which Englishman was assistant referee in the 1998 World Cup Final?

11 Which referee was pushed to the ground by Sheffield Wednesday's Paulo di Canio in a league match with Arsenal in September 1998?

12 Who in December 1995 got booked for "showing" the referee a yellow card after it fell from his pocket?

13 Who were Austria's opponents in 1963 when the referee abandoned the game after two Austrian players were sent off and the rest kicking their counterparts all over the park?

14 Which referee later became a world figure in soccer administration?

15 Which referee reported himself to the FA for sending off the wrong player in an Oxford v Sunderland game?

Answers to page 166

1 Arsenal, **2** Leyton Orient, **3** Aberdeen, **4** Paul and Ron, **5** Paris St. Germain, **6** Kevin Keegan, **7** 1909, **8** 3rd in Premier League (1992-93), **9** Cambridge Utd, **10** Stenhousemuir, **11** Germany, **12** Rangers, **13** Yugoslavia, **14** 1930s, **15** Red.

NOTT FOREST 1

Answers on page 163

1 Forest recorded a 7-0 League Cup win over which club in September 1980?

2 Who succeeded Bob Masters as manager of Forest in 1925?

3 Neil Webb moved from Forest to which club for £1.5m in July 1989?

4 Who scored for Forest in the 1991 Final?

5 In which decade did Forest first win the FA Cup?

6 Who moved from Barnsley to Forest in 1991 to set a club record for a transfer fee received?

7 Which Forest player was fouled in the incident leading to the penalty in the 1970s League Cup Final replay v Liverpool?

8 Who was the only League ever present for Forest in 1995-96?

9 Teddy Sherringham moved from Forest to which club for £2.1m in September 1992?

10 In which decade did Forest first win the Championship?

11 Who were Forest's main rivals for the signature of Birmingham City's Trevor Francis?

12 Who scored Forest's European Cup Final goal to beat Hamburg?

13 Which club did Peter Withe join on leaving Forest?

14 Who beat Forest 2-1 in the 1991 FA Cup Final?

15 Which player of the 1990s with Forest has the middle name of Rasdal?

Answers to page 163

1 1974, **2** Sweden, **3** Ajax, **4** Liverpool won 6-1, **5** Wimbledon, **6** Aztec Gold, **7** Lawrie Sanchez, **8** Dennis Wise, **9** Celtic, **10** Coventry City, **11** Anderlecht, **12** Mark Lawrenson, **13** Arsenal, **14** England, **15** Bobby Robson.

QUIZ 104

Answers on page 164

1 What was Martin Keown's first League club?

2 Frank Clark managed which London side?

3 Who beat Hearts 3-0 in the 1986 Scottish FA Cup Final?

4 What was the names of the Futcher twins?

5 Which French club did Ray Wilkins join after leaving AC Milan?

6 Which former Scunthorpe player sang solo on *Top of the Pops* in 1979?

7 What year this century was the Scottish FA Cup withheld after two draws between Rangers and Celtic?

8 What is the highest position Norwich City have ever achieved in the League?

9 At which club did Andy Sinton make his League debut?

10 Which side provided a great Scottish Cup shock by knocking Aberdeen out in 1995?

11 Alan Shearer hit the quickest goal of a game in Euro 96 against which side?

12 Who beat Kilmarnock 2-0 in the 1960 Scottish FA Cup Final?

13 Which country became the first to lose two European Championship Finals, the first in 1960 and then again in 1968.

14 In which decade did Arsenal first win the FA Cup?

15 What is the main colour of Crewe Alexandra's shirts?

Answers to page 164

1 Danish, **2** David Elleray, **3** Denis Howell, **4** English, **5** Green (change strip: black), **6** He was Suspended by UEFA, **7** Ian Wright, **8** Jack Taylor, **9** Manchester City, **10** Mark Warren, **11** Paul Alcock, **12** Paul Gascoigne, **13** Scotland, **14** Stanley Rous, **15** Stephen Lodge.

QUIZ 105

Answers on page 169

1 Who was nicknamed The Lion Of Vienna?

2 Paxton Road goes by the ground of which club?

3 Viv Anderson was with which club when he made his international debut?

4 Whose shot from the halfway line won the 1995 Final for Barcelona against Paris St Germain?

5 Which disease claimed the life of England defender Jeff Hall?

6 Tommy Coyne was at which club when he made his international debut?

7 Paul Gascoigne moved from Tottenham Hotspur to which club for £5.5m in July 1991?

8 Peter Ndlovu plays for which African country?

9 Which Division Two side were losing 5-1 to Huddersfield but fought back to win 7-6 in 1957?

10 Bill Riding was boss of which team from 1951?

11 Kernaghan and Slaven played for which promoted team?

12 Who scored Manchester Utd's goals in the 1991 European Cup Winners' Cup Final against Barcelona?

13 Which team were beaten 4-1 in the first post-World War Two FA Cup Final?

14 Who was the first German captain to claim the World Cup?

15 Iwan Roberts moved from Huddersfield Town to which club for £300,000 in October 1993?

Answers to page 169

1 Uruguay, **2** Blackburn Rovers, **3** Gianluca Vialli, **4** Paolo Rossi, **5** Dean Holdsworth, **6** Les Sealey, **7** Barcelona, **8** Coventry City, **9** Morris, **10** West Brom, **11** AC Milan, **12** Leeds Utd, **13** Diego Simeone, **14** Hull City, **15** Portugal.

QUIZ 106

Answers on page 170

1 Who scored six goals for Croatia in the 1998 World Cup Finals?

2 Which club did John Atyeo score 314 League goals for?

3 At which club has John Aldridge scored his highest number of goals?

4 Airdieonians and Clyde have shared which ground?

5 Whose hat-trick at Wembley in 1998 helped Charlton secure a place in the Premiership?

6 Danny Wallace moved from Southampton to which club for £1.2m in September 1989?

7 What is Ruel Fox's middle name?

8 Perry Groves appeared in a League Cup final for which club?

9 Which Blackburn player was sent off after three minutes of his debut against Everton?

10 In the 74 fixtures up to 1997, how many different teams have appeared in it?

11 In which country was Jimmy Nicholl born?

12 Burnley recorded a 9-0 FA Cup win over which club in November 1984?

13 Bristol City recorded a 11-0 FA Cup win over which club in November 1960?

14 Who played for Parma against Antwerp from his native Belgium in the 1993 Cup Winners' Cup Final?

15 Which country did Adam Blacklaw play for?

Answers to page 170

1 Real Sociedad, **2** Sampdoria, **3** Swansea City, **4** Yes, **5** 13, **6** 62, **7** AS Roma, **8** Bill Shankly, **9** Bruges, **10** Dean Saunders, **11** Fulham, **12** Ian Rush, **13** John O'Hare, **14** Kenny Dalglish, **15** Mark Lawrenson.

QUIZ 107

Answers on page 167

1 Who won the 1950 World Cup?

2 Before joining Everton, where was Howard Kendall player/manager?

3 Who scored both goals for Samdoria in their 2-0 victory over Anderlecht in the 1990 Cup Winner's Cup Final?

4 Who scored six goals for Italy in the 1982 World Cup Finals?

5 Who did Bolton Wanderers buy in the 1997-98 season for a club ecord £3.5 million?

6 Who was in goal for manchester Utd in the Final replay against Crystal Palace in 1990?

7 Who lost 2-1 to Manchester Utd in the 1991 Cup-Winners' Cup Final?

8 Bobby Gould followed Dave Sexton as manager of which club?

9 Which Republic of Ireland defender Chris won cricket honours for Cornish schools?

10 David Mills moved from Middlesborough to which club for £482,000 in January 1979?

11 Who lost to Ajax in the 1973 Super Cup?

12 Which club did David Rocastle leave to join Manchester City?

13 Which Argentinian player did David Beckham kick which resulted in his red card in the 1998 World Cup Finals?

14 Eddie Gray followed Brian Horton as manager of which club?

15 Which country lost 2-1 to England in the 1966 World Cup Semi-Final?

Answers to page 167

1 Nat Lofthouse, **2** Tottenham Hotspur, **3** Nottingham Forest, **4** Nayim, **5** Polio, **6** Celtic, **7** Lazio, **8** Zimbabwe, **9** Charlton Athletic, **10** Bolton Wanderers, **11** Middlesborough, **12** Mark Hughes, **13** Charlton Athletic, **14** Fritz Walter, **15** Leicester City.

LIVERPOOL 6

Answers on page 168

1 After scoring 50 goals in 83 appearances for Liverpool, John Aldridge moved to which Spanish club?

2 Graeme Souness moved from Liverpool to which club for £650.000 in June 1984?

3 Liverpool recorded a 8-0 FA Cup win over which club in January 1990?

4 Was Kenny Dalglish Liverpools' manager when they won the Premiership title?

5 How many years was Bruce Grobbelaar at Liverpool?

6 How old was Joe Fagan when he became manager of Liverpool?

7 Who did Liverpool beat on penalties in the 1984 European Cup Final?

8 Which former player and manager was honoured in 1998 at Liverpool with a statue?

9 Who did Liverpool beat in the 1976 UEFA Cup Final?

10 Who joined Liverpool from Derby County for £2.9m in July 1991?

11 Liverpool player Robbie Fowler scored 5 goals in a match in October 1993. Who were the opponents?

12 Which player scored 32 League goals for Liverpool in 1983-84?

13 Which Nottingham Forest player was fouled in the incident leading to the penalty in the 1970s League Cup Final replay v Liverpool?

14 Which ex-Liverpool player holds Scotland's most capped record?

15 Which ex-Liverpool star was boss at Oxford Utd for a short time in 1988?

Answers to page 168

1 Davor Suker, **2** Bristol City, **3** Tranmere Rovers, **4** Broadwood stadium, **5** Clive Mendonca, **6** Manchester Utd, **7** Adrian, **8** Arsenal, **9** Garry Flitcroft, **10** 40, **11** Canada, **12** Penrith, **13** Chichester City, **14** Georges Grun, **15** Scotland.

DEBUT GAMES

Answers on page 173

1 Which Colin marked his Southampton debut in 1986 with a hat-trick?

2 Who scored a double hat-trick on his Newcastle Utd debut in the 1950s?

3 Who, at 17 years and 44 days, became the Premier League's youngest player when he made his Chelsea debut in February 1996?

4 John Burns became the first British player to be sent off on his debut. What club was he playing for on this eventful day in 1923?

5 Who scored within 71 seconds of his Fulham debut in 1977?

6 What was the most notable feature of David Platt's debut for Bari?

7 Which Manchester Utd player scored on his English League debut v Watford in August 1984?

8 Which 17 year old made his debut as left-back for AC Milan in 1985 and was holding the position ten years later?

9 How old was Duncan Edwards when he made his League debut?

10 Who scored debut goals for Chelsea, Tottenham Hotspur, West Ham Utd and England?

11 At which club did Eric Cantona's brother make his English League debut?

12 What links the debuts of Alan Shearer, Robert Lee and Dennis Wise?

13 Which current Liverpool player scored on his League, League Cup, FA Cup and European debuts?

14 Which Blackburn player was sent off after three minutes of his debut against Everton?

15 Against which club did West Ham's Joe Cole make his League debut?

Answers to page 173

1 Ian Wright, **2** White, **3** Celtic, **4** Everton, **5** Everton and Manchester Utd, **6** Peter Bonetti, **7** The Republic of Ireland, **8** Manchester Utd, **9** Gary Shaw (In a European Cup game against Dinamo Bucharest in November 1982), **10** Rotherham Utd, **11** Denis Law, **12** 1974, **13** Coventry, **14** Five, **15** San Siro.

QUIZ 108

Answers on page 174

1. Which is the only Hungarian club to have won a European trophy?
2. What was Vinny Samway's first League club?
3. Which football club does Danny Baker support?
4. Which country did Billy Hamilton play for?
5. Which 1990s goalkeeper has played soccer and cricket for Scotland?
6. In which decade was Bryan Hamilton born?
7. Nigel Worthington first played in an FA Cup Final for which team?
8. How did keeper Alex Stepney dislocate his jaw in August 1975?
9. Who was travelling on a bus when he learnt that he had been made England skipper?
10. Which team were beaten 2-1 by Tottenham Hotspur in the 1967 FA Cup Final?
11. Who was Germany's top scorer in Euro 96 and with how many goals?
12. Fullback David Peach scored for which club in a League Cup Final?
13. What is Andy Hinchcliffe's middle name?
14. Leicester City player John Duncan scored 6 goals in a match in December 1924. Who were the opponents?
15. Colin McKee's only Manchester Utd appearance, in the last game of 1993-94, came when which club were champions?

Answers to page 174

1 Sutton Utd, **2** Gary Stevens, **3** 1950, **4** Hearts, **5** West Ham Utd, **6** Northampton Town, **7** Lincoln City, **8** Wim Kieft, **9** Chelsea, **10** Woking, **11** Tony Adams, **12** The Robins, **13** Motherwell, **14** A one year ban from European games, **15** None.

QUIZ 109

Answers on page 171

1 Which England player got four against San Marino in November 1993?

2 What colour are Charlton's home shorts?

3 Who beat Rangers 1-0 in the 1989 Scottish FA Cup Final?

4 Which club was Bob Latchford with when he was First Division leading scorer in 1977-78?

5 But for UEFA's ban, which two sides would have represented England in the Euro Cup Winners' competition in 1985-86?

6 Who kept goal as England lost to West Germany in the 1970 World Cup?

7 Which country did Tony Galvin Play for?

8 Ray Wilkins moved from Chelsea to which club for £825.000 in August 1979?

9 Who scored Aston Villa's first ever hat-trick in European football?

10 Grimsby Town recorded a 6-0 League Cup win over which club in November 1984?

11 Who scored six for Manchester City in an abandoned FA Cup game?

12 In which year did George Best last play for Manchester Utd?

13 Bobby Gould was born in which city where he went on to manage the football team?

14 How many minutes of extra-time were needed in the Euro 96 Final?

15 What is the name of the impressive stadium shared between AC Milan and Inter Milan?

Answers to page 171

1 Clarke, **2** Len Shackleton, **3** Jody Morris, **4** Rochdale, **5** George Best, **6** He missed a penalty, **7** Gordon Strachan, **8** Paolo Maldini, **9** 16, **10** Jimmy Greaves, **11** Stockport County, **12** They all scored, **13** Michael Owen, **14** Garry Flitcroft, **15** Manchester Utd.

QUIZ 110

Answers on page 172

1 Norwich City recorded a 8-0 FA Cup win over which club in January 1989?

2 In the 1986 World Cup which two England players in the squad had the same name?

3 In which year did England first enter the World Cup competition?

4 With 44 goals, Barney Battles set a League season scoring record at which Scottish club?

5 In the 1960s, cricketer Jim Standen played for which London club?

6 Who plays at home at Sixfields Stadium?

7 Which club had a fanzine called Derranged Ferret

8 Which Ajax player won the 1981-82 Golden Boot award?

9 Dave Beasant and Andy Townsend were in the same team at which club?

10 Which non-league side hit a last minute goal to draw at Coventry in 1997?

11 Who scored for both sides in the 1988 friendly between England and Holland?

12 What is Swindon Town's nickname?

13 Tommy Coyne joined which club when he left Tranmere Rovers?

14 Rangers' Euro Cup Winners' Cup victory was marred by hooligan trouble. What was the Scottish team's penalty for this trouble?

15 How many games did England lose in Spain in 1982?

Answers to page 172

1 Ferencvaros, **2** Tottenham Hotspur, **3** Millwall, **4** Northern Ireland, **5** Andy Goram, **6** 1940s, **7** Sheffield Wednesday, **8** By shouting at his teammates, **9** Billy Wright, **10** Chelsea, **11** Jurgen Klinsmann, three, **12** Southampton, **13** George, **14** Port Vale, **15** Manchester Utd.

QUIZ 111

Answers on page 177

1 Who began his international career by scoring 2,3,2,2, then 3 goals in successive matches?

2 Which club has a fanzine called *United We Stand*?

3 Which goalkeeper did QPR sell for £1.3 in 1989-90?

4 Keegan's last game as Newcastle United's manager was an FA Cup tie against which London Club?

5 What is the highest position Oldham Athletic have ever achieved in the League?

6 Andy Walker moved from Bolton Wanderers to which club for £550,000 in June 1994?

7 What was the first club that Arthur Cox managed?

8 Paul Stewart moved from Manchester City to which club for £1.7m in June 1988?

9 At which Scottish club did Dave Mackay start his career?

10 Who did Italy beat 2-1 after extra time to win the second World Cup Final in 1934?

11 Who was the goalkeeper in the controversial "Hand Of God" goal?

12 When did Scotland first appear in the World Cup?

13 In which decade was Roy Evans born?

14 How many hat-tricks did Alan Shearer score for Blackburn Rovers in their 1995-96 season?

15 Who beat Chelsea 4-0 in the 1994 FA Cup Final?

Answers to page 177

1 2-1, **2** 3-2, **3** 2-1, **4** 1894, **5** First subs to be used in a Final, **6** 1894, **7** 1909, **8** Celtic, **9** Four, **10** George McCluskey, **11** 23, **12** 1-0, **13** 1-0, **14** 1-0, **15** 2-1.

• MANCHESTER UTD 4 •

Answers on page 178

1 Who scored Arsenal's last minute winner against Manchester Utd in the 1979 FA Cup Final?

2 Which Dutch master joined Manchester Utd from Ipswich Town?

3 In Manchester Utd's 1968 Euro trail who was the unlikely scorer of the last goal against Real Madrid?

4 Which two Manchester Utd survivers of the Munich crash played in the 1968 European Cup Final?

5 Which ex-Manchester Utd star scored the goal that condemned his old club to relegation?

6 Who was top scorer when Manchester Utd were Champions in 1993-94?

7 Which Manchester Utd star was named European Footballer of the Year in 1968?

8 Which Manchester Utd and Republic of Ireland player was known as 'Gentleman John'?

9 Which team were beaten 2-1 by Manchester Utd in the 1977 FA Cup Final?

10 Which property dealer abandoned his hopes of owning Manchester Utd?

11 Which Mike of Manchester Utd won his only England cap in 1989?

12 Manchester Utd recorded a 5-0 League Cup win over which club in October 1988?

13 Who missed his third penalty in succession for Manchester Utd during their 1-0 Premiership victory over Aston Villa?

14 Manchester Utd recorded a 8-0 FA Cup win over which club in February 1949?

15 In which season did Manchester Utd lose the first 12 games?

Answers to page 178

1 His Leg, **2** Hungary, **3** Finland, **4** Matthias Sammer, **5** Borussia Dortmund, **6** Gusztav Sebes, **7** Jan Tomaszewski, **8** Alan Ball, **9** Sheffield Wednesday, **10** Fulham, **11** Brussels, **12** 1940s, **13** Vancouver Whitecaps, **14** Southampton, **15** Dundee.

OLD FIRM

Answers on page 175

1 What was the score when Celtic beat Rangers in the 1971 Scottish FA Cup Final replay?

2 What was the score when Rangers beat Celtic in the 1973 Scottish FA Cup Final?

3 What was the score when Rangers beat Celtic after extra-time in the 1991 Scottish League Cup Final?

4 In what year did Rangers play Celtic in the Scottish Cup final for the first time?

5 What did Celtic's Chalmers and Rangers' Wilson achieve when they went out for the 1966-67 Scottish League Cup Final?

6 In what year was the first Old Firm Cup Final played?

7 What year this century was the Scottish FA Cup withheld after two draws between Rangers and Celtic?

8 Who won the first game between Celtic and Rangers back in 1888?

9 How many players were red carded in the 1991 League game between Rangers and Celtic?

10 Which player scored the only goal in the Celtic v Rangers 1980 Scottish FA Cup Final?

11 How many times have Rangers and Celtic met in the Scottish FA Cup Final?

12 What was the score when Celtic beat Rangers in the 1989 Scottish FA Cup Final?

13 What was the score when Celtic beat Rangers in the 1980 Scottish FA Cup Final?

14 What was the score when Celtic beat Rangers in the 1977 Scottish FA Cup Final?

15 What was the score when Rangers beat Celtic in the 1987 Scottish League Cup Final?

Answers to page 175

1 Dixie Dean, **2** Manchester Utd, **3** David Seaman, **4** Charlton Athletic, **5** 2nd Division 1 (1914-15), **6** Celtic, **7** Chesterfield, **8** Tottenham Hotspur, **9** Hearts, **10** Czechoslovakia, **11** Peter Shilton, **12** 1954, **13** 1940s, **14** Five, **15** Manchester Utd.

QUIZ 112

Answers on page 176

1 What did Gazza manage to break in a training match at Lazio?

2 Which country do Ferencvaros come from?

3 In which European nation does the football season usually run from April to October?

4 Who was the first native East German to play for the unified national side?

5 Who became the first German winners of the Cup Winners' Cup when they beat Liverpool in the 1966 Final?

6 Which coach created the "Magic Magyars" of the 1950s?

7 Who kept goal for Poland at Wembley in the 1974 World Cup qualifier?

8 Which England midfielder played in white boots for Everton?

9 Danny Wilson played in an FA Cup Final for which side?

10 Allen Clarke became the first £150,000 man when he moved to Leicester City from which club?

11 Where was the 1996 European Cup Winners' Cup Final held?

12 In which decade was Geoff Hurst born?

13 Which Canadian side did Peter Beardsley play for?

14 Which club has a fanzine called *Red Stripe*?

15 Ranger's Colin Hendry began his career with which Scottish club?

Answers to page 176

1 Alan Sunderland, **2** Arnold Muhren, **3** Billy Foulkes., **4** Bobby Charlton and Bill Foulkes, **5** Denis Law, **6** Eric Cantona, **7** George Best, **8** Johnny Carey, **9** Liverpool, **10** Michael Knighton, **11** Phelan, **12** Rotherham Utd, **13** Teddy Sherringham, **14** Yeovil Town, **15** 1930-31.

QUIZ 113

Answers on page 181

1. Who did Kenny dalglish replace as skipper of Celtic?
2. Ossie Ardiles followed Jim Smith as manager of which club?
3. Who were the opponents for Terry Venables' first game as boss of England?
4. Before the 1990s when did Brazil last win the World Cup trophy?
5. What is the name of Derby County's new stadium?
6. Which country did Oscar Ruggeri play for?
7. Who is the Secretary of the French Football Federation after whom the European Championship trophy was named?
8. In Scotland, which club has it's ground nearest to the sea?
9. In what year did Holland make World Cup history by becoming the first country to be awarded a penalty in a Final?
10. Which 17 year old made his debut as left-back for AC Milan in 1985 and was holding the position ten years later?
11. When did Bobby Charlton first play for Manchester Utd?
12. Which English club did Roy Hodgson manage before he took over the Swiss national side?
13. Who succeeded Bob Masters as manager of Nottingham Forest in 1925?
14. In which country were the 1930 World Cup Finals held?
15. At which club did Steve Ogrizovic make his League debut?

Answers to page 181

1 Bournmouth, **2** Gary McAllister, **3** 1913, **4** Bristol Rovers, **5** Jack Taylor, **6** 1994, **7** Kevin Reeves, **8** Portsmouth, **9** 1961, **10** Ferenc Puskas, **11** 1930, **12** Wolves, **13** 68 points, **14** St Mirren, **15** Mark Hughes.

QUIZ 114

Answers on page 182

1 How many goals did Phil Neal score in his League career?

2 Who was the German national coach from 1964 to 1978?

3 Where was the 1971 European Cup Winners' Cup Final replay held?

4 Who won the European Champions Cup five years running?

5 Which player has scored most FA Cup goals in total since 1945?

6 Which Brazilian made his international debut in the 1998 World Cup Semi-Final against Holland?

7 Which millionaire businessman owns Crystal Palace?

8 Who captained Argentina against West Germany in the 1990 World Cup Final?

9 Where was the 1985 European Cup Winners' Cup Final held?

10 Terry Conroy scored in a League Cup Final for which club?

11 Which Irish club did Ronnie Whelan come from?

12 Who is the manager of the Italian national side?

13 Which club was once known as Headington?

14 Which country did Noel Brotherston play for?

15 Barry Kitchener set a League appearance record for which club?

Answers to page 182

1 Alec Stepney, **2** Arsenal, **3** Birmingham City, **4** Bolton Wanderers, **5** Denis Law, **6** Eric Cantona, **7** George Best, **8** Juventus, **9** Liverpool - 1977, **10** Newcastle Utd, **11** Portsmouth, **12** Sheffield Wednesday, **13** Three, **14** York City, **15** 1945.

QUIZ 115

Answers on page 179

1 Which was Jamie Redknapp's first League club?

2 Who was unable to captain Scotland in the 1998 World Cup because of an injury?

3 In what year were Arsenal relegated for the first time in their history?

4 Blackburn Rovers player Tommy Briggs scored 7 goals in a match in February 1953. Who were the opponents?

5 Which British referee was in charge of the 1974 World Cup Final?

6 In which year was the World Cup Final held at the Rose Bowl?

7 Who was the first £1 million pound player to leave Norwich City?

8 What was the first club that Alan Ball managed?

9 In what year was the first Euro Cup Winners' Cup Final first played?

10 Who played for Hungary 84 times and for Spain four times?

11 In what year were Everton first relegated?

12 Graham Turner followed Brian Little as manager of which club in October 1986?

13 Under the 2 points for a win system how many points did Liverpool gain to create a record in 1979?

14 Who was the only Scottish winner of the Anglo-Scottish Cup, which ran from 1976-1981?

15 Which Welsh player, rejected by Barcelona, scored the winning goal against the Spanish side in the 1991 Euro Cup Winners' Cup Final?

Answers to page 179

1 Billy McNeill, **2** Newcastle United, **3** Denmark, **4** 1970, **5** Pride Park, **6** Argentina, **7** Henri Delaunay, **8** Arbroath, **9** 1974, **10** Paolo Maldini, **11** 1956, **12** Bristol City, **13** Jack Baynes, **14** Italy, **15** Chesterfield.

• MANCHESTER UTD 5 •

Answers on page 180

1 Which Manchester Utd keeper was club joint top scorer in mid-season 1974-75 because of his spot kick success?

2 In the 1960s David Herd left which club to join Manchester Utd?

3 Where did Danny Wallace go when he left Manchester Utd?

4 Who beat Manchester Utd 2-0 in the 1958 FA Cup Final?

5 Which Manchester Utd great made a trademark of pulling his cuffs over his hands?

6 Which Manchester Utd star was sent off after the final whistle in 1993?

7 Which player hit 147 goals in 411 league games for Manchester Utd?

8 Who beat Manchester Utd at home in their first European defeat of the 1990s?

9 After Manchester Utd's 1968 victory in the European Cup, who became the next British team to win it, and in what year?

10 Manchester Utd recorded a 7-2 League Cup win over which club in October 1976?

11 Which club did Graeme Hogg move to from Manchester Utd?

12 What Division 2 team defeated Manchester Utd in the 1991 Rumbelows Cup Final?

13 How many times did Bryan Robson win the FA Cup as Manchester Utd skipper?

14 Who knocked Manchester Utd out of the 1995-96 Coca-Cola Cup?

15 In what year did Sir Matt become Manchester Utd's manager?

Answers to page 180

1 73, **2** Helmut Schon, **3** Athens, **4** Real Madrid, **5** Ian Rush, **6** Ze Carlos, **7** Mark Goldberg, **8** Diego Maradona, **9** Rotterdam, **10** Stoke City, **11** Home Farm, **12** Dino Zoff, **13** Oxford Utd, **14** Northern Ireland, **15** Millwall.

CHELSEA 1

Answers on page 185

1 For which club did Graeme Le Saux leave Chelsea?

2 How much did the transfer of Ruud Gullit cost Chelsea?

3 Robert Di Matteo joined Chelsea from which club?

4 Which club did John Spencer leave to join Chelsea?

5 Who became Chelsea's record signing when he joined the club for £1.6m in 1990?

6 Who did Chelsea sell to Spurs for £2.2m in July 1991?

7 Who was Chelsea's manager when they won the League in 1954-55?

8 Gordon Durie moved from Chelsea to which club for £2.2 million in August 1991?

9 How much did AC Milan pay Chelsea in 1961 for the goal-scoring services of Jimmy Greaves?

10 Joe Allon moved to Chelsea in 1991 to set a record for a transfer fee received at which club?

11 What is the highest position Chelsea have ever achieved in the League?

12 Where was the Chelsea v Leeds Utd replayed FA Cup final held?

13 Which team were beaten 2-1 by Chelsea in the 1970 FA Cup Final replay?

14 Who was boss when Chelsea were Division 2 champions in 1988-89?

15 Who, at 18, became Chelsea's youngest ever captain in 1975?

Answers to page 185

1 Sullivan, **2** Six, **3** Hungary, Spain, **4** Franz Beckenbauer, **5** Alan McDonald, **6** Arsenal, **7** 1993, **8** Andy Roxburgh, **9** Crewe Alexandra, **10** The Ball Burst, **11** 8, **12** Liverpool, **13** Luton Town, **14** Tony Brown, **15** 16.

QUIZ 116

Answers on page 186

1 Where was the 1968 European Cup Final held?

2 Which famous former Liverpool manager died in 1981?

3 John Barnes first played in an FA Cup Final for which team?

4 In which decade was Darren Anderton born?

5 Colin Hendry moved from Blackburn Rovers to which club for £700,000 in November 1989?

6 Which Portuguese side won the World Cup Championship in 1987?

7 Where was the 1994 European Cup Winners' Cup Final held?

8 Which German club did Karl-Heinz Rummenigge play for?

9 Which Middlesborough manager signed Fabrizio Ravanelli?

10 Which newspaper sponsored the Football League in the 1980s?

11 Which two players were sent off in the "spitting incident" in the 1988 European Championship?

12 Before the 1998 World Cup, what was the highest number of red cards to be shown in one finals?

13 Which club has won the Austrian League Championship most often?

14 Hereford United had four players sent off in one game in September 1992. Who were their opponents?

15 Who qualified for the 1990 World Cup finals after a 0-0 draw with Poland?

Answers to page 186

1 Sir Matt Busby, **2** Gordon Strachan (Coventry City), **3** Ron Atkinson, **4** Pongo, **5** Dave Mackay (Derby County), **6** Darren Huckerby, **7** 9-1, **8** Hewitt, **9** 61, **10** Leicester City, **11** Wigan, **12** 4th Division 2, (1946-47), **13** Clyde, **14** Watford, **15** Blackburn Rovers.

QUIZ 117

Answers on page 183

1 Who started the game in goal for Scotland when they drew against Colombia in a friendly in May 1998?

2 How many different nations had won Football's World Cup up to the start of the 1944 event?

3 Ferenc Puskas played international soccer for which two countries?

4 Which Bayern Munich player was 1972 European Footballer of the Year?

5 Which Northern Ireland star is QPR's most capped player?

6 Joe Mercer was nearly 38 when he played in an FA Cup Final for which club?

7 In which year did the FA Premier League become known as the FA Carling Premiership?

8 Who did Craig Brown replace in charge of the Scottish team?

9 Which club did David Platt leave to join Aston Villa?

10 What happened to hold up both the 1946 and 1947 FA Cup Finals?

11 How many caps did Alex James get for Scotland?

12 Who lost 2-1 to Borussia Dortmund after extra time in the 1966 Cup-Winners' Cup Final?

13 Mick Hartford scored in a League Cup Final for which club?

14 Which West Brom forward became the first player to score in every round of the competition?

15 How many goals did Liverpool's mean machine defence concede in the 42 League games of 1978-79?

Answers to page 183

1 Blackburn Rovers, **2** Nothing he came on a free transfer, **3** Lazio, **4** Rangers, **5** Dennis Wise, **6** Gordon Durie, **7** Ted Drake, **8** Tottenham Hotspur, **9** £80,000, **10** Hartlepool Utd, **11** Division 1 (1st) (1954-55), **12** Old Trafford, **13** Leeds Utd, **14** Bobby Campbell, **15** Ray Wilkins.

QUIZ 118

Answers on page 184

1 Which soccer manager was knighted in 1968?

2 Who in 1996 was fined £2,000 for refusing to leave the field when sent off in a reserve game?

3 Who was sacked to be replaced by Alex Ferguson at Manchester Utd?

4 What was the nickname of Aston Villa's 1930s player Thomas Waring?

5 Which member of the Tottenham Hotspur double-winning side went on to manage a Championship team?

6 Who moved from Lincoln City to Newcastle United in 1995 to set a club record for a transfer fee received?

7 England's biggest win over Wales was at Cardiff in 1896. What was the score?

8 Who scored Aberdeen's winner in the 1983 Cup Winners' Cup Final?

9 How many players did Barry Fry sign during his three-year stay at Birmingham City?

10 In 1997 which team led 3-1 at Newcastle United in the Premiership but lost 4-3 to a Shearer hat-trick completed in the last minute?

11 Keith Gillespie made his League debut while on loan at which club?

12 What is the highest position Chesterfield have ever achieved in the League?

13 At which Scottish club did Steve Archibald make his League debut?

14 Which club was once known as West Herts?

15 Which club in the north of England did Ossie Ardiles play for?

Answers to page 184

1 Wembley, **2** Bill Shankly, **3** Watford, **4** 1970s, **5** Manchester City, **6** Porto, **7** Copenhagen, **8** Bayern Munich, **9** Bryan Robson, **10** Today, **11** Frank Rijkaard and Rudi Voller, **12** Sixteen, **13** Rapid Vienna, **14** Northampton, **15** England.

QUIZ 119

Answers on page 189

1 Who beat Hibernian 3-0 in the 1985-86 Scottish League Cup Final?

2 Who scored the first ever goal in World Cup history?

3 Which team first beat England at Wembley in a World Cup game?

4 What first was achieved in the 1960 Blackpool against Bolton game?

5 Which League do FC Sion play in?

6 Which club dropped from First to Fourth Divisions between 1984-86?

7 Which manager said of Mark Hughes, "He's playing better and better, even if he is going grey and looks like a pigeon"?

8 David Swindlehurst moved from Crystal Palace to which club for £400,000 in April 1980?

9 How many League goals did Alan Shearer score for Southampton?

10 Which English player was labelled 'El Beatle' by the Portuguese media?

11 Who said "Barnes' problem is that he gets injured on a *Question of Sport*!"?

12 What is Phil Babb's middle name?

13 Which was the first team since the Second World War to win the championship two seasons in a row?

14 Apart from England, which other country took part in two penalty shoot-outs in Euro '96?

15 Which club's ground has the Warwick Road End?

Answers to page 189

1 Manchester Utd, **2** Manchester Utd, **3** Rangers, **4** Doug Rougvie, **5** Montrose, **6** Rangers, **7** 1940s, **8** 1989-90, **9** Eoin Jess, **10** Never, **11** Rangers, **12** 3, **13** Hamburg, **14** Oldham, **15** Rangers.1983

SPURS 3

Answers on page 190

1 Spurs player Les Allen scored 5 goals in a match in February 1960. Who were the opponents?

2 Who scored Spurs' penalty to beat QPR in an FA Cup Final replay?

3 Who said "For those of you watching in Black and White, Spurs are in the yellow shirts"?

4 Which team were beaten 3-2 by Spurs in the 1981 FA Cup Final replay?

5 Richard Gough moved to which club for £1.5m in September 1997?

6 Who resigned as Spurs manager in June 1976?

7 What year did Tottenham Hotspur first win the FA Cup?

8 Steve Archibald moved from Spurs to which club for £1.5m in July 1984?

9 Who became Britain's most expensive player when he moved from Spurs to Marseille for £4.5m in 1989?

10 Which England winger did Spurs buy from Portsmouth for £1.75m in June 1992?

11 Who did Chelsea sell to Spurs for £2.2m in July 1991?

12 Which Spurs player from 1968-1979 retired from playing to become assistant manager at White Hart Lane, before moving to Nigeria to take up a coaching position?

13 Chris Waddle moved from Spurs to which club for £4.5m in June 1989?

14 Who was in goal when Spurs won the FA Cup Final in 1987?

15 Which Arsenal and Spurs boss also managed Northern Ireland?

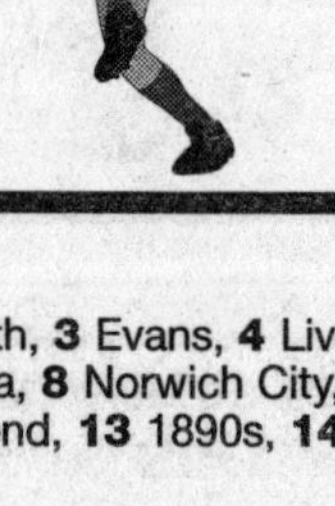

Answers to page 190

1 Yes (once in 1971), **2** Heath, **3** Evans, **4** Liverpool, **5** 0-0, **6** Preston North End, **7** Czechoslovakia, **8** Norwich City, **9** Laurie Cunningham, **10** 1970s, **11** Twice, **12** Southend, **13** 1890s, **14** Wembley Stadium, **15** Clive Allen (Spurs).

ABERDEEN 2

Answers on page 187

1 Which club did Gordon Strachan join on leaving Aberdeen?

2 Who beat Aberdeen 2-1 in the 1993 Scottish FA Cup Final?

3 Which Aberdeen player was sent off in the 1978-79 Scottish League Cup Final?

4 Geographically, which is the nearest club to Aberdeen?

5 Who beat Aberdeen 4-0 in the 1946-47 Scottish League Cup Final?

6 In which decade did Aberdeen first win the Scottish FA Cup?

7 What season did Aberdeen beat Rangers and Celtic in major Cup Finals?

8 Coventry City paid £1.75m for which Aberdeen player in 1996?

9 How many times were Aberdeen relegated in the 50 years following the Second World War?

10 Who beat Aberdeen 2-1 in the 1978-79 Scottish League Cup Final?

11 How many Scottish premier titles did Alex Ferguson win as manager of Aberdeen?

12 Who did Aberdeen beat to win the European Super Cup in 1983?

13 In 1995 Aberdeen paid just over £1m for Paul Bernard, which club did he sign from?

14 Who beat Aberdeen 3-2 in the 1988-89 Scottish League Cup Final?

15 In which year did Aberdeen win the European Cup Winners Cup and the Scottish Cup?

Answers to page 187

1 Aberdeen, **2** Lucien Laurent, **3** Italy, **4** First Live TV match, **5** Swiss League, **6** Wolves, **7** Ruud Gullit, **8** Derby County, **9** 23, **10** George Best, **11** Tommy Docherty, **12** Andrew, **13** Portsmouth, **14** France, **15** Carlisle Utd.

QUIZ 120

Answers on page 188

1 Did Liverpool hard man Tommy Smith ever play for England?

2 Which Adrian became manager of Burnley in March 1996?

3 Which Maurice became boss of Oxford Utd in 1985?

4 Peter Cormack was an FA Cup winner with which club?

5 What was the 90-minute score in the Arsenal v Liverpool 1971 FA Cup Final?

6 Which soccer team does politician Cecil Parkinson support?

7 Who were the opponents when Viv Anderson became England's first black international footballer?

8 Ashley Ward joined Derby County from which club?

9 Which former West Brom and England striker was killed in a car crash in Madrid in July 1989?

10 In which decade was Daniel Amokachi born?

11 How many times have Manchester Utd done the League Cup double?

12 Crystal Palace recorded a 8-0 League Cup win over which club in September 1990?

13 In what decade was the first Hearts v Hibs Scottish FA Cup Final?

14 Northern Ireland beat Italy at which English ground to qualify for the 1958 World Cup?

15 Who scored within 120 seconds of the 1987 Tottenham Hotspur v Coventry City FA Cup Final?

Answers to page 188

1 Crewe Alexandra, **2** Glenn Hoddle, **3** John Motson, **4** Manchester City, **5** Rangers, **6** Terry Neill, **7** 1901, **8** Barcelona, **9** Chris Waddle, **10** Darren Anderton, **11** Gordon Durie, **12** John Pratt, **13** Marseille, **14** Ray Clemence, **15** Terry Neill

QUIZ 121

Answers on page 193

1 Which famous player died at Goodison at the 1980 Merseyside derby?

2 Who became known in Brazil as 'The White Pele'?

3 How far did the Republic of Ireland progress in the 1994 World Cup finals?

4 The Brazilian Denilson moved from Sao Paulo to which club for £22m in August 1997?

5 Which is the only Irish team to have won both the Northern Irish and Irish championships?

6 How many international goals did Kevin Beattie score?

7 Who is Liverpool's longest serving player, with 640 appearances between 1960 and 1978?

8 Perry Groves played in a League Cup Final for which club?

9 A win in the final game of the 1994-95 season would have made Manchester Utd Premiership winners. Which team held them to a draw?

10 Peter Hucker was in goal as which club reached the First Division?

11 Which was Mark Bowen's first League club?

12 At which ground do Marseille play?

13 Which club has a fanzine called *The Voice of the Valley*?

14 What is Chris Armstrong's middle name?

15 Leeds Utd recorded a 5-1 League Cup win over which club in September 1963?

Answers to page 193

1 Blue and White, **2** Dennis Wise, **3** Rangers, **4** None, **5** Aston Villa, **6** Hartlepool, **7** 1910, **8** Roto Volgograd, **9** Rangers, **10** Leeds Utd, **11** John Trollope (770), **12** Mark Hughes, **13** Vittorio Pozzo, **14** 14, **15** 1974.

QUIZ 122

Answers on page 194

1 Bolton Wanderers player J Cassidy scored 5 goals in a match in February 1890. Who were the opponents?

2 Which teams were in the first all-British European Final?

3 With which club did John Lukic play his first League game?

4 Joe Baker set a most goals in a season record at which British club?

5 Which Glenn was Newcastle United skipper when Gazza started out?

6 Who succeeded J Sirrell as manager of Sheffield Utd in 1978?

7 Which Brazilian player joined Newcastle United in 1987?

8 Arthur Cox followed Roy McFarland as boss of which club in 1984?

9 Who lost to Porto in the 1987 Super Cup?

10 Gordon Milne followed Joe Mercer as manager of which club?

11 The gate for a Paul Elliott benefit game in July 1995 was boosted by which two new Chelsea signings?

12 Which member of England's 1966 World Cup winning side played first class cricket with Essex?

13 Who was Port Vale's top league scorer in 1995-96?

14 At which club did Gary Parker make his League debut?

15 Who scored debut goals for Chelsea, Tottenham Hotspur, West Ham Utd and England?

Answers to page 194

1 John Bond and Ken Brown, **2** Wales, **3** 3rd in Premier League (1992-93), **4** John Deehan, **5** Walsall, **6** 42, **7** John Deehan, **8** Watford, **9** Bristol City, **10** Ken Brown, **11** Bryan Gunn, **12** Kevin Reeves, **13** Chris Sutton, **14** Manchester Utd, **15** Crewe Alexandra.

QUIZ 123

Answers on page 191

1 What are the main colours on QPR's home shirts?

2 Which midfielder did Glenn Hoddle make skipper of Chelsea?

3 Which club did Nigel Spackman leave to join Chelsea for the second time?

4 Which club honours did Johnny Haynes gain in his 18 years at Fulham?

5 Terry Donovan moved from Grimsby Town to which club for £125,000 in July 1979?

6 Who, in the 1992-93 season, set a new record of going 13 League and Cup games without scoring a goal?

7 To five years, when did Newcastle Utd first win the FA Cup?

8 Peter Schmeichel scored in a UEFA game against which club?

9 Alex Ferguson appeared in a Scottish Cup Final for which team?

10 Haddock and Swan were in the same team at which club?

11 Between 1970 and 1980, which Swindon Town player made more appearances than any other Football League player has ever made for any club?

12 Who scored both Manchester Utd goals when they beat Barcelona 2-1 to win the Cup Winners' Cup in 1991?

13 Who took Italy to World Cup triumphs in the 1930s?

14 How many players did Villa use in their 1980s Championship success?

15 In which year was the FA Amateur Cup replaced by the FA Vase?

Answers to page 191

1 Dixie Dean, **2** Zico, **3** To the second round, **4** Real Betis, **5** Derry City, **6** One, **7** Ian Callaghan, **8** Arsenal, **9** West Ham Utd, **10** QPR, **11** Tottenham Hotspur, **12** Stade Velodrome., **13** Charlton Athletic, **14** Peter, **15** Mansfield Town.

NORWICH CITY

Answers on page 192

1 Which two ex-West Ham Utd players have managed Norwich City in the post-war period?

2 Norwich City coach David Williams took charge of which country for one game?

3 What is the highest position Norwich City have ever achieved in the League?

4 Who was Norwich City manager when Chris Sutton left for £5 million?

5 Norwich City player Roy Hollis scored 5 goals in a match in December 1951. Who were the opponents?

6 What is the distance between Norwich City and Ipswich Town?

7 Who succeeded Mike Walker as manager of Norwich City in 1994?

8 Tim Sherwood moved to Norwich City from which club?

9 Which club did Rob Newman leave to join Norwich City?

10 Who was boss when Norwich City were 1986 Second Division Champions?

11 Who was the regular keeper for Norwich City in their 1994-95 relegation season?

12 Who was the first £1 million pound player to leave Norwich City?

13 Who moved from Norwich City for £5.5 million in July 1994 to set a club record for a transfer fee received?

14 Which club did Mark Robins leave to join Norwich City?

15 Which club did Ashley Ward leave to join Norwich City?

Answers to page 192

1 Sheffield Utd, **2** Tottenham Hotspur v Wolves (UEFA Cup 1972), **3** Leeds Utd, **4** Hibernian, **5** Roeder, **6** C Coldwell, **7** Mirandinha, **8** Derby County, **9** Ajax, **10** Coventry City, **11** Ruud Gullit and Mark Hughs, **12** Geoff Hurst, **13** Tony Naylor, **14** Luton Town, **15** Jimmy Greaves.

PETER SHILTON

Answers on page 197

1 Steve McCall followed Peter Shilton as manager of which club?

2 In what year did Peter Shilton first play for England?

3 Who was Peter Shilton playing for when he was sent off for the first time in his career?

4 What was Peter Shilton's first club?

5 Which club did Peter Shilton join on leaving Stoke City?

6 Which club did Peter Shilton leave to become the player/manager at Plymouth?

7 Who were England's opponents in June 1989 when Peter Shilton equalled Bobby Moore's record of 108 international appearances?

8 Which club was Peter Shilton playing for when he made his 1,000 League appearance?

9 How many times did Peter Shilton play for England?

10 How many times did Peter Shilton captain England?

11 With which club did Peter Shilton experience relegation in 1990-91?

12 How many World Cup finals matches did Peter Shilton play in?

13 With which club did he make his only FA Cup Final appearance?

14 How many clean sheets did Peter Shilton keep whilst playing for England?

15 How old was he when he appeared in an FA Cup Final for the only time?

Answers to page 197

1 Andreas Moller, **2** Nottingham Forest, **3** Argentina 6 Peru 0, **4** Lother Emmerich, **5** Tranmere Rovers, **6** Ruud Gullit, **7** Andy Moller, **8** Slaven Bilic, **9** Morocco, **10** Royal Engineers, **11** Moldova, **12** Chelsea, **13** David Beckham, **14** Blackburn Rovers, **15** Tottenham Hotspur.

QUIZ 124

Answers on page 198

1 Where was the 1967 European Cup Final played?

2 How much to the nearest million did Kevin Keegan spend in transfer fees at Newcastle Utd?

3 Who played every game in goal in Manchester City's 1995-96 relegation season?

4 Which country did Tony Norman play for?

5 With which club did Ian Wright make his league debut?

6 Aberdeen side Bon Accord were thrashed 36-0 in the Scottish Cup by which club?

7 With 209 goals Charlie Buchan is all-time top League scorer at which club?

8 In which prison did Duncan Ferguson do time?

9 Who teamed up with Henry Cooper to advertise Brut?

10 Which midfielder did Ron Atkinson call 'The Crab' because he was always moving sideways?

11 Frank Saul scored in an FA Cup Final for which club?

12 Which Spanish club did John Aldridge play for?

13 Which goalkeeper is Sweden's most capped player?

14 Which club won the European Cup three years running 1971, 1972 & 1973?

15 Which English midfielder scored in a World Cup Final?

Answers to page 198

1 Benfica, **2** France 2 Brazil 0, **3** Gary Lineker, **4** Ted Drake, **5** Brighton, **6** Crewe Alexandra, **7** Coventry City, **8** Ted Harper, **9** Watford, **10** The Grecians, **11** Dragan Dzajic, **12** Reading, **13** Bobby Moore, **14** Merthyr Tydfil, **15** 1940s.

QUIZ 125

Answers on page 195

1 After Gareth Southgate's famous miss for England who took the winning spot-kick for Germany?

2 Trevor Francis moved from Birmingham City to which club for £1.18m in February 1979?

3 What was the score in the 1978 World Cup quarter final game between Argentina and Peru ?

4 Which Borussia Dortmund player created a Cup Winners' individual goal scoring record with 14 goals in 1965-66?

5 Harold Bell made a 401 consecutive appearances for which club?

6 Who was captain of the 1988 Dutch European Champions?

7 Who took the final spot kick in the England V Germany Euro 96 game?

8 Who claimed that he had been struck by Laurent Blanc when the French captain was sent off in the semi-finals of the 1998 World Cup?

9 From which country does Said Belqola, the referee of the 1998 World Cup Final come from ?

10 Who were the first team to lose an FA Cup Final?

11 Where was England's first 1998 World Cup qualifying game played?

12 Hinton and Houseman played for which 1970s FA Cup Finalists?

13 There were two new caps in England's first qualifying game for the 1998 World Cup. Andy Hinchcliffe was one, who was the other?

14 Alan Shearer moved from Southampton to which club in July 1992?

15 Teddy Sherringham moved to which club in September 1992?

Answers to page 195

1 Andreas Moller, **2** Nottingham Forest, **3** Argentina 6 Peru 0, **4** Lother Emmerich, **5** Tranmere Rovers, **6** Ruud Gullit, **7** Andy Moller, **8** Slaven Bilic, **9** Morocco, **10** Royal Engineers, **11** Moldova, **12** Chelsea, **13** David Beckham, **14** Blackburn Rovers, **15** Tottenham Hotspur.

QUIZ 126

Answers on page 196

1 Who, outside England, plays at The Stadium Of Light?

2 What was the half-time score in the 1998 World Cup Final in Paris?

3 A club record fee received stood for ten years when which player left Everton for Tottenham Hotspur in the mid 1980s?

4 Which Arsenal player scored seven goals in a game against Aston Villa in 1935?

5 Which club did Ron Greenwood become director of in 1983?

6 Which club did Ashley Ward leave to join Norwich City?

7 Swan Lane and Thackhall Street lead to which club's ground?

8 Which player scored 43 League goals for Blackburn Rovers in 1925-26?

9 Graham Taylor followed Glenn Roeder as manager of which club?

10 What is the nickname of Exeter City?

11 Who made the most appearances for the former Yugoslavia?

12 Martin Hicks set a League appearance record at which club?

13 Who was voted best defender in the world by journalists after the 1970 World Cup?

14 Bristol Rovers recorded a 6-0 FA Cup win over which club in November 1987?

15 In which decade was Pat Jennings born?

Answers to page 196

1 Lisbon, **2** £60 million, **3** Eike Immel, **4** Wales, **5** Crystal Palace, **6** Arbroath, **7** Sunderland, **8** Barlinnie, **9** Kevin Keegan, **10** Ray Wilkins, **11** Tottenham Hotspur, **12** Real Sociedad, **13** Thomas Ravelli, **14** Ajax, **15** Martin Peters.

QUIZ 127

Answers on page 201

1 In what year did Peter Shilton first play for England?

2 Swindon Town recorded a 6-0 League Cup win over which club in September 1992?

3 Where was the 1993 European Cup Winners' Cup Final held?

4 Coventry City recorded a 5-0 League Cup win over which club in December 1980?

5 Who were the last Fourth Division Champions?

6 In what decade did Manchester Utd first win the FA Cup?

7 To date only two teams have won the Charity Shield on penalties. Who were they?

8 William McGregor, who pushed for the formation of a League, was a director of which club?

9 In which decade was Jimmy Greaves born?

10 What is the main colour of Rochdale's home shirts?

11 Which club has a fanzine called *The Ugly Inside*?

12 Which keeper Steve of the 70s,80s, and 90s shares his name with a fruit?

13 To what did Dinamo Zagreb change their name in 1991?

14 Which team plays at home in front of the Kippax Stand?

15 Mick Harford scored in a League Cup Final for which club?

Answers to page 201

1 Escape to Victory, **2** 2, **3** West Ham United, **4** Two, **5** Chelsea, **6** 90, **7** Peter Morris, **8** 1, **9** 108, **10** FA Cup, **11** European Cup Winners' Cup, **12** Picked up the ref's whistle and blew to stop play, **13** 1993, **14** A bracelet, **15** Seattle Sounders.

ARSENAL 4

Answers on page 202

1 Who joined Arsenal for a record British fee in December 1971?

2 Who scored Arsenal's last minute winner against Manchester Utd in the 1979 FA Cup Final?

3 Who was Arsenal's first double-winning manager?

4 Who created the first £10,000 transfer fee joining Arsenal from Bolton?

5 Which England batsman played in the 1950 FA Cup Final for Arsenal?

6 Who scored two of Swindon Town's goals to defeat Arsenal in the 1969 League Cup?

7 Which Arsenal player was Footballer of the Year in 1971?

8 Which Arsenal player moved to Le Harve in the early 1990s?

9 Which Arsenal striker called referee Robert Hart a 'muppet'?

10 Who played for Arsenal and Everton and managed Aston Villa, Manchester City and England?

11 Who scored the only goal of the game as Arsenal beat Manchester Utd at Old Trafford in 1997-98?

12 In the pre shoot-out days, how many hours of play did the 1979 FA Cup tie between Arsenal and Sheffield Wednesday last for?

13 Which Arsenal player was fined £800 for an assault on a taxi driver in Hong Kong?

14 Which club did David Platt leave to join Arsenal?

15 In 1970-71 Arsenal were 2-0 down to which team in an FA Cup semi-final?

Answers to page 202

1 Celtic, **2** Bruce Rioch, **3** Austria, **4** Chile, **5** Wycombe Wanderers, **6** Paul McGrath (45 caps for the Republic of Ireland), **7** Carlisle Utd, **8** Paul Gascoigne, **9** Scunthorpe Utd, **10** Alf Ramsey, **11** 47 days, **12** Swansea City, **13** Colchester Utd, **14** Darwen, **15** LKS and Widzew.

BOBBY MOORE

Answers on page 199

1 Which film featured Bobby Moore and Pele?

2 How many international goals did Bobby Moore score?

3 Which club was Bobby Moore with when he became England captain?

4 How many international goals did Bobby Moore score?

5 Which team name was one of Bobby Moore's names?

6 In how many games was Bobby Moore skipper of England?

7 Who managed Southend Utd before Bobby Moore?

8 How many goals did Bobby Moore score in his 124 appearances for Fulham?

9 How many England Caps did Bobby Moore win?

10 Which trophy did Bobby Moore win with West Ham in 1964?

11 Which trophy did Bobby Moore win with West Ham in 1965?

12 What did he do when he knocked out the referee in a match in 1970?

13 In which year did Bobby Moore die of cancer?

14 What was Bobby Moore falsely accused of stealing during the 1970 World Cup finals?

15 Which club did Bobby Moore finish his playing career with?

Answers to page 199

1 1970, **2** Torquay Utd, **3** Wembley, **4** Watford, **5** Burnley, **6** 1900s, **7** Liverpool (1974) Manchester Utd (1993), **8** Aston Villa, **9** 1940s, **10** Blue, **11** Southampton, **12** Cherry, **13** Croatia Zagreb, **14** Manchester City, **15** Luton Town.

QUIZ 128

Answers on page 200

1 Who beat Rangers 1-0 in the 1977 Scottish FA Cup Final?

2 Who succeeded Phil Neal as manager of Bolton Wanderers in 1992?

3 Hugo Meisl was manager and general secretary of which country from 1906 to 1937?

4 Which country lost 4-2 to Brazil in the 1962 World Cup Semi-Final?

5 Which club are nicknamed The Chairboys?

6 Who is Aston Villa's most-capped player?

7 Which club did Bob Stokoe manage on three separate occasions?

8 Which player burst into tears after England's World Cup semi final defeat in 1990?

9 With which league club did Kevin Keegan start his career?

10 Which England boss was born in Dagenham in 1920?

11 How long was John Toshack manager of Wales for?

12 Liverpool recorded a 8-0 FA Cup win over which club in January 1990?

13 Which was Mike Walker's first club as manager?

14 Arsenal recorded a 11-1 FA Cup win over which club in January 1932?

15 Which two Polish clubs play at home in the city of Lodz?

Answers to page 200

1 Alan Ball, **2** Alan Sunderland, **3** Bertie Mee, **4** David Jack, **5** Denis Compton, **6** Don Rogers, **7** Frank McLintock, **8** Graham Rix, **9** Ian Wright, **10** Joe Mercer, **11** Marc Overmars, **12** Nine, **13** Ray Parlour, **14** Sampdoria, **15** Stoke City.

QUIZ 129

Answers on page 205

1. Which London club announced plans to move to Wembley?
2. Which three teams were in the Republic of Ireland's group in USA 94?
3. How many penalty goals did Francis Lee get in 1971-72?
4. What was the cost of the original FA Cup trophy?
5. Which country did Scotland beat in the 1990 World Cup finals?
6. Leeds Utd were taken over in a £20m deal by which company?
7. Which country lost 2-1 to West Germany in the 1966 World Cup semi-final?
8. At which club did Tim Flowers make his League debut?
9. Who were the only team to beat Manchester Utd home and away in the 1993-94 season?
10. What was the first English club that Alex James played for?
11. What was the French novelist Albert Camus's position when he played football for Algiers?
12. Which player scored 24 League goals for Cambridge Utd in 1985-86?
13. At which club did Wilf Mannion end his career?
14. Which country did George Wood play for?
15. Who succeeded Joe Fagan as manager of Liverpool in 1985?

Answers to page 205

1 Hans Segers, **2** Manager Walter Smith, **3** Arsene Wenger (Arsenal), **4** Frank Burrows, **5** Arsenal, **6** Wilson, **7** Javier Clemente, **8** Ted Drake, **9** Watford, **10** Chelsea, **11** Ferencvaros, **12** Wales, **13** Nottingham Forest, Norwich City and Sheffield Wednesday, **14** Manchester Utd, **15** Jairzinho.

QUIZ 130

Answers on page 206

1 Which soccer team does politician Neil Kinnock support?

2 Who was in goal for Oldham Athletic in the 1990 League Cup Final?

3 In which year did Arsenal first win the FA Cup?

4 In which country were the 1934 World Cup Finals held?

5 What is Steve Bruce's middle name?

6 What were the forenames of the Dutch Koeman brothers?

7 Who plays at home at the Millmoor Ground?

8 Who was the player-manager of the beaten 1994 London fianalists?

9 Which country did Paul Price play for?

10 Stefan Schwarz left Arsenal for which club?

11 Which foreign club did Ray Wilkins play for?

12 What was first broadcast on August 22, 1964?

13 In which city was Liam Brady born?

14 Which Dennis has been boss at Bristol City, Oxford, Sunderland and York?

15 Who did Blackburn Rovers play in the 1994 Charity Shield match?

Answers to page 206

1 Northampton, **2** Richard Money, **3** Scotland, **4** Swansea City and Crewe Alexandra, **5** 16, **6** 68 points, **7** Aston Villa, **8** Billy Liddell, **9** Candy, **10** Dean Saunders, **11** Fulham, **12** Ian Rush, **13** John Scales, **14** Kenny Dalglish, **15** Matt McQueen.

QUIZ 131

Answers on page 203

1 Which keeper along with Grobbelaar was involved in the alleged 1990s match fixing charges?

2 Who announced in October his intention to leave Rangers at the end of the 1997-98 season?

3 Who was the first ever non-British manager to win the English league Championship?

4 Who succeeded John Gregory as manager of Portsmouth?

5 Which team played at Plumstead Common from 1886-87?

6 Which Danny became boss of Barnsley in June 1994?

7 Who was Spain's coach in Euro '96?

8 Which player scored 42 League goals for Arsenal in 1934-35?

9 Rostron and Gilligan scored Euro goals in the same game for which club?

10 Which London club pulled out of the first European Cup Competition?

11 Who lost 3-0 to Dynamo Kiev in the 1975 Cup-Winners' Cup Final?

12 Norwich City coach David Williams took charge of which international side for one game?

13 Which three English clubs has Chris Woods played for in League Cup Finals?

14 Property developer Michael Knighton had his £10m bid to buy which club accepted at the start of the 1989-90 season?

15 How is Brazil's Jair Ventura Filho better known?

Answers to page 203

1 Arsenal, **2** Italy Mexico and Norway, **3** 13, **4** £20, **5** Sweden, **6** Caspian, **7** Soviet Union, **8** Wolves, **9** Chelsea, **10** Preston North End, **11** Goalkeeper, **12** David Crown, **13** Hull City, **14** Scotland, **15** Kenny Dalglish.

LIVERPOOL 7

Answers on page 204

1 Which club did Phil Neal play for before he joined Liverpool?

2 Who moved from Fulham to Liverpool for £333,000 in 1980 to set a club record for a transfer fee received?

3 Liverpool's legendary striker Billy Liddell came from which country?

4 Ian Callaghan played in 88 FA Cup games, mostly with Liverpool, but with which other two clubs?

5 How many goals did Liverpool's mean machine defence concede in the 42 League games of 1978-79?

6 Under the 2 points for a win system how many points did Liverpool gain to create a record in 1979?

7 Who finished second when Liverpool won the League in 1989-90?

8 Which Liverpool and Scottish international star played twice for Great Britain against the Rest of Europe?

9 What was the largest word on Liverpool's shirts when they played in the 1989 FA Cup Final?

10 Who scored a 1991 UEFA Cup hat-trick for Liverpool v Swarovski Tirol?

11 Liverpool beat which club 10-0 in the League Cup in September 1986?

12 Which Liverpool player won the 1983-84 Golden Boot award?

13 Which defender played 240 games for Wimbledon before joining Liverpool?

14 Who hit Liverpool's last league goal in the 1985-86 double season?

15 Who succeeded Dave Ashworth as manager of Liverpool in 1923?

Answers to page 204

1 Brentford, **2** Andy Rhodes, **3** 1930, **4** Italy, **5** Roger, **6** Ronald and Erwin, **7** Rotherham Utd, **8** Glenn Hoddle, **9** Wales, **10** Fiorentina, **11** AC Milan, **12** Match of The Day, **13** Dublin, **14** Smith, **15** Manchester Utd.

GOALKEEPERS 1

Answers on page 209

1 Which goalkeeper made 394 consecutive League appearances between August 1981 and October 1990?

2 Who was the first keeper to skipper a World Cup winning side?

3 David Beckham scored from the halfway line in the opening game of the 1997-98 season. Which keeper did he beat?

4 Singer Julio Iglesias was reserve team goalkeeper for which club?

5 Who was the first goalkeeper to save a penalty in an FA Cup Final?

6 Which keeper along with Grobbelaar was involved in the alleged 1990s match fixing charges?

7 Which goalkeeper staged a goalmouth sit-in during the half-time break in 1990?

8 Which international keeper of the 1990s has the nickname 'El Loco'?

9 Who was the first goalkeeper to captain his side to victory in an FA Cup Final?

10 Keeper Andy Goram was at which club when he scored v Morton?

11 Which England goalkeeper did Bristol Rovers sell to Crystal Palace in November 1989?

12 Who performed the 'scorpion kick' at Wembley?

13 Which keeper spent 20 years with Portsmouth?

14 Which goalkeeper said, "It's not nice going down to the supermarket and the woman at the till thinking 'dodgy keeper'"?

15 Which keeper did Alec Ferguson sign from his former club Aberdeen?

Answers to page 209

1 Chris Waddle, **2** Juventus, **3** Hamburg, **4** Lou Macari, **5** Arthur Rowley, **6** Bo Johannsen, **7** 12, **8** Cooper, **9** Blackburn Rovers, **10** West Ham Utd, **11** Notts County, **12** Gary Mabbutt, **13** John Gregory, **14** Clemence, **15** Manchester Utd.

QUIZ 132

Answers on page 210

1 With 700 plus games, which player set a League appearance record for Southampton?

2 What is the middle name of ex-Liverpool ace Mark Walters?

3 Terry Fenwick was at which club when he made his international debut?

4 Which country lost 6-1 to West Germany in the 1954 World Cup semi-final?

5 The minimum size of a pitch is 50 yards by how many yards?

6 Who replaced Billy McNeill as manager of Celtic?

7 Which club, formed in 1881, were originally known as Stanley?

8 What was Mervyn Day's first League club?

9 Who did Crystal Palace buy from Juventus for £1.7 million?

10 Who scored a hat-trick in Manchester Utd's 7-0 Premiership defeat of Barnsley?

11 QPR recorded an 8-1 League Cup win over which club in October 1983?

12 In the 1998 World Cup finals who was the first of 22 players to receive the red card?

13 What are the two colours of Reading's home shirts?

14 Don Howe followed Terry Neill as boss of which club?

15 Who scored a hat-trick for Coventry on the opening day of the 1997-98 season at home against Chelsea?

Answers to page 210

1 The first man to score in an FA Cup Final, **2** Roy Dwight, **3** Division 1 (3rd 1985-86), **4** Division I champions 1977-78, **5** Ayr, **6** Bobby Charlton, **7** Tony Adams, **8** Bristol City, **9** Division 1 champions (4 times), **10** Arsenal, **11** Denis Law, **12** Branco, **13** His collar bone (the very first injury), **14** Ian Rush, **15** Height 8 Feet - Width 8 yards.

QUIZ 133

Answers on page 207

1 Which England international played for Marseille in the 1991 European Cup Final?

2 Roberto Baggio cost £10 million when he moved to AC Milan from where?

3 Which German club won the European Cup in 1983?

4 Who succeeded Dave Mackay as manager of Birmingham City in 1990?

5 Who holds the career record for League goals, with 434 strikes?

6 Who took over from Richard Moller-Nielsen as Denmark manager in 1996?

7 How many games had Alan Shearer not scored for England before Euro '96?

8 Which keeper Paul played over 400 games for Ipswich Town?

9 During Euro '96 which League club was Alan Shearer playing for?

10 John Hartson left which club to join Wimbledon in January 1999?

11 Which was the first team to play 3,000 Football League matches?

12 Whose skull was fractured in a clash with Wimbledon striker John Fashanu?

13 Who took over from Brian little as manager of Aston Villa?

14 Which Ray became boss of Barnet in January 1994?

15 Neil Webb moved from Nottingham Forest to which club for £1.5m in July 1989?

Answers to page 207

1 Dave Beasant, **2** Gianpietro Combi (1934 Italy), **3** Neil Sullivan, **4** Real Madrid, **5** Dave Beasant (Wimbledon), **6** Hans Segers, **7** Neville Southall, **8** Rene Higuita (Colombia), **9** Dave Beasant (Wimbledon), **10** Hibernian, **11** Nigel Martyn, **12** Rene Higuita (Colombia), **13** Alan Knight, **14** David James, **15** Jim Leighton.

QUIZ 134

Answers on page 208

1 What was the historic achievement of A.H. Chequer?

2 What was the name of Elton John's footballing uncle?

3 What is the highest position West Ham Utd have ever achieved in the League?

4 What is the highest position Nottingham Forest have ever achieved in the League?

5 George Burley was player/manager of which Scottish side?

6 Who scored a record 199 League goals in a record 606 appearances Manchester Utd?

7 Which other England regular was controversially sent off for a foul on Alan Shearer in December 1996?

8 Which club did Rob Newman leave to join Norwich City?

9 What is the highest position Newcastle United have ever achieved in the League?

10 Brian Marwood and Martin Hayes were in the same side at which club?

11 Who is the only player to have scored 38 goals in FA Cup matches?

12 Which 1994 World Cup winner later played for Middlesborough?

13 What did Lt. Creswell break during the very first Cup Final to get his name in the record books?

14 Who won the Golden Boot as Europe's top soccer scorer with 32 goals in the 1983/84 season?

15 What is the height and width of the goals in football?

Answers to page 208

1 Terry Paine, **2** Everton, **3** QPR, **4** Austria, **5** 100 yards, **6** Liam Brady, **7** Newcastle Utd, **8** West Ham Utd, **9** Michele Padovano, **10** Andy Cole, **11** Crewe, **12** Anatoli Nankov (Bulgaria), **13** Blue and White, **14** Arsenal, **15** Dion Dublin.

QUIZ 135

Answers on page 213

1 In which decade was Brian Kidd born?

2 Which are the two leading football clubs in Munich?

3 Where was the 1973 European Cup Final held?

4 Which Bournmouth striker hit nine goals in an FA Cup tie?

5 In 1995 which English club was incensed when their player was injured against Sweden?

6 Which three other clubs were in Manchester Utd's 1997-98 Champions' League Group?

7 Which Newcastle Utd centre forward came off as Gazza came on as substitute for his debut?

8 What is the South American equivalent of the European Cup?

9 In which city do Anderlecht play?

10 Dino Zoff became coach and later president of which Italian club?

11 Which Italian Serie B club reached the Cup Winners' Cup semi-final in 1988?

12 Who was on the receiving end of the wild FA Cup Final tackle in which Gazza hurt his knee?

13 Which team were beaten 3-2 by Liverpool in the 1989 FA Cup Final?

14 Which two countries went to war in 1969 over a football match?

15 Which Englishman scored against his own club keeper in Euro '96?

Answers to page 213

1 Nobody remembered to tell him he was playing, **2** Roto Volgograd, **3** Alec Stepney, **4** Dino Zoff, **5** Jimmy Rimmer, **6** Pat Bonner, **7** Sheffield Wednesday, **8** Alex Ferguson, **9** Dino Zoff, **10** Jimmy Rimmer, **11** Pat Jennings, **12** Thomas Ravelli, **13** Andy Goram, **14** Dino Zoff (Italy), **15** Jonathan Gould (Celtic).

SOUTHAMPTON 1

Answers on page 214

1 Which 38-year-old goalkeeper was released by Southampton in May 1996?

2 What is the first name of Southampton defender Benali?

3 Who finished Southampton's joint top scorer in 1995-96 with 7 goals, including a hat-trick in the first game of the season?

4 Southampton recorded a 5-0 League Cup win over which club in August 1979?

5 In which decade did Southampton first win the FA Cup?

6 What type of product was advertised on Southampton's open top bus as it paraded the FA Cup in the 1970s?

7 Which player had his jaw broken by Arsenal's Paul Davis in 1988?

8 Which Southampton striker now breeds and trains racehorses?

9 How many League goals did Alan Shearer score for Southampton?

10 Who was Southampton boss when Alan Shearer made his League debut?

11 Which Second Division side knocked Southampton out of the 1998-99 FA Cup?

12 Which English team knocked Southampton out of the 1970 UEFA Cup competition?

13 Who hit five goals for Ipswich Town v Southampton in 1981-82?

14 Who followed Lawrie McMenemy as boss of Southampton in 1985?

15 Which Southampton boss sold Alan Shearer to Blackburn Rovers?

Answers to page 214

1 Three, **2** Luton Town, **3** Bradford City, **4** Fullback, **5** Johan Cruyff, **6** Richard Gough, **7** Andy Cole, **8** Queen Of The South, **9** Nottingham Forest, **10** Huddersfield Town, **11** Wilkins, **12** Walsall, **13** Scotland, **14** Paris St Germain, **15** Wolverhampton Wanderers.

GOALKEEPERS 2

Answers on page 211

1 Why did Brighton keeper miss a match against Scunthorpe in 1988?

2 Peter Schmeichel scored a UEFA Cup goal against which club?

3 Which Manchester Utd keeper was club joint top scorer in mid-season 1974-75 because of his spot kick success?

4 In the 1970s, which keeper went 1,143 minutes in international soccer without conceding a goal?

5 Which English keeper was on the bench in the 1960s European cup Final and started a 1980s Final?

6 Which was the Republic of Ireland's keeper in the penalty shoot-out against Romania in the 1990 Worl Cup?

7 Against which club did Coventry goalkeeper Steve Ogrizovic score with a long clearance in October 1986?

8 Which manager declared, "Goal keepers are a more protected species than the Golden eagle"?

9 Which goalkeeper helped Juventus win seven league titles?

10 Which goalkeeper played every game in Aston Villa's Championship-winning campaign in 1980-81?

11 Which goalkeeper scored a goal in the 1967 Charity Shield match?

12 Which goalkeeper is Sweden's most capped player?

13 Which 1990s goalkeeper has played soccer and cricket for Scotland?

14 Which goalkeeper has kept the most international clean sheets?

15 Which goalkeeper did Scotland call up at short notice when Andy Goram made his shock withdrawal from the 1998 World Cup?

Answers to page 211

1 1940s, **2** Bayern and 1860, **3** Belgrade, **4** Ted MacDougall, **5** Leeds Utd (Gary McAllister was involved), **6** Feyenoord, Juventus, Kosice, **7** George Reilly, **8** La Copa Libertadores, **9** Brussels, **10** Lazio, **11** Atlanta, **12** Gary Charles, **13** Everton, **14** El Salvador and Honduras, **15** Paul Gascoigne against fellow Rangers player Andy Goram (Scotland).

QUIZ 136

Answers on page 212

1 How many international goals did Terry Butcher score?

2 Mark Pembridge played every 1992 game as which team went down?

3 Which British football stadium saw 56 deaths in a tragic 1985 fire?

4 In which position did Ray Stewart play?

5 Which Barcelona player was European Footballer of the Year in 1973?

6 Which Scottish captain was born in Stockholm?

7 Which player scored 34 League goals for Newcastle Utd in 1993-94?

8 Allan Ball made a record 731 appearances, for which Scottish club between 1963-82?

9 Which club did Peter Shilton join on leaving Stoke City?

10 Which English club was the first ever side to win the First Division titile in three successive years?

11 Which brothers Graham and Ray played at Chelsea in the 1970s?

12 Which club's nickname is The Saddlers?

13 The Wee Blue Devils were a famous forward line of which country?

14 David Ginola and George Weah have played for which French club?

15 England wing-half Billy Wright made 491 appearances for which club?

Answers to page 212

1 Bruce Grobbelaar, **2** Francis, **3** Matt Le Tissier, **4** Wrexham, **5** 1970s, **6** Chewing Gum (Dentyne), **7** Glenn Cockerill, **8** Mick Channon, **9** 23, **10** Chris Nicholl, **11** Fulham, **12** Newcastle Utd, **13** Alan Brazil, **14** Chris Nicholl, **15** Ian Branfoot.

QUIZ 137

Answers on page 217

1 Who moved to Sunderland from Millwall in 1996 to set a club record for a transfer fee paid?

2 Which Borussia Dortmund player scored 14 goals in 1965-66?

3 Which Mick became boss of Scunthorpe in March 1996?

4 How many international goals did Tony Grealish score?

5 Which two foreign teams did Gary Lineker play for?

6 What is the nickname of Montrose?

7 Who was the first professional to play for England against Scotland?

8 Geraint Williams and Dean Saunders were in the same side at which club?

9 Which side knocked Manchester Utd out of the 1995-96 Coca-Cola Cup?

10 The first FA Cup Final hat-trick was scored by William Townley in 1890 for which northern club?

11 Which club had a fanzine called Almighty Brian?

12 Which Leicester-born striker of the 1990s has the middle names William Ivanhoe?

13 How many international goals has Tony Cascarino scored?

14 Who were Britain's last remaining club in Europe in the 1995-96 season?

15 Who was top scorer for both Portsmouth and Aldershot in 1979-80?

Answers to page 217

1 Rio de Janeiro's, **2** Real Sociedad, **3** Mark Huges, **4** Chelsea, **5** Italy, Mexico, France., **6** Everton, **7** QPR, **8** Marseille, **9** Barcelona (four), **10** Tottenham Hotspur, **11** Kevin Keegan on his swift departure from Newcastle Utd, **12** Brian Clough, **13** Leicester City and Stoke City, **14** Ian Edwards, **15** Wycombe Wanderers.

QUIZ 138

Answers on page 218

1 Which club was Frank Worthington with when he was First Division leading scorer in 1978-79?

2 Which country did Gary Waddock play for?

3 Bryan Robson was at which League club when he made his England debut?

4 Which two English League clubs went 50 years after the Second World War with only seven managers?

5 In what Division were Southampton when they won the FA Cup in 1976?

6 Which club did Alan Harper join when he left Everton for the first time?

7 Who started the game in goal for Scotland when they drew against Finland in a friendly in April 1998?

8 Which Italian team did Ian Rush join from Liverpool?

9 Which Manchester Utd player was PFA Player of the Year in 1994?

10 By winning 6-1 at White Hart Lane, which team inflicted Tottenham Hotspur's worst home defeat since 1935?

11 Which club did Russell Osman go to when he left Ipswich Town?

12 Which player scored 147 goals in 411 League games for Manchester Utd?

13 JVC were long-running sponsors of which London club?

14 Which Arsenal defender was sent off in the Premiership match against Aston Villa for handling the ref?

15 Which three other clubs were in Newcastle Utd's 1997-98 Champions' League Group?

Answers to page 218

1 Alex Dawson, **2** Arsenal, **3** Blackburn Rovers, **4** Brian McClair, **5** Denis Law, **6** Everton, **7** Gordon Strachan, **8** Keith Pilkington, **9** Mal Donaghy, **10** No 9, **11** Ray Wilkins, **12** Slavia Prague, **13** Tommy Docherty, **14** York City (3-0 in the Coca-Cola Cup), **15** 1956.

QUIZ 139

Answers on page 215

1 Which City's Maracana Stadium holds 200,000 people?

2 After scoring 50 goals in 83 appearances for Liverpool, John Aldridge moved to which Spanish club?

3 Who is the only English League player to have been twice voted PFA Player of the Year (1989 and 991)?

4 Tony Hateley moved from Aston Villa to which club for £100,000 in October 1966?

5 Which three countries have hosted the World Cup twice?

6 Mark Ward moved from Manchester City to which club for £900.000 in June 1991?

7 Colin Clarke moved from Southampton to which club for £800,000 in March 1989?

8 Chris Waddle moved from Tottenham Hotspur to which club for £4.5m in June 1989?

9 Which club has won the Cup Winners' Cup most often?

10 Paul Allen moved from West Ham Utd to which club for £400.000 in June 1985?

11 Which manager said, "I did not jump. I was pushed. And so abruptly that my salary was cut off immediately"?

12 Who said, "The Trent is lovely, too. I've walked on it for 18 years"?

13 Gordon Banks won the League Cup with which different clubs?

14 Who scored 4 goals in a game for Chester against Malta in October 1978?

15 Who plays at home at Adams Park?

Answers to page 215

1 Alex Rae, **2** Lothar Emmerich, **3** Buxton, **4** Eight, **5** Barcelona & Grampus Eight, **6** The Gable Endies, **7** James Forrest, **8** Derby County, **9** York City, **10** Blackburn Rovers, **11** Nottingham Forest, **12** Emile Heskey, **13** 12, **14** Nottingham Forest, **15** Colin Garwood.

• MANCHESTER UTD 6 •

Answers on page 216

1 Which Manchester Utd player was known as 'The Black Prince'?

2 Who beat Manchester Utd 3-2 in the 1979 FA Cup Final?

3 Which team lost 2-0 to Manchester Utd in the 1994 FA Charity Shield?

4 Who scored his 100th Manchester Utd goal in the 1992 League Cup Final?

5 Who was European footballer of the Year in 1964?

6 Who did Manchester Utd beat 2-1 in the 1985 FA Cup Final?

7 Which Manchester Utd player scored on his English League debut v Watford in August 1984?

8 Who was in goal for Manchester Utd for the 1995-96 league games that Peter Schmeichel missed?

9 In Steve Bruce's first season with Manchester Utd who played most times as his central defensive partner?

10 What shirt number did Mark Hughes usually wear in his first three years at Manchester Utd?

11 Who moved from Chelsea to Manchester Utd in 1979 for a record £825,000 before moving to AC Milan in 1984?

12 Which club did Karel Poborsky leave to join Manchester Utd?

13 Who was boss when Manchester Utd were last promoted?

14 Who inflicted Manchester Utd's only home defeat in their 1995/96 Double Winning season?

15 When did Bobby Charlton first play for Manchester Utd?

Answers to page 216

1 Bolton Wanderers, **2** The Republic of Ireland, **3** West Brom, **4** West Ham Utd and Manchester Utd, **5** Second, **6** Sheffield Wednesday, **7** Leighton, **8** Juventus, **9** Eric Cantona, **10** Chelsea, **11** Leicester City, **12** George Best, **13** Arsenal, **14** Emmanuel Petit, **15** Barcelona, Dynamo Kiev, PSV Eindhoven.

WIMBLEDON 1

Answers on page 221

1 What is the highest position Wimbledon have ever finished in the League?

2 John Scales moved from Wimbledon to which club in August 1994?

3 Which Wimbledon player was sent off in 1995 after tangling with Ruud Gullit?

4 In which decade did Wimbledon first win the FA Cup?

5 Just 3,039 people turned up on Boxing Day 1993 to watch Wimbledon play against which club?

6 Keith Curle moved from Wimbledon to which club for £2.5m in August 1991?

7 Who moved from Wimbledon for £4 million in June 1995 to set a club record for a transfer fee received?

8 Which player with 430 games set a League appearance record for Wimbledon?

9 Whose skull was fractured in a clash with Wimbledon striker John Fashanu?

10 Terry Phelan moved from Wimbledon to which club in September 1992?

11 Which club did Wimbledon beat 7-2 in an FA Cup game in 1980

12 Which player scored 29 League goals for Wimbledon in 1983-84?

13 Which Wimbledon goalkeeper was charged with match-fixing?

14 Which club did Wimbledon buy John Fashanu from?

15 Who did Wimbledon beat 5-0 in a League Cup game in 1985?

Answers to page 221

1 Rangers, **2** York City, **3** Jackie Milburn, **4** 1960s, **5** Faustino Asprilla, **6** Ipswich Town, **7** Fulham, **8** Blackburn Rovers, **9** 2, **10** Nottingham Forest, **11** Harry Catterick, **12** Renel Higuita, **13** Birmingham City, **14** Ossie Ardiles, **15** East Fife.

QUIZ 140

Answers on page 222

1 In which decade was Gary Mabbutt born?

2 How long was Jock Stein manager of Leeds United for?

3 Who was the last player to score a hat-trick against England?

4 Which soccer team does athlete Steve Cram support?

5 Which team did Arsenal beat in the FA Cup Final in the year they first won the double?

6 Terry Cooper followed Lou Macari as boss of which club?

7 Keith Curle moved from Wimbledon to which club for £2.5m in August 1991?

8 Who succeeded Billy Walker as manager of Nottingham Forest in 1960?

9 Who succeeded Jock Wallace as manager of Leicester City in 1982?

10 Who succeeded Syd Owen as manager of Luton Town in 1960?

11 French World Cup squad members Stephane Guivarc'h and Lionel Charbonnier both left which club after the 1998 World Cup?

12 Birmingham City player Jimmy Windridge scored 5 goals in a match in January 1915. Who were the opponents?

13 Which Celtic player was Scottish Footballer of the Year in 1965?

14 Arsenal recorded a 7-0 League Cup win over which club in September 1979?

15 Aston Villa recorded a 8-1 League Cup win over which club in October 1985?

Answers to page 222

1 West Germany (twice), **2** Wally Ardron, **3** Rangers, **4** Billy Bingham, **5** Spartak Moscow, **6** Italy, **7** York City, **8** Brighton, **9** Cambridge Utd, **10** Kenny Dalglish, **11** 44 days, **12** The letter 'S' from the name Hartlepools, **13** Wimbledon, **14** Sheffield Wednesday, **15** Vinnie Jones.

QUIZ 141

Answers on page 219

1 Which club did Paul Rideout Leave to join Everton?

2 Which club became the first team to score 100 points in a season?

3 Who succeeded Alf Ramsey as manager of Ipswich Town?

4 In which decade was Robert Lee born?

5 Who was the first Colombian ever to play in the Football League?

6 Which club was Kevin Beattie with when he first played international soccer?

7 Gordon Davies set a most League goals in total record at which club?

8 Bobby Saxton followed Howard Kendall as manager of which club?

9 How many times did Bob Wilson play for Scotland?

10 Which club used to play at the Town Ground?

11 Which Everton manager captured the League Championship in 1963?

12 Who performed the 'scorpion kick' at Wembley?

13 Which was Julian Dick's first League club?

14 Who took over as boss of Newcastle Utd when Jim Smith resigned?

15 Which Scottish club play at Bayview Park?

Answers to page 219

1 Division 1 (6th 1986-87, 1993-94), **2** Liverpool, **3** Vinnie Jones, **4** 1980s, **5** Everton, **6** Manchester City, **7** Warren Barton, **8** Alan Cork, **9** Gary Mabbutt, **10** Manchester City, **11** Windsor and Eton, **12** Alan Cork, **13** Hans Segers, **14** Millwall, **15** Blackburn.

QUIZ 142

Answers on page 220

1 Which is the only nation to have won the European Championship more than once?

2 Which player scored 38 League goals for Rotherham in 1946-47?

3 Who beat St Mirren 2-0 in the 1962 Scottish FA Cup Final?

4 Which Irishman took charge of the Greek national side in 1970?

5 Which soccer team does Russian President Boris Yeltsin support?

6 Which country beat England in the Third Place Play-Off game in the 1990 World Cup?

7 Who knocked Manchester Utd out of the 1995/96 Coco-Cola Cup?

8 Liam Brady followed Barry Lloyd as manager of which club?

9 Who plays at home at the Abbey Stadium?

10 Who won his 100th Scottish cap in March 1986?

11 How long was Brian Clough manager of Leeds Utd for?

12 What was dropped from Hartlepool Utd in 1968?

13 Paul Merson scored on his debut for two different clubs, Arsenal and Aston Villa, against which club?

14 Against which club did Coventry goalkeeper Steve Ogrizovic score with a long clearance in October 1986?

15 Who was fined £20,000 and given a six-month suspended ban for doing the voice over for the video *Soccer's Hard Men*?

Answers to page 220

1 1960s, **2** 44 days, **3** Marco Van Basten (Holland), **4** Sunderland, **5** Liverpool (2-1), **6** Birmingham City, **7** Manchester City, **8** Andy Beattie, **9** Gordon Milne, **10** Sam Bartram, **11** Auxerre, **12** Glossop, **13** Billy McNeill, **14** Leeds Utd, **15** Exeter.

QUIZ 143

Answers on page 225

1 Which Charlie scored the winner against Liverpool in the 1987 League Cup Final?

2 How long was Jimmy McIlroy manager of Bolton for?

3 Which club is situated in Moss Side?

4 Which club resigned from the League in August 1992?

5 Which club did Peter Shilton leave to become the player/manager at Plymouth?

6 Who was Arsenal's first double-winning manager?

7 Ray Allan made a record 491 appearances, for which Scottish club between 1972-89?

8 Who said his pigs did not squeal as much as Ruud Gullit?

9 In what decade did Manchester City first win the FA Cup?

10 Peter Mellor first played in an FA Cup Final for which team?

11 Steve Harrison followed Dave Bassett as boss of which club?

12 Who scored 23 goals in only 20 games for Scotland?

13 Which Liverpool outfield player was the only one not to score in the 11-0 rout of Stromsgodset in 1974?

14 Which club was once known as Headington?

15 In what year did Paul McStay make his international debut?

Answers to page 225

1 1st Division 1, **2** Ferguson, **3** Mick Mills, **4** Alan Brazil, **5** Florina, **6** Northampton, **7** Alan Brazil, **8** George Burnley, **9** Ray Crawford, **10** Alf Ramsey, **11** Jackie Milburn, **12** Roger Osbourne, **13** Arnold Muhren, **14** Jason Dozzell, **15** Sergei Baltacha.

WEST HAM 1

Answers on page 226

1 Frank McAvennie moved from West Ham Utd to which club for £850,000 in October 1987?

2 Which team were beaten 2-0 by West Ham Utd in the 1975 FA Cup Final?

3 Paul Ince moved from West Ham Utd to which club for £800,000 in September 1989?

4 Who was manager of West Ham Utd's promotion winning side of 1958?

5 In which decade did West Ham Utd first win the FA Cup?

6 What nationality is West Ham Utd's Slaven Bilic?

7 Who succeeded Billy Bonds as manager of West Ham Utd in 1994?

8 Who lost 2-0 to West Ham Utd in the 1965 Cup-Winners' Cup Final?

9 Paul Allen moved from West Ham Utd to which club for £400.000 in June 1985?

10 Which West Ham Utd Player had his red card reduced to yellow after TV evidence showed he was wrongly dismissed v Sheffield Wednesday?

11 Who moved from Walsall to West Ham Utd in 1988 to set a club record for a transfer fee received?

12 Which Chilean World Cup star signed for West Ham in 1998?

13 Paul Goddard moved from West Ham Utd to which club for £400.000 in October 1986?

14 Who scored West Ham Utd's goal to beat Arsenal in the 1980 FA Cup Final?

15 Which team was beaten 1-0 by West Ham Utd in the 1980 FA Cup Final?

Answers to page 226

1 21, **2** David May, **3** Johan Cruyff, **4** The Springetts (Ron and Peter), **5** Reading, **6** Mike Newell, **7** Newcastle Utd, **8** Chris and Neil, **9** Aberdeen, **10** Black, **11** Oxford Utd, **12** Manchester Utd, **13** Luis Suarez, **14** Ron Atkinson, **15** Jack Reynolds.

IPSWICH 1

Answers on page 223

1 What is the highest position Ipswich Town have ever achieved in the League?

2 Which Bobby was Ipswich Town boss from 1982-1987?

3 Which England player set a League appearance record for Ipswich Town?

4 Who hit five goals for Ipswich Town v Southampton in 1981-82?

5 Ipswich Town player Ray Crawford scored 5 goals in a match in September 1962. Who were the opponents?

6 Ipswich Town recorded a 5-0 League Cup win over which club in August 1977?

7 Who was known as "Pele" in his Ipswich Town days?

8 Who succeeded John Lyall as manager of Ipswich Town?

9 Which Ipswich Town player scored five goals in the European Cup?

10 Who was manager of Ipswich Town's championship winning team of the sixties?

11 Who succeeded Alf Ramsey as manager at Ipswich Town?

12 Who scored Ipswich Town's 1978 FA Cup winner against Arsenal?

13 Which Dutch master joined Manchester Utd from Ipswich Town?

14 Which 16-year-old became the First Division's youngest scorer with a goal for Ipswich Town in 1984?

15 Which Ukrainian played in Britain for Ipswich Town and St Johnston?

Answers to page 223

1 Nicholas, **2** 16 days, **3** Manchester City, **4** Maidstone Utd, **5** Derby, **6** Bertie Mee, **7** Cowdenbeath, **8** Vinnie Jones, **9** 1900s, **10** Fulham, **11** Watford, **12** Hughie Gallacher, **13** Brian Hall, **14** Oxford Utd, **15** 1983.

QUIZ 144

Answers on page 224

1 How many goals did Kevin Keegan score for England?

2 Who was the only Premiership player in 1996 to share his name with a calander month?

3 Which Ajax player was European Footballer of the Year in 1971?

4 Who were the goalkeeping brothers to be exchanged in the 60s?

5 Who did Bolton beat 3-2 in the thrilling 1995 play-off Final, having trailed 2-0 at one stage?

6 Who hit Blackburn Rover's hat-trick in the 1995-96 European Cup?

7 Which team won the 1969 UEFA Cup?

8 Which two players called Woods did Graeme Souness bring in from England to Rangers?

9 Who beat Rangers 2-1 in the 1989-90 Scottish League Cup Final?

10 What colour are Fulham's home shorts?

11 Roy Houghton scored in a League Cup Final for which club?

12 David May moved from Blackburn Rovers to which club for £1.25 million in May 1994?

13 Which Barcelona player was European Footballer of the Year in 1960?

14 Which manager told a post-match press conference "It's a game of two halves, and we were crap in both of them"

15 Who was the English trainer of Ajax who led them to their first Dutch Championship in 1918?

Answers to page 224

1 Celtic, **2** Fulham, **3** Manchester Utd, **4** Ted Fenton, **5** 1960s, **6** Croatian, **7** Harry Redknapp, **8** Munich 1860, **9** Tottenham Hotspur, **10** Alvin Martin, **11** David Kelly, **12** Javier Margas, **13** Newcastle Utd, **14** Trevor Brooking, **15** Arsenal.

QUIZ 145

Answers on page 229

1 What is the highest position Bristol City have ever achieved in the League?

2 Who was manager of Stockport at the start of the 1996-1997 season?

3 How many teams entered the first FA Cup tournament?

4 In which decade was Ken Bates born?

5 Who beat Rangers 2-1 in the 1965-1966 Scottish League Cup Final?

6 Which team won the 1978 UEFA Cup?

7 Name the scorer of the goal that took the FA Cup to Coventry for the first time in 1987?

8 Brighton conceded four penalties in a game which had a record five spot-kicks. Who were their opponents, who missed three of the four?

9 Which country did Joe Kinnear play for?

10 What is the first name of Joachim of Leicester City and Aston Villa?

11 Who won a Scottish FA Cup medal for Rangers against Celtic and then for Celtic against Rangers?

12 Which player scored 29 League goals for Wimbledon in 1983-1984?

13 Which country, outside Britain, is the oldest footballing nation?

14 In USA '94 which country scored most goals in the group games yet still went out?

15 Who took over as coach of Tottenham Hotspur after the departure of Gerry Francis?

Answers to page 229

1 Bolton Wanderers, **2** Arsenal, **3** Five, **4** Liverpool, **5** 1973-74, **6** Rene Van Der Kerkhof, **7** 31, **8** Linfield, **9** 7 days, **10** Derby County, **11** Paris St Germain, **12** Southampton, **13** Parma, **14** Terry Venables, **15** Mexico.

QUIZ 146

Answers on page 230

1 What was John Sheridan's first League club?

2 Which Jeff of Arsenal won his only England cap against Yugoslavia in 1972?

3 Which Conference League side was not promoted to the Football League in 1996 because their ground wasn't up to the required standards?

4 Which club did David Seaman leave to join QPR?

5 In what year were Arsenal relegated for the first time?

6 Which England player received a red card in the 1986 Mexico World Cup?

7 What is the highest position Brentford have ever achieved in the League?

8 Who was Sunderland's goalkeeper in their FA Cup Final against Leeds Utd in 1973?

9 Which team have Bobby Gould, Dave Basset and Joe Kinnear all managed?

10 David Beckham scored from the halfway line in the opening game of the 1997-98 season - Which keeper did he beat?

11 Who did Sheffield Wednesday buy from Molde in his native Norway for £800,000?

12 What is Gary Mabutt's middle name?

13 Who beat Liverpool 2-1 in the 1971 FA Cup Final?

14 What is Hereford Utd's nickname?

15 In which decade did Coventry City first win the FA Cup?

Answers to page 230

1 Terry Neill, **2** Tony Adams, **3** 1930, **4** 1935, **5** Alan Shearer, **6** Alan Smith, **7** Bertie Mee, **8** David O'Leary, **9** David Seaman, **10** Eddie Kelly, **11** Fiorentina, **12** He didn't play for anybody else, **13** Ian Wright, **14** Joe Mercer, **15** Manchester Utd.

QUIZ 147

Answers on page 227

1 Which club was once known as Christ Church FC

2 Bobby Gould scored a League Cup Final goal for which club?

3 How many championships did Sir Matt Busby win for Manchester Utd?

4 In which city was Mark Hately born?

5 When did Sunderland appear in the Cup Winners Cup competition?

6 In the 1978 World Cup Final, which Dutchman wore a cast on his arm?

7 How many games were their in Euro '96?

8 Which team has represented Northern Ireland in the European Cup the most times?

9 How long was Tim Ward manager of Exeter for?

10 Where did Charlie George go when he left Arsenal?

11 Which club did Ray Wilkins leave to join Rangers?

12 Who beat Manchester Utd 1-0 in the 1976 FA Cup Final?

13 Faustino Asprilla scored the winning goal against AC Milan to end a record 58 match unbeaten run. Who was he playing for?

14 Who succeeded Tommy Docherty as manager of QPR in 1980?

15 Which country were top of the Republic of Ireland's Group in USA 1994?

Answers to page 227

1 Runners-up Division 1, (1906-07), **2** Dave Jones, **3** 15, **4** 1930s, **5** Celtic, **6** PSV Eindhoven, **7** Keith Houchen, **8** Crystal Palace, **9** The Republic of Ireland, **10** Julian, **11** Alfie Conn, **12** Alan Cork, **13** Argentina, **14** Russia, **15** Christian Gross.

ARSENAL 5

Answers on page 228

1 Which Arsenal and Tottenham Hotspur manager was also team boss of Northern Ireland in 1996?

2 Who was Arsenal's youngest ever captain when he took over the arm band in 1988?

3 What year did Arsenal first win the FA Cup?

4 Arsenal became the second English side to win the First Division title in three successive years, which year did they complete this treble?

5 Which Southampton player became the youngest to score a First Division hat-trick v Arsenal on April 9, 1988?

6 Which Arsenal player was booked for the first time in his career in the 1993 FA Cup Final replay?

7 Which Arsenal boss said "I hadn't planned to be a football manager"

8 Which Arsenal central defender played 558 times for the club between 1975 and 1993?

9 Who played every League game in his first season with the club as Arsenal won the 1990-1991 title?

10 Who came on as a substitute for Arsenal in the 1971 FA Cup Final?

11 Stefan Schwarz left Arsenal for which club?

12 Whch club did Bob Wilson play for after leaving Arsenal?

13 Who was Arsenal's top scorer for six consecutive seasons?

14 Name the Arsenal captain, 1950 footballer of the year, who briefly managed England for a short and glorious period in 1974, between Sir Alf Ramsey and Don Revie?

15 Which team were beaten 3-2 by Arsenal in the 1979 FA Cup Final?

Answers to page 228

1 Leeds Utd, **2** Blockley, **3** Stevenage, **4** Birmingham City, **5** 1913, **6** Ray Wilkins, **7** 5th Division 1, (1935-36), **8** Jim Montgomery, **9** Wimbledon, **10** Neil Sullivan, **11** Petter Rudi, **12** Vincent, **13** Arsenal, **14** United, **15** 1980s.

SUNDERLAND

Answers on page 233

1 Who resigned as Sunderland manager in 1987 as they dropped into Division Three?

2 Who was the regular keeper for Sunderland in their 1990-1991 relegation season?

3 In which decade did Sunderland first win the Championship?

4 Which team was beaten 1-0 by Sunderland in the 1973 FA Cup Final?

5 Who succeeded Johnny Cochrane as manager of Sunderland in 1939?

6 In which decade did Sunderland first win the FA Cup?

7 Which French keeper joined Sunderland in 1996?

8 When did Sunderland appear in the Cup Winners Cup competition?

9 Who beat Sunderland 2-0 in the 1992 FA Cup Final?

10 What is the highest position Sunderland have ever achieved in the League?

11 Who was caretaker manager of Sunderland when he took them to the 1992 FA Cup Final?

12 Who moved to Sunderland from Millwall in 1996 to set a club record for a transfer fee paid?

13 Who moved from Sunderland to Crystal Palace for £1.5 million in 1991?

14 Which Mick became boss of Sunderland in 1993?

15 Sunderland recorded a 7-1 League Cup win over which club in September 1962?

Answers to page 233

1 Arsenal, **2** Borussia Dortmund, **3** 7, **4** Airdrieonians, **5** Preston, **6** Bristol Rovers, **7** Sweden, **8** European Championship 1988, **9** Ian Wright, **10** Austria, **11** West Germany, **12** Ross County, **13** G Milne, **14** Stanley Matthews, **15** Geoff Thomas.

QUIZ 148

Answers on page 234

1 Which was Daniel Amokachi's first English club?

2 In which decade was Johnny Haynes born?

3 Who was sacked in November 1994 by cardiff City then reappointed in march 1995?

4 Vinny Samways first played in an FA Cup Final team for which team?

5 Which soccer team does comedian Eddie Izzard support?

6 Who was the Norwegian agent in the George Graham 'bung' case?

7 Chris Kiwoyma has been leading scorer with which club?

8 Which of the Laudrup brothers did not play when denmark won the European Championship?

9 At which club did Gavin Peacock make his League debut?

10 Which club did Bobby Charlton manage between 1973 and 1975?

11 Who, in December 1995, got sent off playing for Coventry City on his return to his former club Aston Villa?

12 In which decade was Duncan Edwards born?

13 At which Club did Pat Nevin make his Scottish League debut?

14 Who was the first player to miss an FA Cup Final penalty?

15 Which year was the first-ever all Mersyside League Cup final?

Answers to page 234

1 1st Division 1, **2** 5th Division 2, (1930-31), **3** 2nd Division 1, (1955-56), **4** 22nd Division1, (1974-75), **5** Tommy Smith, **6** Leeds Utd, **7** Tanju Colak, **8** Arsenal, **9** Wimbledon, **10** No, second round, **11** Derek Hatton, **12** Millwall, **13** First league substitue, **14** Barry Fry, **15** Alan Shearer.

QUIZ 149

Answers on page 231

1 Martin Hayes scored in a League Cup Final for which club?

2 Which team beat Liverpool in the Euro Cup Winners' Cup in a 1960s Final?

3 How many goals did Andy Gray score for Scotland?

4 Which team were beaten 2-1 by Rangers in the 1992 Scottish FA Cup Final?

5 With whom did Bobby Charlton play his last League match?

6 Luton Town player Joe Payne scored 10 goals in a match in April 1936. Who were the opponents?

7 In which country was Richard Gough born?

8 Kenny Samson played his last England game in which tournament?

9 Who scored the last England goal for Graham Taylor?

10 Who did West Germany beat in the semi-finals of the 1954 World Cup?

11 Which country did Paul Breitner play for?

12 W Herd made a record 124 appearances, for which Scottish club between 1995-98?

13 Who succeeded Joe Mercer as manager of Coventry City in 1981?

14 Which England player was known as 'The Wizard of Dribble'?

15 Who did Bill Dodgin Jnr succeed as manager at Fulham?

Answers to page 231

1 Lawrie McMenemy, **2** Tony Norman, **3** 1890s, **4** Leeds Utd, **5** William Murray, **6** 1930s, **7** Lionel Perez, **8** 1973-74, **9** Liverpool, **10** 1st Division 1, **11** Malcolm Crosby, **12** Alex Rae, **13** Marco Gabbiadini, **14** Buxton, **15** Oldham Athletic.

QUIZ 150

Answers on page 232

1 What is the highest position Ipswich Town have ever achieved in the League?

2 What is the highest position Port Vale have ever achieved in the League?

3 What is the highest position Blackpool have ever achieved in the League?

4 What is the highest position Carlisle Utd have ever achieved in the League?

5 Who had a 1980 book titled I Did It The Hard Way?

6 Howard Wilkinson followed Billy Bremner as boss of which club?

7 Which Galatasaray player won the 1987-1988 Golden Boot award?

8 Gus Caesar played in a League Cup Final for which club?

9 John Scales first played in an FA Cup Final for which team?

10 In 1982, did England progress to the quarter-finals of the World Cup?

11 Who said; "I can cope with being thrown out of the Labour Party, but I can't cope with Liverpool beating Everton 4-1"?

12 Which London soccer team are known as the Lions?

13 What first went to Keith Peacock on the first day of the 1965-1966 season?

14 Who was replaced by Trevor Francis as boss of Birmingham City?

15 Who has scored the most goals in the English Premiership since it began?

Answers to page 232

1 Everton, **2** 1930s, **3** Eddie May, **4** Tottenham Hotspur, **5** Crystal Palace, **6** Rune Hauge, **7** Ipswich Town, **8** Michael, **9** QPR, **10** Preston North End., **11** Kevin Richardson, **12** 1930s, **13** Clyde, **14** John Aldridge, **15** 1984.

QUIZ 151

Answers on page 237

1 Which player scored 42 League goals for West Ham Utd in 1929-1930?

2 How many years was Bruce Grobbelaar at Liverpool?

3 Bryan Robson's last England game was against which country?

4 Larry Lloyd moved from Liverpool to which club for £240.000 in August 1974?

5 Steve Archibald moved from Tottenham Hotspur to which club for £1.5m in July 1984?

6 Terry Phelan moved from Wimbledon to which club for £2.5m in September 1992?

7 Scott Minto moved from Charlton Athletic to which club for £775.000 in May 1994?

8 Who said of Birmingham City "You lose some, you draw some."?

9 Which club's ground is by the River Severn?

10 Tranmere Rovers recorded a 5-1 League Cup win over which club in September 1993?

11 Which fullback captained England in the World Cup in Spain?

12 Which team lost 1-0 to Liverpool in the 1989 FA Charity Shield?

13 Which soccer team does politician Roy Hattersley support?

14 A Brett Angell goal took which team to the Coca-Cola Cup semi-final in 1997?

15 Who was the Brazilian top scorer in the 1994 World Cup tournament?

Answers to page 237

1 Dariusz Dziekanowski, **2** Frank Haffey, **3** Jimmy McGrory, **4** Mo Johnston, **5** Tommy Gemmell and Steve Chalmers, **6** 20, **7** Billy McNeill, **8** Dixie Dean, **9** Frank McAvennie, **10** Jimmy McGrory, **11** Mo Johnston (He joined Rangers), **12** Twice, **13** Aberdeen, **14** Billy McNeill, **15** Dundee.

LEEDS UTD 2

Answers on page 238

1 In which decade did Leeds first win the FA Cup?

2 Which club did Gary Sprake join when he left Leeds?

3 Which England international player won Championship medals with Leeds and Blackburn Rovers in the 1990s?

4 How hit a Charity Shield hat-trick for Leeds in 1992?

5 Who scored Liverpool's extra time winner against Leeds in 1965?

6 Leeds were formed following the demise of which team?

7 Where was the Chelsea v Leeds replayed FA Cup final held?

8 Leeds recorded a 4-0 League Cup win over which club in October 1987?

9 In which year did the song *Leeds United* hit the charts?

10 David Batty moved from Leeds to which club for £2.7m in October 1993?

11 Who was in goal for Leeds in the 1972 and 1973 FA Cup Finals?

12 Ian Snodin moved from Leeds to which club for £850,000 in January 1987?

13 Who made 629 league appearances for Leeds between 1953-1973?

14 Which club did Gary McAllister leave to join Leeds?

15 Which club did Leeds pay £4.5m to for Thomas Brolin in November 1995?

Answers to page 238

1 Naylor, **2** St Petersburg, **3** John Jenson, **4** Sheffield Wednesday, **5** Jurgen Sommer, **6** Argentina Columbia and Spain, **7** Dean Saunders, **8** Manchester Utd, **9** Dave Bassett, **10** 1930s, **11** Celtic, **12** Dennis Bergkamp, **13** David Seaman, **14** Newcastle Utd, **15** 1950.

CELTIC 2

Answers on page 235

1 Which Polish player hit 4 goals for Celtic v Partizan Belgrade in 1989?

2 Which Celtic goalkeeper conceded nine goals in an international match?

3 Who is Celtic's all time top goal scorer?

4 Who said "For a while I did unite Rangers and Celtic fans.There were people in both camps who hated me"?

5 Who scored the goals for Celtic in their 2-1 victory over Internazionale Milan in 1967?

6 How old was Kenny Dalglish when he first played for Celtic?

7 Who retired, as a player in 1975 following the Celtic v Airdrie Scottish Cup Final?

8 Which Celtic player scored a hat-trick in the 1972 Scottish FA Cup Final?

9 Who moved from West Ham Utd to Celtic for £1.5 million in 1992?

10 Who has scored most League goals for Celtic?

11 Which new 'signing' was paraded by Celtic before the Scottish FA Cup Final, only for the player to change his mind and join another club?

12 After winning the Scottish League Cup five years in a row from 1966-1970 how many times did Celtic win the trophy in the following 25 years?

13 Who beat Celtic 3-1 in the 1970 Scottish FA Cup Final?

14 Who followed David Hay as Celtic manager?

15 Who did Celtic beat 5-3 in the 1967-68 Scottish League Cup Final?

Answers to page 235

1 Vic Watson, **2** 13, **3** Turkey, **4** Coventry City, **5** Barcelona, **6** Manchester City, **7** Chelsea, **8** Jasper Carrott, **9** Shrewsbury Town, **10** Oxford Utd, **11** Mick Mills, **12** Arsenal, **13** Sheffield Wednesday, **14** Stockport County, **15** Romario.

QUIZ 152

Answers on page 236

1 Which Tony was Port Vale's top league scorer in 1995-1996?

2 In which Russian city do Zenit play their home matches?

3 Which Arsenal midfielder had the middle name Faxe?

4 Which club did Nigel Worthington leave to join Leeds Utd?

5 Who was the regular keeper in QPR's 1995-96 relegation season?

6 For which three countries did Alfredo di Stefano play international football?

7 Who moved from Derby County to Liverpool in July 1991 to set a club record for a transfer fee received?

8 Which Premiership club has the largest seating capacity?

9 Which manager is known as Harry even though that's not his name?

10 In which decade was Ron Atkinson born?

11 Who did Liverpool meet in the first round of the 1997-1998 UEFA Cup?

12 Which Arsenal player in the 97-1998 season missed an away match in Greece because of his fear of flying?

13 Who was the only ever-present league player for Arsenal in 1995-1996?

14 Which club was Malcolm MacDonald with when he was First Division leading scorer?

15 In what year did Portsmouth last win the Championship?

Answers to page 236

1 1970s, **2** Birmingham City, **3** David Batty, **4** Eric Cantona, **5** Ian St John, **6** Leeds City, **7** Old Trafford, **8** York City, **9** 1972, **10** Blackburn Rovers, **11** David Harvey, **12** Everton, **13** Jack Charlton, **14** Leicester City, **15** Parma.

QUIZ 153

Answers on page 241

1 Where was the 1989 European Cup Winners' Cup Final held?

2 Which club was once known as St Domingo FC?

3 Which English club did Keegan play against in a European Cup Final?

4 Who plays at home at Portman Road?

5 Paul Bracewell was at which club when he made his international debut?

6 Which was Paul Bracewell's first League club?

7 Which Everton player was fouled when Kevin Moran got his 1985 FA Cup Final marching orders?

8 Which team finally landed the League Cup in 1985 in their third Wembley Final?

9 Plymouth Argyle takes its name from the Argyle and Sutherland Highlanders - true or false?

10 From which Spanish club did Everton aquire French international striker Mickael Medar?

11 Who scored 4 goals in a game for Cardiff against Ireland in April 1962?

12 Which manager said, "Napoleon wanted his generals to be lucky. I don't think he would have wanted me"?

13 Conroy and Ritchie scored Euro goals in the same 1970s game for which club?

14 Pat Nevin and Kevin Sheedy were in the same side at which club?

15 Which club had 19 points deducted in 1968 for making illegal payments to players?

Answers to page 241

1 Millwall, **2** Ian Rush, **3** Aberdeen, **4** Juventus, **5** Doncaster Rovers, **6** Lord Justce Taylor, **7** 1920s, **8** Huddersfield Town, **9** Nets in the goals, **10** Andy Townsend, **11** Sweden, **12** Coventry City, **13** The Republic of Ireland, **14** Dudu Georgescu, **15** Nottingham Forest.

QUIZ 154

Answers on page 242

1 David Currie moved from Barnsley to which club for £750.000 in January 1990?

2 John Beresford moved from Barnsley to which club for £300.000 in March 1989?

3 Mick McCarthy moved from Barnsley to which club for £200.000 in December 1983?

4 Who lost 1-0 to Bayern Munich after extra time in the 1967 Cup-Winners' Cup Final?

5 Where was Welsh international Mark Crossley born?

6 Which two Scottish clubs were involved in Colin Stein's £100,000 transfer?

7 Who started his managerial career at Cambridge United and finished with Coventry City?

8 Which club finished third in 1993 in the Premier League but with a 61-65 goal difference?

9 Neill Webb first played in an FA Cup Final for which team?

10 Which Wimbledon player was sent off in 1995 after tangling with Ruud Gullit?

11 In which decade was Trevor Francis born?

12 Which John first became boss of Millwall in 1986?

13 Who won the 1988 European Championship, beating the USSR 2-0 in the final?

14 Which city do the German club team with 1860 in their name come from?

15 Which team were beaten 1-0 by Celtic in the 1989 Scottish FA Cup Final?

Answers to page 242

1 Paul Peschisolido, **2** 46, **3** Glossop, **4** Mackay, **5** 61, **6** Jasper Carrott, **7** Stan Cullis, **8** 6th Division 1 (1955-56), **9** Jim Smith, **10** Stan Cullis, **11** Auto Windscreen Shield, **12** Kenny Burns, **13** Stoke City, **14** Barry Fry, **15** Kevin Francis.

QUIZ 155

Answers on page 239

1 Mick McCarrthy followed Bruce Rioch as boss of which club?

2 "His goals do the talking, but so far he has spoken very much"? Who was the Juventus president talking about?

3 Who beat Celtic 9-8 in the 1990 Scottish FA Cup Final on penalties?

4 At which Italian club did Michel Platini end his career?

5 Which club did Comedian Charlie Williams play for in the 1950s?

6 Who said "The years of patching up grounds...must be over"?

7 In which decade was Jimmy Hill born?

8 Which club had a fanzine called *A Slice of Kilmer Pie*?

9 In 1906 AC Milan became the first club in Italy to install what at their ground?

10 Who said on revealing his new haircut in 1994 at the World Cup Finals, "I asked for a Valderrama and they gave me a Val Doonican"?

11 In which city was the 1994 Cup Winners' Cup final between Arsenal and Parma played?

12 Brian Kilcline was skipper of which FA Cup winning club?

13 Which country did Mick robinson play for?

14 Which Dinamo Bucharest player won the 1974-75 Golden Boot award?

15 Carl Tiler moved from Barnsley to which club for £1.4m in May 1991?

Answers to page 239

1 Berne, **2** Everton, **3** Nottingham Forest, **4** Ipswich Town, **5** Everton, **6** Stoke City, **7** Peter Reid, **8** Norwich City, **9** False, **10** Deportivo La Coruna, **11** Mel Charles, **12** Graham Taylor, **13** Stoke City, **14** Everton, **15** Peterborough.

BIRMINGHAM

Answers on page 240

1 Birmingham City's Managing Director Karen Brady is married to which former Blues player?

2 In the 1995-96 season Birmingham used a record number of players for one season - How many?

3 Birmingham City player Jimmy Windridge scored 5 goals in a match in January 1915. Who were the opponents?

4 Which Dave became boss of Birmingham City in 1989?

5 How many players did Barry Fry sign during his three-year stay at Birmingham City?

6 Who said of Birmingham City, "You lose some, you draw some"?

7 Who was Birmingham City boss between 1965 and 1970?

8 What is the highest position Birmingham City have ever achieved in the League?

9 Who was boss of Birmingham from 1978-1982?

10 Who succeeded Joe Mallett as manager of Birmingham City?

11 Name the trophy won by Birmingham City in 1991?

12 Name the Glaswegian hardman who started at Birmingham City but really made his name under Brian Clough at Nottingham Forest in the late 70s?

13 Jimmy Greenhoff moved from Birmingham City to which club for £100.000 in August 1969?

14 Who was replaced by Trevor Francis as boss of Birmingham City?

15 Who moved from Stockport County to Birmingham City for £800,000 in January 1995?

Answers to page 240

1 Nottingham Forest, **2** Portsmouth, **3** Manchester City, **4** Rangers, **5** Barnsley, **6** Rangers and Hibs, **7** Ron Atkinson, **8** Norwich City, **9** Manchester Utd, **10** Vinnie Jones, **11** 1950s, **12** Docherty, **13** Holland, **14** Munich, **15** Rangers.

RANGERS 2

Answers on page 245

1 Who did Rangers beat 4-1 in the 1981 Scottish FA Cup Final replay?

2 Who did Rangers beat 3-2 in the 1979 Scottish FA Cup Final 2nd replay?

3 Which club did Ray Wilkins leave to join Rangers?

4 When did Rangers first achieve the treble?

5 Who did Rangers beat 2-1 in the 1993 Scottish FA Cup Final?

6 Which Rangers star announced in March 1998 that he would be joining Chelsea at the end of the season?

7 Who did Rangers beat 2-1 in the 1982 Scottish League Cup Final?

8 Who made record 496 appearances for Rangers between 1962-1978?

9 Jim Baxter joined Rangers from which club?

10 What season did Aberdeen beat Rangers and Celtic in major Cup Finals?

11 Who did Rangers beat 4-0 in the 1947 Scottish League Cup Final?

12 Which two players called Woods did Graeme Souness bring in from England to Rangers?

13 Who did Rangers beat 1-0 in the 1985 Scottish League Cup Final?

14 Who did Rangers beat 2-0 in the 1961 Scottish League Cup Final?

15 Who did Rangers beat 2-0 in the 1949 Scottish League Cup Final?

Answers to page 245

1 QPR, **2** Nottingham Forest, **3** Newport, **4** Cambridge Utd, **5** Elland Road, **6** Everton, **7** Wales, **8** Liverpool, **9** Bristol Rovers, **10** Jack Charlton, **11** QPR Manchester City, **12** Tottenham Hotspur, **13** Tottenham Hotspur, **14** Aldershot, **15** The Villains.

QUIZ 156

Answers on page 246

1 Which 46-year-old physiotherapist became Arsenal manager?

2 What colour goes with black on Barnet's home shirts?

3 Which club was once known as Bristol South End?

4 Which Spanish side did Bobby Robson become boss of in 1996?

5 Which club had a fanzine called When Skies Are Grey?

6 With which soccer club did comedian Charlie Williams have trials with?

7 Which club has Doug Ellis been chairman of?

8 Brian Clough won his first championship as manager of which club?

9 Which country inflicted England's first ever defeat at Wembley?

10 Which soccer team does *Fever Pitch* author Nick Hornby support?

11 Which club used to play at Beeston Cricket Ground?

12 Kevin Gallacher moved from Coventry City to which club for £1.5m in March 1993?

13 Who was born on September 29 1939 at Hill O'Beath, Fife?

14 Which Russell has been boss of Bristol City and Cardiff City?

15 *Just Like My Dreams*: was part of the title of which managers book?

Answers to page 246

1 Pele, **2** Grimsby Town, **3** Bob Paisley, **4** Fullback, **5** Merthyr Tydfil, **6** Webb, **7** Fulham, **8** Joe Mercer, **9** England, **10** Aston Villa, **11** Terry Fenwick, **12** Steve Heighway, **13** 33, **14** 3, **15** Stoke City.

QUIZ 157

Answers on page 243

1 Andy Tillson moved from Grimsby Town to which club for £500.000 in December 1990?

2 Middlesborough player Andy Wilson scored 5 goals in a match in October 1923. Who were the opponents?

3 Manchester City player George Smith scored 5 goals in a match in June 1947. Who were the opponents?

4 What was the first League club that Ron Atkinson managed?

5 The first home England international since 1966 to be played away from Wembley was in 1995 v Sweden. Where was it played?

6 Paul Wilkinson moved from Grimsby Town to which club for £300.000 in August 1985?

7 Which country did Malcolm Page play for?

8 Who were the opponents on the day that Dalglish's Blackburn Rovers won the Premiership?

9 Liverpool player John Evans scored 5 goals in a match in September 1954. Who were the opponents?

10 Which Middlesborough boss said "we are on the crest of a slump" days before resigning?

11 Rodney Marsh was capped while playing for which two clubs?

12 Keith Burkinshaw followed Ossie Ardiles as manager of which club?

13 Which London side became the the first club to win the League Cup twice?

14 Which League club went out of business in March 1992?

15 What is Aston Villas nickname?

Answers to page 243

1 Dundee Utd, **2** Hibernian, **3** Paris St Germain, **4** 1948-49, **5** Aberdeen, **6** Brian Laudrop, **7** Dundee Utd, **8** John Greig, **9** Raith Rovers, **10** 1989-90, **11** Aberdeen, **12** Chris and Neil, **13** Dundee Utd, **14** Kilmarnock, **15** Raith Rovers.

QUIZ 158

Answers on page 244

1 Which legendary soccer player was nicknamed "The Black Pearl"?

2 Which soccer team does politician Norman Lamont support?

3 Who was manager of the year in 1976,1977,1980,1982 and 1983?

4 What position did Alf Ramsey play for England?

5 Southend Utd player Jim Shankly scored 5 goals in a match in March 1930. Who were the opponents?

6 Which Dave became boss of Brentford in May 1993?

7 At which club did Cliff Jones finish his playing career?

8 Who played for Arsenal and Everton and managed Aston Villa, Manchester City and England?

9 Which country did Mark Chamberlain play for?

10 Nigel Callaghan moved from Derby County to which club for £525.000 in February 1989?

11 Which Tottenham player was jailed for four months in September 1991 for drink-driving offences?

12 "This is the best amateur footballer I've seen," was Bob Paisley's assessment of which winger?

13 How old was Charles Buchan when he went to Arsenal?

14 How many internationals did Jimmy Greaves play after the 1966 World Cup?

15 Alan Hudson and Geoff Hurst both played for which Midlands team?

Answers to page 244

1 Bertie Mee, **2** Amber, **3** Bristol City, **4** Barcelona, **5** Everton, **6** Doncaster Rovers, **7** Aston Villa, **8** Derby County, **9** Hungary, **10** Arsenal, **11** Notts County, **12** Blackburn Rovers, **13** Jim Baxter, **14** Osman, **15** John Lyall.

QUIZ 159

Answers on page 249

1 Which soccer club was fined £105,000 in 1990 for making irregular payments to players?

2 November 1997 he had the vote of confidence from the board, February 1998, Frank Clark was sacked - who took his place as manager of Manchester City?

3 Which team won the 1988-89 Football League Championship with a 2-0 win in their final match against Liverpool?

4 Which Premier manager was sacked after he admitted taking bungs?

5 Who beat Nottingham Forest 2-1 in the 1991 FA Cup Final?

6 Paul Rideout and Dale Gordon were in the same team at which club?

7 What was John Scale's first League club?

8 Denis Smith followed Brian Horton as boss of which club?

9 Who lost 4-0 to AC Milan in the Final of the 1994 European Cup?

10 Which country did Graham Rix go to play football in?

11 Who was Fred Binney playing for when he was the League's leading scorer in 1972-73?

12 Which government minister handed the 1997-1998 Coca-Cola Cup to Chelsea's player/manager Gianluca Vialli?

13 Eric Skeels set a league appearance record at which club?

14 Laurie Cunningham first played in an FA Cup Final for which team?

15 Which club has a fanzine called Sing When We're Fishing?

Answers to page 249

1 Clive Allen (Spurs), **2** Keith Houchen, **3** Shrewsbury Town, **4** 1980s, **5** Dion Dublin, **6** Kevin Richardson, **7** Sunderland, **8** Arsenal, **9** Dion Dublin, **10** Leeds Utd, **11** Tottenham Hotspur, **12** Assistant manager, **13** Division 1 (6th) 1969-70, **14** Liverpool, **15** Watford.

• LIVERPOOL 8 •

Answers on page 250

1 Which club did Ray Houghton leave to join Liverpool?

2 Liverpool paid £600,000 to Crewe in October 1991 for which defender?

3 Which nickname does Darren Anderton share with Liverpool's Steve McManaman?

4 Which former Liverpool team-mate was assistant manager at Newcastle Utd when Kenny Dalglish arrived?

5 In what decade did Liverpool first win the Championship?

6 How many championship medals did Phil Neal win with Liverpool?

7 Steve Nicol joined Liverpool for £300,000 in 1981 from which club?

8 Which Liverpool manager signed Dalglish?

9 Who did Liverpool meet in the first round of the 1997-1998 UEFA Cup?

10 Who said; "I can cope with being thrown out of the Labour Party, but I can't cope with Liverpool beating Everton 4-1"?

11 Which player scored the first goal in the 1986 Liverpool V Everton FA Cup Final?

12 Which Liverpool player scored from a free-kick to beat Blackburn Rovers in the last game of the 1994-1995 season?

13 Which ex-Liverpool player has managed Wales?

14 Which manager brought Ian Rush back to Liverpool from Juventus?

15 Who scored a first-half hat-trick for Liverpool against Newcastle in Ruud Gullits first game in charge?

Answers to page 250

1 Manchester Utd, **2** Manchester Utd, **3** Dean Saunders, **4** Eyal Berkovic hit John Moncur (both West Ham players), **5** West Brom, **6** Johnny Haynes, **7** Coventry City, **8** Leeds Utd, **9** Twice, **10** Manchester City, **11** Nottingham Forest, **12** Marseille, **13** Torquay Utd, **14** 200.000, **15** Cardiff City.

COVENTRY 1

Answers on page 247

1 Who scored within 120 seconds of the 1987 Tottenham Hotspur v Coventry City FA Cup Final?

2 Name the scorer of the goal that took the FA Cup to Coventry for the first time in 1987?

3 Which club did Coventry sign Steve Ogrizovic from?

4 In which decade did Coventry City first win the FA Cup?

5 Who scored a hat-trick for Coventry on the opening day of the 1997-98 season at home against Chelsea?

6 Who, in December 1995, got sent off playing for Coventry City on his return to his former club Aston Villa?

7 Coventry City recorded a 5-0 League Cup win over which club in January 1990?

8 Jeoff Blockley moved from Coventry City to which club for £200.000 in October 1972?

9 In 1996-97 which Coventry City player was dismissed in successive League games?

10 Noel Whelan moved to Coventry for £2m in December 1995 - Which club did he leave?

11 Which team were beaten 3-2 by Coventry in the 1987 FA Cup Final?

12 When Gordon Strachan refused to leave the pitch during a reserve match what was he with Coventry City?

13 What is the highest position Coventry City have ever achieved in the League?

14 Phil Babb moved from Coventry City to which club for £3.75m in August 1994?

15 Coventry City recorded a 5-0 League Cup win over which club in December 1980?

Answers to page 247

1 Chelsea, **2** Joe Royle, **3** Arsenal, **4** George Graham (Arsenal), **5** Tottenham Hotspur, **6** Rangers, **7** Bristol Rovers, **8** Oxford Utd, **9** Barcelona, **10** France, **11** Exeter City, **12** Home Secretary Jack Straw, **13** Stoke City, **14** Wimbledon, **15** Grimsby.

QUIZ 160

Answers on page 248

1 Which club did Stephen Pears leave to join Middlesborough?

2 Gary Bailey played in an FA Cup Final for which team?

3 Who was on the spot for Aston Villa v Manchester Utd in the 1994 League Cup Final?

4 Who hit whom during the 1997-1998 season Premiership match between Chelsea and West Ham Utd ?

5 Which club did Bryan Robson play for before joining Manchester Utd?

6 Who was England's 1962 World Cup captain?

7 Who beat Tottenham Hotspur 3-2 in the 1987 FA Cup Final?

8 Who beat Arsenal 1-0 in the 1972 FA Cup Final?

9 After winning the Scottish League Cup five years in a row from 1966-1970 how many times did Celtic win the trophy in the following 25 years?

10 Who beat Leicester City 1-0 in the 1969 FA Cup Final?

11 Who beat Luton Town 2-1 in the 1959 FA Cup Final?

12 Who lost 5-3 on penalties to red Star Belgrade in the 1991 European Cup Final?

13 Who were the first club to win promotion on a penalty shoot out?

14 What was the estimated crowd at the first Wembley FA Cup Final?

15 Which is the only non-English club to have won the FA Cup?

Answers to page 248

1 Oxford Utd, **2** Rob Jones, **3** Shaggy, **4** Terry McDermott, **5** 1900s, **6** 8, **7** Ayr Utd, **8** Bob Paisley, **9** Celtic, **10** Derek Hatton, **11** Gary Lineker, **12** Jamie Redknapp, **13** John Toshack, **14** Kenny Dalglish, **15** Michael Owen.

QUIZ 161

Answers on page 253

1 From 1933 to 1956 Jimmy Seed was boss of which club?

2 Who was the post war player to score in every round of the FA Cup?

3 Who was the first Celtic manager sacked by Fergus McCann?

4 Who was manager of the West German World Cup winners in 1954?

5 Which club did Phil Neal leave to join Steve Coppell at Manchester City?

6 In 1983-1984, who resigned as Swansea City boss, returned and even played and was sacked in the same season?

7 Billy McNeill followed John Benson as manager of which club?

8 Who was Frankie Bunn playing for when he hit a record six in a League Cup game?

9 In 1980 Steve Murray was manager of Forfar for how long?

10 Who lost 3-0 to Dynamo Kiev in the 1986 Cup-Winners' Cup Final?

11 Brian Clough's last League game as Forest boss was against who?

12 In which year was Eric Cantona born?

13 John Wark hit a penalty hat-trick against which European team?

14 Arsenal became the second English side to win the First Division title in three successive years, which year did they complete this treble?

15 Who was the first Colombian striker to play in English soccer?

Answers to page 253

1 Barcelona, **2** Napoli, **3** Kevin Richardson, **4** 1970s, **5** Mo Johnston, **6** Lev Yashin, **7** Don Revie, **8** 16, **9** Twice, **10** One, **11** Marcel Desailly, **12** Manchester City, **13** Never, **14** Dennis Bergkamp, **15** Three.

QUIZ 162

Answers on page 254

1 Who was the commentator who delivered the immortal words at a World Cup Final: "They think it's all over. . . "?

2 Which other English club, apart from Manchester Utd and Arsenal have also achieved a major trophy-winning double?

3 Which Spanish side did Howard Kendall manage?

4 In which year did goalkeepers have to wear different coloured shirts from their team mates?

5 Steve Clarke and Clive Wilson were in the same side at which club?

6 What colour are Barnsley's home shorts?

7 Which player scored 41 League goals for Ipswich Town in 1956-1957?

8 Who had an answerphone message in 1996 that went," Kristine's out shopping as usual. I'm down the Job Centre looking for employment"?

9 What is Ian Wright's middle name?

10 Who, at 18, became Chelsea's youngest ever captain in 1975?

11 Who bought Andy Hinchcliffe from Everton for £3.million?

12 Which soccer team does West Ham MP and Sports Minister Tony Banks support?

13 Which club did Bob Wilson play for after leaving Arsenal?

14 Which country hosted the World Cup in the wake of a tragic earthquake?

15 Who lost 2-1 to Barcelona in the 1982 Cup-Winners' Cup Final?

Answers to page 254

1 Division 1 (3rd 1985-86), **2** John Bond and Ken Brown, **3** Oldham Athletic, **4** Trevor Sinclair, **5** Australia, **6** Each goal was scored against a different goalkeeper. (The first against Martin Thomas, then outfied substitute Chris Hepworth and finally Peter Beardsley), **7** John Lyall, **8** Paul Allen, **9** Vic Watson, **10** Because he had been convicted of a drink-driving offence, **11** Emley, **12** Karlsruhe, **13** Phil Parkes, **14** Wembley, **15** Billy Bonds.

QUIZ 163

Answers on page 251

1 Brazilian Anderson da Silva moved from AS Monaco for £13m which club bought him?

2 Which team won the 1989 UEFA Cup?

3 Who played in League Cup Finals for Everton, Arsenal and Aston Villa?

4 In what decade did Derby County first win the Championship?

5 Which Scot scored five successive World Cup qualifiers between 1988-1989?

6 Which player, who died in 1990, was awarded the Order of Lenin?

7 Who took over as manager of Leeds Utd in 1961?

8 How old was Diego Maradon when he first played for Argentina?

9 How many times have Liverpool won the UEFA Cup?

10 How many points did Scotland win in their 1998 World Cup group final matches?

11 Which French player received two yellow cards and was sent off in the 1998 World Cup Final?

12 Steve Coppell follwed Alan Ball as manager of which club?

13 Up to the 1990s how many times have Norwich won the FA Cup?

14 Who is Arsenal's most expensive signing?

15 How many international goals did Ronnie Whelan score?

Answers to page 251

1 Charlton Athletic, **2** Jeff Astle, **3** Lou Macari, **4** Josef Herberger, **5** Cardiff City, **6** John Toshack, **7** Manchester City, **8** Oldham Athletic, **9** Five days, **10** Atletico Madrid, **11** Ipswich Town, **12** 1966, **13** Aris Salonika, **14** 1935, **15** Faustino Asprilla.

WEST HAM 2

Answers on page 252

1 What is the highest position West Ham have ever achieved in the League?

2 Which two ex-West Ham players have managed Norwich City in the post-war period?

3 Who beat West Ham 6-1 on their plastic pitch in a League Cup semi-final match in 1990?

4 Which Queen's Park Rangers striker moved to West Ham?

5 West Ham's Stan Lazaridis plays for which country?

6 What was unusual about West Ham defender Alvin Martin's hat-trick in the 8-1 thrashing of Newcastle in 1987?

7 Who succeeded Ron Greenwood as manager of West Ham in 1977?

8 Who became the youngest player ever to play in an FA Cup Final when he appeared for West Ham in 1980?

9 Which player scored 42 League goals for West Ham in 1929-30?

10 Why was West Ham's Rio Ferdinand dropped from the England squad for the game against Moldova?

11 Which non-league side enjoyed a good FA Cup run in 1998 until they suffered a narrow defeat at West Ham?

12 Which club did West Ham sign Slavic Bilic from?

13 Who was in goal when West Ham won the FA Cup in 1980?

14 West Ham played their first Cup Winners Cup Final in which stadium?

15 Who was Trevor Brooking's 'minder' on the pitch at West Ham?

Answers to page 252

1 Kenneth Wolstenholme, **2** Chelsea (Coca-Cola Cup), **3** Athletic Bilbao, **4** 1913, **5** Chelsea, **6** White, **7** Ted Phillips, **8** Barry Fry, **9** Matthew, **10** Ray Wilkins, **11** Sheffield Wednesday, **12** Chelsea, **13** He didn't play for anybody else, **14** Mexico, **15** Standard Liege.

• INTERNATIONAL REDS •

Answers on page 257

1 How many red cards were shown in the 1998 World Cup tournament?

2 Which England player was sent off in 1973 against Poland?

3 Which team in 1990, became the first ever to have a player sent off in the World Cup Final?

4 Which Northern Ireland player became the first to receive a red card in a British Home International match?

5 Which Argentinian player did David Beckham kick which resulted in his red card in the World Cup Finals 1998?

6 Who were Argentina playing against in the 1966 World Cup when their captain Rattin was sent off?

7 Which French player received two yellow cards and was sent off in the 1998 World Cup Final?

8 Bolivia had a man sent off in the third minute against Germany in the USA 1994 World Cup finals. What was his name?

9 Name the Dutchman who was sent off in Hollands match with Belgium in the 1998 World Cup finals?

10 England's Alan Ball was sent off in 1973 against which country?

11 Which England player was sent off in the Mexico 1986 World Cup?

12 Which Republic of Ireland player was sent off in 1996 playing against Russia?

13 Who were Austria's opponents in 1963 when the referee abandoned the game after two Austrian players were sent off and the rest kicking their counterparts all over the park?

14 Who claimed that he had been struck by Laurent Blanc when the French captain was sent off in the semi-finals of the 1998 World Cup?

15 Which French player was sent off for stamping against Saudi Arabia in the first round of the World Cup Finals in 1998?

Answers to page 257

1 Brazil v England, **2** 31, **3** John Reynolds, **4** No9, **5** Plymouth Argyle, **6** Denis Law, **7** Kevin Keegan, **8** No, **9** Torino, **10** Ronnie Whelan, **11** Leeds Utd, **12** Trevor Cherry, **13** Henning Berg, **14** Kilmarnock, **15** Salonika.

QUIZ 164

Answers on page 258

1 Kirkwood and Milne scored Euro goals in the same 1980s game for which club?

2 Who won the 1997 Coca-Cola Cup?

3 Who were the only brothers to play on the same side in a 1960's FA Cup Final?

4 Who started the game in goal for Scotland when they lost to Denmark in a friendly in March 1998?

5 Who came on as a sub for Arsenal in the 1971 FA Cup Final?

6 Who were the wing duo for Tottenham Hotspur in their double-winning season?

7 Who played every League game for Liverpool in the 1985-86 double-winning season?

8 Who scored 60 goals for Everton in the 1927-28 season?

9 Who was Joe Mercer's assistant when Manchester City won the Championship?

10 Which Brian became boss of Manchester City in 1993?

11 What did Arsenal lose two of and Manchester Utd only one in the 1990-91 season?

12 Which player scored 38 League goals for Bolton Wanderers in 1920-21?

13 Which country did Jimmy Crapnell play for?

14 Which country lost 2-0 to Italy in the 1982 World Cup semi-final?

15 Which player scored 30 League goals for Manchester Utd in 1963-64?

Answers to page 258

1 Sunderland, **2** Derby County, **3** Swindon Town, **4** Aberdeen, **5** Marco van Basten, **6** Tottenham Hotspur, **7** Rangers, **8** Manchester City, **9** Leeds Utd, **10** Newcastle Utd, **11** Gary Lineker, **12** West Ham Utd (1965), **13** Leicester City, **14** Slovan Bratislava, **15** Rotherham Utd.

QUIZ 165

Answers on page 255

1 Which two countries played in the first ever 0-0 draw in a World Cup finals match?

2 How many League games did Glenn Hoddle play for Chelsea?

3 Which West Brom star of the 1890s , nicknamed 'Baldy' won five caps for Northern Ireland and then eight with England?

4 What shirt number did Mark Hughes usually wear in his first three years at Manchester Utd?

5 Which soccer team does Labour politician Michael Foot support?

6 Which Manchester Utd star was European Footballer of the Year in 1964?

7 Which Hamburg player was European Footballer of the Year in 1979?

8 Were Hibs founder members of the Scottish League?

9 Who lost to Ajax on away goals in the 1992 UEFA Cup Final?

10 Which former Liverpool star is manager of Greek side Panionios?

11 Which team did Arsenal pip to the league title in their first double-winning season?

12 Who was manager of Bradford City at the time of the disastrous fire in 1985?

13 Who was the onle ever present for Blackburn Rovers in the 1995-96 season?

14 Alan Robertson made a record 481 appearances, for which Scottish club between 1972-88?

15 Where was the 1973 European Cup Winners' Cup Final held?

Answers to page 255

1 22, **2** Alan Ball, **3** Argentina, **4** Billy Ferguson, **5** Diego Simeone, **6** England, **7** Marcel Desailly, **8** Marco Etcheverry, **9** Patrik Kluivert, **10** Poland, **11** Ray Wilkins, **12** Roy Keane, **13** Scotland, **14** Slaven Bilic, **15** Zinedine Zidane.

QUIZ 166

Answers on page 256

1 Which club did Niall Quinn join on leaving Manchester City?

2 Goddard and Hebberd were in the same team at which club?

3 Which side won promotion but were not allowed to take their place in the top flight?

4 Who beat Rangers 1-0 in the 1983 Scottish FA Cup Final?

5 Which Dutch player was the 1992 European Footballer of the Year?

6 With which club did Neil Ruddock make his League debut?

7 Who beat Celtic 2-1 in the 1964-65 Scottish League Cup Final?

8 Birtles and Bowyer scored Euro goals in the same game for which club?

9 Mick Jones scored in an FA Cup Final for which club?

10 Which club in the 20th century was the first to retain the FA Cup?

11 Who scored six goals for England in the 1986 World Cup Finals?

12 Who won the first Cup Winners Cup Final played at Wembley?

13 Which club had a fanzine called *The Fox*?

14 Who were the first Eastern European side to win the Cup Winners' Cup?

15 Which club was once known as Thornhill United?

Answers to page 256

1 Dundee Utd, **2** Leicester City, **3** Allan and Ron Harris, **4** Leighton, **5** Eddie Kelly, **6** Cliff Jones & Terry Dyson, **7** Bruce Grobbelaar, **8** Dixie Dean, **9** Malcolm Allison, **10** Horton, **11** Points, **12** Joe Smith, **13** Scotland, **14** Poland, **15** Dennis Law.

QUIZ 167

Answers on page 261

1 Willie Maddren followed Malcolm Allison as manager of which club?
2 Vinnie Jones and Mel Sterland were part of which promoted team?
3 Against which team did Bryan Robson score his last goal in a competitive match?
4 Who did Notts County spend a record £2.5m on in 1992?
5 When was the first European Cup Final played at Wembley?
6 Which 41 year-old hung up his boots in November 1995 after a serious neck injury in a reserve team game?
7 Who beat Celtic 3-1 in the 1956 Scottish FA Cup Final?
8 Francis Burns was at which club when he won his only Scottish cap?
9 Which soccer team does Rugby League international Jonathan Davies support?
10 In which month was the Munich air disaster?
11 Which club did Roy Keane turn down when he joined Manchester Utd?
12 Which two clubs did Gordon Banks play for?
13 Which ex-Manchester Utd star scored the goal that condemned his old club to relegation?
14 Which club do Scottish side Airdrieonians share a ground with?
15 Which country does John Spencer play for?

Answers to page 261

1 Emile Heskey, **2** Mark McGhee, **3** 2nd Division 1 (1928-29), **4** Fulham, **5** Mark McGhee, **6** Alan Shearer, **7** Gordon Banks, **8** Never, **9** Arsenal won the double, so the Shield was contested between Liverpool, the Cup runners-up and Leicester City Division Two Champions., **10** Gordon Lee, **11** Port Vale, **12** Arthur Rowley, **13** Gordon Milne, **14** Portsmouth, **15** Birmingham City.

KENNY DALGLISH

Answers on page 262

1 Which Liverpool manager signed Kenny Dalglish?

2 Which manager gave Kenny Dalglish his first Scottish cap?

3 Who advised Kenny Dalglish, "If you're going to get kicked, get kicked in the box, it's worth it there"?

4 Kenny Dalglish scored the only goal in the 1978 European Cup against which side?

5 Who did Kenny Dalglish succeed as manager of Blackburn Rovers?

6 Which player presented Kenny Dalglish with an award when he made his 100th international appearance?

7 Who were the opponents on the day that Kenny Dalglish's Blackburn Rovers won the Premiership?

8 How many Scottish caps did Kenny Dalglish win?

9 Which team did Kenny Dalglish support as a boy?

10 In which year did Kenny Dalglish win his first Scottish Championship medal?

11 How many different Scotland managers did Kenny Dalglish play for?

12 How old was Kenny Dalglish when he first played for Celtic?

13 How many times did Kenny Dalglish win the championship for Liverpool when he was boss?

14 Who did Kenny Dalglish replace as skipper of Celtic?

15 How many World Cup final tournaments did Kenny Dalglish play in?

Answers to page 262

1 Mexico, **2** Plymouth Argyle, **3** Alan Shearer, **4** Martin Peters, **5** Alan Ball, **6** Graeme Souness, **7** Leeds Utd, **8** 130 yards, **9** Norwich City, **10** Dennis Bergkamp, **11** 0-0 after extra time, **12** Chris Armstrong, **13** Innsbruk, **14** Blackpool, **15** Rangers.

LEICESTER CITY

Answers on page 259

1 Which Leicester-born striker of the 1990s has the middle names William Ivanhoe?

2 Who did Martin O'Neill succeed as manager of Leicester City?

3 What is the highest position Leicester City have ever achieved in the League?

4 Allen Clarke became the first £150,000 man when he moved to Leicester City from which club?

5 Who was boss when Leicester City went down in 1994-95?

6 Who hit a 1997 hat-trick for Newcastle Utd, who were losing 3-1, into a 4-3 victory over Leicester City?

7 Who was the Leicester City keeper in the 1961 FA Cup Final?

8 In which decade did Leicester City win the FA Cup before the 1990s?

9 Despite never having won either the League Championship or the FA Cup, Leicester City won the 1971 Charity Shield. How come?

10 Who succeeded David Pleat as manager of Leicester City in 1991?

11 Leicester City player John Duncan scored 6 goals in a match in December 1924. Who were the opponents?

12 Which player scored 44 League goals for Leicester City in 1956-57?

13 Who succeeded Jock Wallace as manager of Leicester City in 1982?

14 Leicester City player Arthur Chandler scored 6 goals in a match in October 1928. Who were the opponents?

15 Steve Claridge joined Leicester City from which club?

Answers to page 259

1 Middlesborough, **2** Leeds Utd, **3** Oldham Athletic, **4** Craig Short, **5** 1963, **6** Jimmy Case, **7** Hearts, **8** Manchester Utd, **9** Chelsea, **10** February 1958, **11** Blackburn Rovers, **12** Leicester City and Stoke City, **13** Denis Law, **14** Clyde, **15** Scotland.

QUIZ 168

Answers on page 260

1 In which country were the 1986 World Cup Finals held?

2 Which club did Peter Shilton join as a player/manager in 1992?

3 Who was the leading scorer in Euro '96, with five goals in the tournament?

4 Which World Cup winner was born in Plaistow in 1943?

5 Who was the first person to play a 100 League games for four different clubs?

6 Which former Liverpool star made his only appearance for Spurs as a substitute in a UEFA Cup game before transferring to Middlesborough?

7 David Harvey played over 300 games for which club?

8 What is the maximum length of a soccer pitch?

9 Gary Megson followed Martin O'Neill as manager of which club?

10 Which player did Bruce Rioch buy in 1995 to set a new English club record?

11 What was the score in the 1991 Arsenal v Spurs FA Charity Shield?

12 Who moved from Crystal Palace for £4.5 million in June 1995 to set a club record for a transfer fee received.

13 In which Austrian city do FC Tirol play their home games?

14 Charnley, Murdie and Perry have all scored more than 100 goals for which club?

15 Who beat Celtic 1-0 in the 1966 Scottish FA Cup Final replay?

Answers to page 260

1 Bob Paisley, **2** Tommy Docherty, **3** Bob Paisley, **4** Bruges, **5** Don Mackay, **6** Franz Beckenbaur, **7** Liverpool, **8** 102, **9** Rangers, **10** 1972, **11** Six, **12** 20, **13** Three, **14** Billy McNeill, **15** Three.

QUIZ 169

Answers on page 265

1 Who scored a double hat-trick on his debut for Newcastle Utd in the 1950s?

2 Nottingham Forest recorded a 7-0 League Cup win over which club in September 1980?

3 Who succeeded Dick Graham as manager of Crystal Palace in 1966?

4 Who was Everton's skipper in the 1985 European Cup Winners' Cup?

5 Thomas Brolin joined Leeds Utd from which Italian club?

6 Who succeeded Billy Bonds as manager of West Ham Utd in 1994?

7 Ron Atkinson followed Dave Sexton as boss of which club?

8 Which Spanish club signed Ronaldo for over £13m?

9 Who succeeded John Bond as manager of Manchester City in 1983?

10 Which club had a fanzine called *In The Loft*?

11 Who succeeded Howard Kendall as manager of Everton in 1994?

12 In which year did Ipswich Town play their first League game?

13 Which two internationals - one Welsh, one English - did Graeme Souness sign in July 1992?

14 Which club did the first English double of the 20th century?

15 Which French international played in three consecutive European Cup Finals in 1993,1994,1995?

Answers to page 265

1 Tom Finney, **2** Hristo Stoichkov, **3** 1930s, **4** Mick Mills, **5** Arsenal, **6** Italy, **7** Bobby Gould, **8** Cardiff City, **9** Lionel Perez, **10** Real Madrid, **11** Jones, **12** Carlisle Utd, **13** Pickles, **14** Peter Shilton, **15** Hans Krankl.

QUIZ 170

Answers on page 266

1 Who was the first Welsh player to be sent off in an international?

2 Who played every League game in his first season with Arsenal when they won the Championship in 1990-91?

3 Who lost to Juventus in the 1984 Super Cup?

4 Which Liverpool player was harangued in the press in 1996 for not living nearer to the club?

5 Which country did Lawrie Sanchez play for?

6 What is Blackpool's nickname?

7 Greg Downs played in an FA Cup Final for which team?

8 How many matches did England play in the 1966 World Cup tournament?

9 How many games was Joe Mercer caretaker manager of England for?

10 Who lost to Valencia on away goal difference in the 1980 Super Cup?

11 In 1982 Scotland played New Zealand in the first of their three group matches. What was the score?

12 The only goal in the 1990 World Cup Final came from a penalty awarded to West Germany. Who was the scorer?

13 Which club did Norwich City sell Justin Fashanu to for £1m?

14 Which country did George Berry play for?

15 Including penalty shoot-outs, who scored England's last goal in Euro '96?

Answers to page 266

1 Kevin Richardson, **2** Paul McGrath (45 caps for the Republic of Ireland), **3** Steve Harkness, **4** Alan Wright, **5** Chris Nicholl of Aston Villa, **6** George Ramsey, **7** Leeds Utd, **8** Peter McParland, **9** The Villains, **10** Andy Gray, **11** Crewe Alexandra, **12** Graham Taylor, **13** Leicester City, **14** Peter Withe, **15** Tom Waring.

QUIZ 171

Answers on page 263

1 Who was the first player to score thirty goals for England?

2 Who scored six goals for Bulgaria in the 1994 World Cup Finals?

3 In which decade was Sir John Hall born?

4 Which England player set a League appearance record for Ipswich Town?

5 Which club has a fanzine called *One Nil Down. . . Two One Up*?

6 In which country were the 1990 World Cup Finals held?

7 Who was Wimbledon manager when they won the FA Cup in the 1980s?

8 Which Welsh football team is known as the Bluebirds?

9 Which French keeper joined Sunderland in 1996?

10 After losing just 8 out of 64 games, John Toshack was sacked as manager of which Spanish club?

11 Who started the game in goal for Wales when they drew against Jamaica in a friendly in March 1998?

12 Who plays at home at Brunton Park?

13 What was the name of the dog who found the stolen World Cup in 1966?

14 Who was the regular keeper for Derby in their 1990-91 relegation season?

15 Which Austrian striker has scored in European Cup Winners' Cup finals for both Barcelona and Rapid Vienna?

Answers to page 263

1 Len Shackleton, **2** Bury, **3** Arthur Rowe (Acting), **4** Kevin Ratcliffe, **5** Parma, **6** Harry Redknapp, **7** Manchester Utd, **8** Barcelona, **9** John Benson, **10** QPR, **11** Mike Walker, **12** 1938, **13** Dean Saunders, Mark Wright, **14** Tottenham Hotspur, **15** Marcel Desailly.

ASTON VILLA 2

Answers on page 264

1 Who, in December 1995, got sent off playing for Coventry City on his return to his former club Aston Villa?

2 Who is Aston Villa's most-capped player?

3 Which Liverpool player did Stan Collymore accuse of making racist remarks to him during Aston Villa's visit to Anfield?

4 Which defender played in all Aston Villa's 1995-96 League games?

5 Who scored all the goals in Aston Villa's 2-2 draw with Leicester City in 1976?

6 Aston Villa became only the second club to do the League and Cup 'double' in 1897. Who was their manager at the time?

7 Which club did Mervyn Day leave to join Aston Villa?

8 Who was Aston Villa's two goal hero in the 1957 FA Cup Final?

9 What is Aston Villas nickname?

10 Which Aston Villa forward won the Young Player of the Year award in 1977?

11 Which club did David Platt leave to join Aston Villa?

12 Which manager brought Dwight Yorke to Villa Park?

13 Which club did Mark Draper leave to join Aston Villa?

14 Who scored a UEFA Cup hat-trick for Aston Villa against Victor Guimaraes in September 1983?

15 Which player scored 49 League goals for Aston Villa in 1930-31?

Answers to page 264

1 Trevor Hockey, **2** David Seaman, **3** Liverpool, **4** Stan Collymore, **5** Northern Ireland, **6** The Tangerines/Seasiders, **7** Coventry City, **8** Six, **9** 7, **10** Nottingham Forest, **11** Scotland won 5-2, **12** Andy Brehme, **13** Nottingham Forest, **14** Wales, **15** Teddy Sheringham.

OFF IN THE CUP

Answers on page 269

1 Which Manchester Utd player was sent off in the 1994 League Cup Final?

2 At which club was Paul Warhurst sent off in a European Cup game?

3 Darren Peacock was sent off as which London club knocked Newcastle United out of the 1995-96 FA Cup?

4 Which Newcastle United player was sent off in a 1996- Coca-Cola quarter final after clashing with Arsenals Lee Dixon?

5 What was the offence for which Kanchelskis was sent off in Manchester Utd's 1994 League Cup Final?

6 Which Aberdeen player was sent off in the 1978-79 Scottish League Cup Final?

7 How many players were sent off in the 1967 World Club Championship between Celtic and Racing Club?

8 Which Manchester Utd player did referee Peter Willis send off in an FA Cup Final?

9 Duncan McKenzie was sent off in a European game playing for which club?

10 Which Ranger's player saw red in the 1996 European Cup game against Borussia Dortmund in Germany?

11 Who was sent off in Manchester Utd's 1990s European Champions League 3-1 defeat in Gothenburg?

12 Which keeper was sent off in the quarter-finals of the 1994 FA Cup Final?

13 Who are the only club to have had two players sent off in a game at Wembley?

14 In 1972, John Ritchie was sent off within 30 seconds as appearing in a Euro game for which club?

15 Vinnie Jones was sent off after receiving two yellow cards, the first after just three seconds of the match. Which club was he playing for?

Answers to page 269

1 Michel Platini, **2** Northern Ireland, **3** Leeds Utd, **4** Kenny Dalglish, **5** Juventus, **6** Brian Clough, **7** Stoke City, **8** 1950s, **9** Millwall, **10** Everton, **11** Chelsea, **12** Portsmouth, **13** Phil Thompson, **14** Leeds United, **15** Colchester Utd.

QUIZ 172

Answers on page 270

1. Kenny Sansom moved from Crystal Palace to which club for £1.35m in August 1980?
2. Which Second Division side reached the Final of the League Cup and the semis of the FA Cup in the same season?
3. Which keeper Peter was with Stoke City throughout the entire 1980s?
4. Who scored all of Liverpool's five goals in a 1993-94 League Cup tie against Fulham?
5. Which club had a fanzine called *Not The 8502*?
6. Which club did Mel Sterland leave to join Rangers?
7. Which club did Julian Dicks join on leaving Liverpool?
8. Which club did Jim Leighton join when he finally left Manchester Utd?
9. How many goals did John Petrie score in his sides 36-0 win over Scottish Cup opponents Bon Accord in September 1885?
10. Gordon McQueen scored in an FA Cup Final for which club?
11. Which country did David Langan play for?
12. Paul Jonquin made a record 523 appearances, for which Scottish club between 1962-79?
13. Who were the first Dutch club to reach the European Cup Final?
14. Pat Crerand became assistant to which Manchester Utd manager?
15. Which famous manager once worked for Grimsby in 1951 and Workington in 1953?

Answers to page 270

1 Bryan Robson, **2** Terry Venables, **3** Hall, **4** Dumbarton, **5** Brighton, **6** 24, **7** Barcelona, **8** Viv Richards, **9** He missed a penalty, **10** Ossie Ardiles, **11** Everton, **12** Bruce Grobbelaar, **13** Leeds Utd, **14** 1890s, **15** Coventry City.

QUIZ 173

Answers on page 267

1 Who resigned as coach of France in July 1992?

2 Which country did Danny Blanchflower play for?

3 With which team did John Lukic make his League debut?

4 Which ex-Liverpool player holds Scotland's most capped record?

5 Which club beat Liverpool to win the 1984 European Super Cup?

6 Who was the young Middlesborough striker who made his England debut against Wales in 1959?

7 Alan Hudson was at which club when he made his international debut?

8 In what decade did Tottenham Hotspur first win the Championship?

9 Paul Goddard moved from Derby County to which club for £800,000 in December 1989?

10 Pat Nevin moved from Chelsea to which club for £925,000 in July 1988?

11 Which soccer team does Lord Richard Attenborough support?

12 Who won the last FA Cup Final before the Second World War?

13 Who was Liverpool skipper for the 1981 European Cup triumph of 1981?

14 Which club did Gordon Strachan join on leaving Manchester Utd?

15 Crewe Alexandra player Tony Naylor scored 5 goals in a match in April 1993. Who were the opponents?

Answers to page 267

1 Andrei Kanchelskis, **2** Blackburn Rovers, **3** Chelsea, **4** David Ginola, **5** Deliberate handball, **6** Doug Rougvie, **7** Five, **8** Kevin Moran, **9** Leeds Utd, **10** Paul Gascoigne, **11** Paul Ince, **12** Peter Schmeichel, **13** Stockport (1994 Play-off final against Burnley), **14** Stoke City, **15** Chelsea.

QUIZ 174

Answers on page 268

1 Which England skipper was born in Chester-le-street in 1957?

2 Which Australian manager got off to a winning start in January 1997?

3 Which Stuart said on live radio, "Lee Sharpe has got dynamite in his shorts"?

4 With 297 goals Andy Jardine became all-time top League scorer at which Scottish club?

5 Which club has a fanzine called *Gulls Eye*?

6 How many England goals did Geoff Hurst score?

7 Which club beat Werder Bremen to win the European Super Cup in 1992?

8 Which West Indian batsman played for Antigua in the 1978 World Cup qualifying games?

9 What was the most notable feature of David Platt's debut for Bari?

10 Who was the manager at Spurs when Jurgen Klinsmann joined them for the first time?

11 Manchester City player Tom Johnson scored 5 goals in a match in September 1928. Who were the opponents?

12 Who was Liverpool's only League ever-present in the 85-86 double-winning season?

13 Which team won the 1968 UEFA Cup?

14 In what decade did Dumbarton first win the Scottish Championship?

15 Keith Houchen scored in an FA Cup Final for which club?

Answers to page 268

1 Arsenal, **2** Oldham Athletic, **3** Fox, **4** Robbie Fowler, **5** Bournmouth, **6** Leeds Utd, **7** West Ham Utd, **8** Dundee, **9** 13, **10** Manchester Utd, **11** The Republic of Ireland, **12** Airdrieonians, **13** Ajax, **14** Tommy Docherty, **15** Bill Shankly.

QUIZ 175

Answers on page 273

1 Which boss said, "Nobody has the right to win anything they haven't earned"?

2 Who plays at home at the Underhill Stadium?

3 Which club has a fanzine called *The Square Ball*?

4 Who lost 1-0 to AC Milan in the Final of the 1990 European Cup?

5 What is the name of York City's ground?

6 Which John of Villa won his only England cap in 1977?

7 Which Arsenal player said after his team lost 1-0 "I do not feel guilty about it, I made the decision three years ago"?

8 Which two countries did Scotland lose to in their 1998 World Cup group?

9 Which international defender moved from Leeds Utd to Manchester Utd on a free transfer?

10 Which Scottish player is known as 'Juke Box'?

11 Who lost 4-3 to Real Madrid in the Final of the 1956 European Cup?

12 Which club was once known as St Jude's?

13 How much did Marseille pay for Trevor Stevens?

14 Which European country hosted the 1954 Football World Cup finals?

15 Which was Stuart Pearce's first League club?

Answers to page 273

1 Ted Harper, **2** 24, **3** David Batty, **4** Henning Berg, **5** Manchester Utd, **6** Tim Flowers, **7** 7 Stuart Ripley 11 Jason Wilcox, **8** David Batty, **9** Ian Branfoot, **10** Matt Le Tissier, **11** Tony Parkes, **12** Alan Shearer, **13** David May, **14** Jack Marshall, **15** Mick McGrath.

WIMBLEDON 2

Answers on page 274

1 Warren Barton moved to which club for £4m in June 1995?

2 Who became manager of Wimbledon in January 1992?

3 Who was Wimbledon boss before Joe Kinnear?

4 In 1984 Dave Bassett left Wimbledon, but returned after only a few days spent at which club?

5 Who succeeded Peter Withe as manager of Wimbledon?

6 Which ground did Wimledon previously play at?

7 Who succeeded Allen Batsford as manager of Wimbledon in 1978?

8 Which defender played 240 games for Wimbledon before going to Liverpool?

9 Dennis Wise joined Wimbledon after which club released him?

10 Who moved from Brentford to Wimbledon in 1992 to set a club record for a transfer fee received?

11 Which Wimbledon player scored the only goal of the 1988 FA Cup Final?

12 Wimbledon player Alan Cork scored 4 goals in a match in February 1979. Who were the opponents?

13 Which Wimbledon striker was a model for fashion company Top Man?

14 Which player hit his first Newcastle Utd hat-trick against Wimbledon in October 1995?

15 How many times was Wimbledon hardman Vinnie Jones sent off whilst playing for The Dons?

Answers to page 274

1 Airdrionians, **2** Brondby, **3** Florence, **4** Webb, **5** Rod Stewart, **6** 24, **7** Graeme Le Saux, **8** James, **9** Manchester, **10** 70, **11** Ray Clemence, **12** Grimsby Town, **13** Southend Utd, **14** Dariusz Dziekanowski, **15** Peterborough.

BLACKBURN 1

Answers on page 271

1 Which player scored 43 League goals for Blackburn in 1925-26?

2 How many FA Cup games have Blackburn gone without defeat?

3 Which England international player won Championship medals with Leeds Utd and Blackburn in the 1990s?

4 Who was the only ever present for Blackburn in 1995-96?

5 Who did Blackburn play in the 1994 Charity Shield match?

6 Who became England's most expensive keeper when he moved to Blackburn in 1993?

7 Who were the regular numbers 7 and 11 who supplied Alan Shearer in Blackburn's championship-winning season?

8 Who moved from Blackburn in 1996 for £3,750,000 to set a club record for a transfer fee received?

9 Which Southampton boss sold Alan Shearer to Blackburn Rovers?

10 Who won the *Match of the Day* 'Goal of the Season' in 1995 for a 35 yard chip shot against Blackburn Rovers?

11 Who was acting manager at Blackburn when Kenny Dalglish arrived?

12 In July 1992 the move of which player to Blackburn broke the British transfer record?

13 Which ex-Blackburn defender faced his old team in the 1994 Charity Shield?

14 Who succeeded Dally Duncan as manager of Blackburn in 1961?

15 Who scored an own goal for Blackburn in the 1960 FA Cup Final?

Answers to page 271

1 Bob Paisley, **2** Barnet, **3** Leeds Utd, **4** Benfica, **5** Bootham Crescent, **6** Gidman, **7** Dennis Bergkamp on missing the UEFA Cup match at Salonika because he will not fly, **8** Brazil and Morocco, **9** Dennis Irwin, **10** Gordon Durie, **11** Reims, **12** QPR, **13** Five, **14** Switzerland, **15** Coventry City.

QUIZ 176

Answers on page 272

1 Which Scottish club used to be called Excelsior?

2 At which club did the Laudrup brothers begin their careers?

3 Which city is the home of Fiorentina?

4 Which David was boss of Chelsea in 1993?

5 Which pop singer said after the birth of his daughter, "It's like seeing Scotland score a goal. You never got used to it"?

6 How many teams competed in the 1982 World Cup in Spain?

7 Which England international was born in Jersey in October 1968?

8 What is Ian Rush's middle name?

9 In which city was Andy Hinchcliffe born?

10 How many League goals did Jack Charlton score?

11 Which England goalkeeper was awarded an MBE in the Queen's Birthday Honours' List in 1987?

12 Which club did Gary Croft leave to join Blackburn Rovers?

13 Which team does singer Alison Moyet support?

14 Which Polish international hit 4 goals for Celtic against Partizan Belgrade in 1989?

15 Who was Terry Bly playing for when he hit 52 goals in 1960-61?

Answers to page 272

1 Newcastle Utd, **2** Joe Kinnear, **3** Peter Withe, **4** Crystal Palace, **5** Joe Kinnear, **6** Plough Lane, **7** Dario Gradi, **8** John Scales, **9** Southampton, **10** Dean Holdsworth, **11** Lawrie Sanchez, **12** Torquay Utd, **13** Dean Holdsworth, **14** Les Ferdinand, **15** Twelve.

QUIZ 177

Answers on page 277

1 With which club did goalkeeper Mark Bosnich make his English League debut?

2 Who managed the English team who won the 1963 Cup Winners Cup ?

3 Who was Luton's boss when they were relegated in 1992?

4 Peter Swales was the chairman of which football club?

5 Liverpool sold Larry Lloyd to which club?

6 Paul Ince moved from Manchester Utd to which club for £7m in July 1995?

7 Tim Sherwood moved to Norwich City from which club?

8 Which English First Division clubs made up the so called Big five early in the 1980s?

9 Who in 1969, became the first Eastern Europe club to win the Cup Winners' Cup?

10 Which club was once known as Heaton Norris Rovers?

11 Between 1981-1990 how many clubs did Dave Beasant play for?

12 Which manager has led two British clubs to Cup Winners' Cup victory?

13 Billy McNeill succeeded John Benson as manager at which club?

14 Liam Brady finished his playing career at which club?

15 How many red cards were shown in the 1998 World Cup finals?

Answers to page 277

1 FA Cup Final, **2** Trevor Phillips, **3** Joao Havelange, **4** Gary Lineker v Malaysia, **5** Tottenham Hotspur, **6** Andy Brehme, **7** Fernando Gomez, **8** Ryan Green (Wolves), **9** Malta, **10** Michael Thomas, **11** Boston Utd, **12** George McCluskey, **13** Paul Gascoigne, **14** Four, **15** Sampdoria.

QUIZ 178

Answers on page 278

1 Which English official was assistant referee in the 1998 World Cup Final?

2 Who were the first host country to win the World Cup?

3 Chris Whyte and George Wood were in the same team at which club?

4 Which Peter became boss of Southend Utd in 1993?

5 What is the highest position Bristol Rovers have ever achieved in the League?

6 Which team won the 1974 UEFA Cup?

7 Who plays at home at Boothferry Park?

8 Which Dynamo Kiev player was European Footballer of the Year in 1975?

9 Where was the 1986 European Cup Winners' Cup Final held?

10 What two colours are in Hamburgs strip?

11 John Rudge has spent more than ten years as boss of which club?

12 Which club in Belgium did Mike Small play for?

13 Who provided the free-kick from which David Platt hit the late goal against Belgium in Italia '90?

14 For which club did Alex Matthie make his League debut?

15 Which club has a fanzine called *Mad As A Hatter*?

Answers to page 278

1 Danish, **2** Holland, **3** One, **4** Ze Carlos, **5** Argentina, **6** Davor Suker, **7** Japan's, **8** Paraguay, **9** Zinedine Zidane, **10** Bleach their hair (The goal-keeper was bald), **11** Davor Suker, **12** Jim Leighton (Scotland), **13** Patrik Kluivert, **14** Zinedine Zidane, **15** Brazil and Morocco.

QUIZ 179

Answers on page 275

1 The severe weather of 1963 caused which event to be put back three weeks?

2 Which FA commercial director had "Not necessarily" resigned in 1996?

3 Name the successor to Sir Stanley Rous, who took over as president of FIFA just before the 1974 World Cup?

4 Who scored England's first hat-trick in the 90s and against which country?

5 Tuttle and Durie scored Euro goals in the same game for which club?

6 Which German player scored the only goal of the 1990 World Cup Final?

7 Which Porto player won the 1982-83 Golden Boot award?

8 Who is the youngest player to earn a full Welsh Cap?

9 Against which country did Wolves teenager Ryan Green make his international debut?

10 Who scored Arsenal's last minute goal against Liverpool at Anfield to win the League title in 1989?

11 Which non-League side does John Motson follow?

12 Which player scored the only goal in the Celtic v Rangers 1980 Scottish FA Cup Final?

13 Who was Britain's first £2m footballer?

14 How many 1980s FA Cup Finals did Graeme Sharp take part in?

15 Who did Barcelona beat 1-0 in the 1992 European Cup final?

Answers to page 275

1 Manchester Utd, **2** Bill Nicholson, **3** David Pleat, **4** Manchester City, **5** Coventry City, **6** Inter Milan, **7** Watford, **8** Arsenal, Everton, Liverpool, Manchester Utd and Tottenham Hotspur, **9** Slovan Bratislava, **10** Stockport County, **11** Three, Wimbledon, Newcastle Utd and Chelsea, **12** Alex Ferguson, **13** Manchester City, **14** West Ham Utd, **15** 22.

• WORLD CUP 1998 2 •

Answers on page 276

1 What nationality is Kim Milton Nielsen, the referee who sent Beckham off in the 1998 World Cup finals?

2 Argentina conceded two goals in each of their final matches of the 1998 finals England was one of there opponents who was the other?

3 How many points did Scotland win in their 1998 World Cup group final matches?

4 Which Brazilian made his international debut in the 1998 World Cup semi-final against Holland?

5 In the 1998 World Cup finals which team was the only one not to concede a goal in their three group matches?

6 Who scored six goals for Croatia in the 1998 World Cup finals?

7 Which country's supporters cleaned up the stadia after each match they attended at the World Cup Finals in 1998?

8 Which team did France knock out with a Golden Goal in the World Cup Finals 1998?

9 Which French player was sent off for stamping against Saudi Arabia in the first round of the World Cup finals in 1998?

10 What did every Romanian player, except their goalkeeper, do before their final group match in France 1998?

11 Who scored the first goal in the 1998 semi-final match between France and Croatia?

12 Who was the oldest player in the 1998 World Cup finals?

13 Name the Dutchman who was sent off in Hollands match with Belgium in the 1998 World Cup finals?

14 Who scored two headed goals in the 1998 World Cup Final for France?

15 Name the two teams Scotland lost to in their 1998 World Cup group?

Answers to page 276

1 Mark Warren, **2** Italy (1934), **3** Arsenal, **4** Taylor, **5** 6th Division 2, (1955-56, 1958-59), **6** Feyenoord, **7** Hull City, **8** Oleg Blokhin, **9** Lyon, **10** White and Red, **11** Port Vale, **12** Standard Liege, **13** Paul Gascoigne, **14** Celtic, **15** Luton Town.

DERBY COUNTY 1

Answers on page 281

1 What is the highest position Derby have ever achieved in the League?

2 Paul Goddard moved from Derby to which club for £800,000 in December 1989?

3 Derby recorded a 7-0 League Cup win over which club in October 1992?

4 In which decade did Derby first win the FA Cup?

5 Which Kevin was a scoring machine for Derby in the 1970s?

6 Ashley Ward joined Derby from which club?

7 Who scored 5 goals in a game for Derby against Wales in March 1896?

8 In what decade did Derby first win the Championship?

9 In 1984, who at Derby became the Leagues youngest club chairman?

10 Which club did Dean Yates leave to join Derby?

11 Who were Derby's Premiership visitors on the night the floodlights went out during a match?

12 When did Derby move to their new ground?

13 Which player scored 37 League goals for Derby in 1930-31?

14 Which two Johns were with Clough's champions at Derby and Nottingham Forrest?

15 Nigel Callaghan moved from Derby to which club for £525,000 in February 1989?

Answers to page 281

1 1906, **2** Exeter City, **3** Norwich City, **4** Tranmere Rovers, **5** Celtic, **6** Wales, **7** Hamburg, **8** Jimmy Quinn, **9** Dave Bassett, **10** Liverpool, **11** Billy Bingham, **12** Total Football, **13** 1976, **14** Teddy Sherringham, **15** Tommy Docherty.

QUIZ 180

Answers on page 282

1 Mike Flannigan moved from Charlton Athletic to which club for £650,000 in August 1979?

2 Who scored his first and Manchester Utd's last goal of the 1992-93 season?

3 Bristol City recorded a 4-0 League Cup win over which club in October 1979?

4 Who has played in League Cup Finals for Luton Town and Nottingham Forest?

5 Who beat Dunfermline 2-0 in the 1991-92 Scottish League Cup Final?

6 Which soccer team does TV chef Delia Smith support?

7 Which country did John McClelland play for?

8 Who beat Morton 5-0 in the 1963-64 Scottish League Cup Final?

9 Which club have a River End Stand and City Stand at their ground?

10 Oldham Athletic recorded a 7-0 League Cup win over which club in October 1989?

11 Stan Seymour won the FA Cup once as a player and twice as a manager of which club?

12 Which Stan hit an FA Cup Final hat-trick in the 1950s?

13 Which club had a fanzine called *Our Days Are Numbered*?

14 Which Ipswich Town player hit two hat-tricks in 1980-81 UEFA Cup games?

15 At which Scottish club did Steve Nicol make his League debut?

Answers to page 282

1 Roy Keane, **2** Keegan and Brooking, **3** Juventus, **4** Roeder, **5** Losers climbed the steps first, **6** Paris and Rome, **7** Wales, **8** Kevin Moran, **9** First subs to be used in a Final, **10** Norwich City, **11** White, **12** Manchester City, **13** Tommy Lawton, **14** Celtic, **15** Sunderland.

QUIZ 181

Answers on page 279

1 When did Everton first win the FA Cup?

2 At which ground was the Cowshed covered terrace?

3 Which club used to play at The Nest?

4 With which club did 'Dixie' Dean make his League debut?

5 Who beat Rangers 2-1 in the 1982-83 Scottish League Cup Final?

6 Which country did Mark Aizlewood play for?

7 At which club did Kevin Keegan have Manfred Kaltz as a team-mate?

8 Which Celtic striker was known as 'The Iron Man'?

9 In 1994, after going down, which boss said, "If you continually play Russian roulette eventually you're going to get the bullet"?

10 Which club first won the League Cup for three consecutive years?

11 Which Irishman took charge of the Greek national side in 1970

12 What name was given to the playing style invented by Ajax in the 1970s?

13 In which year did Kevin Keegan first captain England?

14 Including penalty shoot-outs, who scored the last England goal under Terry Venables?

15 Who was boss when Manchester Utd were last relegated?

Answers to page 279

1 Division 1 Champions (1971-72, 1974-75), **2** Millwall, **3** Southend, **4** 1940s, **5** Hector, **6** Norwich City, **7** Steve Bloomer, **8** 1970s, **9** Ian Maxwell, **10** Notts County, **11** Wimbledon, **12** 1997, **13** Jack Bowers, **14** O'Hare and McGovern, **15** Aston Villa.

QUIZ 182

Answers on page 280

1 Who was stripped of the captaincy of the Republic of Ireland in 1996 for taking a holiday without informing his boss?

2 Ron Greenwood's 1982 World Cup campaign was marred by injuries to which two key players?

3 Who lost to Leeds Utd on the away goals rule in the 1971 UEFA Cup Final?

4 Which Glenn left as Watford boss in February 1996?

5 What FA Cup Final tradition was altered in 1992?

6 Which two cities were the first to have hosted the European Championship Finals twice?

7 Which country did Peter Nicholas play for?

8 Which Manchester Utd player did referee Peter Willis send off in an FA Cup Final?

9 What did Celtic's Chalmers and Rangers' Wilson achieve when they went out for the 1966-67 Scottish League Cup Final?

10 Ron Ashman set an appearance record at which club?

11 What colour are the socks of the German team?

12 Peter Reid was the first managerial casulaty of the 1993-94 season. Which club sacked him?

13 Timed at 17 seconds in 1947, who scored England's fastest goal?

14 Who beat Hibernian 6-3 in the 1974-75 Scottish League Cup Final?

15 Which club did Niall Quinn join on leaving Manchester City?

Answers to page 280

1 Crystal Palace, **2** Bryan Robson, **3** Peterborough Utd, **4** Kingsley Black, **5** Hibernian, **6** Norwich City, **7** Northern Ireland, **8** Rangers, **9** Norwich City, **10** Scarborough, **11** Newcastle Utd, **12** Mortensen, **13** Liverpool, **14** John Wark, **15** Ayr.

QUIZ 183

Answers on page 285

1 Who succeeded Billy Bingham as manager of Everton in 1977?

2 Chris Woods has appeared for which three sides in League Cup Finals?

3 Which country did Gerry Daley play for?

4 Huddersfield Town recorded a 7-0 FA Cup win over which club in November 1991?

5 In what year was the first World Cup played?

6 Which team were beaten 1-0 by Celtic in the 1995 Scottish FA Cup Final?

7 Arsenal tube station is the only train station in Britain to be named after a football club. What was it called originally?

8 John Harkes first played in an FA Cup Final for which team?

9 Who did England meet in their first match in the 1966 finals?

10 What is Darren Huckerby's middle name?

11 Who won the first Scottish FA Cup Final to be decided on penalties?

12 Illgner was in goal for which World Cup winning country?

13 In 1885, what famous first happened in a Birmingham shop?

14 Who was Bob Paisley's first buy for Liverpool?

15 In which year did the FA Cup Final become an all ticket game?

Answers to page 285

1 Andrew Impey, **2** Don Howe, **3** Oxford, **4** Stan Bowles, **5** Birmingham City, **6** Doncaster Rovers, **7** QPR, **8** Terry Venables, **9** Blue and White, **10** Francis, **11** Ray Wilkins followed Gerry Francis, **12** Tottenham Hotspur, **13** Bruce Rioch, **14** Glenn Hoddle, **15** Les Ferdinand.

LIVERPOOL 9

Answers on page 286

1 Who scored Middlesborough's first goal in the second leg of their Coca-Cola Cup semi-final against Liverpool?

2 Which Liverpool defender made his England debut at the age of 20?

3 Which Liverpool player was lambasted in the press in 1996 for not living near the club?

4 How many times did Kenny Dalglish win the championship for Liverpool when he was boss?

5 In which year did Bob Paisley play in a Championship-winning side at Liverpool?

6 How many different Liverpool players scored in their 9-0 win over Crystal Palace in September 1989?

7 What was Alan Kennedy's nickname at Liverpool?

8 Who became the first German winners of the Cup Winners' Cup when they beat Liverpool in the 1966 Final?

9 Larry Lloyd moved from Liverpool to which club for £240,000 in August 1974?

10 Kevin Keegan's last game for Liverpool was in which competition?

11 Which important spectator created a first at the Burnley v Liverpool 1914 FA Cup Final?

12 Which Danish midfielder was loaned from Liverpool to Barnsley in 1995?

13 Which Welshman was Kevin Keegan's main Liverpool strike partner?

14 Who succeeded Joe Fagan as manager of Liverpool in 1985?

15 Which current Liverpool player scored on his League, League Cup, FA Cup and European debuts?

Answers to page 286

1 Andy Cole, **2** Anderlecht, **3** Billy Bremner, **4** Jimmy Dickinson, **5** Gray, **6** Mick McGrath, **7** Denmark, **8** Dusseldorf, **9** Mick McCarthy, **10** Kirkcaldy, **11** Laurent Blanc (For France against Paraguay in 1998), **12** Norwich City, **13** West Ham Utd, **14** Georgi Slavkov, **15** Tottenham Hotspur.

QPR 2

Answers on page 283

1 Which QPR winger of the 1990s has the middle name of Rodney?

2 Who succeeded Trevor Francis as manager of QPR in 1990?

3 QPR player Alan Wilks scored 5 goals in a match in October 1967. Who were the opponents?

4 Who made 34 separate transfer requests to leave QPR?

5 Who did David Seaman play for before his move to QPR?

6 Rufus Brevett moved for £250,000 to QPR in 1991 to set a record for a transfer fee received at which club?

7 Which club did Clive Wilson leave to join Tottenham Hotspur?

8 Who succeeded Tommy Docherty as manager of QPR in 1980?

9 What are the main colours on QPR's home shirts?

10 Who became QPR manager in 1988?

11 At QPR which ex-England midfielder followed another ex-England midfielder as manager?

12 Who beat QPR in an FA Cup Final replay?

13 Who was sacked as manager of QPR in the 1997-98 season?

14 Who scored the penalty to beat QPR in an FA Cup Final replay?

15 Who moved from QPR for £6 million in June 1995 to set a club record for a transfer fee received?

Answers to page 283

1 Steve Burtenshaw, **2** Nottingham Forest, Norwich City & Sheffield Wednesday, **3** The Republic of Ireland, **4** Lincoln City, **5** 1930, **6** Airdrie, **7** Gillespie Road, **8** Sheffield Wednesday, **9** Uruguay, **10** Carl, **11** Aberdeen, **12** West Germany, **13** FA Cup was stolen, **14** Phil Neal, **15** 1924.

QUIZ 184

Answers on page 284

1 Who hit a 1997-98 Champions League hat-trick for Manchester Utd in their 3-1 win at Feyenoord?

2 Who lost 2-0 to Hamburg in the 1977 Cup-Winners' Cup Final?

3 Which former Leeds Utd and Scotland star died in December 1997?

4 Who made 764 appearances for Portsmouth between 1946-1965?

5 Which Andy of Palace won his only England cap in 1991?

6 Who scored an own goal for Blackburn in the 1960 FA Cup Final?

7 Gazza made his international debut against which country?

8 Where was the 1981 European Cup Winners' Cup Final held?

9 Who replaced Jack Charlton as manager of the Republic of Ireland?

10 In which city do Raith Rovers play?

11 Who scored the first ever Golden Goal in the World Cup Finals?

12 Which football club is known as the Canaries?

13 For which team did 1966 World Cup starts, Hurst, Moore and Peters all play?

14 Which Trakia Plovdiv player won the 1980-81 Golden Boot award?

15 Who beat QPR 1-0 in the 1982 FA Cup Final replay?

Answers to page 284

1 Strasbourg, **2** Wimbledon, **3** 1-1, **4** 1981, **5** Arsenal, **6** Bill Shankly, **7** Bristol Rovers, **8** David James, **9** Everton in 1890-91, before Liverpool were formed, **10** Ian Callaghan, **11** John Barnes, **12** Juventus, **13** Mark Lawrenson, **14** Nicholas, **15** Real Madrid.

QUIZ 185

Answers on page 289

1 Major Frank Buckley and Raich Carter have both managed which club in the 1940s and 1950s?

2 Howard Wilkinson was player/manager at which non-League side?

3 In which decade did Manchester City first win the League Championship?

4 Who was the first person to play for two different English League Champions sides and then become manager of champions?

5 Carlton Palmer first played in an FA Cup Final for which club?

6 With which club did Frank Worthington make his League debut?

7 Which manager developed the 'push and run' style of soccer?

8 What was formed in 1958 to change the English League?

9 The adopted Italia '90 anthem Nessun Dorma comes from which opera?

10 Don Revie was manager of England for 29 games, how many of these did he lose?

11 Which country did Tele Santana manage?

12 How many international goals did Colin Bell score?

13 Which manager was offered the jon of managing Nottingham Forest when he was on holiday in Barbados?

14 David Cross first played in an FA Cup Final for which team?

15 Which Nigel has played in Mersey, Glasgow and London derby games?

Answers to page 289

1 Bayern Munich, **2** Sheffield Wednesday, **3** 1951, **4** Stoke City, **5** AS Roma, **6** Eight, **7** Eusebio, **8** Leeds Utd, **9** Turkey, **10** Keith Pilkington, **11** Coventry City, **12** Peter Reid, **13** Preston North End, **14** Arsenal, **15** Milkman.

QUIZ 186

Answers on page 290

1 Which German striker was known as "Der Bomber"?

2 When did Manchester Utd first win the League Cup?

3 Which club had a fanzine called *The Number Nine*?

4 Who scored five Premiership hat-tricks in 1995-96?

5 Tommy Docherty managed only 29 days at which club in 1968?

6 Ray Hartford followed Malcolm MacDonald as manager of which club?

7 The Bridgford Stand is part of the ground of which club?

8 Strachan and Shutt scored Euro goals in the same game for which club?

9 Mick Channon first played for which club in a League Cup Final?

10 Which Rangers and Watford defender featured in Leeds Utd's 1992 triumph?

11 Who were Villa's opponents in the first League Cup Final needing a replay?

12 Which Manchester Utd great made a trademark of pulling his cuffs over his hands?

13 Which Scottish player became Charlton Athletic's most capped player?

14 Which two Scottish teams met in the last game of the 1990-91 season to decide which of them were champions?

15 Who was the first player to appear in three League Cup Finals with different clubs?

Answers to page 290

1 Division 1 (3rd 1913-14), **2** Liverpool, **3** Stockport County, **4** Andy Payton, **5** Emerson, **6** Manchester Utd, **7** Todd, **8** Aston Villa, **9** FC Porto, **10** Manchester Utd, **11** WBA, **12** Atletico Madrid, **13** Gary Pallister, **14** Manchester Utd, **15** Wilf Gillow.

QUIZ 187

Answers on page 287

1 Which German team is the most successful in domestic competitions?

2 Jim McCalliog scored in an FA Cup Final for which club?

3 In which year did Arsenal install floodlights at Highbury?

4 Terry Conroy scored in a League Cup Final for which club?

5 Who lost on penalties to Liverpool in the 1984 European Cup Final?

6 How many times was Stan Flashman supposed to have sacked Barry Fry at Barnet?

7 Who was leading scorer in the 1966 World Cup tournament?

8 Which club has the Revie Stand in their ground?

9 Bryan Robson got his only England hat-trick in an 8-0 rout of which country in 1984?

10 Who was in goal for Manchester Utd for the 1995-96 League games that Peter Schmeichel missed?

11 Who was Dion Dublin playing for when he hit three against Sheffield Wednesday in 1995 and still ended up on the losing side?

12 Which manager was dismissed by Manchester City 12 days into the 1993-94 season?

13 Which team did not concede an FA Cup goal in their double-winning season?

14 Which club used to be called Dial Square?

15 What work did Pat Jennings do before he became a footballer?

Answers to page 287

1 Leeds Utd, **2** Boston United, **3** 1930s, **4** Joe Mercer, **5** Sheffield Wednesday, **6** Huddersfield Town, **7** Arthur Rowe, **8** The Fourth Division, **9** Turandot, **10** 7, **11** Brazil, **12** Nine, **13** Ron Atkinson, **14** West Ham Utd, **15** Spackman.

• MIDDLESBROUGH 1 •

Answers on page 288

1 What is the highest position Middlesborough have ever achieved in the League?

2 Craig Johnston moved from Middlesborough to which club for £575,000 in April 1981?

3 Who knocked out Blackburn, West Ham and Southampton before losing to Middlesborough in the semi-finals of the 1996-97 Coca-Cola Cup?

4 Who moved from Hull to Middlesborough for £750,000 in 1991 to set a club record for a transfer fee paid?

5 Which Brazilian star could not settle in Middlesborough?

6 Which club did Bryan Robson leave to take over as player/manager at Middlesborough?

7 Which Colin became boss of Middlesborough in 1990?

8 Middlesborough player George Camsell scored 5 goals in a match in September 1935. Who were the opponents?

9 Which club did Emerson leave to join Middlesborough?

10 Gary Pallister moved from Middlesborough to which club for £2.3m in August 1989?

11 David Mills moved from Middlesborough to which club for £482,000 in January 1979?

12 Brazilian player Juninho moved from Middlesborough for £12m, which club did he move to?

13 Who moved from Middlesborough in August 1989 to set a club record for a transfer fee received?

14 Which club did Stephen Pears leave to join Middlesborough?

15 Who succeeded Peter McWilliam as manager of Middlesborough in 1934?

Answers to page 288

1 Gerd Muller, **2** 1992, **3** Newcastle Utd, **4** Alan Shearer, **5** QPR, **6** Fulham, **7** Nottingham Forest, **8** Leeds Utd, **9** Norwich City, **10** John McClelland, **11** Everton, **12** Denis Law, **13** John Hewie, **14** Aberdeen & Rangers, **15** George Graham.

WEST BROM 2

Answers on page 293

1 Who beat WBA 1-0 in the 1912 FA Cup Final replay?

2 Which former WBA and England striker was killed in a car crash in Spain in July 1989?

3 Who holds the WBA League appearance record?

4 WBA player Jimmy Cookson scored 6 goals in a match in September 1927. Who were the opponents?

5 Who succeeded Bobby Gould as manager of WBA in 1992?

6 Which player scored 39 League goals for WBA in 1935-36?

7 Who moved from WBA for £1.5m in 1981 to set an English record for a transfer fee received?

8 Which team were beaten 3-2 by WBA in the 1954 FA Cup Final?

9 Which *Fantasy Football* star supports WBA?

10 WBA recorded a 6-1 League Cup win over which club in November 1965?

11 In December 1997, which manager left WBA to take over the reins at Queen's Park Rangers?

12 At which ground do WBA play?

13 Which team were beaten 1-0 by WBA in the 1968 FA Cup Final?

14 What was the first name of ex-WBA and Ipswich Town player Zondervan?

15 What was Tony Brown's nickname?

Answers to page 293

1 Diego Maradona, **2** QPR, **3** Manchester Utd, **4** Joey Jones, **5** Decorate his kitchen, **6** Mark Lawrenson, **7** John Motson, **8** Jimmy Melia, **9** Peter Fox, **10** Ricky Villa, **11** West Ham Utd, **12** Amsterdam Arena, **13** Six, **14** AC Milan, **15** Huddersfield Town.

QUIZ 188

Answers on page 294

1 Who lost to Gothenburg in the 1987 UEFA Cup Final?

2 Which club finished third in the 1992-93 Premier League but had a minus goal difference?

3 Which club played at the White City in the 1930s and in the 60s?

4 Who scored an amazing 46 goals in the European Cup for Benfica?

5 Which two London clubs were denied a merger by the Football League Management Committee?

6 Pat Jennings played his last international game against which team?

7 Who lost 1-0 to Liverpool in the Final of the 1981 European Cup?

8 Which two English clubs have a badge with a horse on it?

9 Who is the record goal-scorer for the Republic of Ireland?

10 Who used to play at Abbsfield, Fulwell?

11 Which Alan went on from non-League Alvechurch to play for England?

12 When Millwall's Malcolm Allen was red-carded in 1992-93 what unwelcomed first did he achieve?

13 Who was Manchester Utd's victorious Cup Winners' cup skipper in 1991?

14 John Aldridge was in which side promoted to the top flight?

15 Which club had a fanzine called *Exceedingly Good Pies*?

Answers to page 294

1 Wolves, **2** 21, **3** Bristol Rovers, **4** Dumbarton, **5** Mansfield Town, **6** Crystal Palace, **7** Middlesborough, **8** Newcastle Utd, **9** West Ham Utd, **10** Bill Nicholson (Spurs), **11** Colin Clarke, **12** Alan Shearer, **13** Ayr Utd, **14** Huddersfield Town, **15** Preston North End.

QUIZ 189

Answers on page 291

1 Who joined Napoli from Barcelona for a record £6.9 million fee?

2 Michael Robinson played in 1980s League Cup Finals for Liverpool and which other club?

3 Which club has a fanzine called *Red Issue*?

4 Who beat Ivor Allchurch's appearance record - 20 years after it was set?

5 What had Denmark's manager Richard Moller Nielsen reputedly planned to do during Euro '92, before his team's surprise late call up?

6 In August 1981 Brighton received £900,000 from Liverpool for which player?

7 Who said "For those of you watching in Black and White, 'Spurs are in the yellow shirts"?

8 In 1992-93 Brighton reached the FA Cup Final and were relegated in the same season. Who was their manager at the time?

9 Which veteran keeper became player/manager of Exeter in 1995?

10 Which friend and Argentinian team-mate joined Ossie Ardiles in his move from Argentina to England?

11 Holland and Jennings scored Euro goals in the same game for which club?

12 In which stadium do Ajax play their home games?

13 How many goals did Gary Lineker score in the 1986 World Cup?

14 Who beat Leeds Utd in the 1973 Cup Winners' Cup Final?

15 Malcolm Macdonald briefly took over as manager of which club in 1987?

Answers to page 291

1 Barnsley, **2** Laurie Cunningham, **3** Tony Brown, **4** Blackpool, **5** Ossie Ardiles, **6** 'W.G.' Richardson, **7** Bryan Robson, **8** Preston North End, **9** Frank Skinner, **10** Coventry City, **11** Ray Harford, **12** The Hawthorns, **13** Everton, **14** Romeo, **15** Bomber.

QUIZ 190

Answers on page 292

1 Which side from the Midlands used to play at Goldthorn Hill?

2 How many international goals did Mike Channon score?

3 At which club did Keith Curle make his League debut?

4 At which Scottish club did Graham Sharp make his League debut?

5 Which club had a fanzine called *Follow The Yellow Brick Road*?

6 Phil Barber played in an FA Cup Final for which team?

7 With which club did Stuart Ripley make his League debut?

8 Bob Stokoe won an FA Cup winners medal with which club?

9 Which club did Paul Ince make his League debut?

10 Who was the first person to play in and manage League Championship sides at the same club?

11 Who marked his 1986 debut for Southampton with a hat-trick?

12 Who was Blackburn Rovers' only league ever present in 1994-95?

13 The Honest Men is the nickname of which Scottish club?

14 Former Prime Minister Wilson supported which club?

15 Nobby Stiles succeeded Harry Catterick as manager at which club?

Answers to page 292

1 Dundee Utd, **2** Norwich City, **3** QPR, **4** Eusebio, **5** Fulham and QPR, **6** Brazil, **7** Real Madrid, **8** Gillingham and Ipswich Town, **9** Frank Stapleton (20), **10** Sunderland, **11** Smith, **12** First British club to have four players sent of in a game, **13** Steve Bruce, **14** Oxford Utd,**15** Rochdale.

QUIZ 191

Answers on page 297

1 Whose last game for Scotland was the 1978 World Cup defeat by Peru in which he missed a penalty?

2 Who were the first team to win the Scottish League Cup in the 1990s on a penalty shoot out?

3 Who were the Dutch scorers in their European Championship Final victory over Russia?

4 What was the first club that Bobby Gould managed?

5 Artificial turf was first used in which stadium?

6 Ian Wilson first played in an FA Cup Final for which team?

7 Which Martin was boss of Bury from 1984 to 1989?

8 In what year was the first Old Firm Cup Final played?

9 Which club did Nigel Clough join on leaving Nottingham Forest?

10 Bond, Brown and Bovington played for which 1960's FA Cup Finalists?

11 Who were the first host country to win the European Championship?

12 How many international goals did Northern Ireland's Johnny Crossan score in the 1960s?

13 Which club did Gareth Southgate leave to join Aston Villa?

14 Which club did John Hartson leave to join Arsenal?

15 In which year did Spain win the European Championship trophy?

Answers to page 297

1 A one year ban from European games, **2** Aberdeen, **3** Chris Woods, **4** East Fife, **5** Leeds Utd, **6** Recreation Park (Alloa), **7** Aberdeen, **8** Aberdeen, **9** Chris Woods and Terry Butcher, **10** Everton, **11** Manager Walter Smith, **12** Scottish League Cup, **13** Aberdeen, **14** Airdrieonians, **15** Davie Cooper.

• MANCHESTER UTD 8 •

Answers on page 298

1 Who beat Manchester Utd 2-1 in the 1957 FA Cup Final?

2 Which lost 4-2 to Manchester Utd in the 1948 FA Cup Final?

3 Who scored Manchester Utd's last goal of the 1992-93 season?

4 Which international defender moved from Leeds Utd to Manchester Utd on a free transfer?

5 Which three other clubs were in Manchester Utd's 1997-98 Champions' League Group?

6 Who was Manchester Utd's first ever £200,000 signing back in 1972?

7 What was the nickname of Manchester Utd's early 20th century player Enoch Walker?

8 Who scored the only goal of the game as Arsenal beat Manchester Utd at Old Trafford in 1997-98?

9 How many home matches did Manchester Utd play on their way to the 1990 FA Cup Final?

10 Which team had Manchester Utd played before the Munich air crash?

11 Kevin Moran left Manchester Utd in 1988 for which club?

12 Pat Crerand became assistant to which Manchester Utd manager?

13 When did Manchester Utd first win the League Cup?

14 Manchester Utd's highest league win is 9-0 against Ipswich in March 1995. Who scored 5 goals in that game?

15 Which team came second and how many points behind were they when Manchester Utd won the first Premier League?

Answers to page 298

1 Bristol City, **2** Neil Sullivan, **3** Three, **4** First player to be sent off at Wembley, **5** Jamie Redknapp, **6** 1990, **7** Sao Paulo, **8** 1894, **9** Foulkes, **10** East Sterlingshire and Falkirk, **11** France, **12** Ted Bates, **13** Manchester City, **14** Dean Saunders, **15** Ayr Utd.

RANGERS 3

Answers on page 295

1 Rangers' Euro Cup Winners' Cup victory was marred by hooligan trouble. What was the Scottish team's penalty for this trouble?

2 Who did Rangers beat 2-1 in the 1979 Scottish League Cup Final?

3 Who in July 1986 moved to Rangers for £600,000, a new record fee for a keeper?

4 Who did Rangers beat 3-0 in the 1950 Scottish FA Cup Final?

5 Which club did Mel Sterland leave to join Rangers?

6 At which ground do Rangers play their reserve team games?

7 Who did Rangers beat 2-1 in the 1993 Scottish FA Cup Final?

8 Who did Rangers beat 3-2 in the 1989 Scottish League Cup Final?

9 Which two Rangers players were found guilty of disorderly conduct likely to provoke a breach of the peace following a brawl in the Old Firm game in October 1987?

10 Which club did Paul Rideout leave join after leaving Rangers?

11 Who announced in October his intention to leave rangers at the end of the 1997-98 season?

12 When Rangers won the Scottish Southern Cup in 1946 it was the forerunner of which tournament?

13 Who beat Rangers 4-1 in the 1982 Scottish FA Cup Final?

14 Who did Rangers beat 2-1 in the 1992 Scottish FA Cup Final?

15 Which former Scotland and Rangers winger died from a brain haemorrhage at the age of 39 in March 1995?

Answers to page 295

1 Don Masson, **2** Raith Rovers, **3** Gullit and Van Basten, **4** Bristol Rovers, **5** Houston Astrodome, Texas, **6** Everton, **7** Dobson, **8** 1894, **9** Liverpool, **10** West Ham Utd, **11** Spain 1964, **12** 10, **13** Crystal Palace, **14** Luton Town, **15** 1964.

QUIZ 192

Answers on page 296

1 Which team was relegated in 1980, 1981 and 1982?

2 Who failed to stop a shot from the halfway line on the opening day of the 1997-98 Premier League season?

3 How many quarter-finals went to extra time in the 1986 World Cup?

4 What famous first goes to Boris Stankovic?

5 Which Liverpool player scored from a free-kick to beat Blackburn Rovers in the last game of the 1994-95 season?

6 Which year saw the first all-seater FA Cup Final?

7 Which club did Middlesborough buy Juninho from?

8 In what year did Rangers play Celtic in the Scottish Cup Final for the first time?

9 Which Bill of Manchester Utd won his only England cap in 1954?

10 Which Scottish clubs with grounds half a mile apart are also alphabetically next to each other?

11 In which country were the 1998 World Cup finals held?

12 Who succeeded George Roughton as manager of Southampton in 1955?

13 Which soccer team does England's World Cup referee Paul Durkin support?

14 Mark Lawrenson was fired as Oxford manager for complaining about the sale of which player to Derby?

15 Steve Nicol made his League debut with which Scottish club?

Answers to page 296

1 Aston Villa, **2** Blackpool, **3** Bryan Robson, **4** Dennis Irwin, **5** Feyenoord, Juventus, Kosice, **6** Ian Storey Moore, **7** Knocker, **8** Marc Overmars, **9** None, **10** Red Star Belgrade, **11** Sporting Gijon, **12** Tommy Docherty, **13** 1992, **14** Andy Cole, **15** Aston Villa ten points behind with 74.

QUIZ 193

Answers on page 301

1 Paul Goddard moved from West Ham Utd to which club for £400,000 in October 1986?

2 George Curtis followed Don Mackay as manager at which club?

3 Who was the Sheffiled Wednesday striker who had a leg amputated?

4 In what decade did Rangers first win the Championship?

5 Which ex-Manchester City keeper recommended Eike Immel to his old club?

6 Which team was the first to win the newly-named UEFA Cup in 1972?

7 Which Danish international broke his leg in the opening match of the 1984 finals?

8 When did Manchester Utd first win the FA Cup?

9 What is Teddy Sheringham's middle name?

10 The resignation of Director Richard Thompson in May 1996 meant that which club was up for sale?

11 Who succeeded John Lyall as manager of Ipswich Town in 1995?

12 Which Tottenahm Hotspur player was the First Division leading scorer in 1986-87?

13 Which London club signed Slaven Bilic?

14 Dario Gradi followed Malcolm Allison as manager of which club?

15 How many Premiership and English sides are called 'United'?

Answers to page 301

1 Everton, **2** Aberdeen, **3** Newcastle Utd, **4** France, **5** Rotterdam, **6** Sunderland, **7** West Germany, **8** Crystal Palace, **9** USA, **10** QPR, **11** Bournmouth, **12** Basle, **13** Manchester City, **14** Tottenham Hotspur, **15** Liverpool.

QUIZ 194

Answers on page 302

1 Who beat Dundee 5-3 in the 1967-68 Scottish League Cup Final?

2 Who beat Stade de Reims 4-3 in the 1956 European Cup Final?

3 Who lost 1-0 to Nottingham Forest in the Final of 1980 European Cup?

4 Which manager, still living in England, was dismissed by Celtic in June 1994?

5 At which club did Dean Saunders make his League debut?

6 Simon Garner and Mark Atkins were in the same side at which club?

7 Which England manager was born in Worksop?

8 Who was Birmingham City boss between 1965 and 1970?

9 Who was the German skipper who broke his arm in his first game in the1992 European Championship in Sweden?

10 Who managed the Great Britain team in the 1948 Olympic games?

11 How many international goals did Jim Baxter score?

12 Which competition started as the Fairs Cup in 1955?

13 Vinny Samways first played in an FA Cup Final for which team?

14 When was the start of the First Division as it is today?

15 Where do Shrewsbury Town play at home?

Answers to page 302

1 Durie, **2** Poland, **3** 10, **4** European Cup Winners' Cup, **5** Sagittarius, **6** 67, **7** 1991, **8** Everton, **9** Scotland, **10** 44, **11** Four, **12** Six, **13** 48, **14** For never being booked or sent off in his playing career, **15** Spain.

QUIZ 195

Answers on page 299

1 Stuart McCall made his international debut while at which club?

2 Which team were beaten 2-1 by Rangers in the 1993 Scottish FA Cup Final?

3 At which club did Kevin Keegan have Imre Varadi as a strike partner?

4 Which country lost 2-0 to West Germany in the 1986 World Cup semi-final?

5 Where was the 1968 European Cup Winners' Cup Final held?

6 Which club has a fanzine called *A Love Supreme*?

7 Which country lost 3-1 to Sweden in the 1958 World Cup semi-final?

8 Which club reached the semi-finals of the FA and League Cups in the 1994-95 season and were relegated from the Premiership?

9 In which country were the 1994 World Cup finals held?

10 Which club did Clive Wilson leave to join Tottenham Hotspur?

11 From which club did Liverpool sign Jamie Redknapp?

12 Where was the 1969 European Cup Winners' Cup Final held?

13 Which club did defenders Booth and Caton play for?

14 Which team won the 1984 UEFA Cup?

15 Which team won the 1973 UEFA Cup?

Answers to page 299

1 Newcastle Utd, **2** Coventry City, **3** Derek Dooley, **4** 1890s, **5** Bert Trautmann, **6** Tottenham Hotspur, **7** Allan Simonsen, **8** 1909, **9** Paul, **10** QPR, **11** George Burnley, **12** Clive Allen, **13** West Ham Utd, **14** Crystal Palace, **15** 16.

• GARY LINEKER 2 •

Answers on page 300

1 Which Gordon was Gary's regular strike partner in his last League season in England?

2 Who were the opponents for the World Cup hat-trick Gary scored in Mexico?

3 How many goals has Gary scored in World Cup finals?

4 What was the only major European Trophy that Gary won?

5 What is Gary's star sign?

6 How many goals did Gary score in his 105 games for Spurs?

7 In which year did Gary win an FA Cup winner's medal?

8 At which club did Gary hit his best League goals total of 30 in a season?

9 Against which country did Gary make his international debut?

10 How many goals did Gary score in his 99 League games for Barcelona?

11 Gary was on the spot twice against Cameroon in Italia '90, but before the game how many years had gone by without an English penalty award?

12 How many goals did Gary score in the 1986 World Cup?

13 How many goals did Gary score for England?

14 Why was he awarded £20,000 by FIFA?

15 Gary scored all four of England's goals in games against Malaysia and which other country?

Answers to page 300

1 Celtic, **2** Real Madrid, **3** Hamburg, **4** Lou Macari, **5** Swansea City, **6** Blackburn Rovers, **7** Graham Taylor, **8** Stan Cullis, **9** Rudi Voller, **10** Matt Busby, **11** Three, **12** UEFA Cup, **13** Tottenham Hotspur, **14** 1992, **15** Gay Meadow.

CELTIC 3

Answers on page 305

1 Who was league ever-present for Celtic in 1995-96?

2 Which Celtic striker was known as 'The Iron Man'?

3 Who did Celtic beat 1-0 in the 1951 Scottish FA Cup Final?

4 Who quit as Celtic boss after winning the League in 1998?

5 Who beat Celtic 2-1 in the 1984 Scottish FA Cup Final?

6 Who did Kenny Dalglish replace as skipper of Celtic?

7 Who beat Celtic 1-0 in the 1974 Scottish League Cup Final?

8 Who beat Celtic 3-1 in the 1956 Scottish FA Cup Final?

9 Which Celtic player hit the first hat-trick in a Scottish FA Cup final?

10 Which English club did Celtic's fullback Tommy Gemmell play for?

11 Who beat Celtic 9-8 on penalties in the 1990 Scottish FA Cup Final?

12 Who holds the League appearance record at Celtic?

13 Who did Celtic beat 2-1 in the 1985 Scottish FA Cup Final?

14 Who did Celtic beat 6-2 in the 1969 Scottish League Cup Final?

15 Which Celtic goalkeeper was called up at short notice by Scotland when Andy Goram made his shock withdrawal from the 1998 World Cup?

Answers to page 305

1 Nigeria, **2** Manchester Utd, **3** Australia, **4** Coventry City, **5** Leeds Utd, **6** Hamilton Academical, **7** Harvey, **8** Stoke City, **9** 1959, **10** Aberdeen, **11** Manchester City, **12** Leeds Utd, **13** 1970s, **14** They failed to qualify, **15** Gold.

QUIZ 196

Answers on page 306

1 Which company was the first to sponsor Tottenham Hotspur's shirts?

2 In December 1997, which manager left West Bromwich Albion to take over the reins at Queen's Park Rangers?

3 Who moved from Sampdoria to Juventus for a world record £12m in 1992?

4 From which club did John Gregory join Aston Villa as new boss?

5 Steve Spriggs set an appearance record at which club?

6 Which Brondby and future Arsenal player scored the opening goal for Denmark in the 1992 European Championship Final against Germany?

7 Which English club was the first to field three Spanish players in the same team?

8 Which was Jimmy Quinn's first League club?

9 Which club had players in 148 consecutive England internationals between October 1938 and April 1963?

10 Bobby Robson became boss of which Spanish giants in 1996?

11 Who broke his neck in the 1956 FA Cup Final?

12 Which Norwegian international was bought from Bayern Munich to replace Larry Lloyd at Nottingham Forest in 1980-81?

13 Who beat Benfica 1-0 in the 1964 European Cup Final?

14 Who beat Eintracht Frankfurt 7-3 in the 1960 European Cup Final?

15 David Clarke made a record 517 appearances, for which Scottish club between 1968-86?

Answers to page 306

1 1992-1993, **2** Sampdoria, **3** Manchester Utd, **4** Derby County, **5** Bari, **6** Wimbledon, **7** Sunderland, **8** G Petchley, **9** Mel Machin, **10** Athletico Bilbao, **11** Leicester City, **12** Brentford, **13** Squash, **14** Nottingham Forest, **15** Andy Goram.

QUIZ 197

Answers on page 303

1 Steve McManaman made his international debut as a sub in November 1994, against which country?

2 Which team was beaten 2-0 by Bolton in the 1958 FA Cup Final?

3 Ned Zelic has captained which country?

4 Kevin Gallacher and Paul Furlong were in the same team at which club?

5 Which club did Richard Jobson join on leaving Oldham?

6 Which team are known as the Accies?

7 Which Colin became manager of Everton in 1987?

8 Which club has a fanzine called the *Victoria Voice*?

9 Tom Finney last played for England in which year?

10 Willie Miller seta League appearance record at which club?

11 David White and Keith Curle were in the same team at which club?

12 Which was Scott Sellar's first League club?

13 In what decade was Juninho born?

14 At what stage did France get knocked out of the 1994 World Cup?

15 What colour are Dumbarton's home shirts?

Answers to page 303

1 Gordon Marshall, **2** Jimmy Quinn, **3** Motherwell, **4** Wim Jansen, **5** Aberdeen, **6** Billy McNeill, **7** Dundee, **8** Hearts, **9** Jimmy Quinn, **10** Nottingham Forrest, **11** Aberdeen, **12** Billy McNeill, **13** Dundee Utd, **14** Hibernian, **15** Jonathan Gould.

QUIZ 198

Answers on page 304

1 Which year was the first season of the Premiership?

2 Graeme Souness moved from Liverpool to which club for £650,000 in June 1984?

3 Eric Cantona moved from Leeds Utd to which club for £1.2m in November 1992?

4 Bruce Rioch moved from Aston Villa to which club for £200,000 in March 1974?

5 David Platt moved from Aston Villa to which club for £5.5 million in July 1991?

6 Everton beat which club 8-0 in the League Cup in August 1978?

7 Coventry City recorded a 5-0 League Cup win over which club in January 1990?

8 Who succeeded Gordon Jago as manager of Millwall in 1977?

9 Who succeeded Alan Clarke as manager of Barnsley in 1980?

10 With which Spanish team did Aston Villa draw 0-0 in the 1997-98 UEFA Cup second round first leg?

11 Which team were beaten 3-1 by Wolves in the 1949 FA Cup Final?

12 As a teenager Rod Stewart had trials at which club?

13 Rangers player Marco Negri was unfit to play part of the 97-98 season because of an eye injury sustained playing which other sport?

14 Hans Van Breukelen first played for which English club?

15 Who in 1991 became Scotland's most expensive keeper?

Answers to page 304

1 Holsten, **2** Ray Harford, **3** Gianluca Vialli, **4** Wycombe Wanderers, **5** Cambridge Utd, **6** John Jensen, **7** Wigan Athletic, **8** Swindon Town, **9** Wolves, **10** Barcelona, **11** Bert Trautmann, **12** Einer Aas, **13** Internazionale, **14** Real Madrid, **15** East Fife.

QUIZ 199

Answers on page 309

1 Which year in the 1950s saw the first floodlit Football League match?

2 In March 1998, who won the African Cup of Nations?

3 Who missed the fourth spot kick for Holland during their semi-final shoot-out against Brazil in the 1998 World Cup?

4 Richard Gough moved from Tottenham Hotspur to which club for £1.5m in September 1997?

5 What is the main colour of Rotherham's home shirts?

6 Which Scottish striker won the 1992-93 Golden Boot award, despite missing a month of the season with a broken leg?

7 Which A C Milan player was European Footballer of the Year in 1992?

8 Which Moscow Dynamo player was European Footballer of the Year in 1963?

9 Who was fined in 1996 for a newspaper article criticising Ruud Gullit?

10 Who beat Wolves 4-1 in the 1949 FA Cup Final?

11 Who beat Arsenal 1-0 in the 1980 FA Cup Final?

12 Who beat Manchester City 3-2 in the 1981 FA Cup Final replay?

13 Which team were beaten 1-0 by Leeds Utd in the 1972 FA Cup Final?

14 Which team came second in the first Premirt League and how many points behind Manchester Utd did they finish?

15 Manchester Utd recorded a 8-0 FA Cup win over which club in February 1949?

Answers to page 309

1 Alex McLeish, **2** Hearts, **3** Rangers, **4** Real Madrid, **5** Alex Smith, **6** Hearts, **7** Rangers, **8** Red, **9** Celtic, **10** Hewitt, **11** Rangers, **12** St Mirren, **13** The Whites, **14** Peterhead, **15** Benny Yorston.

BLACKBURN 2

Answers on page 310

1 Who was Blackburn's only League ever present in 1994-95?

2 Who did Kenny Dalglish succeed as manager of Blackburn?

3 Who is the multi-millionaire owner of Blackburn?

4 Who moved from Sheffield Wednesday to Blackburn in 1993 to set a club record fee for a transfer received?

5 Where did Alan Shearer score an away hat-trick in 1995-96?

6 Manchester City in 1995 and Blackburn in 1996 both played how many League games before a win?

7 Which left-back was displaced by Graeme Le Saux at Blackburn?

8 How many hat-tricks did Alan Shearer score for Blackburn Rovers in their 1995-96 season?

9 Who scored from a free-kick for Liverpool to beat Blackburn in the last game of the 1994-95 season?

10 Simon Barker moved from Blackburn to which club for £400,000 in July 1988?

11 Who beat Blackburn 3-0 in the 1960 FA Cup Final?

12 In which decade did Blackburn first win the FA Cup?

13 What does Alan Shearer eat with chicken before every game?

14 Which Blackburn player was sent off after three minutes of his debut against Everton?

15 Kevin Hird moved from Blackburn Rovers to which club for £357,000 in February 1979?

Answers to page 310

1 Nottingham, **2** Paris St Germain, **3** Black, **4** Jason Dozzell, **5** Ray Wood, **6** AC Milan, **7** Charlie Nicholas, **8** Turin, **9** Charlton Athletic, **10** Martyn, **11** Ian Rush, **12** 30, **13** Preston North End, **14** Kenny Dalglish, **15** Everton.

ABERDEEN 3

Answers on page 307

1 Which Aberdeen defender made 77 appearances for Scotland between 1980-93?

2 Who did Aberdeen beat 3-0 in the 1986 Scottish FA Cup Final?

3 Who beat Aberdeen 2-1 in the 1993 Scottish FA Cup Final?

4 Who lost 2-1 to Aberdeen after extra time in the 1983 Cup-Winners' Cup Final?

5 Who succeeded Ian Porterfield as manager of Aberdeen?

6 Which team were beaten 3-0 by Aberdeen in the 1986 Scottish FA Cup Final?

7 Who did Aberdeen beat 1-0 in the 1983 Scottish FA Cup Final?

8 What colour are Aberdeen's home shorts?

9 Who did Aberdeen beat 3-1 in the 1970 Scottish FA Cup Final?

10 Who scored Aberdeen's winner in the 1983 Cup Winners' Cup Final?

11 Who did Aberdeen beat 2-1 in the 1990 Scottish League Cup Final?

12 Who did Aberdeen beat 2-1 in the 1956 Scottish League Cup Final?

13 What were Aberdeen originally nicknamed before they became The Wasps, and then The Dons?

14 Which club did they beat 13-0 in February 1923?

15 Which Aberdeen player scored 38 goals in the 1929-30 season?

Answers to page 307

1 1956, **2** Egypt, **3** Frank De Boer, **4** Rangers, **5** Red, **6** Ally McCoist, **7** Marco Van Basten, **8** Lev Yashin, **9** Vinnie Jones, **10** Portsmouth, **11** West Ham Utd, **12** Tottenham Hotspur, **13** Arsenal, **14** Aston Villa 74 points, **15** Yeovil Town.

QUIZ 200

Answers on page 308

1 In which city was Andy Cole born?

2 Which French club won the 1996 European Cup Winners' Cup?

3 What colour are Bradford City's home shorts?

4 Who moved from Ipswich Town to Tottenham Hotspur in 1993 to set a club record for a transfer fee received?

5 Which keeper was injured in the 1957 FA Cup Final?

6 Which club did Ray Wilkins join on leaving Manchester Utd?

7 Which player's leaving caused Jimmy Greaves to say, "Stringfellows will miss him"?

8 In which City was the 1990 England against West Germany World Cup semi-final held?

9 England cricketer Mickey Stewart played for which Football League side?

10 Which Nigel went on from non League St Blazey to play for England?

11 Who moved from Chester for £300,000 in 1980 to set a club record for a transfer fee received?

12 How many points did Newcastle Utd get from the first 10 games of the 1992-93 promotion season?

13 Which side beat Hyde 26-0?

14 Which Liverpool player appeared three times at Wembley in 1977-78, his first season in England?

15 At which club did Gary Lineker score 30 goals in a season?

Answers to page 308

1 Alan Shearer, **2** Don Mackay, **3** Jack Walker, **4** Paul Warhurst, **5** Whitehart Lane, **6** 12, **7** Alan Wright, **8** Five, **9** Jamie Redknapp, **10** QPR, **11** Wolverhampton Wanderers, **12** 1880s, **13** Beans, **14** Garry Flitcroft, **15** Leeds Utd.

QUIZ 201

Answers on page 313

1 Who did Chelsea beat 2-1 in the 1971 Cup-Winners' Cup Final replay?

2 Which league club did England captain Billy Wright begin his career at in 1941?

3 Which London side won 6-2 at home on the first leg of a UEFA Cup game in the 1980s and were beaten 4-0 away?

4 Which club beat Barcelona to win the European Super Cup in 1982?

5 How many players were sent off in the League game between Rangers and Celtic in March 1991?

6 Who scored twice for Colchester Utd in the 1970s as they toppled Leeds Utd in the FA Cup?

7 Hughie Gallacher joined Newcastle Utd from which club?

8 Who moved from Leeds Utd for £3.5 million in June 1996 to set a club record for a transfer fee received?

9 Which Graeme bacame boss of Oldham Athletic in November 1994?

10 What was the first London club that Chris Armstrong played for?

11 What was formed in Paris on May 21, 1904?

12 Where was Raich Carter born?

13 How many games did Preston North End lose in their first League season?

14 Steve Hodge first played in an FA Cup Final for which team?

15 Which football executive said, " People think I'm a short, fat bloke, whereas I'm really a tall fat Bloke"?

Answers to page 313

1 Southampton, **2** Leeds Utd, **3** Aston Villa, **4** Red, **5** Terry Venables, **6** Gerd Muller, **7** 3rd Division 1, (1890-91, 1900-01), **8** Strachan, **9** Birmingham City, **10** Aston Villa, **11** Mo Johnston, **12** Blackburn, **13** England, **14** Given, **15** Glasgow Rangers.

QUIZ 202

Answers on page 314

1 In which decade was Roy Keane born?

2 What financial breakthrough was made by goalkeeper Nigel Martyn when he was transferred from Bristol Rovers to Crystal Palace in 1989?

3 Who scored 7 goals in a game for Iraq against Maldives in June 1996?

4 Which England player was pictured in a Portugese nightclub shortly before the 1998 World Cup Finals?

5 Which club does former *EastEnders* actor Tom Watt support?

6 In the 1994 World Cup first round stage Russia was knocked out having been beaten by which two countries?

7 Which international manager was born in Middlesborough in 1927?

8 Which player wrote *So Far So Good*?

9 Which London club was the first to be relegated from the FA Premier League?

10 Who beat Roma 4-2 in the 1984 European Cup Final on penalties?

11 Which Dave became boss of Birmingham City in 1989?

12 Which team won the 1985 UEFA Cup?

13 Which Liverpool manager signed Kenny Dalglish?

14 Which member of the Tottenham Hotspur double side went on to manage a Championship team?

15 Who were the first club to win promotion on a penalty shoot-out?

Answers to page 314

1 Branco, **2** George Camsell, **3** Nottingham Forest, **4** Brian Clough, **5** Graeme Souness, **6** Olympique Marseille, **7** Brighton and Hove Albion, **8** Graham Le Saux, **9** Paul Merson, **10** Bryan Robson, **11** Jack Charlton, **12** Sao Paulo, **13** Bryan Robson, **14** Jack Charlton, **15** Southampton.

QUIZ 203

Answers on page 311

1 Armstrong and Moran scored Euro goals in the same game for which club?

2 Jock Stein followed Jimmy Armfield as boss of which club?

3 Charlie Aitken set a League appearance record at which club?

4 What colour are Barnsley's home socks?

5 Which manager said that Alan Shearer was "so good it's frightening"?

6 Which Bayern Munich player won the 1969-70 Golden Boot award?

7 What is the highest position Notts County have ever achieved in the League?

8 Which midfielder Gordon was awarded an OBE in 1993?

9 Alberto Tarantini came from Argentina to which British club?

10 Which was Tony Dorigo's first League club?

11 Who said "For a while I did unite Rangers and Celtic fans.There were people in both camps who hated me"?

12 Tony Gale won a Championship medal at which club?

13 Which country won the Euro '96 tournament Fair Play Award?

14 Who started the game in goal for the Republic of Ireland when they lost to Argentina in a friendly in April 1998?

15 Trevor Steven moved from Everton to which club for £1.5m in June 1989?

Answers to page 311

1 Real Madrid, **2** Wolverhampton, **3** QPR, **4** Aston Villa, **5** 4, **6** Ray Crawford, **7** Airdrie, **8** Gary Speed, **9** Sharp, **10** Millwall, **11** FIFA, **12** Sunderland, **13** None, **14** Tottenham Hotspur, **15** Graham Kelly.

• MIDDLESBROUGH 2 •

Answers on page 312

1 Which 1994 World Cup winner later played for Middlesborough?

2 Which player scored 59 League goals for Middlesborough in 1926-27?

3 Middlesborough player Andy Wilson scored 5 goals in a match in October 1923. Who were the opponents?

4 Who was the young Middlesborough striker who made his England debut against Wales in 1959?

5 Which former Liverpool star made his only appearance for Spurs as a substitute in a UEFA Cup game before transferring to Middlesborough?

6 To which French club was Fabrizio Ravanelli eventually transferred from Middlesborough for £5 million?

7 Middlesborough player Brian Clough scored 5 goals in a match in August 1958. Who were the opponents?

8 Which Blackburn Rovers and England defender suffered a long-term injury against Middlesborough in December 1995?

9 Who scored Middlesborough's first goal in the second leg of their Coca-Cola Cup semi-final against Liverpool?

10 Which 40-year-old was registered at Middlesborough as a player-manager?

11 Which manager took Middlesborough into the top flight for the first time?

12 Which club did Juninho play for before joining Middlesborough?

13 Which Middlesborough manager signed Fabrizio Ravanelli?

14 Which Middlesborough manager said - days before resigning - "We are on the crest of a slump"?

15 David Armstrong moved from Middlesborough to which club for £600,000 in August 1981?

Answers to page 312

1 1970s, **2** He was the first million pound goalkeeper, **3** Karim Bagheri, **4** Teddy Sheringham, **5** Arsenal, **6** Sweden and Brazil, **7** Don Revie, **8** Liam Brady, **9** Crystal Palace, **10** Liverpool, **11** Mackay, **12** Real Madrid, **13** Bob Paisley, **14** Dave MacKay (Derby), **15** Torquay Utd.

ARSENAL 6

Answers on page 317

1 In which city did Arsenal first win the Cup Winners Cup?

2 Who scored Ipswich Town's 1978 FA Cup winner against Arsenal?

3 Which Arsenal player dropped his shorts to the crowd in a 1979 game against Coventry City?

4 In which city was the 1994 Cup Winners' Cup Final between Arsenal and Parma played?

5 Who scored 42 League goals for Arsenal in season 1934-35?

6 Who did Arsenal beat in the final league game of the 70s double season?

7 In what decade did Arsenal first win the Championship?

8 Who scored Arsenal's first goal in the 1988-89 title decider at Anfield?

9 Which 46-year-old physiotherapist became Arsenal manager?

10 Who followed George Swindin as manager of Arsenal?

11 Which former player is the goalkeeping coach at Arsenal?

12 Ian Wright broke Arsenal's goal-scoring record with a hat-trick against which team?

13 Who managed Arsenal before Arsene Wenger?

14 Charlie Nicholas left which club to join Arsenal?

15 Who holds the Arsenal League appearance record?

Answers to page 317

1 RSC Anderlecht, **2** Norwich City, **3** Internazionale, **4** Jimmy Hill, **5** Aston Villa, **6** Bruges, **7** Manchester City, **8** Division 1, Champions (1920-21, 1959-60), **9** Leicester City, **10** Kevin Keegan, **11** Manchester Utd, **12** Steve Chalmers, **13** Tommy Lawton, **14** Rangers, **15** Jack Taylor.

QUIZ 204

Answers on page 318

1 Who was top scorer for Norwich City in the 1993-94 UEFA Cup campaign?

2 Who moved from Sheffield Utd to Leeds Utd for £2.7m in 1993 to set a club record for a transfer fee received?

3 How long was Bill Lambton manager of Scuthorpe Utd for?

4 How many days did Brian Clough reign as boss of Leeds Utd in 1974?

5 Who hit 42 goals in a season for Arsenal in the 1930s?

6 In which year did Bill Shankly retire?

7 Jimmy Frizzell was boss of which club from 1970 to 1982?

8 Who has scored most goals in for Blackburn Rovers?

9 Which Italian club did John Charles play for?

10 John Bailey first played in an FA Cup Final for which team?

11 In which decade was Dave Beasant born?

12 What replaced goal average when calculating Football League positions after 1974?

13 Steve Walford first played in an FA Cup Final for which team?

14 In the 1997-98 season which Nationwide First Division side knocked Manchester Utd out of the Coca-Cola Cup in the third round?

15 Who moved from Barnsley to Nottingham Forest in 1991 to set a club record for a transfer fee received?

Answers to page 318

1 Blackburn Rovers, **2** MBE, **3** Wimbledon, **4** Bobby Charlton, **5** Zidane, **6** Gerd Muller, **7** Johnny Giles, **8** Carlisle Utd, **9** Matt Le Tissier, **10** Andrei Kanchelskis, **11** Gerd Muller, **12** Sheffield Wednesday, **13** Craig Johnston (took it to show family in Australia), **14** First own goal in a Final, **15** John Jensen.

QUIZ 205

Answers on page 315

1 Which club beat Liverpool to win the European Super Cup in 1978?

2 Millwall player Richard Parker scored 5 goals in a match in August 1926. Who were the opponents?

3 Which team won the 1991 UEFA Cup?

4 Which manager took Coventry City into the first division in the 1960s?

5 Which club has a fanzine called *Heroes and Villains*?

6 Who did Liverpool beat in the 1976 UEFA Cup Final?

7 Which soccer team do the Oasis brothers Liam and Noel Gallagher support?

8 What is the highest position Burnley have ever achieved in the League?

9 Which club had a fanzine called *Where's The Money Gone*?

10 Which Hamburg player was European Footballer of the Year in 1978?

11 Gordon Hill first played in an FA Cup Final for which team?

12 Who scored Celtic's 1967 European Cup Final winner?

13 Which England player hit 22 goals in 23 international games?

14 Who beat Hearts 3-1 in the 1976 Scottish FA Cup Final?

15 Which English referee officiated in the 1974 World Cup Finals?

Answers to page 315

1 Paris, **2** Roger Osbourne, **3** Sammy Nelson, **4** Sweden, **5** Ted Drake, **6** Tottenham Hotspur, **7** 1930s, **8** Alan Smith, **9** Bertie Mee, **10** Billy Wright, **11** Bob Wilson, **12** Bolton, **13** Bruce Rioch, **14** Celtic, **15** David O'Leary.

QUIZ 206

Answers on page 316

1 Which club did Ossie Ardiles join on loan in March 1988?

2 Which honour did England goalkeeper Ray Clemence receive in the Queen's Birthday Honours' List in 1987?

3 Andy Thorn first played in an FA Cup Final for which team?

4 Who became England's all-time leading scorer when he netted against Sweden in 1968?

5 Who was the scorer of France's two first-half goals in the 1998 World Cup Final against Brazil?

6 Which Bayern Munich player won the 1971-72 Golden Boot award?

7 Which ex-West Brom manager said, "the only certainty about management is the sack"?

8 Alan Ross set a League record for appearances at which club?

9 Who won the *Match of the Day* 'Goal of the Season' in 1995 for a 35 yard chip shot against Blackburn Rovers?

10 Which player hit a hat-trick in the November 1994 Manchester derby?

11 Who scored ten goals for Germany in the 1970 World Cup finals?

12 At which club did Chris Turner make his debut?

13 Which player took the actual FA Cup out of England and why?

14 What famous first went to Lord Kinnaird in the 1877 FA Cup Final?

15 Who scored a great Final Euro '92 goal and then moved to play in London?

Answers to page 316

1 Jeremy Goss, **2** Brian Deane, **3** 3 days, **4** 44, **5** Ted Drake, **6** 1974, **7** Oldham Athletic, **8** Simon Garner, **9** Juventus, **10** Everton, **11** 1950s, **12** Goal Difference, **13** Arsenal, **14** Ipswich Town, **15** Carl Tiler.

QUIZ 207

Answers on page 321

1 Who moved from Norwich City for £5.5 million in July 1994?

2 Newcastle Utd played which club in the first English League game to be played under floodlights?

3 Dario Gradi said that which ex-Crewe Alexandra player "can go on to become a truly great player"?

4 In 1996 Kevin Keegan was incensed by Alex Ferguson's comments concerning which opposing team?

5 Who were the first team to beat Tottenham Hotspur in an FA Cup Final?

6 In which decade was Des Lynam born?

7 Which ex-footballer's bad language on *Wogan* in 1990 brought accusations that he was drunk?

8 Who has played for Leeds Utd, Wimbledon, Manchester City, Chelsea, and Everton?

9 How many times were Aberdeen relegated in the 50 years following the Second World War?

10 Which former Liverpool player became manager of Brighton?

11 What was the score in the first round, first leg of Chelsea's Cup Winners' Cup second round tie in Tromso, Norway?

12 How many times did Ray Wilkins play for England?

13 What are the two main colours on Bournemouth's home shirts?

14 Outside which football ground were the Hovis adverts filmed?

15 Kevin Moran and Colin Hendry were in the same team at which club?

Answers to page 321

1 Kevin Keegan, **2** Mary Poppins, **3** Robledo, **4** 1910, **5** Bobby Moncur, **6** Each goal was scored against a different goalkeeper. (The first against Martin Thomas, then outfied substitute Chris Hepworth and finally Peter Beardsley), **7** Kevin Keegan on his swift departure from Newcastle, **8** Michael Owen, **9** Roeder, **10** 27, **11** Charlton Athletic, **12** Faustino Asprilla, **13** Leicester City, **14** Mirandinha, **15** Shaka Hislop.

ASTON VILLA 3

Answers on page 322

1 With which Spanish team did Aston Villa draw 0-0 in the 1997-98 UEFA Cup second round, first leg?

2 Who scored a penalty for Aston Villa against Manchester Utd in the 1994 League Cup Final?

3 Who succeeded Billy McNeil as manager of Aston Villa in 1987?

4 Which club did Mervyn Day leave to join Aston Villa?

5 Who scored the only goal to win the European Cup Final for Aston Villa?

6 Who was Aston Villa's winger when they won the 1981 title?

7 Who lost to Aston Villa in the 1982 Super Cup?

8 Which European Cup winner and Aston Villa captain played more than 700 matches between 1969 and 1984?

9 Who succeeded Tony Barton as manager of Aston Villa in 1984?

10 Which club did Paul McGrath leave to join Aston Villa?

11 What was the nickname of Aston Villa's 1930's player Thomas Waring?

12 Shaun Teale went to which club after leaving Villa?

13 David Platt moved from Aston Villa to which club for £5.5 million in July 1991?

14 Bruce Rioch moved from Aston Villa to which club for £200,000 in March 1974?

15 Who scored 5 goals in a game for Aston Villa against Ireland in February 1882?

Answers to page 322

1 Juventus, **2** Wimbledon, **3** Piet Keizer, **4** Hamburg, **5** Alan Hanson, **6** Barnsley, **7** Northern Ireland and the Republic of Ireland, **8** Chris Waddle and Stuart Pearce, **9** Newcastle Utd, **10** Leeds Utd, **11** Berti Vogts, **12** Mark Hughes, **13** Red, **14** Chelsea, **15** Groningen.

NEWCASTLE 2

Answers on page 319

1 Which boss took Newcastle Utd into the Premier League?

2 With which film character did Newcastle directors Hall and Shepherd compare Alan Shearer?

3 What was the surname of 1950s Newcastle Utd brothers Ted and George?

4 When did Newcastle Utd first win the FA Cup?

5 Which Newcastle Utd player hit his first goals for seven years in the 1969 Inter-Cities Fairs Cup Final?

6 What was unusual about West Ham defender Alvin Martin's hat-trick in the 8-1 thrashing of Newcastle in 1987?

7 Which manager said, "I did not jump. I was pushed. And so abruptly that my salary was cut off immediately"?

8 Who scored a first-half hat-trick for Liverpool against Newcastle in Ruud Gullits first game in charge?

9 Which Glenn was Newcastle Utd skipper when Gazza made his debut?

10 How many points did Newcastle Utd take from their first ten games of the 1995-96 League season?

11 Keegan's last game as Newcastle Utd's manager was an FA Cup tie against which London Club?

12 Which Newcastle player was booked because he put his shirt on the corner flag and raised it to the crowd after scoring a UEFA Cup goal against Metz?

13 Which club did Alan Shearer score his first Newcastle Utd hat-trick against?

14 Which Brazilian player joined Newcastle Utd in 1987?

15 Who moved from reading to Newcastle Utd in August 1995 to set a club record for a transfer fee received?

Answers to page 319

1 Chris Sutton, **2** Portsmouth, **3** David Platt, **4** Leeds Utd, **5** Coventry City, **6** 1940s, **7** George Best's, **8** Terry Phelan, **9** Never, **10** Jimmy Case, **11** Tromso 3 Chelsea 2, **12** 84, **13** Red and Black, **14** Ewood Park, Blackburn, **15** Blackburn Rovers.

QUIZ 208

Answers on page 320

1 Which foreign team did Liam Brady move to in 1980?

2 Which team was John Scales playing for when he made his first FA Cup Final appearance?

3 Which Ajax star of the 70s was Holland's first full-time soccer professional?

4 At which German club did Franz Beckenbauer end his playing days?

5 Which defender was born in Alloa on 13 June 1955?

6 Viv Anderson was player/manager of which club in 1993-94?

7 Which two football teams met for the first time when they played at Lansdowne Road, Dublin on September 10th 1978?

8 Which two England players missed penalties in Italia '90?

9 Which team were beaten 3-0 by Liverpool in the 1974 FA Cup Final?

10 Which team were beaten 2-1 by Chelsea in the 1970 FA Cup Final replay?

11 Who was in charge of the German Euro '96 team?

12 Who scored a last gasp equaliser for Manchester Utd against Oldham in a 1990s semi-final?

13 What colour are Doncaster's home shirts?

14 Tony Dorigo was at which club when he made his international debut?

15 At which club did Ronald Koeman start his League career?

Answers to page 320

1 Athletico Bilbao, **2** Dean Saunders, **3** Graham Taylor, **4** Leyton Orient, **5** Peter Withe, **6** Tony Morley, **7** Barcelona, **8** Dennis Mortimer, **9** Graham Turner, **10** Manchester Utd, **11** Pongo, **12** Tranmere Rovers, **13** Bari, **14** Derby County, **15** Howard Vaughton.

QUIZ 209

Answers on page 325

1 Frank McAvennie moved from West Ham Utd to which club for £850,000 in October 1987?

2 Martin Keown moved from Everton to which club in January 1993?

3 Who won the FA Charity Shield for the third time in four years in 1996?

4 Who did AC Milan beat to win the 1990 European Super Cup?

5 Which team did George Ramsay guide to the double?

6 Which Spanish club did Terry Venables manage?

7 What Division 2 team defeated Manchester Utd in the 1991 Rumbelows Cup Final?

8 Andy Ritchie and Michael Robinson were in the same team at which club?

9 Who was Blackburn Rovers' chairman when Kenny Dalglish went to Ewood Park?

10 Which Roy became manager of Bolton Wanderers in 1995?

11 Who moved from Celtic to Chelsea in 1991 to set a club record for a transfer fee received?

12 Who bought Fulham FC?

13 Who 'bit yer leg'?

14 Kevin Drinkell, Matt Tees and Ron Rafferty were all big scorers for which club?

15 Who scored the winning goal for Real Madrid in the 1998 European Cup final against Juventus?

Answers to page 325

1 Beans, **2** Poland, **3** Manchester Utd, **4** Anderlecht, **5** Aberdeen, **6** 16, **7** France, **8** Tottenham Hotspur, **9** Luton Town, **10** They all scored, **11** Michael Knighton, **12** Morocco, **13** Vinnie Jones, **14** West Ham Utd, **15** 1870s.

QUIZ 210

Answers on page 326

1 Which Ian became Southampton manager in 1991?

2 In which decade did Blackburn Rovers first win the FA Cup?

3 Who were the first team outside the First Division to win the FA Cup after the second World War?

4 What trophy was won with Celtic's 200th goal of the season in 1967?

5 Barry Murphy set an appearance record at which Yorkshire club?

6 Frank Yallop and Neil Thompson were fullbacks at which club?

7 Atkinson, Kendall and Walker were in contention for which management job in August 1995?

8 Which club did Dave Beasant join on leaving Chelsea?

9 In which city was Ivor Allchurch born?

10 Derek Reeves scored 39 League goals for which club?

11 What is Jason Wilcox's middle name?

12 Which Rangers star announced in March 1998 that he would be joining Chelsea at the end of the season?

13 Southampton recorded a 6-0 FA Cup win over which club in February 1995?

14 Sheffield Utd recorded a 5-1 League Cup win over which club in October 1982?

15 Port Vale recorded a 5-1 League Cup win over which club in September 1983?

Answers to page 326

1 Dave Basset (Nottingham Forest), **2** Kenny Burns, **3** Norwich City, **4** Trevor Francis (Nottingham Forest), **5** Andy Beattie, **6** Des Walker, **7** Kevin Keegan, **8** Ron Atkinson, **9** Valencia, **10** Andy Marriott, **11** Division I Champions 1977-78, **12** Kingsley Black, **13** Runcorn, **14** Wally Ardron, **15** Barcelona.

QUIZ 211

Answers on page 323

1 At Blackburn Rovers, Alan Shearer said before a match he always ate chicken and what?

2 England's Alan Ball was sent off in 1973 against which country?

3 Who were the first English team to play in the European Cup?

4 Who were the first team to compete in three consecutive Cup Winners' Cup Finals?

5 Which British side won the Cup Winners' Cup and their national cup in the same season?

6 In the 1960s Sporting Lisbon set a record by scoring how many goals in a Cup Winners Cup game?

7 Bernard Lama Played for which country in Euro 96?

8 Which club was Teddy Sheringham with when he was Premier League leading scorer in 1992-93?

9 Which club banned away fans in April 1986?

10 What links the debuts of Alan Shearer, Robert Lee and Dennis Wise?

11 Which property dealer abandoned his hopes of owning Manchester Utd?

12 Against which country was England's Ray Wilkins sent off?

13 Who was booked within five seconds of the start of the Chelsea against Sheffield Utd 1992 FA Cup tie?

14 Slater and Small were in the same team at which London club?

15 In what decade was the corner-kick first taken?

Answers to page 323

1 Celtic, **2** Arsenal, **3** Manchester Utd, **4** Sampdoria, **5** Preston North End, **6** Barcelona, **7** Sheffield Wednesday, **8** Brighton, **9** Bill Fox, **10** McFarland, **11** Paul Elliott, **12** Mohamed al Fayed, **13** Norman Hunter (Leeds Utd), **14** Grimsby Town, **15** Predrag Mijatovic.

NOTT FOREST 2

Answers on page 324

1 Which manager was sacked in January 1999?

2 Which Glaswegian hardman started at Birmingham City before making his name under Brian Clough at Nott Forest in the late 70s?

3 Which club did David Phillips leave to join Nott Forest?

4 Who scored on his European Cup Final debut in 1979?

5 Who succeeded Billy Walker as manager of Nott Forest in 1960?

6 Which defender played for Nott Forest, Sampdoria and Sheffield Wednesday?

7 Which England international played against Nott Forest in the 1980 European Cup Final?

8 Who took over as boss of Nott Forest in January 1999?

9 Who beat Nott Forest to win the European Super Cup in 1980?

10 Who was in goal for Nott Forest in the 1992 League Cup Final?

11 What is the highest position Nott Forest have ever achieved in the League?

12 Who has played in League Cup Finals for Luton Town and Nott Forest?

13 Ian Woan joined Nott Forest from which non-League club?

14 Which player scored 36 League goals for Nott Forest in 1950-51?

15 Which club did Nott Forest beat to win the European Super Cup in 1979?

Answers to page 324

1 Branfoot, **2** 1950s, **3** Sunderland, **4** European Cup, **5** Barnsley, **6** Ipswich Town, **7** Manager of Wales, **8** Southampton, **9** Swansea, **10** Southampton, **11** Malcolm, **12** Brian Laudrop, **13** Luton Town, **14** Grimsby, **15** Wrexham.

• CRYSTAL PALACE •

Answers on page 329

1 Who did Palace buy from Juventus for £1.7 million?

2 How long was Dave Bassett manager of Palace for?

3 David Swindlehurst moved from Palace to which club for £400,000 in April 1980?

4 Who became England's most expensive goalkeeper when he moved to Palace in 1989?

5 What is the highest position Palace have ever achieved in the League?

6 Palace player Peter Simpson scored 6 goals in a match in October 1930. Who were the opponents?

7 Who was the regular keeper in Palace's 1994-95 relegation season?

8 How many different Liverpool players scored in their 9-0 win over Palace in September 1989?

9 What was the title of Palace's 1990 FC Cup Final song?

10 Which player scored 46 League goals for Palace in 1930-31?

11 Ian Wright moved from Palace to which club for £2.5m in September 1991?

12 Which Andy of Palace won his only England cap in 1991?

13 Which Alan became manager of Palace in March 1993?

14 Kenny Sansom moved from Palace to which club for £1.35m in August 1980?

15 Who came off of the bench to hit two goals in a final for Palace?

Answers to page 329

1 Jimmy Hampson, **2** Oldest Player (41 Years 257 days), **3** Hampden Park, Glasgow, **4** Hearts, **5** Loughborough Town, **6** Stan Flashman, **7** Robert Maxwell, **8** George Graham, **9** Sheffield Wednesday, **10** Bari, **11** Liverpool, **12** Juventus, **13** Ted Drake, **14** West Brom, Manchester City & Norwich City, **15** 1-1.

QUIZ 212

Answers on page 330

1 Which international footballer played 125 times for his country, 34 of them whilst he played for Derby County?

2 Which England player was stamped on by Roy Keane in an FA Cup semi-final replay in 1995?

3 Which Arsenal midfielder of the 1990s has the middle name Faxe?

4 From which club did Arsenal buy Dutch striker Dennis Bergkamp?

5 Who was the first ever non-British manager to take charge of Arsenal?

6 Which soccer team does Sporty Spice Mel C support?

7 What is Chris Sutton's middle name?

8 How much did Atletico Madrid pay for Italian Christian Vieri when they bought him from Juventus in July 1997?

9 Which country lost 1-0 to Italy in the 1934 World Cup semi-final?

10 Gary Bull established a record for most League goals in a season at which club?

11 How was Austria's goal machine of the 1930s Franz Binder known?

12 Which football player was known as 'The Vulture'?

13 At which two grounds were the Euro '96 semi-finals held?

14 Which soccer team does the Boo Radley's Rob Cieka support?

15 Which player did Chelsea sign from Celtic in 1991 to set a club record for a transfer received?

Answers to page 330

1 RSC Anderlecht, **2** Real Madrid, **3** Mark Hughes, **4** Celtic, **5** Sheffield Wednesday, **6** Rangers, **7** Nigel Martyn, **8** Glenn Hoddle and Mark Hateley, **9** Ipswich Town, **10** Bobby Charlton, **11** Ipswich Town, **12** Newcastle Utd, **13** 10th Division 1, (1992-93), **14** Joe Mercer, **15** Sheffield Wednesday.

QUIZ 213

Answers on page 327

1 Which player scored 45 League goals for Blackpool in 1929-30?

2 What did Newcastle Utd's Bill Hampson achieve in the 1924 FA Cup Final?

3 Which is the largest football stadium in the British Isles?

4 Who beat Partick Thistle 5-1 in the 1959 Scottish League Cup Final?

5 Arsenal's biggest win and heaviest defeat both came against which club?

6 Which Barnet chairman was said to have sacked manager Barry Fry eight times?

7 Which chairman sold his stake in Derby County for £5.6m to a consortium led by Brian Fearn?

8 Who was the first player to score in three League Cup Finals with different clubs?

9 Chris Waddle scored in an FA Cup Final for which club?

10 David Platt missed a penalty on his debut for which Italian club?

11 Which side beat Tottenham Hotspur 7-0 to inflict their heaviest League defeat?

12 Which foreign team did Liam Brady join in 1980?

13 Who scored seven goals in one game for Arsenal against Aston Villa in December 1935?

14 Which three teams has Asa Hartford played for in League Cup Finals?

15 What was the score after normal time in the 1989 Merseyside FA Cup Final?

Answers to page 327

1 Michele Padovano, **2** 3 days, **3** Derby County, **4** Nigel Martyn, **5** 3rd Division 1 (1990-91), **6** Exeter, **7** Nigel Martyn, **8** 8, **9** *Glad All Over*, **10** Peter Simpson, **11** Arsenal, **12** Gray, **13** Smith, **14** Arsenal, **15** Ian Wright.

QUIZ 214

Answers on page 328

1 Which club beat Liverpool to win the European Super Cup in 1978?

2 Who beat AC Milan 3-2 in the 1958 European Cup Final?

3 Who scored Manchester Utd's goals against Barcelona in the 1991 European Cup Winners' Cup Final?

4 Who beat Rangers 1-0 in the 1967 Scottish League Cup Final?

5 Chelsea paid £2.3m for Dan Petrescu in November 1995. Which club did he leave?

6 Who beat Aberdeen 2-1 in the 1979 Scottish League Cup Final?

7 Which England goalkeeper did Bristol Rovers sell to Crystal Palace in November 1989?

8 In 1988 which Englishmen played for the French Champions?

9 At which club did Brian Talbot make his League debut?

10 Who captained the Manchester Utd team to lift the 1968 European Cup?

11 Kevin Steggles was a Euro scorer for which English team?

12 Jim Lawrence set an appearance record at which club?

13 What is the highest position Peterborough Utd have ever achieved in the League?

14 Who was the first person to play for two different English League Champions sides and then become manager of champions?

15 Bart-Williams and Warhurst scored Euro goals in the same game for which club?

Answers to page 328

1 Peter Shilton, **2** Gareth Southgate, **3** John Jensen, **4** Inter Milan, **5** Arsene Wenger, **6** Liverpool, **7** Roy, **8** £12.5m, **9** Austria, **10** Barnet, **11** "Bimbo", **12** Emilio Butragueno, **13** Old Trafford and Wembley, **14** Crewe Alexandra, **15** Paul Elliott.

QUIZ 215

Answers on page 333

1 What decoration was Kenny Dalglish awarded in February 1985?

2 Who was Portsmouth's manager when they went down from the top flight in 1988?

3 Which ex-Manchester Utd player set up the Bobby Stokes FA Cup winner?

4 Which England manager was born in Burnley?

5 Which former Liverpool player was Blackburn Rover's top scorer in their 1992 promotion season?

6 What colour are Brighton's home shorts?

7 Which German player had an extra-time 'goal' disallowed against England in Euro '96?

8 Thomas Doll went from Hamburg to which club in June 1991?

9 Which two foreign teams did Gary Lineker play for?

10 How many players did Hereford Town have sent off against Northampton in September 1992?

11 Who lost to Aberdeen in the 1983 Super Cup?

12 Which manager sold Gary Lineker to Tottenham Hotspur?

13 For which club did Brian Talbot score an FA Cup Final goal?

14 At which club did Emlyn Hughes make his League debut?

15 Mark Bright first played in an FA Cup Final for which team?

Answers to page 333

1 Doncaster Rovers, **2** He read it on Teletext, **3** Leeds Utd, **4** 0-2, **5** Tromso 3 Chelsea 2, **6** Bobby Tambling, **7** Ray Wilkins, **8** 18, **9** Manchester Utd, **10** Everton, **11** Parma, **12** Hollins, **13** Brian Laudrup, **14** Real Madrid, **15** Vinnie Jones.

MANCHESTER CITY

Answers on page 334

1 Which club did Phil Neal leave to join Steve Coppell at Manchester City?

2 Who lost 2-1 to Manchester City in the 1970 Cup-Winners' Cup Final?

3 Manchester City player George Smith scored 5 goals in a match in June 1947. Who were the opponents?

4 Which player scored 38 League goals for Manchester City in 1928-29?

5 Manchester City in 1995 and Blackburn in 1996 both played how many League games before a win?

6 Which English side knocked out Manchester City in the 1971 Cup Winners's Cup Competition?

7 Who replaced Frank Clarke as manager of Manchester City?

8 Who was signed by Manchester City from Liverpool in January 1996?

9 Manchester City recorded a 6-0 League Cup win over which club in October 1983?

10 In what decade did Manchester City first win the FA Cup?

11 Which Gerry went from Portsmouth to Manchester City in 1995?

12 Who succeeded John Bond as manager of Manchester City in 1983?

13 Who moved from Manchester City to Tottenham Hotspur for £1.7m in 1988 to set a club record for a transfer received?

14 Which rotund comedian once had trials with Manchester City?

15 In which decade did Manchester City first win the League Championship?

Answers to page 334

1 Springfield Park, **2** David Trezeguet, **3** Paris, **4** Rioch, **5** Crystal Palace, **6** Huddersfield Town, **7** Escape to Victory, **8** Coventry City, **9** Munich, **10** Everton, **11** Tommy Docherty, **12** Dave Beasant, **13** Boston Utd, **14** Celtic, **15** Leeds Utd.

CHELSEA 2

Answers on page 331

1 Chelsea recorded a 7-0 League Cup win over which club in November 1960?

2 How did Ruud Gullit discover he was being replaced as Chelsea boss by Gianlucca Vialli?

3 Tony Dorigo moved from Chelsea to which club for £1.7 million in June 1991?

4 What was the half time score in the Chelsea v Liverpool 1997 4th Round FA Cup game, which Chelsea went on to win 4-2?

5 What was the score in the snowy first round leg of Chelsea's Cup Winners' Cup second round tie in Tromso, Norway?

6 Which player of the 1950s and 1960s set up Chelsea's record for most League goals for the club?

7 Who moved from Chelsea to Manchester Utd in 1979 for a record £825,000 before moving to AC Milan in 1984?

8 How old was Ray Wilkins when he was made captain at Chelsea?

9 Mark Hughes joined Chelsea from which club?

10 Pat Nevin moved from Chelsea to which club for £925,000 in July 1988?

11 Which club did Gianfranco Zola play for before his move to Chelsea?

12 Which John became manager of Chelsea in March 1985?

13 Which Rangers star announced in March 1998 that he would be joining Chelsea at the end of the season?

14 Who lost 2-1 to Chelsea after a replay in the 1971 Cup-Winners' Cup Final?

15 Who was booked within five seconds of the start of the Chelsea v Sheffield Utd 1992 FA Cup tie?

Answers to page 331

1 MBE, **2** Alan Ball, **3** Jim McCalliog, **4** Ron Greenwood, **5** David Speedie, **6** Blue, **7** Stefan Kuntz, **8** Lazio, **9** Barcelona and Grampus Eight, **10** Four, **11** Hamburg, **12** Johan Cruyff, **13** Arsenal, **14** Blackpool, **15** Crystal Palace.

QUIZ 216

Answers on page 332

1 What is Wigan Athletic's ground called?

2 Whose goal for Monaco knocked Manchester Utd out of the 1997-98 Champion's League?

3 In which city did Arsenal first win the Cup Winners' Cup?

4 Which Bruce became boss of Millwall in 1992?

5 Mark Bright first played in an FA Cup Final for which team?

6 With which League team did Denis Law make his debut?

7 Which film featured Bobby Moore and Pele?

8 Who were Nottingham Forest's main rivals for the signature of Birmingham City's Trevor Francis?

9 Where was the 1997 European Cup Final held?

10 Who beat Manchester Utd 1-0 in the 1995 FA Cup Final?

11 Which manager is famous for the remark 'I've had more clubs than Jack Nicklaus'?

12 Who became the first goalie to save a penalty in a Wembley FA Cup Final?

13 Howard Wilkinson was player/manager for which non-League club?

14 Who beat St Johnstone 1-0 in the 1970 Scottish League Cup Final?

15 Noel Whelan moved to Coventry for £2m in December 1995. Which club did he leave?

Answers to page 332

1 Cardiff City, **2** Gornik Zabrze, **3** Newport, **4** Tom Johnson, **5** 12, **6** Chelsea, **7** Joe Royle, **8** Nigel Clough, **9** Torquay Utd, **10** 1900s, **11** Creaney, **12** John Benson, **13** Paul Stewart, **14** Eddie Large, **15** 1930s.

QUIZ 217

Answers on page 337

1 Which club did Peter Withe join on leaving Nottingham Forest?

2 Which player scored 42 League goals for Bournmouth in 1970-71?

3 Where was the 1961 European Cup Final held?

4 What is the inscription above the Bill Shankly gates at Anfield?

5 Which club did Andy Thorn leave to join Newcastle Utd?

6 What is Torquay's nickname?

7 How many international goals did Billy Bremner score?

8 Which club was Bobby Moore with when he became England captain?

9 In which year did all four British teams qualify for the World Cup Finals for the only time?

10 Which manager sold Gary Lineker to Tottenham Hotspur?

11 In which decade did Motherwell first win the Scottish FA Cup?

12 Which player made 655 league appearances for Chelsea between 1962-80?

13 Manchester Utd player George Best scored 6 goals in a match in February 1970. Who were the opponents?

14 What is the highest position Manchester Utd have ever achieved in the League?

15 Whose home until May 1997, was the Baseball Ground?

Answers to page 337

1 1911, **2** David O'Leary, **3** Sammy Nelson, **4** Birmingham City, **5** 37, **6** Stamford Bridge, **7** Dumbarton, **8** Ray Harford, **9** Aston Villa, **10** 1990, **11** Steve Stone, **12** Green and White, **13** West Ham Utd, **14** Frank, **15** Gerd Muller.

QUIZ 218

Answers on page 338

1 Which great international forward became known as 'The Little Cannon'?

2 Dave Stringer followed Ken Brown as boss of which club?

3 In a 1994 England game the goalkeeper and two centre halves all came from which club?

4 Ruud Gullit became the worlds most expensive player when he moved from which club to AC Milan in 1987?

5 Who hit his first England hat-trick in the 7-1 thrashing of San Marino?

6 What is Dean Holdsworth's middle name?

7 What was Bruce Grobbelaar's first English League club?

8 At which three clubs did the Futcher twins play together?

9 Who was the Scottish Player of the Year in 1994-95?

10 Which Mel became boss of Bournmouth in August 1994?

11 Major Frank Buckley and Raich Carter both managed which club in the 1940s and 1950s?

12 Who followed Alf Ramsey as manager of Ipswich Town?

13 Rick Holden played in a League Cup final for which team?

14 Kevin Keegan moved from Liverpool to which club for £500,000 in June 1977?

15 Brighton and Hove Albion player Arthur Attwood scored 6 goals in a match in October 1932. Who were the opponents?

Answers to page 338

1 Derby County, **2** Glasgow Rangers, **3** Kevin Ratcliffe, **4** Peter Reid, **5** The Sultan of Brunei, **6** 1981, **7** Billy Bingham, **8** Derek Hatton, **9** Graeme Sharp, **10** Kidd, **11** Peter Reid, **12** Tony Cottee, **13** 1985, **14** Blackburn Rovers, **15** Duncan Ferguson.

QUIZ 219

Answers on page 335

1 When did Bradford City first win the FA Cup?

2 Which Arsenal central defender played 558 times for the club between 1975 and 1993?

3 Which Arsenal player dropped his shorts to the crowd in a 1979 game against Coventry City?

4 Steve Claridge joined Leicester City from which club?

5 How many international caps did George Best win?

6 Where were the FA Cup Finals played immediately before the opening of Wembley?

7 Which soccer team does *Talking Head's* David Byrne support?

8 Who succeeded Malcolm Macdonald as boss of Fulham?

9 John and James Cowan played for which double winners?

10 When did the Republic of Ireland first qualify for the World Cup Finals?

11 Which England player went to the same school as Gazza?

12 What are the first-choice colours of Plymouth Argyle shirts?

13 Which club was once know as Thames Ironworks FC?

14 What is Jamie Redknapp's middle name?

15 Which Bayern Munich player was European Footballer of the Year in 1970?

Answers to page 335

1 Newcastle Utd, **2** Ted MacDougall, **3** Berne, **4** *You'll Never Walk Alone*, **5** Wimbledon, **6** The Gulls, **7** Three, **8** West Ham Utd, **9** 1958, **10** Johan Cruyff, **11** 1950s, **12** Ron Harris, **13** Northampton Town, **14** Division 1 and Premiership Champions (9 times), **15** Derby County.

EVERTON 2

Answers on page 336

1 Craig Short joined Everton from which club?

2 Stuart McCall moved from Everton to which club for £1.25m in August 1991?

3 Who was Everton's skipper in the 1985 European Cup Winners' Cup?

4 Who wrote *Everton Winter Mexican Summer: A Football Diary*?

5 In November of the 1997-98 season it was widely reported that which mega-rich foreigner was interested in buying Everton?

6 When did Neville Southall make his Everton League debut?

7 Who is the Luton Town and Everton forward who went on to manage Northern Ireland?

8 Who said; "I can cope with being thrown out of the Labour Party, but I can't cope with Liverpool beating Everton 4-1"?

9 Which 1980s and 1990s striker hit 111 Everton League goals?

10 Which Brian of Everton got an early bath in a 1980 FA Cup semi-final?

11 Which Everton player was fouled when Kevin Moran got his 1985 FA Cup Final marching orders?

12 Who moved from West Ham Utd to Everton in July 1988 to set a club record for a transfer fee received?

13 In which year was Neville Southall voted Footballer of the Year?

14 Before joining Everton, where was Howard Kendall player/manager?

15 Who was sold to Newcastle Utd against the wishes of Everton manager Walter Smith?

Answers to page 336

1 Ferenc Puskas, **2** Norwich City, **3** Arsenal (Seaman, Adams, Bould), **4** PSV Eindhoven, **5** Ian Wright, **6** Christopher, **7** Crewe Alexandra, **8** Chester, Luton, Manchester City, **9** Brian Laudrup, **10** Machin, **11** Leeds Utd, **12** Jackie Milburn, **13** Oldham Athletic, **14** S V Hamburg, **15** Shoreham.

SPURS 4

Answers on page 341

1 In what decade did Spurs first win the Championship?

2 Which club did Jurgen Klinsmann join on leaving Spurs ?

3 Who replaced Gerry Francis as coach of Spurs ?

4 Which member of the Spurs double-winning side went on to manage a Championship team?

5 Who was the first player to be convicted of feigning an injury to try to get an opponent sent off?

6 Who dived full length on the pitch after his first goal for Spurs in the Premiership?

7 Who was in goal for Spurs when they won the FA Cup in 1981?

8 Spurs player Ted Harper scored 5 goals in a match in August 1930. Who were the opponents?

9 Who was boss at Spurs when Gazza arrived?

10 How many league games did Spurs win in 1960-61, creating a record for most wins in a season?

11 Who resigned from Spurs saying "Players have become impossible"?

12 Which two German-speaking footballers had a row in the Spurs tunnel?

13 Who succeeded Peter Shreeves as manager of Spurs in 1986?

14 Spurs recorded a 5-0 FA Cup win over which club in September 1990?

15 Which Spurs manager signed Ossie Ardiles and Ricky Villa in 1978?

Answers to page 341

1 Northampton, **2** Paul Gascoigne, **3** Southampton, **4** Billy Bonds (West Ham Utd), **5** West Brom, **6** 19, **7** Strasbourg, **8** John Cochrane, **9** Ron Saunders, **10** 104 years, **11** Kingstown, Jamaica, **12** Diego Maradona, **13** Neil Ruddock, **14** Chester, **15** England.

QUIZ 220

Answers on page 342

1 Which club did Paul McGrath leave to join Aston Villa?

2 Who retired from football, aged 50, in April 1965?

3 Where was the 1967 European Cup Final held?

4 Who beat Airdrieonians 2-1 in the 1992 Scottish FA Cup Final?

5 Who beat Rangers 4-1 in the 1982 Scottish FA Cup Final?

6 Which country's football team was defeated in the 1982 and 1986 World Cup finals?

7 Where was the 1977 European Cup Final held?

8 Eric Cantona and Steve Hodge were in the same team at which club?

9 Who was Kenny Dalglish's Liverpool skipper for the 1986 double-winning side?

10 Which Scotsman managed Galatasaray in 1995?

11 Which American has played in England for Derby County, Sheffield Wednesday and West Ham Utd?

12 Schmeichel played all but two games for Manchester Utd in 1993-94. Who played in those games?

13 Which Mel became boss of Manchester City in 1987?

14 Which team were beaten 3-1 by Newcastle Utd in the 1955 FA Cup Final?

15 At which club did Kevin Hitchcock make his League debut?

Answers to page 342

1 10th Division 1 (1988-89), **2** Vic Buckingham, **3** 5th Division 1 (1934-35), **4** Oldham, **5** Everton, **6** Walsall, **7** 1970s, **8** Perth, **9** Czechoslovakia, **10** Nick Barmby, **11** For the first match against Moldova, **12** Luton Town, **13** 1930s, **14** Liverpool and Arsenal, Arsenal won on goal difference., **15** Five.

QUIZ 221

Answers on page 339

1 Which club did Phil Neal play for before he joined Liverpool?

2 Who said "I never make predictions and I never will"?

3 Dave Merrington was manager of which Premiership side in 1995-96?

4 Who 'bit yer bum'?

5 Which soccer team does comedian Frank Skinner support?

6 How many international goals did Don Givens score?

7 Who beat Liverpool 3-0 in the 1997-98 UEFA Cup second round, first leg?

8 Who succeeded Billy Butler as manager of Reading in 1939?

9 Who succeeded Nobby Stiles as manager of West Brom in 1986?

10 How long had the old Football League been going?

11 Where was John Barnes born?

12 Who went from Argentinos Juniors to Boca Juniors in 1981?

13 Who wanted a 'Loyalty' payment from Tottenham Hotspur before moving to Liverpool?

14 Oldham Athletic player Eric Gemmill scored 7 goals in a match in January 1953. Who were the opponents?

15 Which country did Mike Bailey play for?

Answers to page 339

1 1950s, **2** Bayern Munich, **3** Christian Gross, **4** Dave Mackay (Derby County), **5** Gordon Durie (Tottenham), **6** Jurgen Klinsmann, **7** Milija Aleksic, **8** Reading, **9** Terry Venables, **10** 31, **11** Bill Nicholson, **12** Christian Gross and Jurgen Klinsmann, **13** David Pleat, **14** Hartlepool Utd, **15** Keith Burkinshaw.

QUIZ 222

Answers on page 340

1 What is the highest position Millwall have ever achieved in the League?

2 Who was the English manager of Dutch side Ajax in the 1970s?

3 What is the highest position Grimsby Town have ever achieved in the League?

4 Where was Walter Winterbottom born?

5 Pat van Den Hauwe first played in an FA Cup Final for which team?

6 Which club has a fanzine called *Blazing Saddlers*?

7 In which decade did Ipswich Town first win the FA Cup?

8 In which city do St Johnstone play?

9 Which country won the European Championship on penalties in 1976?

10 Which English player scored twice in the 3-0 defeat of China in 1996?

11 When was Alan Shearer appointed captain of England?

12 Which team was beaten 2-1 by Nottingham Forest in the 1959 FA Cup Final?

13 In which decade was Gordon Banks born?

14 The 1988-89 League Championship ended with two teams at the top on equal points, who were they and how was a winner decided?

15 From 1974, how many consecutive World Cup finals did Scotland reach?

Answers to page 340

1 Manchester Utd, **2** Stanley Mathews, **3** Lisbon, **4** Rangers, **5** Aberdeen, **6** West Germany's, **7** Rome, **8** Leeds Utd, **9** Alan Hansen, **10** Graeme Souness, **11** John Harkes, **12** Gary Walsh, **13** Machin, **14** Manchester City, **15** Mansfield Town.

QUIZ 223

Answers on page 345

1 Which Juventus player was European Footballer of the Year in 1961?

2 Which non-League side did Graham Roberts quit as boss of in 1998?

3 Which soccer team does TV Pundit John McCririck support?

4 Which Chilean World Cup star signed for West Ham in 1998?

5 In September 1987 who became the 1,000th England player?

6 In the 1994 World Cup quarter-finals, Romania equalised at the death against which country?

7 Which Danish midfielder was loaned from Liverpool to Barnsley in 1995?

8 Who was Sheffield Wednesday boss in the 1990-91 season?

9 Who beat Motherwell 4-2 in the 1955 Scottish League Cup Final?

10 How many Premiership points were deducted from Tottenham Hotspur because of financial irregularities?

11 Who beat Huddersfield 2-0 in the 1930 FA Cup Final?

12 Jim Fallon made a record 620 appearances for which Scottish club between 1968-86?

13 What is the highest position Reading have ever achieved in the League?

14 Which soccer team does The Spice Girl's Mel B support?

15 What is the highest position Portsmouth have ever achieved in the League?

Answers to page 345

1 David Speedie (Chelsea), **2** John Bond, **3** Peter Reid, **4** Tottenham Hotspur, **5** 1969, **6** Denis Law, **7** Leeds Utd, **8** Roy Gatrix, **9** Andy Dibble, **10** Division 1 Champions (2 times 1936-37, 1967-68), **11** Leicester City, **12** Sampdoria, **13** Barnes, **14** Eike Immel, **15** Machin.

RANGERS 4

Answers on page 346

1 Who has won most Scottish caps during their time with Rangers?

2 Who said "For a while I did unite Rangers and Celtic fans.There were people in both camps who hated me"?

3 Rangers player Marco Negri was unfit to play part of the 97-98 season because of an eye injury sustained playing which other sport?

4 Who beat Rangers 1-0 in the 1983 Scottish FA Cup Final?

5 Which club beat Rangers to win the European Super Cup in 1972?

6 Who moved from Dundee Utd to Rangers for £4 million in 1993 to set a club record for a transfer fee received?

7 Mel Sterland moved from Sheffield Wednesday to which club for £800,000 in March 1989?

8 Who was the first Catholic player to be signed by Rangers?

9 Richard Gough moved to Rangers from which club for £1.5m in September 1997?

10 Who beat Rangers 2-1 in the 1989-90 Scottish League Cup Final?

11 Who was the only League ever present for Rangers in 1995-96?

12 Who beat Rangers 3-2 in the 1951-52 Scottish League Cup Final?

13 Which Rangers manager was fined £5,000 for breaking a touchline ban imposed earlier?

14 Which new 'signing' was paraded by Celtic before the Scottish FA Cup Final, only for the player to change his mind and join another club?

15 Rangers signed which player from Atlanta in the late 1980s?

Answers to page 346

1 Raith Rovers, **2** Barcelona, **3** Newcastle Utd, **4** Leeds Utd, **5** Arrigo Saachi, **6** Bolton Wanderers, **7** Moscow Dynamo, **8** Middlesborough and Wimbledon, **9** Vienna, **10** Juventus, **11** Liverpool, **12** Notts County, **13** Ron Flowers, **14** Alan Shearer, **15** Bury.

• MANCHESTER CITY 2 •

Answers on page 343

1 Who hit a hat-trick when Chelsea beat Manchester City 5-4 in the Full Members Cup?

2 Which Manchester City boss bought his own son Kevin?

3 Who was sacked at Manchester City 12 days into the 1993-94 season?

4 Who beat Manchester City 3-2 in the 1981 FA Cup Final replay?

5 Before the 1990s, when did Manchester City last win the FA Cup?

6 Who scored six for Manchester City in an abandoned FA Cup game?

7 Which club did David Rocastle leave to join Manchester City?

8 Which defender played 415 league games for Blackpool and Manchester City and never scored?

9 Who was Manchester City's keeper in the 1989 promotion to top flight?

10 What is the highest position Manchester City have ever achieved in the League?

11 Which team were beaten 1-0 by Manchester City in the 1969 FA Cup Final?

12 Trevor Francis moved from Manchester City to which club for £800,000 in July 1982?

13 What was the surname of dad Ken and son Peter both of Manchester City?

14 Who was Manchester City's keeper in the 1995-96 relegation season?

15 Which Mel became boss of Manchester City in 1987?

Answers to page 343

1 Omar Sivori, **2** Yeovil, **3** Newcastle Utd, **4** Javier Margas, **5** Neil Webb, **6** Sweden, **7** Jan Molby, **8** Ron Atkinson, **9** Hearts, **10** Six, **11** Arsenal, **12** Clydebank, **13** 2nd Division 1, (1994-95), **14** Leeds Utd, **15** 1st Division 1, (1948-49, 1949-50).

QUIZ 224

Answers on page 344

1 McAnespie and Rougier scored Euro goals in the same 1990s game for which club?

2 Who lost to Aston Villa in the 1982 Super Cup?

3 With which club did Stan Seymour win the FA Cup once as a player and twice as a manager?

4 Howard Wilkinson followed Billy Bremner as boss of which club?

5 Who was in charge of Italy for Euro '96?

6 Eddie Hopkinson set a League appearance record at which club?

7 Who lost 3-2 to Rangers in the 1972 Cup-Winners' Cup Final?

8 In the 1996-97 season, which two Premiership clubs had never appeared in any of the major European competitions?

9 Where was the 1995 European Cup Final held?

10 Which team won the 1993 UEFA Cup?

11 David Burrows won a Championship medal with which club?

12 Which club has a fanzine called *No More Pie In The Sky*?

13 Who scored England's first ever European Championship goal?

14 Which player scored England's first goal in Euro '96?

15 With which club did Terry McDermott make his League debut?

Answers to page 344

1 George Young, **2** Mo Johnston, **3** Squash, **4** Aberdeen, **5** Ajax, **6** Duncan Ferguson, **7** Glasgow Rangers, **8** Mo Johnston, **9** Tottenham Hotspur, **10** Aberdeen, **11** Alan McLaren, **12** Dundee, **13** Graeme Souness, **14** Mo Johnston (He joined Rangers), **15** Trevor Francis.

QUIZ 225

Answers on page 349

1 Everton player Jack Southwork scored 6 goals in a match in December 1893. Who were the opponents?

2 Which striker at Leeds Utd was known as 'The Shark'?

3 Who is the chairman of Leyton Orient?

4 Paul Power first played in an FA Cup Final for which team?

5 Regis and Atkinson were the strike force at which club?

6 At the time of the 1974 World Cup, Dutch players Rep, Han and Krol were all with which club?

7 Who was the first ever winner of the Golden Boot award?

8 For which club did Bobby Gould score a League Cup Final goal?

9 Who succeeded Mick Mills as manager of Stoke City in 1989?

10 Who scored Nottingham Forest's goal in the European Cup Final to beat Hamburg?

11 Which two clubs went to court to fight for the services manager Terry Yorath?

12 What was the Gazza rap record called?

13 Which two Scottish teams met in the final game of the 1990-91 season to decide which of them were champions?

14 How many different Scotland managers did Kenny Dalglish play for?

15 Hughes and Tueart scored Euro Goals in the same 70s game for which club?

Answers to page 349

1 12, **2** C Harper, **3** Garrincha, **4** Sam Longston, **5** Spurs v Manchester Utd (1963-64), **6** San Marino, **7** Halifax Town, **8** Glasgow, **9** Had advertising on shirts in a match, **10** Vancouver Whitecaps, **11** AC Milan, **12** Brown, **13** Carl, **14** Liverpool, **15** Dave Russell.

QUIZ 226

Answers on page 350

1 Who succeeded Graham Taylor as manager of Watford in 1987?

2 Robert Fleck has hit three in a Euro game for which club?

3 Which German player has appeared in five World Cup Finals?

4 Who did Marseille beat 1-0 in the 1993 European Cup Final?

5 Who was captain of Arsenal's FA Cup winning side of 1930?

6 *Fantasy Football* celebrity Frank Skinner supports which team?

7 Who is Dundee's all-time top scorer?

8 Which goalkeeper made 394 consecutive League appearances between August 1981 and October 1990, before a broken finger forced him to sit out a game?

9 In the 1920s, 1930s and 1940s which club used to play at the Recreation Ground, Hanley?

10 Which Arsenal defender brought Paul Allen down from behind in 1980 when he was clear on goal?

11 Kenny Dalglish replaced Kevin Keegan at Liverpool. Which transfer cost most?

12 Who was sacked by Cardiff City in November 1994?

13 What colour are Barcelona's home shorts?

14 Graeme Souness was first capped while at which club?

15 Which Colin became boss of Middlesborough in 1990?

Answers to page 350

1 Partick Thistle, **2** Aberdeen, **3** Brian McClair, **4** Dundee Utd, **5** Hibernian, **6** Kenny Dalglish, **7** Paul Elliott, **8** Aberdeen, **9** Brian McClair, **10** Dunfermline, **11** Hibernian, **12** Liam Brady, **13** Pierre Van Hooijdonk, **14** Airdrie, **15** Clyde.

QUIZ 227

Answers on page 347

1 How many international goals did Gerry Armstrong score?

2 Who succeeded R Sproson as manager of Port Vale in 1977?

3 Which football player was known as Little Bird?

4 Who was the Derby County Chairman when Brian Clough resigned?

5 Who were the first English clubs to meet in the Cup Winners' Cup competition?

6 Which team did Wales beat 5-0 in their first game in the 1998 World Cup campaign?

7 Which team did Wycombe Wanderers replace in the Football League in 1993?

8 In which city do Queen's Park play?

9 What did Kettering do before any other club in the 1970s?

10 Which foreign team did Peter Beardsley play for?

11 Which Italian club did Luther Blisset join?

12 Which Tony of West Brom was First Division leading scorer in 1970-71?

13 What is the name of Glenn Hoddle's footballing brother?

14 Who beat Fulham 10-0 in a League Cup game in 1986?

15 Who succeeded Walter Galbraith as manager of Tranmere Rovers in 1961?

Answers to page 347

1 West Brom, **2** Joe Jordan, **3** Barry Hearn, **4** Manchester City, **5** Aston Villa, **6** Ajax, **7** Eusebio, **8** Arsenal, **9** Alan Ball, **10** John Robertson, **11** Bradford and Swansea, **12** 'Geordie Boys', **13** Aberdeen and Rangers, **14** Six, **15** Sunderland.

CELTIC 4

Answers on page 348

1 Who beat Celtic 4-1 in the 1972 Scottish League Cup Final?

2 Who did Celtic beat 2-1 in the 1954 Scottish FA Cup Final?

3 Which Celtic player was Footballer of the Year in 1987?

4 Who did Celtic beat 2-1 in the 1988 Scottish FA Cup Final?

5 Who did Celtic beat 6-3 in the 1975 Scottish League Cup Final?

6 Which former Celtic player scored 30 goals in 102 appearances for Scotland?

7 Which player did Chelsea sign from Celtic in 1991 to set a club record for a transfer received?

8 Who did Celtic beat 2-0 in the 1967 Scottish FA Cup Final?

9 Which Celtic player score four times in their 8-3 win over Hamilton in January 1987?

10 Who did Celtic beat 3-2 in the 1965 Scottish FA Cup Final?

11 Which team were beaten a record 6-1 by Celtic in the 1972 Scottish FA Cup Final?

12 Which former Celtic manager became manager of Brighton?

13 Which Dutch international said that a £7,000 a week wage increase was “Good enough for the homeless but not for an international striker”?

14 Who did Celtic beat 1-0 in the 1995 Scottish FA Cup Final?

15 Who beat Celtic 1-0 in the 1955 Scottish FA Cup Final replay?

Answers to page 348

1 Dave Bassett, **2** Rangers, **3** Lothar Matthaus, **4** AC Milan, **5** Tom Parker, **6** West Brom, **7** Alan Gilzean, **8** Dave Beasant, **9** Port Vale, **10** Willie Young, **11** Keegan’s, **12** Eddie May, **13** Blue, **14** Middlesborough, **15** Todd.

IPSWICH TOWN 2

Answers on page 353

1 The side beaten by Ipswich in a UEFA Cup Final was prefixed by which two letters?

2 Which Ipswich player hit two hat-tricks in 1980-81 UEFA Cup games?

3 Who was bought by Ipswich in 1994 at a club record fee?

4 In which decade did Ipswich enter the League?

5 Who succeeded Jackie Milburn as manager of Ipswich in 1964?

6 Which Scottish player has joined Ipswich on three occasions?

7 Ipswich recorded a 6-1 League Cup win over which club in November 1985?

8 In which decade did Ipswich first win the Championship?

9 Which keeper Paul played over 400 games for Ipswich?

10 Which club did Russell Osman go to when he left Ipswich?

11 Which Ipswich player Adam was banned after a drugs test?

12 In which decade did Ipswich first win the FA Cup?

13 Who was the regular keeper for Ipswich in their 1994-95 relegation season?

14 Which manager John took Ipswich up as Second Division Champions?

15 Which player scored 41 League goals for Ipswich in 1956-57?

Answers to page 353

1 Newcastle Utd, **2** Nottingham Forest, **3** Motherwell, **4** Aston Villa, **5** Blue and White, **6** 7 Stuart Ripley 11 Jason Wilcox, **7** Mark Bright, **8** Hearts, **9** Trevor Brooking, **10** Southend, **11** 1974, **12** Johan Neeskens of Holland, **13** Stuttgart, **14** Tony Morley, **15** 1950s.

QUIZ 228

Answers on page 354

1 Who handed out Fulham's record 10-0 defeat in a League Cup game in 1986?

2 Roy Sproson set a League appearance record for which club?

3 Kenny Dalglish's first home game as Newcastle Utd's boss was against which team in the FA Cup?

4 In which country did Kevin Keegan briefly take part in a World Cup tournament?

5 Which Porto player won the 1984-85 Golden Boot award?

6 Who were Tottenham Hotspur's wing duo in their double season?

7 Which managers picked Kenny Dalglish's teams in his 1986 testimonial?

8 In the 50 years following the Second World War which clubs had the fewest managers?

9 Who moved from Stockport County to Birmingham City for £800,000 in January 1995?

10 Kevin Keegan's first three internationals were all against which country?

11 Who scored for England in the Swedes 2 v Turnips 1 game?

12 Which fourth division side appeared in the 1962 League Cup Final?

13 What is buried under the North Bank at Highbury and is said to bring the club good luck?

14 Who did Internazionale beat in the 1991 UEFA Cup Final?

15 Which goalkeeper holds the record for the most international clean sheets?

Answers to page 354

1 Graham Taylor, **2** Vienna, **3** Blackburn Rovers, **4** QPR, **5** Alan Smith, **6** Walsall, **7** Leeds City, **8** Shinguards, **9** Paolo Maldini, **10** Jimmy Hill, **11** West Germany (1954), **12** Real Sociedad, **13** Ruud Gullit (Euro 88), **14** Liverpool, **15** Bari.

QUIZ 229

Answers on page 351

1 Terry Dermott first played in an FA Cup Final for which team?

2 Which club did Lee Chapman leave to join Leeds Utd the first time?

3 Coyne and Kirk scored Euro goals in the same 1990s game for which club?

4 Which club's ground includes the Doug Ellis Stand?

5 What colour are the stripes on Chester's home shirts?

6 Who were the regular numbers 7 and 11 who supplied Alan Shearer in Blackburn Rover's championship-winning season?

7 Who scored the winning goal in the 1993 all Sheffield FA Cup semi-final?

8 Which team were beaten 3-0 by Aberdeen in the 1986 Scottish FA Cup Final?

9 Who scored West Ham Utd's goal to beat Arsenal in the 1980 FA Cup Final?

10 Which club did manager Barry Fry join after being sacked by Barnet for the eigth time?

11 In which year was the Charity Shield first played at Wembley?

12 Who scored the first penalty in a World Cup Final match?

13 Where was the 1988 European Cup Final held?

14 Who was Aston Villa's flying winger when they won the 1981 title?

15 In what decade did Chelsea first win the Championship?

Answers to page 351

1 AZ (Alkmaar), **2** John Wark, **3** Steve Sedgley, **4** 1930s, **5** Bill McGarry, **6** John Wark, **7** Swindon, **8** 1960s, **9** Cooper, **10** Leicester City, **11** Tanner, **12** 1970s, **13** Craig Forest, **14** Lyall, **15** Ted Phillips.

QUIZ 230

Answers on page 352

1 Wolves appointed which former England manager in April 1994?

2 Where was the 1990 European Cup Final held?

3 Which team were beaten 3-0 by Wolves in the 1960 FA Cup Final?

4 Which club was once known as St Jude's?

5 Who went on when Gary Lineker was sustituted in his last international game?

6 Which club lost 15 consecutive games in Division 2 in 1988-89?

7 Leeds Utd were formed following the demise of which team?

8 Samuel Widdowson of Nottingham Forest is credited with inventing what?

9 Who was Italy's captain in the 1997 World Cup qualifier at Wembley?

10 Which former player and television personality took over when a linesmen was injured during an Arsenal and Liverpool match in 1972?

11 Turek was in goal for which World Cup-winners?

12 Dalian Atkinson moved from Sheffield Wednesday to which club for £1.7m in August 1990?

13 Who was the first Dutch skipper to lift a major international trophy for his country?

14 Ray Kennedy moved from Arsenal to which club for £450,000 in July 1974?

15 Which club did David Platt join on leaving Aston Villa?

Answers to page 352

1 Liverpool, **2** Port Vale, **3** Charlton Athletic, **4** Spain, **5** Fernando Gomez, **6** Cliff Jones and Terry Dyson, **7** Tommy Docherty and Alex Ferguson, **8** West Ham Utd and Manchester Utd, **9** Kevin Francis, **10** Wales, **11** David Platt, **12** Rochdale, **13** A workman's horse (it died in an accident during construction), **14** AS Roma, **15** Dino Zoff (Italy).

QUIZ 231

Answers on page 357

1 What was Gary Mabbutt's scoring record in the 1987 Spurs against Coventry Cup Final?

2 Paul Furlong scored three times in the 1994-95 Cup Winners' Cup competition for which club?

3 Which club did England's Bob Crompton play for?

4 In 1984, who at Derby County became the League's youngest club chairman?

5 Jimmy Neighbour played for which two clubs in League Cup Finals?

6 Which language must all FIFA referees be able to speak?

7 In which season was the European Cup first held?

8 Which is the oldest Scottish team?

9 Eddie Large was a trainee at which club?

10 Which Howard became boss of Notts County in 1995?

11 George Ramsay guided which team to the double?

12 David Platt's first England hat-trick was against which country?

13 Which club beat Arsenal to win the European Super Cup in 1995?

14 Steve Bruce first played in a League Cup Final for which club?

15 How many goals did Billy Bremner score for Scotland?

Answers to page 357

1 European Cup Winner's Cup, **2** Leeds Utd, **3** Played behind closed doors, **4** White, **5** Billy Bonds, **6** Everton, **7** Lou Macari, **8** Preston North End, **9** Billy Bonds (West Ham Utd), **10** Eyal Berkovic hit John Moncur (both West Ham players), **11** Luton Town, **12** Sunderland, **13** Bury, **14** Frank McAvennie, **15** Manchester City.

SPURS 5

Answers on page 358

1 Who wanted a 'Loyalty' payment before moving to Liverpool?

2 Who did Spurs beat in the 1984 UEFA Cup Final?

3 Which sacked boss said, "I feel like Robin Hood - feared by the bad, loved by the good"?

4 What shirt number did Gazza wear at Spurs?

5 Who won the championship as a player and a manager with Spurs?

6 Which Welsh player capped over 50 times, won the double with Spurs?

7 What is the highest position Spurs have ever achieved in the League?

8 What was Gary Mabbutt's scoring record in the 1987 Spurs against Coventry FA Cup Final?

9 Paul Gascoigne moved from Spurs to which club in July 1991?

10 A 1994 League Cup defeat by Notts County was the sign for which Spurs boss that his days were numbered?

11 Which Peter became Spurs manager in 1991?

12 Who was in goal for Spurs for the 1984 UEFA Cup triumph, achieved after a shoot out?

13 Which future England manager won a championship medal with Spurs in 1951?

14 Spurs player Alf Stokes scored 5 goals in a match in September 1957. Who were the opponents?

15 Who were the wing duo for Spurs in their double-winning season?

Answers to page 358

1 Ron Aitkinson, **2** Terry Butcher, **3** Sampdoria, **4** 10, **5** Three, **6** (Oldham Athletic), **7** Schillachi, **8** Tottenham Hotspur, **9** Gerry Hitchens, **10** Gillingham, **11** Sweden, **12** Ian St John, **13** Chile, **14** Valencia, **15** Arsenal.

WEST HAM 3

Answers on page 355

1 Which European trophy was won by West Ham in 1965?

2 West Ham player Vic Watson scored 6 goals in a match in February 1929. Who were the opponents?

3 What was strange about West Ham's 1980 European Cup Winners' Cup game against Castilla ?

4 What colour are West Ham home shorts?

5 Who played 663 times to set West Ham League appearance record?

6 Tony Cottee moved from West Ham to which club for £2m in July 1988?

7 Which manager has spent the shortest time as boss of West Ham?

8 Which team were beaten 3-2 by West Ham in 1964 FA Cup Final?

9 Who 'bit yer bum'?

10 Who hit whom during the 1997-98 season Premiership match between Chelsea and West Ham?

11 Before meeting up with West Ham, where had Tim Breaker and Les Sealey been in the same side?

12 West Ham player Geoff Hurst scored 6 goals in a match in October 1968. Who were the opponents?

13 West Ham recorded a 10-0 League Cup win over which club in 1984?

14 Who moved from West Ham to Celtic for £1.5 million in 1992?

15 Which club did Ian Bishop leave to join West Ham?

Answers to page 355

1 He scored two goals - one for each team, **2** Chelsea, **3** Blackburn Rovers, **4** Ian Maxwell, **5** Tottenham Hotspur and Norwich City, **6** English, **7** 1955-56, **8** Queen's Park, **9** Manchester City, **10** Kendall, **11** Aston Villa, **12** San Marino, **13** AC Milan, **14** Norwich City, **15** Three.

QUIZ 232

Answers on page 356

1 Who is the only Manchester Utd boss never to have lost to Manchester City?

2 Who succeeded Malcolm Crosby as manager of Sunderland in 1993?

3 Who lost 1-0 to Barcelona in the Final of the 1992 European Cup?

4 How many international goals did Leighton James score?

5 How many international goals did Chris Nichol score?

6 At which ground would you find the Lookers Stand and the George Hill Stand?

7 Which Italian player scored six goals in Italia '90?

8 Which team does *Between The Lines* actor Neil Pearson support?

9 Who was the first player to be capped for England while playing for a foreign team?

10 Portsmouth player Alf Strange scored 5 goals in a match in January 1923. Who were the opponents?

11 Gary Lineker played his last internatonal against which country?

12 Who scored an extra-time winner for Liverpool against Leeds Utd in 1965?

13 Which country did Michael Owen make his international debut?

14 Who beat Nottingham Forest to win the European Super Cup in 1980?

15 Brian Talbot scored in an FA Cup Final for which club?

Answers to page 356

1 Neil Ruddock, **2** RSC Anderlecht, **3** Terry Venables (Spurs), **4** 8, **5** Bill Nicholson, **6** Cliff Jones, **7** Division 1 Champions (1950-51, 1960-61), **8** He scored two goals - one for each team, **9** Lazio, **10** Ossie Ardiles, **11** Shreeves, **12** Tony Parks, **13** Alf Ramsey, **14** Birmingham, **15** Cliff Jones & Terry Dyson.

QUIZ 233

Answers on page 361

1 Which club score in two FA Cup Finals is 10 for and none against?

2 Which club did Gary Taggart join on leaving Manchester City?

3 Philllip Albert's 90th minute goal did not save Belgium being knocked out of 1994 World Cup by which team?

4 Jimmy Gabriel first played in an FA Cup Final for which team?

5 Which team were the first to arrive at Wembley by helicopter?

6 Which club had a fanzine called *Red Issue*?

7 What is Mark Hateley's middle name?

8 Who beat Rangers 3-2 in the 1952 Scottish League Cup Final?

9 Where was the 1991 European Cup Final held?

10 Which brothers were together at Villa for 18 years from the late 1930s?

11 What is the link between Harrow Chequers, Hitchin Town and Reigate Priory?

12 Which team got promotion via the play-offs in their first season in the League in 1993-94?

13 Which Manchester Utd manager signed Gordon Strachan?

14 Who beat Hibernian 3-0 in the 1951 Scottish League Cup Final?

15 Which football player was known as 'The Giraffe'?

Answers to page 361

1 Vienna, **2** Teddy Sherringham, **3** Aberdeen, **4** Manchester City, **5** Keith Burkinshaw, **6** 4, **7** 5, **8** Red Star Belgrade, **9** Robert, **10** Ray Parlour, **11** Brighton & Hove Albion, **12** Rochdale, **13** Stan Anderson, **14** Marseille, **15** Norwich City.

QUIZ 234

Answers on page 362

1 How many times did Arsenal win the FA Cup in the 1980s?

2 Who created the first £10,000 transfer fee joining Arsenal from Bolton?

3 Which club used to play at the Antelope Ground?

4 Which English club got a 0-4 home drubbing from Juventus in the 90s?

5 Who succeeded B McEwan as manager of Sheffield Utd in 1988?

6 Which club has a fanzine called *Hanging On The Telephone*?

7 Derek Fazackerley set a League appearance record at which club?

8 John Neal followed Geoff Hurst as manager of which club?

9 Chairman Francis Lee flew to Marbella to sign which holidaymaker as his club manager?

10 Mark Wright moved from Derby County to which club for £2.2m in June 1991?

11 Who replaced Peter Reid as boss of Manchester City?

12 Irving Natrass played for which two rival sides?

13 Which Italian team were the first winners of the Cup Winners' Cup in 1961?

14 Mickey Stockwell was ever present as which club made the top flight?

15 Which London soccer ground was partly declared a Grade Two listed building in 1987?

Answers to page 362

1 Peter Rodrigues, **2** Liverpool, **3** Colin Clarke, **4** Leeds, **5** QPR, **6** Alan Shearer, **7** Crystal Palace, **8** Leeds Utd, **9** Rochdale, **10** Black, **11** Dave Merrington, **12** Leicester, **13** Ron Davies, **14** Blackburn Rovers, **15** David Lee.

QUIZ 235

Answers on page 359

1 Where was the 1964 European Cup Final held?

2 Which player scored 33 League goals for Millwall in 1990-91?

3 Who beat Celtic 2-1 in the 1984 Scottish FA Cup Final?

4 Peter Barnes was at which club when he made his international debut?

5 Which Spurs manager signed Ossie Ardiles and Ricky Villa in 1978?

6 How many World Cup Finals did Walter Winterbottom's England qualify for?

7 How many players were sent off in the 1997 Chesterfield v Plymouth Argyle League game?

8 Who lost to Manchester Utd in the 1991 Super Cup?

9 What is Darren Anderton's middle name?

10 Which Arsenal player was fined £800 for an assault on a taxi driver in Hong Kong?

11 Which team's fans invaded the pitch in 1996 to protest about plans to share Portsmouth's ground?

12 Which club had a fanzine called *Exceedingly Good Pies*?

13 Who succeeded Ian Greaves as manager of Bolton Wanderers in 1980?

14 Who lost 5-3 on penalties to Red Star Belgrade in the final of the 1991 European Cup?

15 Which club has a fanzine called *I Can Drive A Tractor*?

Answers to page 359

1 Bury, **2** Barnsley, **3** Germany, **4** Everton, **5** Brighton, **6** Manchester Utd, **7** Wayne, **8** Dundee, **9** Bari, **10** Moss Brothers, **11** Entered the first FA Cup competition, **12** Wycombe Wanderers, **13** Ron Atkinson, **14** Motherwell, **15** Jack Charlton.

SOUTHAMPTON 2

Answers on page 360

1 Who was Southampton skipper in their 1970s triumph in the FA Cup Final?

2 Who beat Southampton 7-1 in the Premier League in January 99?

3 Who marked his 1986 debut for Southampton with a hat-trick?

4 Southampton player Derek Reeves scored 5 goals in a match in December 1960. Who were the opponents?

5 Colin Clarke moved from Southampton to which club for £800,000 in March 1989?

6 Which Southampton player became the youngest to score a First Division hat-trick in April 1988?

7 Which club did Iain Dowie leave to join Southampton?

8 Rodney Wallace moved from Southampton to which club for £1.6m in July 1991?

9 Who did Southampton beat 5-0 in the League Cup in September 1990?

10 What colour are Southampton's home shorts?

11 Which manager was replaced by Graeme Souness?

12 Southampton player Charlie Wayman scored 5 goals in a match in October 1948. Who were the opponents?

13 Who scored half of Southampton's 74 goals in the 1966-67 season?

14 Where did Alan Shearer move to on leaving Southampton?

15 Who moved from Bury to Southampton for £375,000, in October 1991 to set a club record for a transfer fee received?

Answers to page 360

1 Never, **2** David Jack, **3** Southampton, **4** Rangers, **5** Dave Bassett, **6** Huddersfield Town, **7** Blackburn Rovers, **8** Chelsea, **9** Alan Ball, **10** Liverpool, **11** Brian Horton, **12** Middlesborough & Newcastle Utd, **13** Florentina, **14** Ipswich Town, **15** Fulham's Craven Cottage.

WORLD CUP 1966 2

Answers on page 365

1 Who scored England's first in the 1966 World Cup Final?

2 How many matches did England play in the 1966 World Cup finals?

3 Can you name all the ever-present players in every England game of the 1966 World Cup finals?

4 Who scored first for West Germany in the 1966 World Cup Final?

5 Which country lost 2-1 to West Germany in the 1966 World Cup semi-final?

6 Who sent the ball forward for Geoff Hurst's final goal in the 1966 World Cup Final?

7 Who managed West Germany in the 1966 World Cup Final?

8 What was the nationality of the referee in the 1966 World Cup Final?

9 Which winger John was in England's 1966 World Cup squad?

10 In the 1966 World Cup quarter-finals which injured player did Geoff Hurst replace?

11 Who did England meet in their first match in the 1966 finals?

12 Who was manager of Italy in the 1966 World Cup finals, later to be sacked?

13 Of the six games England played during the 1966 World Cup finals how many resulted in defeat?

14 Which was the only country to deny England victory in the 1966 World Cup finals?

15 Who scored nine goals for Portugal in the 1966 World Cup finals?

Answers to page 365

1 Yugoslavia, **2** Bobby Smith, **3** Berwick Rangers, **4** Manchester City, **5** Birmingham City, **6** Stuttgart, **7** Mike England, **8** Aston Villa, **9** Waldie, **10** Brighton, **11** Derby County, **12** Bottom (22nd), **13** Liverpool, **14** 1970s, **15** Cardiff City.

OWN GOALS

Answers on page 366

1 Who scored an own goal in the Aston Villa v Everton replayed League Cup Final in the 70s?

2 Who was George Chisholm playing for when he scored a League Cup Final own goal?

3 Who scored all the goals in Aston Villa's 2-2 draw with Leicester City in 1976?

4 Who scored an own goal for Blackburn in the 1960 FA Cup Final?

5 Who scored for both sides in the 1988 friendly between England and Holland?

6 Which Scot scored an own goal against Brazil in the 1998 World Cup Finals?

7 Pat Kruse scored an own goal after just 3 seconds in a match against Cambridge Utd in January 1977. Which side did he play for?

8 Which England and Fulham player scored an own goal after just 30 seconds, before any player from the opposing side had even touched the ball?

9 Which team was Bert Turner playing for when he scored for both sides in the 1946 FA Cup Final?

10 Which team was Tommy Hutchison playing for when he scored for both sides in the 1981 FA Cup Final?

11 Which team was Gary Mabbutt playing for when he scored for both sides in the 1987 FA Cup Final?

12 Robert Stewart scored five own goals in a season whilst playing at which club?

13 Which Colombian scored an own goal in the 1994 World Cup Finals and was shot dead when he returned home?

14 George Cox scored an own goal on the first day of the first season of the English League. What club did he play for?

15 Who scored an own goal in the 1877 FA Cup final?

Answers to page 366

1 1967-68, **2** Nine, **3** Graham Turner, **4** Manchester City, **5** Crystal Palace, **6** Tom Keetley, **7** Blackpool v Bolton Wanderers, **8** Sheffield Utd, **9** Southend, **10** Exeter, **11** Hearts and Kilmarnock, **12** Three, **13** Two, **14** West Ham Utd, **15** AC Milan.

QUIZ 265

Answers on page 363

1 Who was shown the first yellow card of the 1998 World Cup finals?

2 Sheffield Wednesday player Douglas Hunt scored 6 goals in a match in November 1938. Who were the opponents?

3 Howard Wilkinson was player-manager of which non-League side?

4 Which Dutch side did Bobby Robson take charge of after leaving England?

5 Who beat Dundee Utd 1-0 in the 1985 Scottish League Cup Final?

6 Which team did "El Tel" lose to in the 1896 European Cup Final?

7 Who is Celtic's all time top goal scorer?

8 Who was the regular keeper for Ipswich Town in their 1994-95 relegation season?

9 Which soccer team plays its home matches at Upton Park?

10 Ian Snodin moved from Leeds Utd to which club for £850,000 in January 1987?

11 Which manager was sacked by one club in January 1998 and parted company with another in April 1998?

12 Who kept goal for Northern Ireland in the 1958 World Cup?

13 Who succeeded Jim Smith as manager of Newcastle Utd in 1991?

14 Who succeeded Sammy Chapman as manager of Wolverhampton Wanderers in 1986?

15 Goals from which Dutch striker knocked out Norwich from the 1993-94 UEFA Cup?

Answers to page 363

1 Cesar Sampaio, **2** Norwich, **3** Boston Utd, **4** PSV Eindhoven, **5** Rangers, **6** Steaua Bucharest, **7** Jimmy McGrory, **8** Craig Forest, **9** West Ham Utd, **10** Everton, **11** Chris Kamara (Bradford City & Stoke City), **12** Harry Gregg, **13** Ossie Adiles, **14** Brian Little, **15** Dennis Bergkamp.

QUIZ 237

Answers on page 364

1 In which season did it become compulsory for all 92 League clubs to enter the English FA Cup?

2 How many international goals did Liam Brady score?

3 Who succeeded Tony Barton as manager of Aston Villa in 1984?

4 John Bond followed Malcolm Allison as boss of which club?

5 In 1990, Liverpool beat which club 9-0 in the League and lost to them in an FA Cup semi-final?

6 Which player scored 39 League goals for Notts County in 1930-31?

7 Which derby was England's first live TV match in September 1960?

8 Which club had a fanzine called *The Greasy Chip Buttie*?

9 Derby County recorded a 7-0 League Cup win over which club in October 1992?

10 Crystal Palace player Peter Simpson scored 6 goals in a match in October 1930. Who were the opponents?

11 Which two Scottish teams met in the final game of the 1964-65 season to decide which of them were champions?

12 How many times did Bryan Robson win the FA Cup as Manchester Utd skipper?

13 How many international goals did Frank Worthington score?

14 Which club provided three England players for the World Cup-winning squad of 1966?

15 Which foreign club did Ray Wilkins play for?

Answers to page 364

1 Roger Kenyon (Everton), **2** Sunderland, **3** Chris Nicholl of Aston Villa, **4** Mick McGrath, **5** Tony Adams, **6** Tom Boyd, **7** Torquay Utd, **8** Alan Mullery, **9** Charlton Athletic, **10** Manchester City, **11** Tottenham Hotspur, **12** Middlesborough, **13** Escobar, **14** Aston Villa, **15** Lord Kinnaird.

QUIZ 238

Answers on page 369

1 Which Scottish winger was nicknamed 'The Flea'?

2 Which manager was nicknamed 'El Tel' when he managed Barcelona?

3 Which Bobby became Wimbledon manager in 1987?

4 Goalkeeper Bill Brown joined Spurs from which club?

5 Who created a record for Derby County by playing 486 League games?

6 Which German player won the Footballer of the Year in 1995?

7 What was the score after extra-time in the France v West Germany 1982 World Cup semi-final?

8 Jim Ryan followed Ray Harford as manager of which club?

9 Which club has a fanzine called *Hello Albert*?

10 Leeds Utd player Gordon Hodgson scored 5 goals in a match in October 1938. Who were the opponents?

11 Which sport was played professionally by Ryan Gigg's father?

12 Who was top scorer in Euro '88?

13 Bill Dodgin Jnr followed Alec Stock as manager of which club?

14 Which club chairman was forced to apologise for remarks he made about black players in a television programme?

15 Which Fourth Division side competed in the 1962 League Cup Final?

Answers to page 369

1 Bobby Moore, **2** Soviet Union, **3** Brazil and West Germany, **4** 1-0 to England, **5** 1-0 to England, **6** Allan Clarke, **7** Alan Mullery, **8** 3-2 to West Germany, **9** Italy, **10** Franz Beckenbauer, **11** Azteca Stadium, **12** Albertosi, **13** Alberto, **14** Facchetti, **15** East German.

SHEFFIELD WED 2

Answers on page 370

1 What is the highest position Wednesday have ever achieved in the League?

2 Who moved from Wednesday to Blackburn Rovers in 1993 to set a club record fee for a transfer received?

3 Brian Marwood moved from Wednesday to which club for £600,000 in March 1988?

4 Mel Sterland moved from Wednesday to which club for £800,000 in March 1989?

5 Who did Wednesday buy from Molde, Norway for £800,000?

6 Ron Atkinson pledged himself to Wednesday just three days before he joined which club?

7 Who succeeded Jack Charlton as manager of Wednesday in 1983?

8 Dalian Atkinson moved from Wednesday to which club for £1.7m in August 1990?

9 Paul Warhurst moved from Wednesday to which club for £2.7m in August 1993?

10 Who moved from Port Vale to Wednesday for £1 million in 1994 to set a club record for a transfer fee received?

11 Who in 1991 said he would be "bananas" to leave Wednesday?

12 Who was in goal when Wednesday lost the FA Cup Final in 1993?

13 After they were thrashed 7-1 by Wednesday in the FA Cup, which caretaker manager said, "The Cup is the icing on the cake, but at the moment we haven't got any cake"?

14 Who was Wednesday boss in the 1998-99 season?

15 Who was Dion Dublin playing for when he hit three against Wednesday in 1995 and still ended up on the losing side?

Answers to page 370

1 Bristol Rovers, **2** Newcastle United, **3** Dundee United, **4** Brian Clough, **5** Micky Adams, **6** 1956, **7** Marseille, **8** Howard Wilkinson, **9** Tottenham Hotspur, **10** West Brom, **11** Steve Chalmers, **12** Nottingham Forest, **13** Glentoran, **14** Chelsea, **15** Manchester City.

• WORLD CUP 1970 2 •

Answers on page 367

1 Who was imprisoned during the 1970 World Cup Finals, wrongly accused of stealing a bracelet?

2 Which team faced Mexico in the opening game of the 1970 World Cup Finals?

3 Which two nations had 100% records after the group stages of the 1970 World Cup Finals?

4 What was the score in the England v Czechoslovakia game in the 1970 World Cup Finals?

5 What was the score in the England v Romania game in the 1970 World Cup Finals?

6 Who scored England's penalty against Czechoslovakia in the 1970 World Cup Finals?

7 Who scored his only goal for England against West Germany in the quarter-finals of the 1970 World Cup Finals?

8 What was the score after extra-time of the England v West Germany quarter-final in the 1970 World Cup Finals?

9 Who did West Germany lose to in the semi-final of the 1970 World Cup Finals?

10 Which West German player took to the field wearing a sling in the 1970 World Cup Finals?

11 In which stadium did the 1970 World Cup Final take place?

12 Who played in goal for Italy in the 1970 World Cup Final?

13 Who was Brazil's captain in the 1970 World Cup Final?

14 Who was Italy's captain in the 1970 World Cup Final?

15 What was the nationality of Rudi Glockner, the 1970 World Cup Final referee?

Answers to page 367

1 Jimmy Johnstone, **2** Terry Venables, **3** Gould, **4** Dundee, **5** Kevin Hector, **6** Jurgen Klinsmann, **7** 3-3, **8** Luton Town, **9** Chester City, **10** Liecester City, **11** Rugby League, **12** Marco van Basten, **13** Fulham, **14** Ron Noades (Crystal Palace), **15** Rochdale.

QUIZ 239

Answers on page 368

1 Which club had a fanzine called *Trumpton Times*?

2 Which club rejected a young Alan Shearer after giving him a trial in goal?

3 Eamonn Bannon's goal in April 1983 clinched the Scottish Championship for which team?

4 Who succeeded Tim Ward as manager of Derby County in 1967?

5 In November 1998 who was appointed manager of Brentford to succeed to David Webb?

6 When was the first Manchester derby in the FA Charity Shield?

7 Who beat AC Milan 1-0 in the 1993 European Cup Final before being stripped of the title?

8 Who succeeded Jack Charlton as manager of Sheffield Wednesday in 1983?

9 Which soccer team does actor Warren Mitchell support?

10 Who beat Everton 1-0 in the 1966 FA Cup Final?

11 Who scored the winning goal for Celtic in the 1967 European Cup Final?

12 Who were the first club to retain the League Cup?

13 Danny Blanchflower started out with which Irish club?

14 Birchenall and Boyle scored Euro goals in the same 60s game for which club?

15 Ray Ransom first played in an FA Cup Final for which team?

Answers to page 368

1 Division 1 (1st), **2** Paul Warhurst, **3** Arsenal, **4** Glasgow Rangers, **5** Petter Rudi, **6** Aston Villa, **7** Howard Wilkinson, **8** Real Sociedad, **9** Blackburn Rovers, **10** Ian Taylor, **11** Ron Atkinson, **12** Chris Woods, **13** Kenny Swain (Grimsby Town), **14** Danny Wilson, **15** Coventry City.

QUIZ 240

Answers on page 373

1 Robert Bell became the first player to score a League triple hat-trick but for which club?

2 Barry Venison first played in an FA Cup Final for which team?

3 In 1994, who equalised for Italy three minutes from time v Nigeria and in the next round hit the winner v Spain two minutes from time?

4 Neil Warnock followed John Barnwell as manager of which club?

5 Which soccer team does politician Derek Hatton support?

6 Tottenham Hotspur player Les Allen scored 5 goals in a match in February 1960. Who were the opponents?

7 Which player scored 28 League goals for Hartlepool Utd in 1990-91?

8 Which ground installed the first ever 'dug-outs' requested by the coach so that he could study his players footwork?

9 Which soccer team does snooker player Steve Davis support?

10 In what year was the penalty kick introduced?

11 Which non League side did Ian Wright play for?

12 Which two Johns were with Clough's champions at Derby County and Nottingham Forest?

13 In which year did Aberdeen win the European Cup Winners' Cup and the Scottish Cup?

14 In 1972, John Ritchie was sent off within 30 seconds as appearing in a Euro game for which club?

15 Which club received a £125,000 fine for poaching their manager from another club?

Answers to page 373

1 Wimbledon, **2** Bradford, **3** Fulham, **4** Scunthorpe, **5** Arsenal, **6** Chris Morris, **7** John Rudge, **8** Wales, **9** Norwich City, **10** Shaun, **11** Mike Keen, **12** Burnley, **13** Montrose, **14** Westley, **15** Sheffield Utd.

QUIZ 241

Answers on page 374

1 Who was the skipper of the 1970 Brazilian World Cup team?

2 Tommy Robson played 482 League games for which club?

3 Which team won the 1983 UEFA Cup?

4 Which player scored 39 League goals for Southampton in 1959-60?

5 Which soccer team does the Manic Street Preacher's James Dean Bradfield support?

6 How many players were sent off in the 1967 World Club Championship between Celtic and Racing Club?

7 Charlton Athletic player Wilson Lennox scored 5 goals in a match in February 1929. Who were the opponents?

8 For which club did David Speedie make his League debut?

9 Which player scored 36 League goals for Chester City in 1946-47?

10 Which soccer team does classical violinist Nigel Kennedy support?

11 Who succeeded Andy Nelson as manager of Charlton Athletic in 1980?

12 Southampton player Charlie Wayman scored 5 goals in a match in October 1948. Who were the opponents?

13 Who, in 1975, became the first English soccer club banned from international competition due to its hooligan supporters?

14 Which player scored 29 League goals for Exeter City in 1936-37?

15 In 1911 a new FA Cup was made in - and then won by the team from which place?

Answers to page 374

1 Einer Aas, **2** Liverpool, **3** Sammy Chapman, **4** Barry Fry, **5** Hamburg, **6** Liverpool, **7** Sampdoria, **8** Bob Houghton, **9** Ian Storey Moore, **10** Luton Town, **11** Shinguards, **12** Brian Clough, **13** Ipswich Town, **14** Malmo, **15** Stan Collymore.

QUIZ 242

Answers on page 371

1 Terry Phelan first played in an FA Cup Final for which team?

2 England's cricket captain Brian Close played soccer in the 1950s for which team?

3 Liverpool recorded a 10-0 League Cup win over which club in September 1986?

4 Which Football League club did Ian Botham play for?

5 Martin Hayes scored in a League Cup Final for which club?

6 Which Republic of Ireland defender of the 1990s has the middle name Barry?

7 Who took over as manager of Port Vale in 1983 and was still there in 1999?

8 Which country did Phil Woosnam play for?

9 At which club did Robert Fleck make his English League debut?

10 Who is Peter Reid's soccer playing brother?

11 Who succeeded George Kirby as manager of Watford in 1973?

12 Aston Villa player Len Capwell scored 5 goals in a match in August 1925. Who were the opponents?

13 Geographically, which is the nearest club to Aberdeen?

14 Which Terry was in charge at Luton Town during 1995?

15 Which soccer team does The Beautiful South's Paul Heaton support?

Answers to page 371

1 Tranmere Rovers, **2** Liverpool, **3** Roberto Baggio, **4** Notts County, **5** Everton, **6** Crewe Alexandra, **7** Joe Allon, **8** Pittodrie (Aberdeen), **9** Charlton Athletic, **10** 1891, **11** Greenwich Borough, **12** O'Hare and McGovern, **13** 1983, **14** Stoke City, **15** Everton (Mike Walker from Norwich City).

NOTT FOREST 3

Answers on page 372

1 Which Norwegian international was bought from Bayern Munich to replace Larry Lloyd, but played only 20 games for Forest in 1980-81?

2 Which club did Nigel Clough join on leaving Forest?

3 In 1971 Forest had a player sent off for the first time in 32 years. Who was the player involved?

4 Who was boss at Southend Utd when Stan Collymore moved to Forest for £2m in 1993?

5 Who lost 1-0 to Forest in the Final of 1980 European Cup?

6 Stan Colymore moved from Forest to which club in July 1995?

7 Des Walker moved from Nottingham to which club for £1.5m in May 1992?

8 Who was Malmo's English manager when they met Forest in the European Cup Final?

9 Arriving in 1972 from Forest, who was Manchester Utd's first ever £200,000 signing?

10 Which team was beaten 2-1 by Forest in the 1959 FA Cup Final?

11 Samuel Widdowson of Forest is credited with which innovation?

12 Which manager dealt with four fans who invaded the pitch in a League Cup match at the City ground in 1989?

13 Brian Clough's last League game as Forest boss was against who?

14 Who lost 1-0 to Forest in the Final of the 1979 European Cup?

15 In January 1996, which former striker lost his appeal for a pay-off from Forest?

Answers to page 372

1 Carlos Alberto, **2** Peterborough, **3** Anderlecht, **4** Derek Reeves, **5** Nottingham Forest, **6** Five, **7** Exeter, **8** Barnsley, **9** Dick Yates, **10** Aston Villa, **11** Mike Bailey, **12** Leicester, **13** Leeds Utd, **14** Rod Williams, **15** Bradford.

WORLD CUP 1974 2

Answers on page 377

1 Who, during the 1974 World Cup finals, was the first player to make 55 appearances for Scotland?

2 Which goalkeeper saved penalties against Sweden and West Germany in the 1974 World Cup finals?

3 Who scored the winning goal in the 1974 World Cup Final?

4 Who kept goal for Poland at Wembley in the 1974 World Cup qualifier?

5 Which team were the only unbeaten team in the 1974 World Cup finals?

6 In which city was the 1974 World Cup Final staged?

7 Which Celtic star was diagnosed diabetic after playing in the 1974 World Cup squad?

8 Which Dutchman scored two goals against Argentina in the 1974 World Cup finals?

9 Who scored the first goal of the 1974 World Cup finals?

10 Who was top scorer for the Dutch in both 1974 and 1978 World Cups?

11 Who scored the only goal of the game in the Poland v West Germany game in the 1974 World Cup finals?

12 How many red cards were shown in the 1974 World Cup finals?

13 Which country beat Zaire 9-0 in the 1974 World Cup finals to equal the then record?

14 Who played in goal for West Germany in the 1974 World Cup Final?

15 Which countries were in Scotland's group in the 1974 World Cup finals?

Answers to page 377

1 8, **2** Shaggy, **3** Black and White, **4** Leeds Utd, **5** The Republic of Ireland, **6** 1978, **7** Steaua Bucharest, **8** Leeds Utd, **9** David Platt, **10** 1950s, **11** None, **12** Belgium, **13** Dean Saunders, **14** Ajax, **15** Manchester City.

QUIZ 243

Answers on page 378

1 Paul Warhurst moved from Sheffield Wednesday to which club for £2.7m in August 1993?

2 Who scored a first minute penalty for Holland in the 1974 World Cup Final?

3 Chris Waddle scored in an FA Cup Final for which club?

4 Which Hereford Utd player was the League's leading scorer in 1974-75 and 1975-76?

5 Gordon McQueen scored in an FA Cup Final for which club?

6 Bolivia had a man sent off in the third minute against Germany in the USA 1994 World Cup finals. What was his name?

7 Which Middlesborough manager said - days before resigning - "We are on the crest of a slump"?

8 Which football player said " I don't want to put pressure on the manager here, but I never came to Newcastle United to be a substitute"?

9 Which club was once known as Pine Villa?

10 Who retired from international soccer after the 1974 World Cup game against Zaire?

11 Who made 629 League appearances for Leeds Utd between 1953-73?

12 Which club has a fanzine called *Bert Trautmann's Helmet*?

13 Which club in the 1970s won the Championship while on holiday in Majorca?

14 Which future England player was born in Rotherham in 1963?

15 Who scored a hat-trick in the Manchester derby in November 1994?

Answers to page 378

1 Red Star Belgrade, **2** Tennents, **3** Colchester, **4** Jimmy Seed, **5** Bristol Rovers, **6** Notts County, **7** Preston North End, **8** Don Howe, **9** Dave Beasant (Wimbledon), **10** Ian St John, **11** Vancouver Whitecaps, **12** Ray Houghton, **13** Brighton, **14** Twelve, **15** Roberto Baggio.

QUIZ 244

Answers on page 375

1 How many Championship medals did Phil Neal win with Liverpool?

2 Which nickname does Darren Anderton share with Liverpool's Steve McManaman?

3 What colour are Grimsby Town's striped home shirts?

4 Which club has a fanzine called *The Square Ball*?

5 Which country did Gerry Peyton play for?

6 Tunisia, England's group rivals in the 1998 World Cup competition, appeared only once before in the finals. In what year?

7 Who did AC Milan beat 4-0 in the 1989 European Cup Final?

8 Which team won the 1971 UEFA Cup?

9 Who scored England's only goal in Euro '92?

10 In what decade did Aberdeen first win the Championship?

11 How many British teams qualified for the 1994 World Cup?

12 Which country did Nico Claesen play for?

13 Who joined Liverpool from Derby County for £2.9m in July 1991?

14 Who lost 1-0 to Mechelen in the 1988 Cup-Winners' Cup Final?

15 Which club was once known as Ardwick FC?

Answers to page 375

1 Denis Law, **2** Tomaszewski (Poland), **3** Gerd Muller, **4** Jan Tomaszewski, **5** Scotland, **6** Munich, **7** Danny McGrain, **8** Johan Cruyff, **9** Breitner, **10** Johan Neeskens, **11** Gerd Muller, **12** 5, **13** Yugoslavia, **14** Maier, **15** Brazil, Yugoslavia and Zaire.

QUIZ 245

Answers on page 376

1 Who beat Marseille on penalties in the 1991 European Cup Final?

2 Who were the Scottish FA Cup sponsors from 1989-1998?

3 Leeds Utd recorded a 4-0 League Cup win over which club in November 1977?

4 Who was manager of Charlton Athletic from 1933-56?

5 Stuart Taylor set a League appearance record at which club?

6 Albert Ironmonger set a League appearance record for which club?

7 Bill Shankly played for which FA Cup-winning side?

8 Who succeeded Trevor Francis as manager of QPR in 1990?

9 Who was the first goalkeeper to save a penalty in an FA Cup Final?

10 Which Motherwell forward hit three goals in three minutes in 1959?

11 Peter Beardsley was sold by Carlisle in April 1981. Which club did he join?

12 Which Irish player scored the winning goal against Italy in the 1994 World Cup finals match?

13 At which club did Eric Young make his League debut?

14 How many times was Wimbledon hardman Vinnie Jones sent off whilst playing for The Dons?

15 Who missed Italy's final penalty in the 1994 World Cup?

Answers to page 376

1 Blackburn Rovers, **2** Johan Neeskens, **3** Sheffield Wednesday, **4** Dixie McNeil, **5** Manchester Utd, **6** Marco Etcheverry, **7** Jack Charlton, **8** David Ginola., **9** Oldham Athletic, **10** Denis Law, **11** Jack Charlton, **12** Manchester City, **13** Derby County, **14** David Seaman, **15** Andrei Kanchelskis.

QUIZ 246

Answers on page 381

1 Where was the 1992 European Cup Final held?

2 Leeds Utd recorded a 4-0 League Cup win over which club in October 1987?

3 Which player was known as Bonzo?

4 What is Matt Le Tissier's middle name?

5 Who beat Manchester Utd 3-1 in the opening day of the 1995-96 season?

6 At which ground do Anderlecht play their home games?

7 Which Colin was Minister for Sport in the 1980s?

8 Who took over as England skipper from Billy Wright?

9 Who scored England's only goal against Romania in the 1998 World Cup finals?

10 Who succeeded Jock Stein as manager of Leeds Utd in 1978?

11 Who was the first 50-year-old to play top-flight football in England?

12 Which country lost 5-1 to Hungary in the 1938 World Cup semi-final?

13 Which country did Spain beat 6-1 in the 1998 World Cup finals?

14 Which England full-back Roger died in the Munich air disaster?

15 Which club has a fanzine called *The Greasy Chip Buttie*?

Answers to page 381

1 Scunthorpe Utd, **2** Barnsley, **3** Everton, **4** Malcolm Allison, **5** Steve Daley, **6** Bert Trautmann, **7** Everton, **8** Malcolm Macdonald, **9** Sunderland, **10** Brian Horton, **11** Germany, **12** Newcastle Utd, **13** They were relegated, **14** Ardwick, **15** 1970.

• WORLD CUP 1978 2 •

Answers on page 382

1 What was the result of Scotland's Group Four game against Iran in the 1978 World Cup finals?

2 In which country were the 1978 World Cup finals held?

3 Which two teams contested the opening game of the 1978 World Cup finals?

4 Whose last game for Scotland was the 1978 World Cup defeat by Peru in which he missed a penalty?

5 How many goals were scored in the 38 games of the 1978 World Cup finals?

6 Peru beat Scotland 3-1 in the 1978 World Cup finals. Who scored Scotland's goal?

7 Who was top scorer for the Dutch in the 1978 World Cup finals?

8 Sergio Gonella refereed the 1978 World Cup Final. From which country did he come?

9 Which Dutchman scored all three goals against Peru in the 1978 World Cup finals?

10 Which Scottish player scored a brilliant solo goal against Holland in a 1978 World Cup match?

11 Who was in goal for Holland in the 1978 World Cup Final?

12 Which country had two players sent off in a game against Argentina in the 1978 World Cup finals?

13 Which team was followed by Ally's Army in the 1978 World Cup?

14 Who was in goal for Argentina in the 1978 World Cup Final?

15 How many goals did West Germany score against Mexico in the 1978 World Cup finals?

Answers to page 382

1 Notts County, **2** Preston North End, **3** Dean, **4** Jackie Milburn, **5** Celtic, **6** Mo Johnston, **7** No internationals, **8** Notts County, **9** Flowers, **10** Liam Brady, **11** Group C, **12** Leicester City, **13** Trevor Morley, **14** Basle, **15** Wrexham.

• MANCHESTER CITY 3 •

Answers on page 379

1 Manchester City recorded a 6-0 League Cup win over which club in September 1974?

2 Which club did Gary Taggart join on leaving Manchester City?

3 Manchester City player Tom Johnson scored 5 goals in a match in September 1928. Who were the opponents?

4 Who was Joe Mercer's assistant when Manchester City won the Championship?

5 Which Wolves player moved for £1 million to Manchester City in 1979?

6 Which ex-Manchester City keeper recommended Eike Immel to his old club?

7 Mark Ward moved from Manchester City to which club in June 1991?

8 Who was the manager of Huddersfield when they lost 10-1 to Manchester City?

9 Which club did Niall Quinn join on leaving Manchester City?

10 Who replaced Peter Reid as boss of Manchester City?

11 In which country was Manchester City goalkeeper Bert Trautmann born?

12 Who beat Manchester City 3-1 in the 1955 FA Cup Final?

13 What happened to Manchester City in 1938 after being champions in 1937?

14 Under what previous name did Manchester City play?

15 In which year did Manchester City win the European Cup Winners' Cup?

Answers to page 379

1 Wembley, **2** York City, **3** Billy Bonds, **4** Paul, **5** Aston Villa, **6** Constant Vanden Stock, **7** Moynihan, **8** Ronnie Clayton, **9** Michael Owen, **10** Jimmy Adamson, **11** Sir Stanley Matthews, **12** Sweden, **13** Bugaria, **14** Byrne, **15** Sheffield Utd.

QUIZ 247

Answers on page 380

1 Who were the first English club to play 3,000 matches in the League?

2 David Beckham has spent time on loan at which Lancashire club?

3 What is Warren Barton's middle name?

4 Who scored England's first ever hat-trick in a World Cup match?

5 Who beat Internazionale 2-1 in the 1967 European Cup Final?

6 Partick Thistle's record fee received was £200,000 in 1981 when which player moved to Watford?

7 What links the teams of Leicester City in 1961, Sunderland in 1973 and Crystal Palace in 1990?

8 Which club has a fanzine called *The Pie*?

9 Who started the game in goal for England when they drew against Switzerland in a friendly in March 1998?

10 Which player wrote *So Far So Good*?

11 Which group were Germany in at the start of Euro '96?

12 Which club did Gary McAllister leave to join Leeds Utd?

13 Which London-based player was stabbed in a domestic row?

14 Where was the 1984 European Cup Winners' Cup Final held?

15 Which club did Joey Jones leave to join Liverpool?

Answers to page 380

1 1-1, **2** Argentina, **3** West Germany and Poland, **4** Don Masson, **5** 102, **6** Joe Jordan, **7** Johan Neeskens, **8** Italy, **9** Robbie Rensenbrink, **10** Archie Gemmill, **11** Jongbloed, **12** Hungary, **13** Scotland, **14** Fillol, **15** 6.

QUIZ 248

Answers on page 385

1 Who was in goal when Leeds Utd won the FA Cup in the 1970s?

2 Who in the 1980s went from Portsmouth to AC Milan?

3 What is the main colour of Gillingham's home shirts?

4 Who wrote *Everton Winter Mexican Summer: A Football Diary*?

5 Which French club did Mo Johnston play for?

6 Who moved from Cambridge in 1992 to Manchester Utd to set a club record for a transfer fee received?

7 Which manager John took Ipswich Town up as Second Division Champions?

8 Kevin Ball first played in an FA Cup Final for which team?

9 Stuart McCall scored in an FA Cup Final for which club?

10 Ray Graydon scored a League Cup Final winner for which club?

11 Irish international John Byrne first played in an FA Cup Final for which team?

12 Who beat Hamburg 1-0 in the 1980 European Cup Final?

13 Who beat FC Bruges 1-0 in the 1978 European Cup Final?

14 Who scored a double hat-trick on his Newcastle Utd debut in the 1950s?

15 Which Juventus player was European Footballer of the Year in 1982?

Answers to page 385

1 Terry Hurlock, **2** Luton Town, **3** Steve Morrow, **4** Bobby Charlton, **5** Mark Draper, **6** England, **7** Gary McAllister, **8** Eric Cantona was born, **9** Howard Kendall (During his second spell), **10** 1940s, **11** West Ham Utd, **12** Brussels, **13** Eric Cantona, **14** Zico, **15** Aston Villa.

QUIZ 249

Answers on page 386

1 Which club originally played at the Red House ground?

2 In which city was Trevor Francis born?

3 Which country does Dariusz Kubicki come from?

4 What was the title of Crystal Palace's 1990 FA Cup Final song?

5 What was the nickname of Brazil's Garrincha?

6 Where was the 1963 European Cup Final held?

7 Which team were beaten 4-3 by Motherwell in the 1991 Scottish FA Cup Final?

8 What is Dave Beasant's middle name?

9 Who lost 1-0 to Chelsea in the 1998 Cup Winners' Cup Final?

10 Which Dinamo Bucharest player won the 1988-89 Golden Boot award?

11 Against which country did Paul Gascoigne make his international debut?

12 Which team went down two seasons after winning the championship in the 60s?

13 Who was Chelsea's manager when they won the League in 1954-55?

14 Which Scottish team are known as The Ton?

15 When did the English League adopt three points for a win?

Answers to page 386

1 30, **2** Charlton Athletic, **3** George Eastham, **4** Ruud Gullit, **5** Notts County, **6** Stevenage Borough, **7** Airdrie, **8** Chelsea, **9** George Reilly, **10** Les Ferdinand, **11** Oldest Player (41 Years 257 days), **12** Terry McDermott, **13** Alan Shearer, **14** Darren Huckerby, **15** Hughie Gallacher.

QUIZ 250

Answers on page 383

1 Which Fulham player amassed a record 61 disciplinary points in the 1994-95 season?

2 Ashley Grimes played in 1980s League Cup Finals for which team?

3 Which Arsenal player broke his arm in a fall after being hoisted in the air by Tony Adams at the end of the 1993 League Cup Final?

4 Who is England's all-time record goalscorer?

5 Which player did Leicester City buy for £1.25m from Notts County and then sell at a £2m profit a year later to Aston Villa?

6 Which country did Mick Channon play for?

7 Which Scottish captain was born in Motherwell in 1964?

8 Why, according to a Nike advertising slogan, was 1966 a good year for English football?

9 Who was manager of Everton before Mike Walker?

10 In which decade was Eusebio born?

11 Parris and Potts played for which relegated side?

12 Where was the 1964 European Cup Winners' Cup Final held?

13 Which Manchester Utd star got a red card after the final whistle in 1993?

14 By what name was Brazil's Artur Antunes Coimbra better known?

15 Which soccer team does Black Sabbath's Geezer Butler support?

Answers to page 383

1 David Harvey, **2** Mark Hateley, **3** Blue, **4** Peter Reid, **5** Nantes, **6** Dion Dublin, **7** Lyall, **8** Sunderland, **9** Everton, **10** Aston Villa, **11** Sunderland, **12** Nottingham Forest, **13** Liverpool, **14** Len Shackleton, **15** Paolo Rossi.

NEWCASTLE 3

Answers on page 384

1 How many points did Newcastle get from the first 10 games of the 1992-93 promotion season?

2 Kenny Dalglish's first home game as Newcastle boss was against which team in the FA Cup?

3 Which player took Newcastle to court?

4 Who replaced Kenny Dalglish as Newcastle manager, promising 'Sexy Football'?

5 Newcastle Utd recorded a 7-1 League Cup win over which club in October 1993?

6 Who forced Newcastle to a replay in the Fourth round of the 1998 FA Cup?

7 Hughie Gallacher joined Newcastle from which club?

8 Gavin Peacock moved from Newcastle to which club for £1.25m in July 1993?

9 Which Newcastle centre forward came off as Gazza came on as sub for his debut?

10 Which player hit his first Newcastle hat-trick against Wimbledon in October 1995?

11 What did Newcastle Bill Hampson achieve in the 1924 FA Cup Final?

12 Which former Liverpool team-mate was assistant manager at Newcastle when Kenny Dalglish arrived?

13 Who hit a 1997 hat-trick for Newcastle, who were losing 3-1, into a 4-3 victory over Leicester City?

14 Who moved from Lincoln City to Newcastle in 1995 to set a club record for a transfer fee received?

15 Which ex-Newcastle player committed suicide on a railway track?

Answers to page 384

1 Rotherham Utd, **2** Plymouth, **3** Poland, **4** *Glad All Over*, **5** The Little Bird, **6** Wembley, **7** Dundee Utd, **8** John, **9** Stuttgart, **10** Dorin Mateut, **11** Denmark (June 1989), **12** Ipswich Town, **13** Ted Drake, **14** Greenock Morton, **15** 1981.

WORLD CUP 1982 2

Answers on page 389

1 Which squad charted in 1982 with *We Have A Dream*?

2 In 1982 Scotland played New Zealand in the first of their three group matches. What was the score?

3 Who was captain of Brazil for the 1982 World Cup finals?

4 Who were the first nation to win a World Cup shoot out in 1982?

5 Who was bought in as coach for England for the 1982 World Cup finals?

6 Who was manager of Northern Ireland in the World Cup finals in 1982?

7 Who was manager of Scotland in the 1982 World Cup finals?

8 Which Scottish player was voted into the world team by newspaper reporters at the 1982 World Cup finals?

9 Which 1978 finalists failed to qualify for the 1982 World Cup finals?

10 Who was manager of Argentina in the 1982 World Cup finals?

11 Which African countries qualified for the World Cup finals for the first time in 1982?

12 In which city was the 1982 World Cup Final held?

13 Which other countries made up England's group in the 1982 World Cup finals

14 Which other countries made up Scotland's group in the 1982 World Cup finals

15 Which Northern Ireland player was sent off in the 1982 World Cup finals game against Spain?

Answers to page 389

1 Basle, **2** Alan Kelly, **3** Billy Bingham, **4** 1967, **5** Maurice, **6** Dumbarton, **7** Arsenal, **8** Bobby Hunt, **9** Nagoya Grampus 8., **10** Chris Balderstone, **11** Rochdale, **12** Martin O'Neill, **13** Moldova, **14** Arsenal, **15** Tottenham Hotspur.

QUIZ 251

Answers on page 390

1 Norwegian goalkeeper Erik Thorstvedt played for which London club?

2 Which Brian of Arsenal won his only England cap in 1988?

3 Which club did Leeds Utd pay £4.5m to for Thomas Brolin in November 1995?

4 What season did Celtic achieve Scotland's first double?

5 Gerry Ryan took temprary charge of which club in November 1991?

6 What is the highest position Middlesborough have ever achieved in the League?

7 Who were the first Cup winners to win the Charity Shield?

8 Who scored for Juventus in their 1997 European Cup Final defeat by Borussia Dortmund?

9 Which club did Bryan Robson leave to take over as player/manager at Middlesborough?

10 How many international goals did Joe Jordan score?

11 Who was aged 60 when he took over as England's caretaker manager?

12 Who was the regular keeper for Sunderland in their 1990-91 relegation season?

13 Which player scored 47 League goals for Swindon Town in 1926-27?

14 Which soccer team does Radio 1 DJ Zoe Ball support?

15 Who is the first player this century to win four FA Cup winners medals?

Answers to page 390

1 Middlesborough, **2** John Toshack, **3** Leicester City, **4** Athletic Bilbao, **5** Barcelona, **6** Lou Macari, **7** Sheffield Utd, **8** Celtic, **9** Blackburn Rovers, **10** Jeremy Goss, **11** Lothar Matthaus, **12** Middlesborough, **13** 33 years, **14** Clarke, **15** Everton.

QUIZ 252

Answers on page 387

1 Where was the 1975 European Cup Winners' Cup Final held?

2 Which keeper set a league appearance record for Preston North End?

3 Who is the Luton Town and Everton forward who went on to manage Northern Ireland?

4 In which year was the first League Cup Final played at Wembley?

5 What is Roy Keane's middle name?

6 Andy Jardine made a record 297 appearances, for which Scottish club between 1957-67?

7 Which soccer team does TV talk-show host Clive Anderson support?

8 Which player scored 37 League goals for Colchester Utd in 1961-62?

9 At which club was Gary Lineker playing when he retired from soccer?

10 Who was stripped of the Carlisle captaincy for playing cricket until the end of the county season?

11 John Burns became the first British player to be sent off on his debut. What club was he playing at the time?

12 Which manager guided Wycombe Wanderers to the Second Division in only their first season in top flight football?

13 Who were the opponents when Alan Shearer was first captain of England?

14 Which London club has a fanzine called *The Gooner*?

15 Who won the 1981 and 1982 FA Cup Finals, both after replays?

Answers to page 387

1 Scotland, **2** Scotland won 5-2, **3** Socrates, **4** West Germany, **5** Don Howe, **6** Billy Bingham, **7** Jock Stein, **8** Gordon Strachan, **9** Holland, **10** Cesar Menotti, **11** Cameroon and Algeria, **12** Madrid, **13** Czechoslovakia, France and Kuwait, **14** Brazil, New Zealand and Soviet Union, **15** Mal Donaghy.

QUIZ 253

Answers on page 388

1 Peter Davenport and Gary Pallister were in the same team at which club?

2 Which ex-Liverpool player has managed Wales?

3 Which team were beaten 2-0 by Tottenham Hotspur in the 1961 FA Cup Final?

4 Which Spanish side did Howard Kendall manage?

5 Who lost 4-0 to AC Milan in the 1994 European Cup Final?

6 Who took Swindon Town to successive promotions in 1986 and 1987?

7 Keith Edwards hit 35 goals in a season to take which club out of the old Fourth Division?

8 Which team does 1998 Snooker Champion John Higgins support?

9 Price and Sellars played in which promotion-winning team?

10 Who was top scorer in Norwich City's UEFA Cup games in 1993-94?

11 Which German captain won the UEFA Cup with Internazionale in 1991?

12 Which soccer team does Chris Rea support?

13 How many years did Stanley Mathews play League soccer in England?

14 Which Colin marked his Southampton debut in 1986 with a hat-trick?

15 Just 3,039 people turned up on Boxing Day 1993 to watch Wimbledon play against which club?

Answers to page 388

1 Tottenham Hotspur, **2** Marwood, **3** Parma, **4** 1906-07, **5** Brighton, **6** Division 1 (3rd 1913-14), **7** Tottenham Hotspur, **8** Alessandro Del Piero, **9** Manchester Utd, **10** 11, **11** Joe Mercer, **12** Tony Norman, **13** Harry Morris, **14** Manchester Utd, **15** Mark Hughes.

QUIZ 254

Answers on page 393

1 Martin Peters had a short stay as boss of which club in 1981?

2 At which club did Brazil and Muhren score in the same European game?

3 Which team recorded a song with Paper Lace?

4 Barlow, Barrett and Bunn played for which League Cup Finalists?

5 What was the added bonus for Stoke City when they won the 1972 League Cup?

6 Which Joe became manager of Bristol City in November 1994?

7 What colour are West Ham Utd's home shorts?

8 Blyth, Gilchrist and Steele played for which 1970's FA Cup Finalists?

9 Mike Newell and Gary McAllister were in the same team at which club?

10 Which Dinamo Bucharest player won the 1986-87 Golden Boot award?

11 Who was the first player to move for £20,000?

12 Who lost 1-0 to Ajax in the 1987 Cup-Winners' Cup Final?

13 Ian Nolan's move to Sheffield Wednesday in August 1994 set a club record for a transfer fee received at which club?

14 Simply Red's cover of *Daydream Believer* was for which manager?

15 What colour are Wolves' home shorts?

Answers to page 393

1 Cameroon, **2** Mark Wright, **3** Toto Schillachi, **4** Chris Waddle and Stuart Pearce, **5** Marseille, **6** Turin, **7** David O'Leary, **8** McCall and Johnston (1 each), **9** Yugoslavia, **10** David Platt, **11** Mick McCarthy, **12** 0-0, **13** Diego Maradona, **14** Gary Lineker, **15** Toto Schillachi.

LEEDS UTD 3

Answers on page 394

1 How long was Brian Clough manager of Leeds for?

2 Which Billy became boss of Leeds in 1985?

3 Who scored Chelsea's winner against Leeds in the replayed 1970 FA Cup Final?

4 Who lost to Leeds in the 1968 Fairs Cup Final?

5 Who was Sunderland's goalkeeper in their FA Cup Final against Leeds in 1973?

6 Leeds player Gordon Hodgson scored 5 goals in a match in October 1938. Who were the opponents?

7 Which team knocked Leeds out of the FA Cup in 1996-97?

8 How long was Jock Stein manager of Leeds for?

9 Who succeeded Don Revie as manager of Leeds in 1974?

10 Which international defender moved from Leeds to Manchester Utd on a free transfer?

11 From 1965 to 1974 what was the lowest position that Leeds finished in the First Division?

12 Who succeeded Jock Stein as manager of Leeds in 1978?

13 Which team lost 4-3 to Leeds in the 1992 FA Charity Shield?

14 Who knocked Leeds out of the 1995-96 UEFA Cup competition?

15 Who beat Leeds in the 1973 Cup Winners' Cup Final?

Answers to page 394

1 Juventus in 1996, **2** Lincoln City, **3** Blackpool v Bolton Wanderers, **4** Roberto Bagio, **5** Lee Sharpe, **6** Harold "Bunny" Bell, **7** Little, **8** PSV Eindhoven, **9** Crosby, **10** Paul Furlong, **11** 1920s, **12** Swansea City and Crewe Alexandra, **13** 10, **14** Hungary, **15** Stoke City.

WORLD CUP 1990 2

Answers on page 391

1 Who did England beat in the 1990 World Cup quarter-final?

2 In Italia '90 who scored England's winner against Egypt?

3 Who scored six goals for Italy in the 1990 World Cup Finals?

4 Which two England players missed penalties in Italia '90?

5 Which club was Chris Waddle at during Italia '90?

6 In which City was the 1990 England v West Germany World Cup semi-final held?

7 Who came on in extra time for the Republic of Ireland in the Italia '90 World Cup game against Romania?

8 Who were Scotland's joint top scorers in Italia '90?

9 Which country lost 4-3 on penalties to Argentina in the 1990 World Cup semi-final?

10 Which England mid-fielder scored the only goal in the World Cup quarter-final against Belgium in Bologna in 1990?

11 Which Republic of Ireland player committed most fouls in Italia '90?

12 What was the score after 90 minutes in the Final of the 1994 World Cup?

13 Who captained Argentina against West Germany in the 1990 World Cup Final?

14 Who took England's first penalty in the shoot-out with Germany?

15 Who scored Italy's winner against England in the third-place play off game?

Answers to page 391

1 Sheffield Utd, **2** Manchester Utd (They never scored together at Ipswich Town), **3** Nottingham Forest, **4** Oldham Athletic, **5** Qualification for Europe, **6** Jordan, **7** White, **8** Southampton, **9** Leicester City, **10** Rodion Camataru, **11** Tommy Lawton, **12** Lokomotive Leipzig, **13** Tranmere Rovers, **14** Peter Reid, **15** Black.

QUIZ 255

Answers on page 392

1 Before Borussia Dortmund in 1997, which was the last team to win the European Cup Final in their own country?

2 Which club was the first to be automatically demoted from the League?

3 Which game was the first match to be shown live on television?

4 Which player joined AC Milan for £10m from Juventus only to spend more time on the subs bench than in his opponent's penalty box?

5 Who moved from Torquay for £600,000 in May 1988 to set a club record for a transfer fee received?

6 Which Tranmere Rovers centre-half made a record 401 consecutive League appearances in the 1950s?

7 Which Alan became boss of York City in 1983?

8 Who knocked Leeds Utd out of the 1995-96 UEFA Cup competition?

9 Which Malcolm became boss of Sunderland in 1992?

10 Who moved from Watford to Chelsea in May 1994 to set a club record for a transfer fee received?

11 In what decade did West Brom first win the Championship?

12 Ian Callaghan played in 88 FA Cup games, mostly with Liverpool, but with which other two Clubs?

13 Joe Payne holds the Third Division (South) record of goals in a game. How many did he score?

14 Which was the first country to lose two World Cup Finals?

15 Freddie Steele is all-time top League scorer at which club?

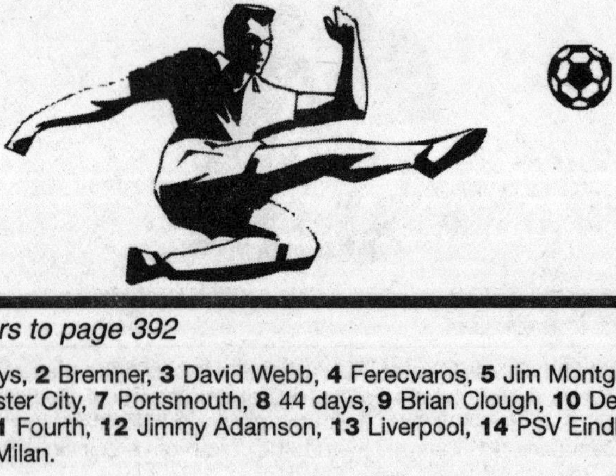

Answers to page 392

1 44 days, **2** Bremner, **3** David Webb, **4** Ferecvaros, **5** Jim Montgomery, **6** Liecester City, **7** Portsmouth, **8** 44 days, **9** Brian Clough, **10** Dennis Irwin, **11** Fourth, **12** Jimmy Adamson, **13** Liverpool, **14** PSV Eindhoven, **15** AC Milan.

QUIZ 256

Answers on page 397

1 How many times did Wolves win the FA Cup under the control of manager Stan Cullis?

2 Which striker was sent off on his on-loan return to Leeds Utd in 1996?

3 Who beat Dunfermline 3-0 in the 1950 Scottish League Cup Final?

4 Which AC Milan player was European Footballer of the Year in 1988 and 1989?

5 Jesper Olsen won an FA Cup winners' medal with which club?

6 Who beat Scotland 5-0 in April 1993, severely damaging their chances of qualifying for the 1994 World Cup?

7 Which two Polish teams play at home in the city of Poznan?

8 Which club replaced Southport in the League in 1978?

9 Who was Italy's captain when they won the World Cup in 1982?

10 Which team scored within 27 seconds against France in the 1982 World Cup?

11 Which Southampton boss sold Alan Shearer to Blackburn Rovers?

12 Which father and son strikers played a total of 16 games for England without managing to score a goal?

13 Which British club did Floretina beat in the only Cup Winners' Cup Final to have been played over two legs?

14 Which Real Madrid player was 1959 European Footballer of the Year?

15 Who saved Gary Lineker's penalty in an FA Cup Final?

Answers to page 397

1 Stirling Albion, **2** Coventry City, **3** Liverpool, **4** Rotherham Utd, **5** Everton, **6** Denis Law, **7** Pat Glover, **8** St Mirren, **9** Wolves, **10** Today, **11** Dennis Violett, **12** Steve Bull, **13** Jimmy Melia, **14** Tranmere Rovers, **15** Motherwell.

QUIZ 257

Answers on page 398

1. For which club did Roger Osborne score an FA Cup Final goal?
2. AC Milan won three consecutive Serie A titles in the 1990s. Which year did they win the first of these three?
3. Who was the first player to be sent off in a live TV League match?
4. Which soccer team does TV comedian Steve Coogan support?
5. In which city do Hibernian play?
6. Which soccer team does singer Elton John support?
7. Which players, with the same surname, scored in consecutive European Championship Finals?
8. Apart from Oxford, Derby County and Reading, which other club did Robert Maxwell try to buy in the 1987-88 season?
9. Which was Trevor Steven's first League club?
10. Which player scored 39 League goals for West Brom in 1935-36?
11. Who beat Dundee 3-0 in the 1981 Scottish League Cup Final?
12. In which city do Espanol play?
13. For which club has Eric Cantona made most appearances?
14. Which team won the FA Cup and then found their single at No.1?
15. Which soccer team does comedian Tim Brooke-Taylor support?

Answers to page 398

1 Harry Catterick, **2** Liverpool, **3** Rangers, **4** Tottenham Hotspur, **5** 349, **6** Bob Latchford, **7** Duncan Ferguson, **8** Harvey, **9** Maine Road, **10** Rangers, **11** Watford, **12** 4-4, **13** Bobby Mimms, **14** Duncan Ferguson, **15** Heath.

QUIZ 258

Answers on page 395

1 Matt McPhee made a record 504 appearances for which Scottish club between 1967-81?

2 Bobby Gould has twice been manager of which club?

3 Brondby knocked which English team out of the UEFA Cup in 1995?

4 At which club did Bobby Mimms make his League debut?

5 At which team did Ian Bishop make his League debut?

6 Which Scot played for Torino in 1961-62?

7 Which player scored 42 League goals for Grimsby Town in 1933-34?

8 Who beat Aberdeen 3-1 in the 1959 Scottish FA Cup Final?

9 In 1960 which club hit 100 goals for a third successive season?

10 Which national newspaper pulled out of a deal to sponsor the Football League?

11 Who set the most League goals in a season record at Manchester Utd with 32 in 1959-60?

12 Who was the first Third Division player in the 1980s to be capped by England?

13 Who was manager of Brighton for the 1983 FA Cup Final?

14 Which club used to play at Steeles Field and Ravenshaws Field?

15 Who beat Dundee 4-0 in the 1952 Scottish FA Cup Final?

Answers to page 395

1 Twice, **2** Lee Chapman, **3** East Fife, **4** Marco Van Basten, **5** Manchester Utd, **6** Portugal, **7** Lech and Warta, **8** Wigan Athletic, **9** Dino Zoff, **10** England, **11** Ian Branfoot, **12** Brian and Nigel Clough, **13** Rangers, **14** Alfredo Di Stefano, **15** Mark Crossley.

EVERTON 3

Answers on page 396

1 Which Everton manager captured the League Championship in 1963?

2 Which club finished second to Everton, nine points adrift, in the race for the 1986-87 title?

3 Which club did Duncan Ferguson leave to join Everton?

4 Which side inflicted a 10-4 thrashing on Everton in season 1958-59?

5 What was Dixie Dean's Everton League goals total?

6 Howard Kendall moved to Birmingham City as part of a deal that took which player to Everton in the 1970s?

7 Peter Johnson, the club Chairman, sold which player to Newcastle against the wishes of manager Walter Smith?

8 Which Colin became manager of Everton in 1987?

9 Where was the replayed League Cup Final between Liverpool and Everton held?

10 Which club did Paul Rideout leave to join Everton?

11 Which team were beaten 2-0 by Everton in the 1984 FA Cup Final?

12 Kenny Dalglish's last game in charge of Liverpool was a 5th round FA Cup game against Everton. What was the score?

13 Who was in goal for Everton in the 1986 FA Cup Final?

14 Which Everton striker spent time in jail in 1995?

15 Which Adrian moved to Espanol from Everton in the 1980s?

Answers to page 396

1 Ipswich Town, **2** 1992, **3** Paul Gascoigne, **4** Manchester Utd, **5** Edinburgh, **6** Watford, **7** Muller (Gerd in 1972, Dieter in 1976), **8** Watford, **9** Burnley, **10** 'W.G.' Richardson, **11** Dundee Utd, **12** Barcelona, **13** Manchester Utd, **14** Manchester Utd, **15** Derby County.

• WORLD CUP 1986 2 •

Answers on page 401

1 In Mexico 1986 who beat the USSR 4-3 after extra time?

2 Who was manager of England in the 1986 World Cup finals?

3 Uruguay's Jose Batista was sent off after just 45 seconds in a 1986 World Cup finals game against Scotland for a foul on which player?

4 Who was captain of Brazil for the 1982 and 1986 World Cups?

5 Who was manager of Northern Ireland in the 1986 World Cup finals?

6 Who did England face in the quarter-finals of the 1986 World Cup tournament?

7 What was the England squad's song for the 1986 World Cup?

8 Which manager collapsed and died thirty minutes after his country qualified for the 1986 World Cup finals?

9 Emilio Butragueno scored four goals as Spain beat which country 5-1 in the 1986 World Cup finals?

10 In which Stadium was the 1986 World Cup Final played?

11 Who was Scotland's caretaker manager during the World Cup finals in 1986?

12 How many hat-tricks were scored in the 1986 World Cup finals?

13 Which injury forced Bryan Robson out of the 1986 World Cup?

14 Which other countries were in England's group for the 1986 World Cup finals?

15 Who did Belgium face in the semi-final of the 1986 World Cup?

Answers to page 401

1 Sheffield Utd, **2** Aston Villa, **3** Martyn, **4** Athens, **5** Dumbarton, **6** Blackburn Rovers, **7** Wycombe Wanderers, **8** Porterfield, **9** Grimsby Town, **10** Falkirk, **11** Pele, **12** Liverpool, **13** Southampton, **14** Reading, **15** Chelsea.

QUIZ 259

Answers on page 402

1 Who was Manchester Utd's first ever £200,000 signing when he moved from Nottingham Forest?

2 Which team won ten successive League titles in East Germany?

3 Who were the opponents of Cesare Maldini's first match as coach?

4 Apart from Athens and Thessaloniki, which is the only other city in Greece to have been home to winners of the Greek League?

5 How many Carling Premiership club players were in France's 1998 World Cup winning side?

6 Who were the first nation to win a World Cup shoot out?

7 Which club had a fanzine called *A Load of Cobbolds*?

8 Which Brazilian scored the only goal of the 1997 European Final for Barcelona against Paris St Germain?

9 At which club did Geoff Thomas make his League debut?

10 In which year did Scotland pull out of the Rous Cup?

11 Who beat Rangers 1-0 in the 1980 Scottish FA Cup Final?

12 Which England international player won eight championship medals in three different countries?

13 Ian Porterfield followed Bobby Campbell as manager of which club?

14 John Greig made a record 496 appearances for which Scottish club between 1962-78?

15 Who scored a hat-trick as Liverpool beat Southampton 7-1 in January 1999?

Answers to page 402

1 Scunthorpe, **2** Kevin Keegan, **3** Little, **4** Nine (three two-legged rounds, a semi-final at home and away and a one off Final), **5** Chelsea, **6** Les Ferdinand, **7** Bradford City, **8** 6, **9** Blackpool, **10** Milkman, **11** 18, **12** Six, **13** 2, **14** Michael Owen, **15** Hearts.

QUIZ 260

Answers on page 399

1 Which club has a fanzine called *The Flashing Blade*?

2 Punk violinist Nigel Kennedy supports which English team?

3 Who started the game in goal for England when they beat Cameroon in a friendly in November 1997?

4 Where was the 1983 European Cup Final held?

5 Which team plays at Boghead Park?

6 Howard Kendall took which team out of the Third Division?

7 Which club used to play at Loakes Park?

8 Which Ian became boss of Sheffield Utd in 1981?

9 At which club did Mick Lyons finish his playing career?

10 Which team were relegated from the Scottish Premier League in 1993 and again in 1996?

11 Who is Edson Arantes do Nascimento?

12 Craig Johnston scored an FA Cup Final goal for which club?

13 At which club did Andy Townshend make his League debut?

14 Roger Smee was a former centre-forward then chairman of which club, where he helped repel Robert Maxwell?

15 Danny Blanchflower followed Ken Shellito as manager of which club?

Answers to page 399

1 Belgium, **2** Bobby Robson, **3** Gordon Strachan, **4** Socrates, **5** Billy Bingham, **6** Argentina, **7** *We've Got The Whole World At Our Feet,* **8** Jock Stein (Scotland), **9** Denmark, **10** The Azteca in Mexico City, **11** Alex Ferguson, **12** 4, **13** Dislocated shoulder, **14** Morocco, Poland and Portugal, **15** Argentina.

QUIZ 261

Answers on page 400

1 Which was Ray Clemence's first League club?

2 Which England international played against Nottingham Forest in the 1980 European Cup Final?

3 Which Brian became Leicester City manager in 1991?

4 Before the adoption of the league system, what was the lowest number of matches required to win the European Cup?

5 Who won the 1997 FA Cup?

6 Who moved from QPR for £6 million in June 1995 to set a club record for a transfer fee received?

7 What was Phil Babb's first League club?

8 How many international goals did Chris Waddle score?

9 Which team were beaten 4-2 by Manchester Utd in the 1948 FA Cup Final?

10 What did Pat Jennings do before he become a footballer?

11 How old was Ray Wilkins when he was made captain at Chelsea?

12 How many goals did Stan Collymore score in his first season at Aston Villa?

13 How many international goals did Viv Anderson score?

14 Who scored a first half hat-trick for Liverpool against Newcastle Utd in 1998-99?

15 Baird and Levein scored Euro goals in the same 1990s game for which Scottish Club?

Answers to page 400

1 Ian Storey Moore, **2** Dynamo Berlin, **3** Northern Ireland, **4** Larissa, **5** Five, **6** West Germany, **7** Ipswich Town, **8** Ronaldo, **9** Rochdale, **10** 1990, **11** Celtic, **12** Trevor Steven, **13** Chelsea, **14** Rangers, **15** Robbie Fowler.

QUIZ 262

Answers on page 405

1 In which decade did West Brom first win the FA Cup?

2 West Brom recorded a 6-1 League Cup win over which club in September 1966?

3 Who previously held the record of most League goals for Arsenal before Ian Wright?

4 Which Scottish side did Paul Hegarty play for in a UEFA Cup Final?

5 Which team was Beaten 3-1 by Liverpool in the 1986 FA Cup Final?

6 In 1984 Dave Bassett left Wimbledon, but returned after only a few days spent at which club?

7 Which Welsh striker moved from West Ham Utd to Wimbledon for over £6m in January 1999?

8 Who were the first club to gain promotion and win the First Division in consecutive seasons?

9 Who was boss when Norwich City were 1986 Second Division Champions?

10 How many years of hurt were there in *Three Lions*?

11 From which club did John Aldridge join Tranmere Rovers?

12 Whose home is Spotland?

13 Which brothers Graham and Ron were at Oxford Utd in the 1960s?

14 Des Walker moved from Nottingham Forest to which club for £1.5m in May 1992?

15 Who won the penalty shoot-out to win the 1994 World Cup Final?

Answers to page 405

1 Rose Bowl, **2** Greece, **3** Roberto Baggio, **4** Andy Townsend, **5** Holland, **6** Roberto Baggio, **7** Bonner and Coyne, **8** Hristo Stoichkov, **9** Romario, **10** Brazil, **11** Italy, **12** Russia, **13** Brazil 3-2, **14** Italy, **15** Sweden.

DERBY 2

Answers on page 406

1 Which American has played in England for Derby, Sheffield Wednesday and West Ham Utd?

2 Which international footballer played 125 times for his country, 34 of them whilst he played for Derby?

3 What was the name of Derby's old ground?

4 Who succeeded Colin Addison as manager of Derby in 1981?

5 Who was the regular keeper for Derby in their 1990-91 relegation season?

6 Who succeeded Tim Ward as manager of Derby in 1967?

7 Who scored five goals in Derby's 12-0 UEFA Cup 1st round, 1st leg win over Finn Harps?

8 What is the name of Derby's new stadium?

9 Which fullback moved from Leicester City to Derby in 1972?

10 Who created a record for Derby by playing 486 League Games?

11 Which chairman sold his stake in Derby County for £5.6m to a consortium led by Brian Fearn?

12 Mark Lawrenson was fired as Oxford manager for complaining about the sale of which player to Derby?

13 Which club did Russell Hoult leave to join Derby?

14 Who was the Derby Chairman when Brian Clough resigned?

15 Who joined Liverpool from Derby for £2.9m in July 1991?

Answers to page 406

1 Falkirk, **2** Hyde Utd, **3** At least 5 feet, **4** Shrewsbury, **5** QPR, **6** Juventus (Lost on away goals rule), **7** Marco Gabbiadini, **8** Torquay Town, **9** Port Vale, **10** 1960s, **11** West Germany, **12** Waddle, **13** Jose Luis Chilavert, **14** 1950s, **15** 1970.

WORLD CUP 1994 2

Answers on page 403

1 In which stadium was the 1994 World Cup Final held?

2 Which country failed to score in the USA 1994?

3 Who missed the final penalty for Italy in the 1994 World Cup Final?

4 Who said on revealing his new haircut in 1994 at the World Cup finals, "I asked for a Valderrama and they gave me a Val Doonican"?

5 Who knocked the Republic of Ireland out of the second round of the 1994 World Cup?

6 Who was Italy's top scorer in the 1994 World Cup finals?

7 20 of the Republic of Ireland's 22-man USA 94 squad played in the English League, which two didn't?

8 Who scored six goals for Bulgaria in the 1994 World Cup finals?

9 Who was the Brazilian top scorer in the 1994 World Cup tournament?

10 Which team knocked Holland out of the 1994 World Cup?

11 An extra time goal by which country sent Nigeria out of the 1994 World Cup?

12 In USA '94 which country scored most goals in the group games yet still went out?

13 Who won the penalty shoot-out to win the 1994 World Cup Final?

14 Which country took the first penalty in the 1994 Final shoot out?

15 Jonas Thern was playing for which country when he got sent off in a 1994 World Cup semi-final?

Answers to page 403

1 1880s, **2** Aston Villa, **3** Cliff Bastin, **4** Dundee Utd, **5** Everton, **6** Crystal Palace, **7** John Hartson, **8** Liverpool, **9** Ken Brown, **10** 30, **11** Real Sociedad, **12** Rochdale, **13** Atkinson, **14** Sampdoria, **15** Brazil 3-2.

QUIZ 263

Answers on page 404

1 In the first £5,000 transfer Syd Puddefoot moved to which Scottish club?

2 Which team conceded 26 goals against Preston North End in an FA Cup game?

3 What should be the minimum height of corner flags?

4 Wolverhampton Wanderers recorded a 6-1 League Cup win over which club in September 1991?

5 In 1996-97, Port Vale were 4-0 up at home yet had to settle for a 4-4 draw against which London team?

6 In 1970-71 which team played 12 UEFA Cup games without defeat yet still failed to win the trophy?

7 Who moved from Sunderland to Crystal Palace for £1.5m in 1991?

8 What were Torquay known as before they took on the name United?

9 Sir Stanley Mathews was manager of which English club?

10 In which decade did West Ham Utd first win the FA Cup?

11 Who was Weber playing for when he hit a World Cup Final equaliser?

12 Which international Chris once worked as a sausage seasoning maker?

13 Which eccentric goalkeeper, who plays for Paraguay, regularly takes penalties?

14 In which decade did Wolves first win the Championship?

15 In what year was the World Cup first transmitted in colour to the UK?

Answers to page 404

1 John Harkes, **2** Peter Shilton, **3** Baseball Ground, **4** John Newman, **5** Peter Shilton, **6** Brian Clough, **7** Kevin Hector, **8** Pride Park, **9** David Nish, **10** Kevin Hector, **11** Robert Maxwell, **12** Dean Saunders, **13** Leicester City, **14** Sam Longston, **15** Dean Saunders.

QUIZ 264

Answers on page 409

1 Which English side knocked out Manchester City in the 1971 Cup Winners's Cup competition?

2 In which decade did Sheffield Wednesday first win the FA Cup?

3 Which player was involved the only time that the British transfer ceiling has been doubled in one move?

4 Walker and Waddle were in the same side at which club?

5 Petrescu and Pembridge were in the same side at which club?

6 Which British football stadium is situated just 50 yards from the North Sea?

7 Which Utd were Third Division Champions in 1984 and Second Division Champions the following season?

8 Tommy Docherty's first signing was which Scottish fullback?

9 Who was manager of the English side that won the UEFA Cup in 1970?

10 Which Arsenal player held the club's scoring record before Ian Wright?

11 Who lost to Napoli in the 1989 UEFA Cup Final?

12 Walter Winterbottom led England into how many World Cups?

13 Who beat Juventus 1-0 in the 1983 European Cup Final?

14 Marshall and Claridge were in the same side at which club?

15 Which production team handled the charity version of *Ferry Across The Mersey*?

Answers to page 409

1 Billy Ferguson, **2** Charlton Athletic, **3** Colchester Utd, **4** Ruud Gullit, **5** Alan Shearer, **6** Simon Garner, **7** Barcelona, **8** Fulham, **9** Norwich City, **10** Billy Wright and Stan Cullis, **11** Gianluca Vialli, **12** Espanol, **13** *Back Home*, **14** Arbroath, **15** Scottish League Cup.

QUIZ 265

Answers on page 410

1 Which country beat Zaire 9-0 in the 1974 World Cup finals to equal the then record?

2 Which player opened the scoring for Spurs in the 1961 FA Cup Final?

3 Which team with a ground in England knocked Rangers out of the 1967 Scottish FA Cup?

4 Steve MacKenzie first played in an FA Cup Final for which team?

5 Which soccer team does comedian Jasper Carrott support?

6 Where was the 1962 European Cup Winners' Cup Final replay held?

7 Which Wales manager was sacked in 1987-88 after eight years in charge?

8 Which team did Lee Sharpe support as a boy?

9 What is Reggie Blinker's middle name?

10 Mike Gatting's brother Steve played in an FA Cup Final for which team?

11 Willems and Van Der Laan were in the same side at which club?

12 What was the highest position that West Brom reached in 1985-86?

13 Byrne, Lawler and Strong played for which 1960s FA Cup Finalists?

14 In which decade did Wales first beat England at Wembley?

15 Phil Dwyer set a League appearance record for which club?

Answers to page 410

1 Denis Bergkamp, **2** Jonathan Gould (Celtic), **3** Saint-Etienne, **4** Brazil won 4-2, **5** Didier Deschamps, **6** Laurent Blanc (For France against Paraguay in 1998), **7** Shearer and Owen (Penalty), **8** Bugaria, **9** Diego Simeone, **10** Lilian Thurman, **11** Slaven Bilic, **12** Cesar Sampaio, **13** Edmundo, **14** Marcel Desailly, **15** Spain.

QUIZ 266

Answers on page 407

1 Which Northern Ireland player became the first to receive a red card in a British Home International match?

2 Hales, Flannigan and Peacock have all scored goals for which club?

3 Micky Cook set a League appearance record at which club?

4 Who did Gianluca Vialli replace as manager of Chelsea?

5 Who is the youngest scorer of a hat-trick in top flight English soccer?

6 Which veteran striker was at Blackburn, West Brom and Wycombe in successive promotion seasons?

7 As a player which club did Johan Cruyff move to when he left Ajax?

8 Which soccer team did comedian Tommy Trinder support?

9 Andy Linighan and Mike Phelan were in the same team at which club?

10 Wolverhampton was the starting place for which two former England skippers?

11 Who was the manager of Chelsea when they won the Coca-Cola Cup in 1998?

12 Who lost on penalties to Bayer Leverkusen in the 1988 UEFA Cup Final?

13 Which football song was No.1 for three weeks in May 1970?

14 Which team holds the British record for a League Victory?

15 When Rangers won the Scottish Southern Cup in 1946 it was the forerunner of which tournament?

Answers to page 407

1 Chelsea, **2** 1890s, **3** Trevor Francis, **4** Sheffield Wednesday, **5** Sheffield Wednesday, **6** Gayfield Park (Arbroath), **7** Oxford, **8** Alex Forsyth, **9** Bertie Mee, **10** Cliff Bastin, **11** Stuttgart, **12** Four, **13** Hamburg, **14** Leicester City, **15** Stock, Aitken and Waterman.

• WORLD CUP 1998 3 •

Answers on page 408

1 Argentina went out of the 1998 World Cup quarter-finals 2-1 to Holland. Which Dutch player scored in the last minute of normal time?

2 Who was the goalkeeper called up at short notice by Scotland when Andy Goram made his shock withdrawal from the 1998 World Cup?

3 In which city were both England and Scotland knocked out of the 1998 World Cup finals?

4 What was the outcome of the penalty shoot-out in the Brazil v Holland 1998 World Cup semi-final?

5 Who deputised as captain in the 1998 World Cup Final for the suspended Laurent Blanc?

6 Who scored the first ever Golden Goal in the World Cup finals?

7 Who scored Englands two goals against Argentina in the 1998 World Cup finals?

8 Which country did Spain beat 6-1 in the 1998 World Cup finals?

9 Which Argentinian player did David Beckham kick which resulted in his red card in the World Cup finals 1998?

10 Which French player scored two goals against Croatia in the 1998 World Cup semi-final?

11 Who claimed that he had been struck by Laurent Blanc when the French captain was sent off in the semi-finals of the 1998 World Cup?

12 Who scored the first goal of the 1998 World Cup finals?

13 Which Brazilian player made way for Ronaldo in the 1998 World Cup Final?

14 Which French player received two yellow cards and was sent off in the 1998 World Cup Final?

15 Which was the only seeded country not to qualify for the second round of the 1998 World Cup finals?

Answers to page 408

1 Yugoslavia, **2** Bobby Smith, **3** Berwick Rangers, **4** Manchester City, **5** Birmingham City, **6** Stuttgart, **7** Mike England, **8** Aston Villa, **9** Waldie, **10** Brighton, **11** Derby County, **12** Bottom (22nd), **13** Liverpool, **14** 1970s, **15** Cardiff City.

CHELSEA 3

Answers on page 413

1 In what decade did Chelsea first win the Championship?

2 Ray Wilkins moved from Chelsea to which club in August 1979?

3 Which David was boss of Chelsea in 1993?

4 Which government minister handed the 1997-98 Coca-Cola Cup to Chelsea's player/manager Gianluca Vialli?

5 Which opposing team's manager was involved in a touchline brawl in January 1999 and ordered from the bench by the referee?

6 Which player made 655 League appearances for Chelsea between 1962-80?

7 Which team did Chelsea beat in the last game of the 1997-98 season, resulting in their relegation?

8 Who hit whom during the 1997-98 season Premiership match between Chelsea and West Ham Utd ?

9 In which decade did Chelsea first win the FA Cup?

10 What was the score in the second leg of Chelsea's Cup Winners' Cup second round tie with Tromso?

11 Which brothers Graham and Ray played at Chelsea in the 1970s?

12 Who beat Chelsea 4-0 in the 1994 FA Cup Final?

13 Who came off the substitutes bench to score Chelsea's winner in the 1998 European Cup Winners Cup Final?

14 Who did Gianluca Vialli replace as manager of Chelsea?

15 Who moved from Watford to Chelsea in May 1994 ?

Answers to page 413

1 Dean, **2** 1972, **3** 105, **4** Hearts, **5** Argentina, **6** West Ham Utd and Ipswich Town, **7** Uruguay, **8** Newcastle Utd, **9** Peter Schmeichel, **10** Sheffield Wednesday, **11** Ron Yeats, **12** Billy Wright, **13** Tottenham Hotspur, **14** Eamon Dunphy, **15** 7.

QUIZ 267

Answers on page 414

1 Kidd and Powell scored Euro goals in the same game for which club?

2 Rick Holden played a League Cup Final for which club?

3 Which former Arsenal player was sent off in a Sweden against Romania World Cup quarter-final?

4 At which club was Paul Warhurst sent off in a European Cup game?

5 Who dropped out of the Scottish League in 1967?

6 Which Nigerian became Leyton Orient's most capped player?

7 Liam Brady's elder brothers Ray and Pat were together at which club?

8 In what year did Tottenham Hotspur first win the FA Cup?

9 Who were Scotland's joint top scorers in Italia '90?

10 Who did Terry Venable's make his England skipper for his first game in charge?

11 Which future Leeds Utd manager was kept out of the 1949 Cup Final by a nose bleed?

12 Danny Bergara followed Asa Hartford as manager of which club?

13 Manager George Allison followed which legend in 1934?

14 Who beat Burnley 1-0 in the 1947 FA Cup Final?

15 Jimmy Mullen followed Frank Casper as manager of which club?

Answers to page 414

1 Stimac, **2** Harford, **3** Terry Harkin, **4** Paul Warhurst, **5** Bertie Mee, **6** Wilf McGuinness, **7** Norway, **8** Oxford Utd, **9** Don Revie, **10** Real Sociedad, **11** Notts County, **12** Ray Wilkins, **13** Frank Newton, **14** 62, **15** Sweden.

QUIZ 268

Answers on page 411

1 What is Mr Windass' first name?

2 In which year did the song *Leeds United* hit the charts?

3 How many times did Wolve's Billy Wright play for England?

4 Who won their first trophy in 50 years when they beat Celtic 3-1 to claim the 1950 Scottish FA Cup?

5 Which team knocked Italy out of Italia '90?

6 In the 1990s John Lyall was at which two clubs in relegation seasons?

7 Which country do the club Penarol come from?

8 Which English team knocked Southampton out of the 1970 UEFA Cup competition?

9 Which keeper was sent off in the quarter-finals of the 1994 FA Cup Final?

10 Which soccer team does MP Roy Hattersley support?

11 Which Liverpool skipper said of compatriot Bill Shankly, "His motivation could move mountains"?

12 Which ex-England skipper died in September 1994?

13 Alan Sugar owns which football club?

14 Which Republic of Ireland international of the 1960s wrote the book *Only A Game* in the 1970s?

15 What was Bryan Robson's shirt number for most of his Manchester Utd career?

Answers to page 411

1 1950s, **2** Manchester Utd, **3** Webb, **4** Home secretary Jack Straw, **5** Gordon Strachan (Coventry City), **6** Ron Harris, **7** Bolton Wanderers, **8** Eyal Berkovic hit John Moncur (both West Ham Utd players), **9** 1970s, **10** Chelsea 7 Tromso 1, **11** Wilkins, **12** Manchester Utd, **13** Gianfranco Zola, **14** Ruud Gullit, **15** Paul Furlong.

QUIZ 269

Answers on page 412

1 Which Igor was the only Croatian to see red in Euro '96?

2 Which Ray became boss of Wimbledon in 1990?

3 Which player scored 35 League goals for Crewe Alexandra in 1964-65?

4 Who moved from Sheffield Wednesday to Blackburn Rovers in 1993 to set a club record fee for a transfer received?

5 Who was the manager of the English club that won the UEFA Cup in 1970?

6 Who followed Sir Matt Busby as manger of Manchester Utd?

7 Which country does Justein Flo come from?

8 Which club started out playing at Headington Quarry?

9 Which manager led Leeds Utd to their first ever League Championship?

10 Which Spanish team did John Aldridge and Kevin Richardson play for?

11 Which club did Dean Yates leave to join Derby County?

12 Who became the first England player to be sent off during the World Cup finals?

13 Which player scored 43 League goals for Fulham in 1931-32?

14 How old was Joe Fagan when he became manager of Liverpool?

15 Jonas Thern was playing for which country when he got sent off in a 1994 World Cup semi-final?

Answers to page 412

1 Manchester City, **2** Oldham Athletic, **3** Stefan Schwartz, **4** Blackburn Rovers, **5** Third Lanark, **6** John Chiedozie, **7** Millwall, **8** 1901, **9** McCall and Johnston (1 each), **10** David Platt, **11** Don Revie, **12** Stockport, **13** Herbert Chapman (Arsenal), **14** Charlton Athletic, **15** Burnley.

QUIZ 270

Answers on page 417

1 Who moved from Charlton in 1996 to become Britain's most expensive teenager?

2 Which country did Red Boys represent in the UEFA Cup competition?

3 Which team knocked Holland out of the 1994 World Cup?

4 Who said "I don't care if he's black or white or yellow with purple spots, if he can do a job for West Bromwich Albion he's in the team."?

5 Which Manchester City boss bought his own son Kevin?

6 Who lost to Parma in the 1995 UEFA Cup Final?

7 Which French player was victim of Schmeichel's appalling challenge in 1984?

8 Who beat Juventus 3-1 in the 1997 European Cup Final?

9 Which player scored 39 League goals for Hull City in 1932-33?

10 Who became manager of Northern Ireland in 1994?

11 Danny Blanchflower followed Ken Shellito as manager of which club?

12 Tommy Docherty was manager of which club for just 29 days in 1968?

13 Rangers signed which player from Atlanta in the late 1980s?

14 To which English team did Ujpest Dozsu lose to in a UEFA Cup Final?

15 John Ward was boss of which club from 1991-1993?

Answers to page 417

1 None, **2** Huddersfield Town, **3** Aberdeen, **4** Huddersfield Town, **5** 171, **6** Torino, **7** Manchester City, **8** Wales, **9** 2, **10** Manchester Utd, **11** Zaire, **12** 41, **13** 1964, **14** 30, **15** 1940.

COVENTRY CITY 2

Answers on page 418

1 Kevin Gallacher moved from Coventry City to which club for £1.5m in March 1993?

2 Coventry City paid £1.75m for which Aberdeen player in 1996?

3 Liverpool paid £3.75m to Coventry in September 1994 for which defender?

4 Which non-league side hit a last minute goal to draw at Coventry in 1997?

5 Who signed Stuart Pearce at Coventry City?

6 Who succeeded Joe Mercer as manager of Coventry City in 1981?

7 Gary Collier moved from Coventry City to which club in March 1980?

8 Which Terry became manager of Coventry City in 1990?

9 Which Leeds Utd midfielder hit a 1995 hat-trick against Coventry City?

10 Who did Gordon Strachan succeed as manager of Coventry City?

11 Coventry City player Cyril Regis scored 5 goals in a match in October 1985. Who were the opponents?

12 Who formed a management partnership with Joe Mercer at Coventry in the 1970s?

13 Who succeeded Phil Neal as manager of Coventry City in 1995?

14 Coventry City recorded a 7-2 League Cup win over which club in October 1985?

15 What was Gary Mabbutt's scoring record in the 1987 Spurs v Coventry Cup Final?

Answers to page 418

1 Internazionale, **2** Ian Taylor, **3** Stamford Bridge, **4** Stoke City, **5** Alan Shearer, **6** Twenty-two, **7** 11, **8** 1945, **9** Paul Cooper, **10** Gerd Muller, **11** Juventus, **12** 1958, **13** Luton Town, **14** Blue and White, **15** Bleach their hair (The goalkeeper was bald).

DENIS LAW

Answers on page 415

1 How many Scottish League clubs did Denis Law play for?

2 With which League team did Denis Law make his debut?

3 In which city was Denis Law born?

4 Which club did Denis Law make his League debut with?

5 How many goals did Denis Law score for Manchester Utd in his 309 League games?

6 Which Italian side did Denis Law sign for in 1961?

7 Which club did Denis Law finish his career with?

8 Against which country did Denis Law make his international debut?

9 How many League Championships did Denis Law win with Manchester Utd?

10 Against which side did Denis Law score his last League goal?

11 Against which country did Denis Law make his last appearance for Scotland?

12 How many FA Cup goals did Denis Law score in setting his record?

13 In which year was Denis Law voted European Footballer of the Year?

14 How many international goals did Denis Law score?

15 In which year was Denis Law born?

Answers to page 415

1 Lee Bowyer, **2** Luxembourg, **3** Brazil, **4** Ron Atkinson, **5** John Bond, **6** Juventus, **7** Patrick Battiston, **8** Borussia Dortmund, **9** Billy McNaughton, **10** Bryan Hamilton, **11** Chelsea, **12** QPR, **13** Trevor Francis, **14** Newcastle Utd, **15** York City.

QUIZ 271

Answers on page 416

1 Which team won the 1994 UEFA Cup?

2 Who moved from Port Vale to Sheffield Wednesday for £1m in 1994 to set a club record for a transfer fee received?

3 Which ground shares its name with a battle in England against the Norman invaders?

4 At which club did Garth Crooks make his League debut?

5 Which former Blackburn player became the first player to score 30 or more league goals in three consecutive seasons in the top division since the 1930's?

6 How many teams started in the first FA Premier League season?

7 How many goals did Stanley Mathews score for England?

8 In what year did Sir Matt Busby become Manchester Utd's manager?

9 Who saved 8 out of 10 penalties he faced in the 1979-80 season?

10 Whose last international goal was a World Cup Final winner?

11 Who beat Borussia Dortmund in the 1993 UEFA Cup Final?

12 When did Wales last qualify for the World Cup?

13 Kamara and Dreyer played in which team leaving the top flight?

14 What colour are FC Porto's shirts?

15 What did every Romanian player, except their goalkeeper, do before their final group match in France '98?

Answers to page 416

1 Blackburn Rovers, **2** Eoin Jess, **3** Phil Babb, **4** Woking, **5** Bobby Gould, **6** G Milne, **7** Portland Timbers, **8** Butcher, **9** Gary McAllister, **10** Ron Atkinson, **11** Chester City, **12** Gordon Milne, **13** Ron Atkinson, **14** Chester City, **15** He scored two goals - one for each team.

QUIZ 272

Answers on page 421

1 Which English team did Roy Keane support as a boy?

2 Perry Groves and Brian Marwood were in the same team at which club?

3 Which club did Gary Sprake join when he left Leeds Utd?

4 How long was Fred Everiss manager of West Brom for?

5 Which player scored 34 League goals for Bradford City in 1961-62?

6 George Best played for which Scottish Club?

7 Who is the multi-millionaire owner of Blackburn Rovers?

8 Which club did Pat Rice join on leaving Arsenal?

9 Who moved from Leyton Orient to Notts County for £600,000 in 1981 to set a club record for a transfer fee received?

10 What is the highest position Leeds Utd have ever achieved in the League?

11 Who is Scotland's youngest player to win a full international cap?

12 Name any of the three teams from the former East Germany that have appeared in Cup Winners' Cup Finals?

13 In what year did Chelsea hit the charts with *Blue Is The Colour*?

14 In which decade did Huddersfield Town first win the Championship?

15 Who beat Steaua Bucharest 4-0 in the 1989 European Cup Final?

Answers to page 421

1 Liverpool, **2** Hungary, **3** Doug Rougvie, **4** Republic of Ireland, **5** George Best, **6** West Brom, **7** The trophy was shared for six months each, **8** Manchester Utd, **9** Walsall, **10** Livingston, **11** Tottenham Hotspur, **12** Two, **13** Graham Moseley, **14** George Best, **15** White.

QUIZ 273

Answers on page 422

1 Which German city is home to FC Schalke '04?

2 Alan Smith and Kevin Campbell were in the same side at which club?

3 Grimsby Town recorded a 10-0 FA Cup win over which club in October 1981?

4 Which team were beaten 2-1 by Arsenal in the 1971 FA Cup Final?

5 In which country were the 1982 World Cup finals held?

6 In 1985-86 David Crown set a record for most League goals in a season at which club?

7 Who scored 10 goals in a game for Germany against Russia in July 1912?

8 Shaun Cunnington moved from Grimsby Town to which club for £650,000 in July 1992?

9 Which country did Mark Lawrenson play for?

10 Who was boss when Chelsea were Division 2 Champions in 1988-89?

11 What year did Tottenham Hotspur first win the FA Cup?

12 With 195 goals scored in the 1960s and 1970s Chris Chilton became all-time top League scorer at which club?

13 Who was Joe Harper playing for when he hit a Scottish League Cup hat-trick and still ended up a loser?

14 Which team were beaten 1-0 by West Brom in the 1968 FA Cup Final?

15 An injury to which knee ended Steve Coppell's career?

Answers to page 422

1 Ray Harford, **2** 1910's, **3** Bill Fox, **4** Gary Croft, **5** Liverpool, **6** Simon Garner, **7** 1950s, **8** Bristol Rovers, **9** Graham Le Saux, **10** Manchester City, **11** Southampton, **12** 1994-95 Premiership Champions, **13** Chris Sutton, **14** Grimsby Town, **15** Manchester Utd.

QUIZ 274

Answers on page 419

1 Mike Hooper and John Barnes were in the same team at which club?

2 Which country did Ujpest Dozsa represent in the UEFA Cup competition?

3 Which Aberdeen player was sent off in the 1978-79 Scottish League Cup Final?

4 Which country did John Aldridge play for?

5 Who scored within 71 seconds of his Fulham debut in 1977?

6 Talbot and Ford were in the same team at which club?

7 Until 1974, what happened to the Charity Shield when the matches were drawn?

8 Which soccer team does The Smith's Morrissey support?

9 Phil Parkes made his League debut at which club?

10 Which Scottish side plays at home at the Almondvale stadium?

11 Steve Perryman set a League appearance record at which club?

12 How many international goals did Danny Blanchflower score?

13 Who was in goal for Brighton in the 1983 FA Cup Final?

14 Which Manchester Utd player was European Footballer of the Year in 1968?

15 What is the main colour of Tranmere Rovers' home shirts?

Answers to page 419

1 Tottenham Hotspur, **2** Arsenal, **3** Birmingham City, **4** 46 years, **5** David Layne, **6** Hibernian, **7** Jack Walker, **8** Watford, **9** John Chiedozie, **10** Division 1 champions (3 times 1968-69,1973-74,1991-92), **11** John Lambie, **12** Carl-Zeis Jena, Locomotiv Leipzig and FC Magdeburg, **13** 1972, **14** 1920s, **15** AC Milan.

BLACKBURN 3

Answers on page 420

1 Who succeeded Kenny Dalglish as manager of Blackburn in 1995?

2 In which decade did Blackburn first win the Championship?

3 Who was chairman when Kenny Dalglish went to Blackburn?

4 Who moved from Grimsby Town to Blackburn for £1m to set a club record for a transfer fee received?

5 Who were the opponents on the day that Blackburn won the Premiership?

6 Who has scored most goals in a career for Blackburn?

7 In which decade did Blackburn first win the FA Cup?

8 Blackburn player Tommy Briggs scored 7 goals in a match in February 1953. Who were the opponents?

9 Which Blackburn and England defender suffered a long-term injury against Middlesborough in December 1995?

10 Colin Hendry moved from Blackburn to which club for £700,000 in November 1989?

11 Tim Flowers became Britain's costliest goalkeeper when he moved to Blackburn for £2m. Which club did he leave?

12 What is the highest position Blackburn have ever achieved in the League?

13 In 1994 which player was transferred to Blackburn for £5.5m?

14 Which club did Gary Croft leave to join Blackburn?

15 David May moved from Blackburn to which club for £1.25m in May 1994?

Answers to page 420

1 Gelsenkirchen, **2** Arsenal, **3** Boston, **4** Liverpool, **5** Spain, **6** Cambridge Utd, **7** Gottfried Fuchs, **8** Sunderland, **9** The Republic of Ireland, **10** Bobby Campbell, **11** 1901, **12** Hull City, **13** Hibernian, **14** Everton, **15** Left.

EURO '96 2

Answers on page 425

1 Who scored Scotland's only goal of Euro '96?

2 Alan Shearer hit the quickest goal of a game in Euro '96 against which side?

3 Which Dutch player scored against England in Euro '96?

4 Who took the final spot kick in the England V Germany Euro '96 game?

5 Who knocked England out of Euro '96?

6 Which Englishman scored against his own club keeper in Euro '96?

7 Name the French keeper who earned 'man of the match' in their quarter-final victory over Holland during Euro '96?

8 Which group were the Germans in at the start of Euro '96?

9 Davor Suker beat which Danish keeper in Euro '96?

10 Who was in charge of the German Euro '96 team?

11 What was historic about Oliver Bierhoff's Euro '96 goal in which Germany beat the Czech Republic?

12 In Euro '96, whose penalty for France was saved in the semi-final shoot-out against the Czech Republic?

13 Which country did Zvonimir Boban play for in Euro '96?

14 Which outfield player saved on the line with his hands in the Scotland v Holland group match in Euro '96?

15 Which German player had an extra-time 'goal' disallowed against England in Euro '96?

Answers to page 425

1 Won all their League games, **2** Coventry City, **3** Hugh McIlmoyle, **4** Arsenal, **5** Manchester Utd, **6** Aston Villa, **7** Swindon Town, **8** 1990, **9** Internazionale, **10** Bobby Charlton and Bill Foulkes, **11** 1960s, **12** Norman Whiteside, **13** Plymouth Argyle, **14** Billy Wright, **15** Gillingham.

QUIZ 275

Answers on page 426

1 Peter Barnes won England caps while at which three clubs?

2 How many international goals did Terry Venables score?

3 Who beat AC Milan 1-0 in the 1993 European Cup Final?

4 Which club has a fanzine called *Ferry Cross The Wensum*?

5 Which soccer team does Cardinal Basil Hume support?

6 Wayne Clarke and Alan Harper were in the same team at which club?

7 On Good Friday, 1936, Swansea travelled to Plymouth. Where did they play the following day?

8 Which team won the first Czech League Championship after the split with Slovakia in the 1993-94 season?

9 In which decade did Aston Villa first win the Championship?

10 Kenny Dalglish scored the only goal in the 1978 European Cup against which side?

11 Who was the first British player to score a hat-trick of penalties in a European game?

12 Five players were sent off in the 1967 World Club Championship game between Celtic and who?

13 What nationality is West Ham Utd's Slaven Bilic?

14 John Gavin is the all-time top scorer at which club?

15 Which player scored 49 League goals for Aston Villa in 1930-31?

Answers to page 426

1 Remi Moses, **2** Oldham Athletic, **3** Turkey, **4** £1.5m, **5** Chester-le-street, **6** Ron Greenwood, **7** Dislocated shoulder, **8** Three, **9** 7, **10** West Brom, **11** 1, **12** 90, **13** 26, **14** Captain Marvel, **15** France.

QUIZ 276

Answers on page 423

1 What did Rangers achieve in season 1898-99

2 Bobby Gould succeeded Dave Sexton as manager of which club?

3 Which player scored 39 League goals for Carlisle Utd in 1963-64?

4 Steve Williams and Brian Talbot were together at which club?

5 Which club was once known as Newton Heath?

6 Who finished second when Liverpool won the League by nine points in the 1989-90 season?

7 Which club did John Moncur leave to join West Ham Utd?

8 In what year did the Scotland World Cup squad release *Say It With Pride*?

9 Who beat Real Madrid 3-1 in the 1964 European Cup Final?

10 Which two Manchester Utd survivers of the Munich crash played in the 1968 European Cup Final?

11 In which decade did Blackpool last play in the top division?

12 Who was 18 years and 14 days old when he played in the Brighton v Manchester Utd FA Cup Final?

13 Steve McCall followed Peter Shilton as manager of which club?

14 Who said that he was 'Supremely grateful' to have played against the great Hungarian side of the 1950s?

15 Who was Tony Cascarino playing for when he won his first cap?

Answers to page 423

1 Ally McCoist, **2** Germany, **3** Patrik Kluivert, **4** Andy Moller, **5** Germany, **6** Paul Gascoigne against fellow Rangers player Andy Goram (Scotland), **7** Bernard Lama, **8** Group C, **9** Peter Schmeichel, **10** Berti Vogts, **11** It was the first time an international had been settled by the 'Golden Goal' method., **12** Reynald Pedros, **13** Croatia, **14** John Collins, **15** Stefan Kuntz.

BRYAN ROBSON

Answers on page 424

1 Which other player joined Manchester Utd as part of the Bryan deal?

2 Against which team did Bryan score his last goal in a competitive match?

3 Bryan got his only England hat-trick in the 8-0 rout of which country in 1984?

4 How much did Bryn cost Manchester Utd when he signed for them?

5 Where was Bryan born?

6 Which England manager gave Bryan his first cap?

7 Which injury forced Bryan out of the 1986 World Cup?

8 How many times did Bryan win the FA Cup as Manchester Utd skipper?

9 What was Bryan's shirt number for most of his Manchester Utd career?

10 Bryan was at which League club when he made his England debut?

11 How many goals did Bryan score for Middlesborough?

12 How many games did Bryan play for England?

13 How many goals did Bryan score for England?

14 What was Bryan's nickname?

15 Against which country did Bryan score a World Cup goal after just 27 seconds?

Answers to page 424

1 Manchester City, West Brom and Leeds Utd, **2** He didn't score any, **3** Olympique Marseille, **4** Norwich City, **5** Newcastle Utd, **6** Everton, **7** Newcastle Utd, **8** Sparta Prague, **9** 1890s, **10** Bruges, **11** John Wark, **12** Racing Club, **13** Croatian, **14** Norwich City, **15** Tom 'Pongo' Waring.

SPURS 6

Answers on page 429

1 Goalkeeper Bill Brown joined Spurs from which club?

2 Which company was the first to sponsor Spurs shirts?

3 Which team were beaten 2-0 by Spurs in the 1961 FA Cup Final?

4 Who was the manager at Spurs when Jurgen Klinsmann joined them for the first time?

5 How many Premiership points were deducted from Spurs because of financial irregularities?

6 Spurs recorded a 5-0 League Cup win over which club in February 1987?

7 Which player, suffering from a broken nose, scored for Spurs in the 1993 FA Cup Final replay?

8 Which player opened the scoring for Spurs in the 1961 FA Cup Final?

9 Which player scored 33 League goals for Spurs in 1986-87?

10 Who was in goal for Spurs in the 1991 FA Cup Final?

11 Which club did Steve Sedgley join on leaving Spurs?

12 What is the name of Clive Allen's dad who was also a Spurs player?

13 Who moved from Manchester City to Spurs for £1.7m in 1988 to set a club record for a transfer received?

14 Which Spurs star played his only international game in 1982 against Iceland?

15 Who scored 5 goals in a game for Spurs against Ireland in November 1938?

Answers to page 429

1 Sunderland, **2** Four, **3** Tommy Docherty, **4** Saint-Etienne, **5** Billy McNeill, **6** Ipswich Town, **7** Nigel, **8** Matt Busby, **9** Kenny, **10** Sydney, **11** 10, **12** Margaret Thatcher, **13** Hamburg, **14** Manchester Utd, **15** An artist.

QUIZ 277

Answers on page 430

1. Which national side did Tele Santana manage?
2. Which club did Gianfranco Zola play for before his move to Chelsea?
3. Which club did Duncan Ferguson leave to join Everton?
4. Who knocked West Ham out of the 1998-99 FA Cup?
5. How did Bill Shankly end the observation that, "Football isn't a matter of life and death. . . "?
6. Which England manager described his players of "running round like headless chickens"?
7. Who were Aston Villa's opponents in the first League Cup Final needing a second replay?
8. Who beat St Mirren 2-1 in the 1956 Scottish League Cup Final?
9. In which country was John Salako born?
10. Which was John Aldridge's first League club?
11. Which was Steve Coppell's first League Club?
12. George Watson made a record 353 appearances for which Scottish club between 1975-87?
13. Alphabetically, which is the last Scottish League club?
14. Tony Fitzpatrick set a Scottish League appearance record at which club?
15. Who was Manchester Utd's first ever League substitute?

Answers to page 430

1 Forty-four, **2** Mark McGhee, **3** Finland, **4** Sunderland, **5** Rome, **6** Nat Lofthouse, **7** Northern Ireland, **8** George Eastham, **9** Liverpool, **10** Luton Town & Manchester Utd, **11** Portsmouth, **12** AC Milan, **13** AC Milan, **14** Nimes, **15** Kees Kist.

QUIZ 278

Answers on page 427

1 Marco Gabbiadini was top scorer for which team on the up in 1990?

2 How many international goals did Neil Webb score?

3 Who was boss when Manchester Utd were last promoted?

4 In which city were both England and Scotland knocked out of the 1998 World Cup finals?

5 Who retired as a player in 1975 following the Celtic v Airdrie Scottish Cup Final?

6 Roger Osborne scored in an FA Cup Final for which club?

7 What is Mark Atkins' middle name?

8 Who succeeded A Scott Duncan as manager of Manchester Utd in 1945?

9 Which forename links Hibbitt and Swain, both sacked as managers on the same day in 1994?

10 What is Peter Beagrie's middle name?

11 How many international goals did Colin Stein score?

12 In 1978, which spectator said, "I thought the No.10 Whymark played exceptionally well", when in fact he hadn't played at all?

13 Who lost to Liverpool in the 1977 Super Cup?

14 Mark Hughes joined Chelsea from which club?

15 According to Eric Cantona, who is "Someone who can light up a dark room"?

Answers to page 427

1 Dundee, **2** Holsten, **3** Leicester City, **4** Ossie Ardiles, **5** Six, **6** West Ham Utd, **7** Andy Linighan, **8** Bobby Smith, **9** Clive Allen, **10** Erik Thorstvedt, **11** Ipswich Town, **12** Les, **13** Paul Stewart, **14** Steve Perryman, **15** Willie Hall.

QUIZ 279

Answers on page 428

1 Jimmy Greaves played for England 57 times. How many goals did he score for them?

2 Who did Martin O'Neill succeed as manager of Leicester City?

3 Which country does Mixu Pastelainen come from?

4 Vic Halom first played in an FA Cup Final for which team?

5 Where was the 1984 European Cup Final held?

6 Who bagged 255 League goals for Bolton in the 1940s and 1950s?

7 Who won the 1986-and-Final - Home international championship?

8 Which player took Newcastle Utd to court?

9 Which team lost 4-3 to Leeds Utd in the 1992 FA Charity Shield?

10 Les Sealey has played in League Cup Finals for which two clubs?

11 Which club has a fanzine called *January 3rd '88*?

12 Who beat Benfica 1-0 in the 1990 European Cup Final?

13 Who beat Ajax 4-1 in the 1969 European Cup Final?

14 What was the last French club Eric Cantona played for?

15 Which AZ67 Alkmaar player won the 1978-79 Golden Boot award?

Answers to page 428

1 Brazil, **2** Parma, **3** Rangers, **4** Swansea, **5** "it's more important than that", **6** Graham Taylor, **7** Everton, **8** Aberdeen, **9** Nigeria, **10** Newport County, **11** Tranmere Rovers, **12** Falkirk, **13** Stranraer, **14** St Mirren, **15** John Fitzpatrick.

QUIZ 280

Answers on page 433

1 Who were Dutch champions in 1994 1995 and 1996?

2 In what year did the first Manchester derby in the FA Charity Shield take place?

3 Jimmy Greenhoff moved from Birmingham City to which club for £100,000 in August 1969?

4 George Beel established a record for most League goals in a season at which club?

5 Who beat Sampdoria 1-0 in the 1992 European Cup Final?

6 In 1966, which Leeds Utd defender won his only Scottish cap?

7 How many caps did Ossie Ardiles win for Argentina?

8 In which year in the 1980s did Liverpool and Everton not contest the Charity Shield?

9 Who beat Manchester Utd 2-0 in the 1958 FA Cup Final?

10 Which team name was one of Bobby Moore's names?

11 Which player scored 46 League goals for Crystal Palace in 1930-31?

12 What was notable about the draw between England and Scotland in the 1970s Home International Championship?

13 Frank Burrows followed John Gregory as manager of which club?

14 Which team did Alan Sunderland score an FA Cup Final goal for?

15 Who retired in 1961 to become a lay preacher and a JP?

Answers to page 433

1 Dean Saunders, **2** England, **3** Faustino Asprilla, **4** Galatasaray, **5** Graeme Souness, **6** Hungary, **7** Ipswich Town, **8** John Wark, **9** London X1, **10** Luxembourg, **11** Napoli, **12** Roto Volgograd, **13** Swansea City, **14** The toss of a coin, **15** Tottenham Hotspur v Wolves (UEFA Cup 1972).

ASTON VILLA 4

Answers on page 434

1 Villa beat which German club to become the fourth English team to win the European Cup?

2 Who was Villa boss in their 1986-87 relegation season?

3 What is the highest position Villa have ever achieved in the League?

4 What is the name of the Villa chairman?

5 Who scored the goals that took Villa through 2-1 in the second leg of their second round UEFA Cup tie with Athletico Bilbao?

6 Who played every game in goal for Villa in the 1981 side?

7 Which team were beaten 2-1 by Villa in the 1957 FA Cup Final?

8 Who moved from Leicester City to Villa in July 1995 to set a club record for a transfer fee received?

9 Which brothers were together at Villa for 18 years from the late 1930?

10 Which Everton player scored an own goal in the League Cup final replay against Villa?

11 Who was manager of Villa when they won the League Cup in 1975?

12 Which Villa striker accused one of his team mates of being, not 'Stan the man' but 'the wrong man'?

13 Villa recorded a 13-0 FA Cup win over which club in October 1886?

14 Andy Gray moved from Villa to which club for £1.75m in September 1979?

15 From which club did John Gregory join Villa as new boss?

Answers to page 434

1 Northampton Town, **2** Stanley Mathews, **3** Workington, **4** Pat Jennings, **5** San Marino, **6** Preston North End, **7** Bob Wilson, **8** Manchester City, **9** 1960s, **10** Tommy Docherty, **11** Wolverhampton, **12** 1930s, **13** Preston, **14** Gornik Zabrze, **15** 32.

UEFA CUP 2

Answers on page 431

1 Who scored a 1991 UEFA Cup hat-trick for Liverpool v Swarovski Tirol?

2 Which country has provided most UEFA Cup winners?

3 Which Newcastle Utd player was booked because he put his shirt on the corner flag and raised it in the air after scoring a UEFA Cup goal against Metz?

4 Which team did Dean Saunders play for in the 1995-96 UEFA Cup?

5 Which former Liverpool star made his only appearance for Spurs as a substitute in a UEFA Cup game before transferring to Middlesborough?

6 Which country did Ujpest Dozsa represent in the UEFA Cup?

7 Trevor Whymark scored four goals in a UEFA game for which club?

8 Which Ipswich Town player hit two hat-tricks in 1980-81 UEFA Cup games?

9 What was the generic title of the first ever team to represent England in the UEFA Cup competition?

10 Which Country do Red Boys represent in the UEFA Cup competition?

11 Which winners of the UEFA Cup did Diego Maradona play for?

12 Peter Schmeichel scored a UEFA Cup goal against which club?

13 Melville and James scored Euro goals in the same game for which club in their only UEFA Cup run?

14 After three drawn games, how was the Racing Strasbourg v Barcelona UEFA game of 1964-65 decided?

15 Which teams were in the first all-British European Final?

Answers to page 431

1 Ajax, **2** 1956, **3** Stoke City, **4** Burnley, **5** Barcelona, **6** Willie Bell, **7** 42, **8** 1981, **9** Bolton Wanderers, **10** Chelsea, **11** Peter Simpson, **12** First goalless draw, **13** Portsmouth, **14** Arsenal, **15** Billy Liddell.

QUIZ 281

Answers on page 432

1 At which club did Phil Neal make his League debut?

2 According to Bobby Charlton who "still had his magic" when nearing 50?

3 John Burridge made his League debut for which club who are now no longer in the League?

4 Which goalkeeper was born in Newry on June 12 1945?

5 Against which country did David Platt score his first England hat-trick?

6 Which Division Two team led Arsenal 2-0 at home before losing 2-4 in the third round of the 1998/99 FA Cup?

7 Which goalkeeper presented BBC's Football Focus?

8 Harry Dowd was in an FA Cup winning 1960s team at which club?

9 In what decade did Dundee first win the championship?

10 Who in the 1970s was sacked six weeks after winning the FA Cup?

11 With which league club did England captain Stan Cullis begin his playing career?

12 In which decade did the Italians first win the World Cup?

13 Who were the first champions of the Football League in the 1888-89 season?

14 Who lost 2-1 to Manchester City in the 1970 Cup-Winners' Cup Final?

15 In 1971, Sammy Chapman became the first Nottingham Forest player to be sent off for how many years?

Answers to page 432

1 Bayern Munich, **2** Billy McNeill, **3** Division 1 Champions, **4** Doug Ellis, **5** Ian Taylor and Dwight Yorke, **6** Jimmy Rimmer, **7** Manchester Utd, **8** Mark Draper, **9** Moss Brothers, **10** Roger Kenyon, **11** Ron Saunders, **12** Savo Milosevic, **13** Wednesday Old Athletic, **14** Wolves, **15** Wycombe Wanderers.

QUIZ 282

Answers on page 437

1 Which club did Vinnie Jones join on leaving Chelsea?

2 After the Second World War Stan Cullis became secretary-manager for which club?

3 Felix was in goal for which World Cup winners?

4 Which soccer team does comedian Phil Jupitus support?

5 Kevin Wilson and Clive Allen were in the same team at which club?

6 What was the first club that Billy Bremner managed?

7 With which club did Ray Wilkins make his League debut?

8 How many caps did Bill Shankly win?

9 Who was the first black player to be named in an England under-21 squad?

10 Which club did Mike Milligan leave to join Everton?

11 Who beat Dundee Utd 1-0 in the 1987 Scottish FA Cup Final?

12 In which four Swedish cities were European Championship finals matches played in 1992?

13 Who beat Fiorentina 2-0 in the 1957 European Cup Final?

14 Watford recorded a 8-0 League Cup win over which club in October 1987?

15 Which AC Milan player was European Footballer of the Year in 1987?

Answers to page 437

1 Stenhousemuir, **2** Fulham, **3** Kenny Sansom, **4** Preston North End, **5** John Toshack, **6** Southport, **7** Bob Paisley, **8** Blackburn Rovers, **9** Belgium, **10** No, **11** Argentina, **12** Coventry City, **13** Chelsea, **14** King, **15** Wolves.

QUIZ 283

Answers on page 438

1 Which soccer team does TV Presenter Nick Hancock support?

2 Adcock, Stewart and White each hit three for which team in the same game in 1987?

3 How many League goals did Dixie Dean score in his record breaking 1927-28 season?

4 Gerhard Hanappi played 93 times for which country?

5 Who scored 4 goals in a game for Wrexam against Ireland in February 1882?

6 Who scored on his European Cup Final debut in 1979?

7 Which club plays at home at Edgar Street?

8 Which goalkeeper is the most capped Swedish international?

9 Who was the first player to score a hat-trick in a European Cup Final?

10 How many times did kenny Dalglish win the championship for Liverpool when he was boss?

11 What is Denis Irwin's real first name?

12 Who were the first Scottish club to play on artificial turf?

13 Which Lewisham-born midfield England player has the first names David Carlyle?

14 Manchester Utd paid £1m to Cambridge for which player in August 1992?

15 Who beat Dundee Utd 3-1 in the 1964 Scottish FA Cup Final?

Answers to page 438

1 AC Milan, **2** Barcelona, **3** Bayern Munich, **4** Benfica, **5** Bobby Charlton, **6** Burnley, **7** Chelsea, **8** Eddie and Frank Gray, **9** Eusebio, **10** Ferenc Puskas, **11** Feyenoord in 1970, **12** Gary Shaw, **13** Hibernian, **14** John Robertson, **15** Linfield.

QUIZ 284

Answers on page 435

1 Archie Rose made a record 360 appearances for which Scottish club?

2 Which London side did Johnny Haynes play for?

3 Who did Tony Adams replace as Arsenal skipper in 1988?

4 Which is the only English League side to go a whole season without losing?

5 Which British manager was sacked by Real Madrid in 1990?

6 At which club, no longer in the League, did Peter Withe make his League debut?

7 Who advised Kenny Dalglish, "If you're going to get kicked, get kicked in the box, it's worth it there"?

8 Ian Pearce first played in an FA Charity Shield for which club?

9 Who were the opponents when Ian Rush hit his record breaking 24th goal for Wales?

10 Have Millwall ever won the FA Cup?

11 In which country was Helenio Herrera born?

12 Leicester City recorded a 8-1 League Cup win over which club in December 1964?

13 Which soccer team does snooker star Jimmy White support?

14 Which Andy became boss of Mansfield in 1993?

15 John Barnwell followed Sammy Chung as manager of which club?

Answers to page 435

1 Wimbledon, **2** Wolverhampton, **3** Brazil (1970), **4** West Ham Utd, **5** Chelsea, **6** Doncaster Rovers, **7** Chelsea, **8** Five, **9** Laurie Cunningham, **10** Oldham Athletic, **11** St Mirren, **12** Stockholm, Gothenburg, Malmo and Norrkoping, **13** Real Madrid, **14** Darlington, **15** Ruud Gullit.

• EUROPEAN CUP 2 •

Answers on page 436

1 Which team appeared in the European Cup Final in 1993,1994 and 1995?

2 Who were the first club to eliminate Real Madrid from the European Cup competition?

3 Aston Villa beat which German club to become only the fourth English team to win the European Cup?

4 Who did AC Milan beat in the final of the 1990 European Cup?

5 Who captained the Manchester Utd team to lift the 1968 European Cup?

6 Which Lancashire town team represented England in the European Cup in 1960-61?

7 Which London club pulled out of the first European Cup Competition?

8 Which brothers played in the 1976 European Cup Final?

9 Who scored an amazing 46 goals in the European Cup for Benfica?

10 Who was the first player to score a hat-trick in a European Cup Final?

11 Which were the first team from Holland to win the European Cup?

12 Who scored a European Cup hat-trick for Aston Villa against Dinamo Bucharest in November 1982?

13 Who were the first British team to compete in the European Cup?

14 Who scored Nottingham Forest's goal in the European Cup final to beat Hamburg?

15 Which team has represented Northern Ireland in the European Cup the most times?

Answers to page 436

1 Stoke City, **2** Manchester City, **3** 60, **4** Austria, **5** John Price, **6** Trevor Francis (Nottingham Forest), **7** Hereford Utd, **8** Thomas Ravelli, **9** Ferenc Puskas, **10** Three, **11** Joseph, **12** Stirling Albion, **13** Rocastle, **14** Dion Dublin, **15** Rangers.

MANCHESTER UTD 8

Answers on page 441

1 Who beat Manchester Utd 2-1 in the 1957 FA Cup Final?

2 Which team lost 4-2 to Manchester Utd in the 1948 FA Cup Final?

3 Who scored his first and Manchester Utd's last goal of the 1992-93 season?

4 Which international defender moved from Leeds Utd to Manchester Utd on a free transfer?

5 Which three other clubs were in Manchester Utd's 1997-98 Champions' League Group?

6 Which defender did Manchester Utd buy for £10.5m in 1998?

7 What was the nickname of Manchester Utd's early 20th century player Enoch Walker?

8 Who did Manchester Utd buy for over £12m from Aston Villa in 1998?

9 How many home matches did Manchester Utd play on their way to the 1990 FA Cup Final?

10 Which team had Manchester Utd played before the Munich crash?

11 Kevin Moran left Manchester Utd in 1988 for which club?

12 Pat Crerand became assistant to which Manchester Utd manager?

13 When did Manchester Utd first win the League Cup?

14 Manchester Utd's highest League win is 9-0 against Ipswich in March 1995. Who scored 5 goals in that game?

15 Which team came second and how many points behind were they when Manchester Utd won the first Premier Division Championship?

Answers to page 441

1 West Ham Utd, **2** County Ground, **3** Stan Collymore, **4** 1962, **5** Albert Quixall, **6** Dundee, **7** Ian Callaghan, **8** David Elleray, **9** The Pilgrims, **10** Sheffield Wednesday, **11** Manchester Utd, **12** Bobby Charlton, **13** Peter Withe, **14** Manchester Utd, **15** Juventus.

QUIZ 285

Answers on page 442

1 Which soccer team does Singer Billy Bragg support?

2 Who resigned as Tottenham Hotspur manager on June 23rd 1976?

3 In 1995-96 Ball and Hall were in the same side at which club?

4 Which soccer team does Robbie Williams support?

5 Trevor Francis was Britain's most expensive player until who moved?

6 Who moved from West Ham Utd to Celtic for £1.5 million in 1992?

7 Which soccer team does Politician David Blunkett support?

8 In 1995-96 Arsenal, Colchester Utd and Preston North End shared what in common?

9 Which club did Graeme Souness join in Italy?

10 Which football commentator, capped 43 times by England, made 568 appearances for Blackpool from 1952-71?

11 What followed West Bromwich before the name Albion was introduced?

12 Who was Keith Edwards playing for when he was the League's leading scorer in 1981-82?

13 Roger Palmer became all time top scorer at which club?

14 In what decade did Portsmouth first win the Championship?

15 Mick Robinson first played in an FA Cup Final for which team?

Answers to page 442

1 Charlton Athletic, **2** John Aldridge, **3** Alfie Conn, **4** Ted Drake, **5** Hull City, **6** Gary Lineker, **7** Plymouth Argyle, **8** George Camsell, **9** David Kelly, **10** Bremner, **11** 2 (Steve Daley and Andy Gray), **12** They play in black and white stripes, **13** Denis Law and Kenny Dalglish, **14** Raymond Kopa, **15** Gardia Warsaw.

QUIZ 286

Answers on page 439

1 Pike and Goddard scored in the same European game for which club?

2 Which ground used to be home to Northampton?

3 In January 1996, who lost his appeal for a pay-off from his old club Nottingham forest?

4 In which year did Fulham install floodlights at Craven Cottage?

5 Quantrill was the first English international whose surname began with the letter Q. Who is the only other one?

6 Doug Cowie made a record 341 appearances for which Scottish club between 1945-61?

7 Who holds Liverpool's record for most league appearances?

8 Which English headmaster was a referee in Euro '96?

9 What is Plymouth Argyles nickname?

10 Carlton Palmer first played in an FA Cup Final for which team?

11 Which club holds the record for most FA Cup wins?

12 Who scored first for Manchester Utd in the 1960s European Cup Final against Benfica?

13 Who scored a UEFA Cup hat-trick for Aston Villa against Victor Guimaraes in September 1983?

14 Which soccer team does cricketer Mike Atherton support?

15 Who beat Ajax 4-2 on penalties in the 1996 European Cup Final?

Answers to page 439

1 Aston Villa, **2** Blackpool, **3** Bryan Robson, **4** Dennis Irwin, **5** Feyenoord, Juventus, Kosice, **6** Jaap Staam, **7** Knocker, **8** Dwight Yorke, **9** None, **10** Red Star Belgrade, **11** Sporting Gijon, **12** Tommy Docherty, **13** 1992, **14** Andy Cole, **15** Aston Villa, 74.

QUIZ 287

Answers on page 440

1 Sam Bartram set a League appearance record at which club?

2 Who is the highest-ever scoring player in English football?

3 Who won a Scottish FA Cup medal for Rangers against Celtic and then another for Celtic against Rangers?

4 Who was the first person in England to win the Championship as a player and as a manager?

5 Which club had a fanzine called *Tiger Rag*?

6 Which England player hit hat-tricks against Turkey in 1985 and 1987?

7 Who was Peter Shilton playing for when he was sent off for the first time in his career?

8 Which player scored 59 League goals for Middlesborough in 1926-27?

9 Who was Newcastle Utd's top scorer in the 1992-93 promotion season?

10 Which Billy became boss of Leeds Utd in 1985?

11 The first £1 million British move was in February 1979, how many more players moved for a million in the same year?

12 Why are Juventus nicknamed the 'Zebras'?

13 Which two players are joint top scorers for Scotland?

14 Which Real Madrid player was European Footballer of the Year in 1958?

15 Under communism, what was the name of the Polish police team?

Answers to page 440

1 West Ham Utd, **2** Terry Neill, **3** Sunderland, **4** Port Vale, **5** Steve Daley, **6** Frank McAvennie, **7** Sheffield Wednesday, **8** Smallest League, **9** Sampdoria, **10** Jimmy Armfield, **11** Strollers, **12** Sheffield Utd, **13** Oldham Athletic, **14** 1940s, **15** Brighton.

QUIZ 288

Answers on page 445

1 Which Wolves player moved for £1 million to Manchester City in 1979?

2 Which team won three Scottish FA Cup Finals in a row - all after extra time?

3 How many times did Kevin Keegan play for England?

4 Which TV expert scored a Final League Cup winner for Wolves?

5 Striker Gary played League soccer with Barnet in the 1990s while brother Steve was scoring goals for which club?

6 Wark and Walsh scored in the same European game for which club?

7 In which decade did Liverpool win the UEFA Cup for the first time?

8 Sheffield Utd recorded a 5-1 League Cup win over which club in September 1985?

9 Neil Warnock followed John Barnwell as manager of which club?

10 Hancock, Pye and Shorthouse played for which 1940s FA Cup fianalists?

11 Which Japanese J-League team did Ossie Ardiles become manager of in 1996?

12 With which club did Trevor Sinclair make his League debut?

13 Which European Cup-winner was the first player over 35 to make his Scottish debut?

14 Who were the first team to win a replayed Scottish FA Cup Final?

15 Who recorded the song that topped the charts for three weeks in May 1970?

Answers to page 445

1 Liverpool, **2** Ossie Adiles, **3** Tottenham Hotspur, **4** Alan Shearer, **5** David Ginola, **6** Jackie Milburn, **7** Malcolm Macdonald, **8** Parma, **9** West Ham Utd, **10** Andy Cole, **11** David Ginola., **12** Joe Harvey, **13** Manchester City, **14** Peter Beardsley, **15** Wim Jonk.

GIANT KILLERS

Answers on page 446

1 Barrie Williams was boss of which 1989 giant-killers?

2 Which giant-killers knocked Leeds Utd out of the 1970-71 FA Cup?

3 Which side knocked Manchester Utd out of the 1995-96 Coca-Cola Cup?

4 Which side provided a Scottish Cup upset by knocking out Aberdeen in 1995?

5 Which Third Division giant-killers reached the 1959 FA Cup semi-final?

6 Who scored the USA goal which beat England in the 1950 World Cup finals?

7 Which Third Division side knocked Premiership side West Ham Utd out of the 1998-99 FA Cup?

8 Which Second Division side knocked Premiership side Southampton out of the 1998-99 FA Cup?

9 Which League side did non League Hereford Utd beat 2-1 in 1972?

10 Which Third Division side beat Arsenal 2-0 in 1933?

11 What was the score when non League Boston Utd beat Derby County in 1955?

12 Who did the Faroe Islands beat in their first ever competitive match?

13 Which Third Division side won the League Cup in 1967?

14 Which Second Division side won the 1972 FA Cup?

15 Which Second Division side won the 1980 FA Cup?

Answers to page 446

1 Kenny Sansom, **2** Claimed to have stolen it in 1890s, **3** AC Milan, **4** Oldham, **5** Wales, **6** Newcastle Utd, **7** Peterborough, **8** Crystal Palace, **9** Cardiff City, **10** Amaros, **11** Hereford Utd, **12** Brentford, **13** West Ham Utd, **14** Leicester City, **15** Aston Villa.

NEWCASTLE 4

Answers on page 443

1 Peter Beardsley moved from Newcastle to which club for £1.9m in July 1987?

2 Who succeeded Jim Smith as manager of Newcastle in 1991?

3 Paul Gascoigne moved from Newcastle to which club for £2.3m in July 1988?

4 Which Newcastle striker and England captain said, "I voted for Zola even though he did do us at Wembley"?

5 Which Newcastle player was sent off in a 1996 Coca-Cola quarter final after clashing with Arsenal's Lee Dixon?

6 Who has scored most goals in a career for Newcastle?

7 Which Newcastle striker scored 5 goals in a game for England against Cyprus in April 1975?

8 From which club did Newcastle buy Faustino Asprilla?

9 Which soccer team does Newcastle and England mid-fielder Rob Lee support?

10 Who did Bristol City buy from Arsenal for £500,000 and sell to Newcastle for £1.75m nine months later?

11 Which football player said " I don't want to put pressure on the manager here, but I never came to Newcastle to be a substitute"?

12 After the 1952 FA Cup Final which Newcastle skipper said, "Joe Mercer is the greatest player I have ever met"?

13 Which team were beaten 3-1 by Newcastle in the 1955 FA Cup Final?

14 As Newcastle manager, which former team-mate did Kevin Keegan sign as a player?

15 Who scored for PSV Eindhoven as they beat Newcastle 1-0 in the 1997-98 Champions' League?

Answers to page 443

1 Steve Daley, **2** Aberdeen, **3** 63, **4** Andy Gray, **5** Wolves, **6** Liverpool, **7** 1970s, **8** Rotherham Utd, **9** Notts County, **10** Wolves, **11** Shimzu S-Pulse, **12** Blackpool, **13** Ronnie Simpson, **14** Queens Park (1876), **15** England World Cup Squad.

QUIZ 289

Answers on page 444

1 Which Arsenal defender was capped 86 times for England between 1979 and 1986?

2 In 1958, 83 year old Harry Burge claimed what link with the FA Cup?

3 Silvio Berlusconi put his money into which club?

4 In 1995 Aberdeen paid just over £1m for Paul Bernard, which club did he sign from?

5 Which country did Peter Rodrigues play for?

6 Bobby Moncur led which team to win the UEFA Cup?

7 Barnsley recorded a 6-0 League Cup win over which club in September 1981?

8 Alan Mullery followed Steve Kember as manager of which club?

9 Bristol City recorded a 5-1 League Cup win over which club in August 1992?

10 Which Manuel holds the appearance record for France?

11 Who was Dixie McNeil playing for when he was the Leagues leading scorer in 1974-75 and 1975-76?

12 Charlton Athletic recorded a 5-0 League Cup win over which club in August 1980?

13 Tony Cottee was a favourite with which London club?

14 Which team did Manchester City beat 1-0 in the 1969 FA Cup Final?

15 Which famous Midlands side was founded by cricketing enthusiasts of the Wesleyan Capel?

Answers to page 444

1 Sutton Utd, **2** Colchester Utd, **3** York City, **4** Stenhousemuir, **5** Norwich City, **6** Larry Gaetjens, **7** Swansea City, **8** Fulham, **9** Newcastle Utd, **10** Walsall, **11** 6-1, **12** Austria (1-0), **13** QPR, **14** Sunderland, **15** West Ham Utd.

QUIZ 290

Answers on page 449

1 How many times did Jimmy Greaves score three or more goals for England?

2 Which club was once known as Belmont AFC

3 Which side resigned from the League in 1962?

4 Which Brian of Burnley made his only England appearance in 1961?

5 Who started the game in goal for Republic of Ireland when they lost to the Czech Republic in a friendly in March 1998?

6 Who beat West Ham Utd 6-1 on their plastic pitch in a League Cup semi-final match in 1990?

7 Which keeper spent 20 years with Portsmouth?

8 Which Portugese side did Graeme Souness manage in 1998?

9 Stuart Ripley first played in an FA Charity Shield for which club?

10 When was the last time Wales qualified for the World Cup finals?

11 Which England midfielder scored the only goal in the World Cup quarter-final against Belgium in Bologna in 1990?

12 Who beat Aberdeen 3-2 in the 1989 Scottish League Cup Final?

13 Who started the game in goal for Wales when they lost to Tunisia in a friendly in June 1998?

14 Which club had a fanzine called *Marching Together*?

15 Who was the first Englishman to play for AC Milan?

Answers to page 449

1 Erwin Van Den Burgh, **2** Andy Cole, **3** Connelly, **4** 3rd Division 1- (1891-92 /1920-21 /1924-25), **5** Blackburn Rovers, **6** Gordon Durie (Tottenham), **7** Rotherham Utd, **8** Michael Knighton, **9** Hull City, **10** Six, **11** Leeds Utd, **12** Aston Villa, **13** 1960s, **14** Sir John Hall of Newcastle Utd, **15** Brussels.

QUIZ 291

Answers on page 450

1 Which England manager was born in Worksop?

2 Alan Shearer's first Newcastle Utd hat-trick was against which side?

3 Who beat Benfica 6-5 in the 1988 European Cup Final on penalties?

4 Who were the first side to lose a Wembley FA Cup Final?

5 Which player scored 30 League goals for Bristol Rovers in 1963-64?

6 Which player of the 1950s and 60s set up Chelsea's record for most League goals for the club?

7 Which Scottish side hit a record 132 Division One goals in 1957-58?

8 How many Championships did Bobby Charlton win with Manchester Utd?

9 How many games did Cambridge Utd go without a win in 1983-84?

10 Which England midfielder's autobiography was called *Rock Bottom*?

11 Which country did John Devine play for?

12 In 1958 which team were relegated for the first time in 68 years?

13 Which CSKA Sofia player won the 1968-69 Golden Boot award?

14 At which Scottish club did Steve Archibald make his League debut?

15 A Charlie George goal won the FA Cup for which team?

Answers to page 450

1 Emmanuel Petit, **2** Herbert Chapman, **3** John Hartson, **4** John Jensen, **5** John Jenson, **6** John Lukic, **7** Kenny Sansom, **8** Liverpool, **9** Liverpool, **10** Liverpool, **11** Loughborough Town, **12** Luton Town, **13** RSC Anderlecht, **14** Ted Drake, **15** Trevor Brooking.

QUIZ 292

Answers on page 447

1 Which Lierse player won the 1979-80 Golden Boot award?

2 Manchester Utd's highest League win is 9-0 against Ipswich Town in March 1995 - Who scored 5 goals in that game?

3 Which winger John was in England's 1966 World Cup squad?

4 What is the highest position Bolton have ever achieved in the League?

5 Ted Harper established a record for most League goals in a season at which club?

6 Who was the first player to be convicted of feigning an injury to try to get an opponent sent off?

7 Manchester Utd recorded a 5-0 League Cup win over which club in October 1988?

8 Which Carlisle chairman once tried to buy Manchester Utd?

9 Manchester Utd recorded a 5-0 League Cup win over which club in September 1987?

10 How many times did Jimmy Greaves score three or more for England?

11 Duncan McKenzie was sent off in a European game playing for which club?

12 Tony Barton followed Ron Saunders as boss of which club?

13 In what decade did Kilmarnock first win the Championship?

14 Which chairman said in 1991, "Lets kill off once and for all that Ossie's job is on the line"?

15 Where was the 1985 European Cup Final held?

Answers to page 447

1 6, **2** Tranmere Rovers, **3** Accrington Stanley, **4** Miller, **5** Given, **6** Oldham Athletic, **7** Alan Knight, **8** Benfica, **9** Blackburn Rovers, **10** 1958, **11** David Platt, **12** Rangers, **13** Marriott, **14** Leeds Utd, **15** Jimmy Greaves.

ARSENAL 7

Answers on page 448

1 Which Arsenal defender was sent off in the Premiership match against Aston Villa for handling the ref?

2 Which former Arsenal manager is said to haunt Highbury?

3 Which Welsh international scored Arsenal's goal in their 2-1 defeat by Real Zaragoza in the 1995 Cup Winners' Cup Final?

4 Which Brondby and future Arsenal player scored the opening goal for Denmark in the 1992 European Championship Final against Germany?

5 Which Arsenal midfielder had the middle name Faxe?

6 Who was Arsenal's regular keeper when they won the Premiership in 1988-89?

7 Which Arsenal defender was capped 86 times for England between 1979 and 1986?

8 Which team were beaten 2-1 by Arsenal in the 1971 FA Cup Final?

9 Michael Thomas moved from Arsenal to which club in December 1991?

10 Ray Kennedy moved from Arsenal to which club in July 1974?

11 Arsenal's biggest win and heaviest defeat both came against which club?

12 Which club did John Hartson leave to join Arsenal?

13 Who lost to Arsenal in the 1970 UEFA Cup Final?

14 Who scored seven goals in one game for Arsenal against Aston Villa in December 1935?

15 Who scored West Ham Utd's goal to beat Arsenal in the 1980 FA Cup Final?

Answers to page 448

1 Graham Taylor, **2** Leicester City, **3** PSV Eindhoven, **4** West Ham Utd, **5** Alfie Biggs, **6** Bobby Tambling, **7** Hearts, **8** 4, **9** 31, **10** Paul Merson, **11** Republic of Ireland, **12** Sunderland, **13** Petar Jekov, **14** Clyde, **15** Arsenal.

GOALKEEPERS 3

Answers on page 453

1 Who kept goal as England lost to West Germany in the 1970 World Cup?

2 Who became England's most expensive keeper when he moved to Blackburn in 1993?

3 Peru's goalkeeper in the 1978 quarter-final match against Argentina in which Peru lost 6-0 was born in which country?

4 What was the nickname of early 20th century keeper Bill Foulke?

5 Which Leicester City keeper said, "Personally, I like a hostile environment maybe because I played at Millwall"?

6 Who was England's first choice goalkeeper in the 1990 Word Cup finals?

7 Which Birmingham City keeper saved a penalty with his first touch in his first match?

8 How did keeper Alex Stepney dislocate his jaw in August 1975?

9 Which Celtic keeper let nine goals in an international match?

10 Les Sealey has played in League Cup Finals for which two clubs?

11 Who was the goalkeeper in the controversial 'Hand Of God' goal?

12 Norwegian goalkeeper Erik Thorstvedt played for which London club?

13 With which club did Gordon Banks make his League debut?

14 Which ex-England keeper, working as a journalist, lost his life in the Munich air disaster?

15 With which club did Mark Bosnich make his English League debut?

Answers to page 453

1 Stephen Lodge, **2** George Camsell, **3** Paul Gascoigne, **4** Alex Ferguson, **5** Morton, **6** Belgium and Holland, **7** 14, **8** Bobby Moore, **9** Bury, **10** Semi-finals, **11** Celtic, **12** Munich 1860, **13** Clydesdale, **14** Cardiff City, **15** Halifax Town.

QUIZ 293

Answers on page 454

1 Which Final had two teams both to be relegated from the top flight in that same season?

2 How many players did Birmingham City use in th 1995-96 season?

3 Who beat Celtic 4-1 in the 1972 Scottish League Cup Final?

4 Ron Ashman set an appearance record at which club?

5 Which Scottish international took Newcastle Utd to the title in 1927?

6 Which football player was known as Budgie ?

7 Which Club has a fanzine called *The Thin Blue Line*?

8 What do the initials USSF stand for?

9 Which team was the first to win the Scottish League Cup on a penalty shoot-out?

10 In which country was John Salako born?

11 Whose 1970 testimonial match was a Manchester derby?

12 Who succeeded George Kerr as manager of Grimsby Town in 1982?

13 How many players were sent off in the 1997 Chesterfield v Plymouth Argyle Division Two League game?

14 Which Liverpool player was fined £2,000 for exceeding 45 disciplinary points during the 1995-96 season?

15 Which club beat Tottenham Hotspur after extra time in a League Cup Final?

Answers to page 454

1 PSG, **2** Steaua Bucherest, **3** Cesare Maldini, **4** Andy Payton, **5** Sunderland, **6** Scotland, **7** It was the first time an international had been settled by the 'Golden Goal' method., **8** Wales, **9** Corinthians, **10** Hibernian, **11** West Brom, Manchester City and Norwich City, **12** Uruguay, **13** Jimmy Greaves, **14** Bobby Moncur, **15** Sampdoria.

QUIZ 294

Answers on page 451

1 Which referee reported himself to the FA for sending off the wrong player in an Oxford v Sunderland game?

2 Who hit a record 59 goals in a season for Middlesborough?

3 Which Lazio player broke his leg during a training session in April 1994?

4 Who was Scotland's caretaker manager in the mid 80s?

5 With which club did Joe Jordan make his League debut?

6 Where will the finals of the 2000 European Championship be held?

7 What number did Johan Cruyff wear for most of his Ajax career?

8 Who provided the pass to Geoff Hurst to score his final goal in the 1966 World Cup Final?

9 At which club did Terry McDermott make his League debut?

10 The 1990 World Cup in Italy saw England reach which stage of the finals?

11 Who beat Aberdeen 2-1 in the 1954 Scottish FA Cup Final?

12 Who lost 2-0 to West Ham Utd in the 1965 Cup-Winners' Cup Final?

13 Who were the first team to lose a Scottish FA Cup Final?

14 Which club has a fanzine called *Watch The Bluebirds Fly*?

15 Norwich City recorded a 7-1 League Cup win over which club in November 1963?

Answers to page 451

1 Peter Bonetti, **2** Tim Flowers, **3** Argentina, **4** Fatty, **5** Kasey Keller speaking about the atmosphere during the Costa Rica - USA World Cup qualifying match, **6** Peter Shilton, **7** Tony Coton, **8** By shouting at his teammates, **9** Frank Haffey, **10** Luton Town and Manchester Utd, **11** Peter Shilton, **12** Tottenham Hotspur, **13** Chesterfield, **14** Frank Swift, **15** Manchester Utd.

QUIZ 295

Answers on page 452

1 Which club did Ossie Ardiles join on loan from Spurs during the Falklands War?

2 Who lost 4-0 to AC Milan in the Final of the 1989 European Cup?

3 Who stepped down as boss of Italy after the World Cup finals in 1998?

4 Who moved from Hull to Middlesborough for £750,000 in 1991 to set a club record for a transfer fee paid?

5 Owers, Atkinson and Armstrong played for which 1990s FA Cup finalists?

6 Bobby Charlton's first international goal was against which country?

7 What was historic about Oliver Bierhoff's Euro '96 goal in which Germany beat the Czech Republic?

8 Which country did Roy Vernon play for?

9 Which club in the 1880s twice provided all the players in the England team?

10 Arthur Duncan made a record 446 appearances for which Scottish club?

11 Which three teams has Asa Hartford played for in League Cup Finals?

12 Which country lost 4-2 to Hungary in the 1954 World Cup semi-final?

13 Which player scored 41 League goals for Chelsea in 1960-61?

14 Which Newcastle Utd player hit his first goals for seven years in the 1969 Inter-Cities Fairs Cup Final?

15 Who lost 2-0 to Barcelona in the 1989 Cup-Winners' Cup Final?

Answers to page 452

1 Norwich City v Sunderland, **2** 46, **3** Partick Thistle, **4** Norwich City, **5** Hugie Gallacher, **6** Johnny Byrne, **7** Cardiff City, **8** United States Soccer Federation, **9** Raith Rovers, **10** Nigeria, **11** Bill Foulkes, **12** Dave Booth, **13** Five, **14** Neil Ruddock, **15** Liverpool.

QUIZ 296

Answers on page 457

1 Who were champions of Serie A in 1995-96?

2 Which Brian of Celtic was Scottish Premier Division leading scorer in 1983-84?

3 Which are the three League teams with an x in them?

4 Which country did Jimmy Quinn play for?

5 Which former England goalkeeper became manager of Barnet?

6 Paul Power was a Championship winner with which club?

7 Which country did Clayton Blackmore play for?

8 Which player scored 34 League goals for Southend Utd in 1928-29?

9 Which country took the first penalty in the 1994 Final shoot out?

10 At which club did John McGinlay make his League debut?

11 What is the first name of Ipswich Town's Ulhenbeek?

12 Which Dynamo Kiev player was European Footballer of the Year in 1986?

13 By what name were the European Football Championships formerly known?

14 What was the first name of ex-West Brom and Ipswich Town player Zondervan?

15 Which Ipswich Town player Adam was banned after a drugs test?

Answers to page 457

1 Jimmy Greaves, **2** Wimbledon, **3** Peter Osgood, **4** 1972, **5** Ruud Gullit and Mark Hughs, **6** Gianfranco Zola, **7** Jimmy Greaves, **8** Dave Sexton, **9** Sheffield Wednesday, **10** 31, **11** Peter Osgood, **12** Wimbledon, **13** David Speedie (Chelsea), **14** Mark Stein, **15** Gianluca Vialli.

ENGLAND 3

Answers on page 458

1 Who was the first player to be capped for England while playing for a foreign team?

2 How many games did England lose in Spain in 1982?

3 How many times did Jimmy Greaves score three or more for England?

4 How many goals did Stanley Matthews score for England?

5 Which England player made his debut against Yugoslavia, just three days before his 20th birthday?

6 Which club in the 1880s twice provided all the players in the England team?

7 Who in 1979 scored on his England debut v Bulgaria?

8 How many full England caps did Steve Bruce win?

9 Which England player was known as 'The Wizard of Dribble'?

10 In what decade was the first official Scotland V England game?

11 Which England player was sent off in 1973 against Poland?

12 Who was made skipper in Terry Venables' first game in charge of England?

13 Which England manager accused his players of "running around like headless chickens"?

14 Which player burst into tears after England's World Cup semi-final defeat in 1990?

15 Who was the first Third Division player in the 1980s to be capped by England?

Answers to page 458

1 Millwall, **2** Stuttgart, **3** Reims, **4** Peter Reid, **5** Ralph Allen, **6** Rotherham United, **7** Tranmere Rovers, **8** Ally McCoist, **9** Jimmy, **10** Yugoslavia, **11** Princess Alexandra, **12** Eight, **13** FIFA, **14** Robbie Rensenbrink, **15** Arnold Muhren.

CHELSEA 4

Answers on page 455

1 Who scored 41 League goals for Chelsea in 1960-61?

2 Chelsea's Dennis Wise was transferred from which other London club?

3 In Chelsea's 13-0 win over Jeunesse Hautcharage in the European Cup Winners' Cup, which player scored five goals?

4 In what year did Chelsea hit the charts with *Blue Is The Colour*?

5 The gate for a Paul Elliott benefit game in July 1995 was boosted by which two new Chelsea signings?

6 Which Chelsea player was voted Footballer of the Year in 1997 only to question how many journalists were sober when they cast their votes?

7 Which Chelsea star finished as the League's top scorer in 1959?

8 Who succeeded Tommy Docherty as manager of Chelsea in 1967?

9 Chelsea paid £2.3m for Dan Petrescu. Which club did he leave?

10 How many League games did Glenn Hoddle play for Chelsea?

11 Which Chelsea player has scored in every round, including the Final of the FA Cup?

12 Which club did Vinnie Jones join on leaving Chelsea?

13 Who hit a hat-trick when Chelsea beat Manchester City 5-4 in the Full Members Cup?

14 Who moved from Stoke City for £1.5m to Chelsea to set a club record for a transfer fee received?

15 Who was the manager of Chelsea when they won the Coca-Cola Cup in 1998?

Answers to page 455

1 AC Milan, **2** McClair, **3** Crewe Alexandra, Exeter and Oxford, **4** Northern Ireland, **5** Ray Clemence, **6** Everton, **7** Wales, **8** Jim Shankly, **9** Italy, **10** Shrewsbury Town, **11** Gus, **12** Igor Belanov, **13** The European Nations Cup, **14** Romeo, **15** Tanner.

QUIZ 297

Answers on page 456

1 Which London club were Rovers, then Athletic, then went to a single name?

2 Who did Napoli beat in the 1989 UEFA Cup Final?

3 Which French team became the first to lose two European Cup Finals?

4 Who was sacked at Manchester City 12 days into the 1993-94 season?

5 Which player scored 32 League goals for Charlton Athletic in 1934-35?

6 Portsmouth recorded a 5-0 League Cup win over which club in October 1993?

7 Frank Worthington followed Bryan Hamilton as manager of which club?

8 Which Scot was Europe's top League scorer in 1991-92?

9 Which christian names link Northern Ireland's McIlroy and Quinn?

10 Which country lost 4-3 on penalties to Argentina in the 1990 World Cup semi-final?

11 Where does the Alexandra come from in Crewe's name?

12 How many goals did England score against Turkey in 1984?

13 Which organisation is based at Hitzigweg 11, CH-8032 Zurich?

14 Which Dutch international scored twice for his club in both the 1976 and 1977 Cup Winners' Cup finals?

15 Who scored the 1980s FA Cup Final replay penalty for Manchester Utd?

Answers to page 456

1 Gerry Hitchens, **2** None, **3** Six, **4** 11, **5** Alan Ball, **6** Corinthians, **7** Glenn Hoddle, **8** None, **9** Stanley Matthews, **10** 1870s, **11** Alan Ball, **12** David Platt, **13** Graham Taylor, **14** Paul Gascoigne, **15** Steve Bull.

QUIZ 298

Answers on page 461

1 Who started the magazine *Football Monthly*?

2 Which Scottish team are known as "The Loons"?

3 In which town was Ruel Fox born?

4 Who beat Huddersfield Town 3-1 in the 1928 FA Cup Final?

5 At which Italian club did Dino Zoff begin his career?

6 Alan Shearer and Iain Dowie were in the same team at which club?

7 Which ex-West Ham Utd player at Celtic was sent off along with Ranger's Butcher and Woods ?

8 Which sacked boss said, "I feel like Robin Hood - feared by the bad, loved by the good"?

9 Notts County recorded a 5-0 League Cup win over which club in August 1988?

10 How many international goals did Francis Lee score?

11 Which country hosted the 1994 World Cup?

12 Who wrote the biography *The Party's Over*?

13 Which manager brought Kevin Keegan back to England after playing in Germany?

14 Which manager won his first Scottish Championship after being in charge of the team for only four weeks?

15 Who did Cameroon beat in the 1990 World Cup opener?

Answers to page 461

1 Jimmy Rimmer, **2** 27, **3** Andy Townsend, **4** Norman Whiteside, **5** Sunderland, **6** Craig Brown, **7** Johnny Giles, **8** Northern Ireland, **9** Arsenal, **10** Franz Beckenbauer, **11** Tottenham Hotspur, **12** Status Quo, **13** Ted Fenton, **14** Lloyd George, **15** 44.

QUIZ 299

Answers on page 462

1 Which Birmingham City keeper saved a penalty with his first touch in his first match?

2 Mark Hughes left which club to join Southampton?

3 Which Ajax player won the 1985-86 Golden Boot award?

4 What happened to the referee after Leeds Utd's defeat in the 1973 Cup Winners' Cup Final?

5 Who moved from reading to Newcastle Utd in August 1995 to set a club record for a transfer fee received?

6 Which QPR player scored 11 goals in the 1976-77 UEFA Cup competition?

7 Who said, "As much as I love women and music, my first love will always be football"?

8 Who joined AC Milan from Portsmouth?

9 Which club dropped Lindsey from its name in the 1950s?

10 Who scored 60 league goals for Everton in 1927-28?

11 Where was the 1971 European Cup Winners' Cup Final held?

12 Alan Durban followed Alan A'Court as manager of which club?

13 Which African side reached the 1990 World Cup quarter-finals?

14 Dutch master Rinus Michels coached which German League side?

15 Who beat Manchester Utd 2-1 in the 1957 FA Cup Final?

Answers to page 462

1 Tommy Docherty, **2** Alex McLeish, **3** Gary McAllister, **4** Portugal, **5** Wembley Wizards, **6** Ally McCoist, **7** Hughie Gallacher, **8** Richard Gough, **9** Andy Goram, **10** Jim Baxter, **11** Ronnie Simpson, **12** 1-1, **13** Austria, **14** Jimmy McMullan, **15** Saint-Etienne.

QUIZ 300

Answers on page 459

1 Which goalkeeper played every game in Aston Villa's Championship-winning campaign in 1980-81?

2 How many points did Newcastle Utd take from their first ten games of the 1995-96 League season?

3 Which Republic of Ireland international was born in Maidstone in July 1963?

4 In 1983, who became the youngest ever player to score a League Cup Final goal at Wembley?

5 Which club plays at the Stadium of Light?

6 Which future national manager was born in Lanarkshire July 1, 1940?

7 Who resigned as the Republic of Ireland manager in April 1980?

8 Which country did keeper Harry Gregg play for?

9 Jeoff Blockley moved from Coventry City to which club for £200,000 in October 1972?

10 Who was the first person to coach and captain World Cup winning teams?

11 Chris Armstrong moved from Crystal Palace to which club for £4.5m in June 1995?

12 Which group helped Manchester Utd to chart success in 1994?

13 Who was manager of West Ham Utd's promotion winning side of 1958?

14 What are the two middle names of Noel Blake?

15 How many goals did Gary Lineker score in his 99 League games for Barcelona?

Answers to page 459

1 Charles Buchan, **2** Forfar, **3** Ipswich Town, **4** Blackburn Rovers, **5** Udinese, **6** Southampton, **7** Frank McAvennie, **8** Terry Venables (Spurs), **9** Mansfield, **10** 10, **11** USA, **12** Jim Baxter, **13** Lawrie McMenemy, **14** Walter Smith, **15** Argentina.

SCOTLAND 2

Answers on page 460

1 Which Scottish manager suffered only three defeats in his twelve games?

2 Which defender won 77 caps for Scotland between 1980 and 1991?

3 Who was unable to captain Scotland in the 1998 World Cup because of an injury?

4 Who beat Scotland 5-0 in April 1993, severely damaging their chances of qualifying for the 1994 World Cup?

5 When Scotland hammered England 5-1 at Wembley in 1928 what nickname were they given?

6 Who scored Scotland's only goal of Euro '96?

7 Who scored 23 goals in only 20 games for Scotland?

8 Which member of the Scotland squad in the 1992 European Championship finals in Sweden was born in Sweden?

9 Which 1990s goalkeeper has played soccer and cricket for Scotland?

10 Who scored twice for Scotland at Wembley in 1963 in the 2-1 victory?

11 Which European Cup-winner was the first player over 35 to make his Scottish debut?

12 What was the result of the Scotland against Iran in the 1978 World Cup?

13 Who did Scotland face in their first 1998 World Cup qualifying game?

14 Who captained the great 1920s 5-1 winning Scottish side?

15 In which city were both England and Scotland knocked out of the 1998 World Cup finals?

Answers to page 460

1 Tony Cotton, **2** Chelsea, **3** Marco Van Basten, **4** He was Suspended by UEFA, **5** Shaka Hislop, **6** Stan Bowles, **7** Rod Stewart, **8** Mark Hateley, **9** Scunthorpe Utd, **10** Dixie Dean, **11** Real Madrid, **12** Stoke City, **13** Cameroon, **14** Bayer Leverkusen, **15** Aston Villa.

EVERTON 4

Answers on page 465

1 Who succeeded Howard Kendall as manager of Everton in 1994

2 Who lost 3-1 to Everton in the 1985 Cup-Winners' Cup Final?

3 Everton player Jack Southwork scored 6 goals in a match in December 1893. Who were the opponents?

4 Which England midfielder played in white boots for Everton?

5 Who was skipper of Everton's 1966 FA Cup winning side?

6 Which Blackburn player was sent off after three minutes of his debut against Everton?

7 Who was the boss who took Gary Lineker to Everton in 1985?

8 Who was the only league ever-present for Everton in 1995-96?

9 Which Everton player scored an own goal in the League Cup Final replay against Aston Villa?

10 Who beat Everton 1-0 in the 1966 FA Cup Final?

11 Who moved from Manchester Utd to Everton for £5.5m in August 1995?

12 Which Everton centre-back played in the 1970 World Cup in Mexico?

13 Which player scored the first goal in the 1986 Liverpool v Everton FA Cup Final?

14 Who was manager of Everton before Mike Walker?

15 What name did Dixie Dean give his daughter, born on the day in 1931 that his club Everton, beat Southampton 9-1?

Answers to page 465

1 Newcastle Utd, **2** Terry Venables, **3** Exeter City, **4** Napoli, **5** Watford, **6** Internazionale, **7** Crystal Palace, **8** Duncan Ferguson, **9** 5, **10** Tommy Docherty, **11** Oldham Athletic, **12** 15th Division 2, (1974-75), **13** Peter Ward, **14** QPR, **15** Frank Haffey.

QUIZ 301

Answers on page 466

1 With which club did Hearts plan to merge in 1989-90?

2 Which player was outjumped by Pele before Banks made his famous save in Mexico 1970?

3 Allan Clarke was at which club when he made his international debut?

4 Which Republic of Ireland player was nicknamed 'Chippy'?

5 Which club did Jurgen Klinsmann join on leaving Tottenham Hotspur?

6 Who was Liverpool's only English born player in the 1986 FA Cup Final?

7 What season did Aberdeen beat Rangers and Celtic in major Cup Finals?

8 In which year did Jack Charlton become manager of the Republic of Ireland?

9 Kenny Dalglish's last game in charge of Liverpool was a 5th round FA Cup game against Everton. What was the score?

10 Aged 29 Frank Sibley became the youngest League manager when he was at which club?

11 Who won the first game between Celtic and Rangers back in 1888?

12 Brian Horton followed Mark Lawrenson as manager of which club?

13 Southend Utd player Billy Best scored 5 goals in a match in July 1968. Who were the opponents?

14 In which decade was extra time first played in an FA Cup Final game?

15 Which team won the 1986 UEFA Cup?

Answers to page 466

1 Andy Marriott, **2** Bonner and Coyne, **3** 1880s, **4** Paul Gascoigne, **5** Sheffield Wednesday, **6** Birmingham City, **7** Andrew, **8** 1880s, **9** Ajax, **10** Juventus, **11** Middlesborough, **12** 1920s, **13** Stanley Matthews, **14** Leeds Utd, **15** Sheffield.

QUIZ 302

Answers on page 463

1 Which club have a ground that contains The Millburn Stand?

2 Which England manager was born in London on 6th January, 1943?

3 Which ground had the Cowshed covered terrace?

4 Which winners of the UEFA Cup did Diego Maradona play for?

5 At which club did John Barnes make his League debut?

6 German players Klinsmann and Matthaus brought which club the Italian League title in 1989?

7 Jim Cannon set a League appearance record at which club?

8 Who moved from Dundee Utd to Rangers for £4 million in 1993 to set a club record for a transfer fee received?

9 How many international goals did Bob Latchford score?

10 Which manager gave Kenny Dalglish his first Scottish cap?

11 Roger Palmer became the all-time top scorer at which club?

12 What is the highest position York City have ever achieved in the League?

13 Which Brighton forward came on as substitute for eight minutes in his only England appearance?

14 Ossie Ardiles and Trevor Francis were in the same team at which club?

15 Which Celtic keeper let nine goals in in an international match?

Answers to page 463

1 Mike Walker, **2** Rapid Vienna, **3** WBA, **4** Alan Ball, **5** Brian Labone, **6** Garry Flitcroft, **7** Howard Kendall, **8** Neville Southall, **9** Roger Kenyon, **10** WBA, **11** Andrei Kanchelskis, **12** Brian Labone, **13** Gary Lineker, **14** Howard Kendall (During his second spell), **15** Nina.

QUIZ 303

Answers on page 464

1 Who was in goal for Nottingham Forest in the 1992 League Cup Final?

2 20 of the Republic of Ireland's 22-man USA 94 squad played in the English League - which two didn't?

3 In which decade did Blackburn Rovers first win the FA Cup?

4 Which Ranger's player was sent off in the 1996 European Cup game against Borussia Dortmund in Germany?

5 Lee Chapman and Mark Chamberlain were in the same team at which club?

6 Trevor Francis was at which club when he made his international debut?

7 What is David Seamans middle name?

8 In which decade did Aston Villa first win the FA Cup?

9 Which club beat Rangers to win the European Super Cup in 1972?

10 Which team are known as the Zebras?

11 Malcolm Allison followed Bobby Murdoch as manager of which club?

12 In which decade was Alfredo Di Stefano born?

13 Which Blackpool and England Player won the 1956 Footballer of the Year award?

14 Which soccer team does TV presenter Richard Whiteley support?

15 Which City has a Wednesday and a United?

Answers to page 464

1 Hibs, **2** Alan Mullery, **3** Leeds Utd, **4** Liam Brady, **5** Bayern Munich, **6** Mark Lawrenson, **7** 1989-90, **8** 1986, **9** 4-4, **10** QPR, **11** Celtic, **12** Oxford Utd, **13** Brentwood, **14** 1870s, **15** Real Madrid.

QUIZ 304

Answers on page 469

1 Which York City player collapsed and died during a game against Lincoln City?

2 John Docherty followed Ron Atkinson as manager of which club?

3 Who was the first substitute to come on in an FA Cup Final?

4 Which club announced in November 1995 they were thinking of moving to Dublin?

5 Who is the oldest player to turn out for Wales?

6 Bobby Campbell scored 121 League goals for which club?

7 Where was the 1979 European Cup Final held?

8 A 1994 League Cup defeat by Notts County was the sign for which Tottenham Hotspur boss that his days were numbered?

9 Which country did Bob McNab play for?

10 Which club has a fanzine called *The Cumberland Sausage*?

11 Who scored Arsenal's last minute winner against Manchester Utd in the 1979 FA Cup Final?

12 How old was Jack Charlton when he stood down as manager of the Republic of Ireland?

13 Who in December 1995 got booked for 'showing' the referee a yellow card after it fell from his pocket?

14 Who scored 5 goals in a game for Aston Villa against Ireland in February 1882?

15 Clough and Harkness were in the same side at which club?

Answers to page 469

1 Brian Deane, **2** Division 1 Champions (3 times 1968-69,1973-74,1991-92), **3** Frank Worthington, **4** Jimmy Greenhoff, **5** Lucas Radebe, **6** Ray Crawford, **7** Allan Clarke, **8** Caspian, **9** Don Revie, **10** Gary McAllister, **11** Joe Jordan, **12** Manchester Utd, **13** Sheffield Utd, **14** Arsenal, **15** Chelsea.

WALES 2

Answers on page 470

1 Which brothers Mel and John played together for Wales in the 1950s?

2 Who started the game in goal for Wales when they lost to Tunisia in a friendly in June 1998?

3 Stuart Williams won 33 of his Welsh caps while at which club?

4 Which Welsh player capped over 50 times, won the double with Spurs?

5 Which Wales manager was sacked in 1987-88 after eight years in charge?

6 At which ground did the last Home International match in 1984 between Wales and England take place?

7 Which Norwich City coach took charge of Wales for one game?

8 Who was Welsh boss for the vital 1977 World Cup qualifier v Scotland?

9 Which Welsh player was the most capped before Neville Southall?

10 Who did wales beat 3-2 to celebrate their FA's centenary in 1951?

11 Who scored 6 goals in a game for Linfield against Wales in February 1930?

12 Which Welsh international was disciplined by Bobby Gould for disrespectful behaviour towards Paolo Maldini?

13 When was the last time Wales qualified for the World Cup Tournament?

14 Which player has scored more goals for Wales than any other player?

15 Which team knocked Wales out of the 1958 World Cup finals?

Answers to page 470

1 Southampton, **2** Tottenham Hotspur, **3** Sheffield Wednesday, **4** Poland, **5** Uruguay, **6** Brian Labone, **7** Bill Perry, **8** Recreation ground, **9** Sweden, **10** Bob Houghton, **11** Kevin Richardson, **12** Roger Kenyon (Everton), **13** 1940s (Rangers 1949), **14** Chile, **15** For staging a half-time sit-down protest in his goal.

LEEDS UTD 4

Answers on page 467

1 Who moved from Sheffield Utd to Leeds for £2.7m in 1993 to set a club record for a transfer fee received?

2 What is the highest position Leeds have ever achieved in the League?

3 Who was joint top scorer with Arthur Graham as Leeds went down in 1982?

4 Who played for Leeds in the first leg of a Fairs Cup Final but was transferred before the second?

5 Which Leeds outfield player took over as goalkeeper twice in 1995-96 and only conceded one goal?

6 Who scored twice for Colchester Utd in the 1970s as they toppled Leeds Utd in the FA Cup?

7 Which Leeds player was nicknamed 'Sniffer'?

8 Leeds were taken over in a £20m deal by which company?

9 Who took over as manager of Leeds in 1961?

10 Which Leeds midfielder hit a 1995 hat-trick against Coventry City?

11 Which Leeds striker was known as 'The Shark'?

12 Eric Cantona moved from Leeds to which club for £1.2m in November 1992?

13 Which club did Vinnie Jones join on leaving Leeds?

14 Which team were beaten 1-0 by Leeds in the 1972 FA Cup Final?

15 Who beat Leeds Utd 2-1 in the 1970 FA Cup Final replay?

Answers to page 467

1 David Longhurst, **2** Cambridge Utd, **3** Dennis Clarke, **4** Wimbledon, **5** Billy Meredith, **6** Bradford City, **7** Munich, **8** Ossie Ardiles, **9** England, **10** Carlisle Utd, **11** Alan Sunderland, **12** 60, **13** Paul Gascoigne, **14** Howard Vaughton, **15** Liverpool.

QUIZ 305

Answers on page 468

1 Neil Shipperley's goals kept which side in the Premiership in 1995-96?

2 At which club did Miller and Hazard score in the same Euro game?

3 Nigel Pearson and Alan Harper were in the same team at which club?

4 Who were England's opponents in June 1989 when Peter Shilton equalled Bobby Moore's record of 108 international appearances?

5 Which South American country both hosted and won the first football World Cup?

6 Which Everton centre-back played in the 1970 World Cup in Mexico?

7 Who hit the winning goal in the 1953 Matthews Final?

8 Which ground do Chesterfield play at?

9 Against which country did Gary Lineker play his last international game?

10 Who was Malmo's English manager when they met Nottingham Forest in the European Cup Final?

11 Which English midfielder joined John Aldridge at Real Sociedad in 1990?

12 Who scored an own goal in the Aston Villa v Everton replayed League Cup Final in the 70s?

13 In what decade was the first treble won in Scotland?

14 Against which country did Michael Owen make his international debut?

15 Why was Everton goalkeeper fined a week's wages at the start of the 1990-91 season?

Answers to page 468

1 Charles, **2** Marriott, **3** West Brom, **4** Cliff Jones, **5** Mike England, **6** Wrexham, **7** David Williams, **8** Mike Smith, **9** Ivor Allchurch, **10** Rest of UK X1, **11** Joe Bambrick, **12** Robbie Savage, **13** 1958, **14** Ian Rush, **15** Brazil.

QUIZ 306

Answers on page 473

1 Craig Brewster scored the only goal to win the Scottish League Cup for which club in 1993-94?

2 At which club did Frank Worthington make his League debut?

3 Kevin Hodges set up a League appearance record at which club?

4 Scotsman Andy Gray first played in an FA Cup Final for which team?

5 Which London side won 6-2 at home in the first leg of a UEFA Cup game in the 1980s but were knocked out on the Away Goals rule after losing 4-0 away?

6 Which member of the winning 1966 World Cup squad went on to manage the Republic of Ireland?

7 Dennis Bergkamp's goal led which team to Euro success in 1992?

8 Which John became manager of Chelsea in March 1985?

9 Who were in the First Division from 1890 until relegation in 1958?

10 What is the highest position Swindon Town have ever achieved in the League?

11 Which is the most isolated British club?

12 Fred Everiss was manager at which club for a record-breaking 46 years?

13 Which Wimbledon player scored the only goal of the 1988 FA Cup Final?

14 Which Jan became boss of Swansea in February 1996?

15 In which decade was Billy Bingham born?

Answers to page 473

1 Southampton, **2** They lost 4-7, **3** Arsenal won the double, so the Shield was contested between Liverpool, the Cup runners-up and Leicester City Division Two Champions., **4** Billy Bonds, **5** *You'll Never Walk Alone*, **6** Seven, **7** Stan Collymore, **8** Celtic, **9** Gianni Rivera, **10** Real Madrid, **11** John Wark, **12** Florian Albert, **13** Ferencvaros, **14** Bayern Munich, **15** White and Blue.

QUIZ 307

Answers on page 474

1 Micky Horswill played for which team in an FA Cup Final?

2 Which country did John Chiedozie play for?

3 Dave Thomas and John Hollins were in the same team at which club?

4 Who managed the teams in the first all-London FA Cup Final in the 20th century?

5 Who became Britain's most expensive player when he moved from Preston North End to Arsenal in 1929?

6 Which club is owned by pop star Elton John?

7 Which Brazilian player made way for Ronaldo in the 1998 World Cup Final?

8 With which soccer club did TV entertainer Des O'Connor have trials with?

9 Which soccer soap was shown on BBC in the mid 1960s?

10 Which club was once known as Riverside Albion?

11 Bryan Robson was with which club when he first played for England?

12 With which soccer club did actor Brian Regan have trials with?

13 In what decade was the first official Scotland V England game?

14 Which Yorkshire team did Bill Shankly manage between 1956 and 1959?

15 Who knocked England out of the European Championship in 1996?

Answers to page 474

1 1990, **2** He argued with the referee, **3** Mick McCarthy, **4** 57, **5** Holland, **6** Pat Bonner, **7** Bonner and Coyne, **8** Italy, **9** Paul McGrath, **10** Brazil, **11** John Aldridge, **12** Roy Keane, **13** David O'Leary, **14** Johnny Giles, **15** Roy Keane.

QUIZ 308

Answers on page 471

1 Osman and Ruddock were in the same team at which club?

2 Barnet's first game in the football League was at home to Crewe Alexander in August 1991 - What was the score?

3 Despite never having won either the League Championship or the FA Cup, Leicester City won the 1971 Charity Shield. How come?

4 Who was Trevor Brooking's 'minder' on the pitch at West Ham?

5 Which Rogers and Hammerstein song became the Anfield anthem?

6 How many English teams have won the Cup Winners' Cup?

7 Who scored a UEFA Cup hat-trick for Aston Villa against Stromsgodset in September 1998?

8 Who lost 2-1 to Feyenoord in the Final of the 1970 European Cup?

9 Which AC Milan player was European Footballer of the Year in 1969?

10 Which Spanish team were the first winners of the European Cup?

11 Which Scot scored 14 goals in the 1980-81 UEFA Cup competition?

12 Which Ferencvaros player was European Footballer of the Year in 1967?

13 Who were the first Eastern European UEFA Cup winners?

14 Who beat Atletico Madrid 4-0 in the 1974 European Cup Final replay?

15 What are the main colours of IFK Gothenburg's home shirts?

Answers to page 471

1 Dundee Utd, **2** Huddersfield Town, **3** Plymouth Argyle, **4** Everton, **5** QPR, **6** Jack Charlton, **7** Ajax, **8** Hollins, **9** Sunderland, **10** 4th Division 2, (1989-90), **11** Carlisle Utd, **12** West Brom, **13** Lawrie Sanchez, **14** Molby, **15** 1930s.

•REPUBLIC OF IRELAND 2•

Answers on page 472

1 When did the Republic of Ireland first qualify for the World Cup Finals?

2 In the 1994 World Cup finals Jack Charlton, manager of the Republic of Ireland was fined and given a touchline ban by FIFA. What offence did he commit?

3 Which Republic of Ireland player committed most fouls in Italia '90?

4 How many appearances did Mick McCarthy make for the Republic of Ireland?

5 A late goal by which team meant the Republic of Ireland failed to reach the semi-finals of the Euro '88 Championship?

6 Who was the Republic of Ireland's goalkeeper in the penalty shoot-out against Romania in the 1990 World Cup?

7 20 of the Republic of Ireland's 22-man USA '94 squad played in the English League. Which two didn't?

8 Who knocked the Republic of Ireland out of the 1990 World Cup finals?

9 Which player has been capped most times by the Republic of Ireland?

10 Which country beat the Republic of Ireland 7-0 in 1982?

11 Which player was involved in the substitute row in the Mexico v the Republic of Ireland 1994 World Cup game?

12 Which Republic of Ireland player was sent off in 1996 playing against Russia?

13 Who came on in extra time for the Republic of Ireland in the Italia '90 World Cup game against Romania?

14 Who resigned as the Republic of Irelands manager in April 1980?

15 Who only lasted less than a week as captain of the Republic of Ireland?

Answers to page 472

1 Sunderland, **2** Nigeria, **3** QPR, **4** Bill Nicholson (Spurs),Tommy Docherty (Chelsea), **5** Alex James, **6** Watford, **7** Edmundo, **8** Northampton Town, **9** "United", **10** Cardiff City, **11** West Brom, **12** Liverpool, **13** 1870s, **14** Huddersfield Town, **15** Germany.

• MANCHESTER UTD 9 •

Answers on page 477

1 Who scored first for Manchester Utd in the 1960s European Cup Final against Benfica?

2 Who were the only team to beat Manchester Utd home and away in the 1993-94 season?

3 Which Manchester Utd player scored the Republic of Ireland's goal in their 1-1 draw with Belgium in the first leg of the 1998 World Cup qualifying play-off?

4 How many championships did Sir Matt Busby win for Manchester Utd?

5 Paul Ince moved from Manchester Utd to which club for £7m in July 1995?

6 In Manchester Utd's founding days what did the letters LYR stand for?

7 Who scored Manchester Utd's goals against Barcelona in the 1991 European Cup Winners' Cup Final?

8 Who was 18 years and 14 days old when he scored in the 1983 FA Cup Final against Brighton?

9 Which other player joined Manchester Utd as part of the Bryan Robson deal?

10 Bobby Charlton's last Manchester Utd League appearance was at which ground?

11 How many times have Manchester Utd done the League-Cup double?

12 What was the score in the drawn Manchester Utd v Brighton FA Cup Final of 1983?

Answers to page 479

1 1950s, **2** The Republic of Ireland, **3** Hamburg, **4** Sunderland, **5** Doug Ellis, **6** 14, **7** Wrexham, **8** Wolves, **9** Diego Maradona, **10** Benfica, **11** Eoin Hand, **12** Cameroon, **13** Barcelona, **14** Norwich City, **15** Bayern Munich.

QUIZ 309

Answers on page 478

1 Ipswich Town recorded a 6-1 League Cup win over which club in November 1985?

2 Who beat Preston North End 3-2 in the 1964 FA Cup Final?

3 At which club did Dean Saunders make his League debut?

4 Who followed Ian St John as manager of Portsmouth?

5 Who became Spurs most expensive player when he moved from Crystal Palace in the summer of 1995?

6 Blackburn Rovers established a record of going how many FA Cup games without defeat?

7 Which country lost 4-3 on penalties to West Germany in the 1990 World Cup semi-final?

8 Keving Hodges set up a League appearance record at which club?

9 Which fullback moved for a record fee from Leicester City to Derby County in 1972?

10 Which Liverpool manager was boss of Huddersfield from 1956-59?

11 Who fractured his skull in a motorbike accident in the 1920s?

12 What was Johan Cruyff's first family links with Ajax?

13 Who scored 42 league goals for Arsenal in season 1934-35?

14 Who plays at the Royal Dublin Society Ground?

15 What was the 90 minute score in the Manchester Utd v Liverpool Charity Shield game?

Answers to page 480

1 Phil Babb, **2** Robbie Fowler, **3** QPR, **4** Tommy Lawrence, **5** 1959, **6** Alan Hansen, **7** Barry Fry, **8** Bournmouth, **9** Craig Johnston, **10** Everton, **11** Graeme Souness, **12** Jason McAteer, **13** John Wark, **14** Kevin Keegan, **15** Michael Thomas.

QUIZ 310

Answers on page 479

1 Bowan and Goss scored Euro goals in the same game for which club?

2 What were there five of in the March 1989 Football match, between Crystal Palace and Brighton to create a record?

3 Which player with 430 games set a League appearance record for Wimbledon?

4 Wimbledon recorded a 5-0 League Cup win over which club in September 1985?

5 Who knocked Dundee out of the 1962-63 European Cup?

6 Dave Gaskell was in an FA Cup winning 1960s team at which club?

7 In the 1960s, which club went from Division 4 to Division 1 and back again?

8 Who did England play to celebrate the centenary of the Football Association?

9 Which manager when he heard about Souness having heart surgery said, "My heart goes out to Graeme Souness"?

10 Which Scottish player scored for the Italian League in 1976?

11 Who is the first striker whose career lasted at least six games but never scored for England?

12 Which Harry was Luton manager from 1972-78?

13 Who beat Marseille 5-3 in the 1991 European Cup Final on penalties?

14 Geographically, which is the nearest club to Aberdeen?

15 Who managed the Great Britain team in the 1948 Olympics?

Answers to page 475

1 Bobby Charlton, **2** Chelsea, **3** Dennis Irwin, **4** Five, **5** Inter Milan, **6** Lancashire and Yorkshire Railway, **7** Mark Hughes, **8** Norman Whiteside, **9** Remi Moses, **10** Stamford Bridge, **11** Twice, **12** 2-2, **13** Andy Cole, **14** Atletico Madrid, **15** Bobby Charlton.

QUIZ 311

Answers on page 480

1 Who came on as a substitute for Arsenal in the 1971 FA Cup Final?

2 Which club had a fanzine called *The Almighty Brian*?

3 Tony Ingham set up a League appearance record at which club?

4 Which Desmond's 1981 book was *The Soccer Tribe*?

5 How many international goals did Kevin Moran score?

6 What colour are Exeter City's striped shirts?

7 Who moved from Fulham to Liverpool for £333,000 in 1980 to set a club record for a transfer fee received?

8 Which Welshman was Kevin Keegan's main Liverpool strike partner?

9 Who did Charlton sell to Newcastle Utd for £750,000 in September 1992?

10 At which ground did terracing collapse in 1902 killing 25 people?

11 Archie Gemmill and John McGovern took over which club in September 1994?

12 Who became the youngest player ever to play in an FA Cup Final when he appeared for West Ham Utd in 1980?

13 Which year did the League Cup become the Milk Cup?

14 Who was in goal for Leeds Utd in the 1972 and 1973 FA Cup Finals?

15 Where was England manager Walter Winterbottom born?

Answers to page 476

1 Swindon, **2** West Ham Utd, **3** Swansea City, **4** Jimmy Dickson, **5** Chris Armstrong, **6** 24, **7** England, **8** Plymouth Argyle, **9** David Nish, **10** Bill Shankly, **11** Dixie Dean, **12** His mother was a cleaner in the offices, **13** Ted Drake, **14** Shamrock Rovers, **15** 1-1.

QUIZ 312

Answers on page 475

1 In which decade was Liam Brady born?

2 Which country did Tony Grealish play for?

3 Who did Aberdeen beat to win the European Super Cup in 1983?

4 Which club once had "and District Teachers' AFC" added to their name?

5 Who in 1994 said, "I Believe Ron to be one of the top three managers in the country" - before sacking him three weeks later?

6 How many players were used by Aston Villa during their Championship-winning season of 1980-81?

7 At which ground did the last Home International match in 1984 between Wales and England take place?

8 Norman Deeley scored twice in an FA Cup Final for which club?

9 Who tested positive for cocaine following a Serie A game?

10 Who beat Real Madrid 5-3 in the 1962 European Cup Final?

11 Who was manager of the Republic of Ireland directly before Jack Charlton?

12 Which was the first black African country to reach the quarter-finals of the World Cup?

13 Who lost to AC Milan in the 1989 Super Cup?

14 Which club's ground is by the River Wensum?

15 Who beat Leeds Utd 2-0 in the 1975 European Cup Final?

Answers to page 477

1 Norwich City, **2** Penalties, **3** Alan Cork, **4** Blackburn, **5** Real Madrid, **6** Manchester Utd, **7** Northampton Town, **8** Rest of the World X1, **9** Brian Clough, **10** Denis Law, **11** Tony Cottee, **12** Haslam, **13** Red Star Belgrade, **14** Montrose, **15** Matt Busby.

LIVERPOOL 10

Answers on page 476

1 Liverpool paid £3.75m to Coventry in September 1994 for which defender?

2 Who scored all of Liverpool's five goals in a 1993-94 League Cup tie against Fulham?

3 Which Liverpool player did Stan Collymore accuse of making racist remarks to him during Aston Villa's visit to Anfield?

4 Which Liverpool player was 'The Flying Pig'?

5 In which year was Bill Shankly appointed manager of Liverpool?

6 Who was Kenny Dalglish's Liverpool skipper for the 1986 double-winning side?

7 Who said "If Liverpool is a danger to your health, try managing Barnet"?

8 From which club did Liverpool sign Jamie Redknapp?

9 Which former Liverpool player invented the Predator boot?

10 Which team was beaten 3-1 by Liverpool in the 1986 FA Cup Final?

11 Which Liverpool manager sold Peter Beardsley?

12 Who did Liverpool sign from Bolton in September 1995?

13 Which Scottish midfielder was Liverpool's top League scorer in 1984-85?

14 Which ex-Liverpool star played only 27 minutes in the final stages of a World Cup to earn the last of his 63 caps?

15 Who scored Arsenal's last minute goal against Liverpool at Anfield to win the League title in 1989?

Answers to page 478

1 Eddie Kelly, **2** Nottingham Forest, **3** Jimmy McMullan, **4** Morris, **5** Six, **6** Red and White, **7** Richard Money, **8** John Toshack, **9** Robert Lee, **10** Ibrox, **11** Rotherham, **12** Paul Allen, **13** 1982, **14** David Harvey, **15** Oldham.